Charles John Abbey

The English Church and its Bishops 1700-1800 by Charles J. Abbey

Vol. II

Charles John Abbey

The English Church and its Bishops 1700-1800 by Charles J. Abbey
Vol. II

ISBN/EAN: 9783743373594

Manufactured in Europe, USA, Canada, Australia, Japa

Cover: Foto ©Lupo / pixelio.de

Manufactured and distributed by brebook publishing software (www.brebook.com)

Charles John Abbey

The English Church and its Bishops 1700-1800 by Charles J. Abbey

THE ENGLISH CHURCH

AND ITS BISHOPS

1700—1800

BY

CHARLES J. ABBEY

RECTOR OF CHECKENDON; LATE FELLOW OF UNIVERSITY COLLEGE, OXFORD
AND JOINT-AUTHOR OF 'THE ENGLISH CHURCH IN THE EIGHTEENTH CENTURY'

IN TWO VOLUMES

VOL. II.

LONDON
LONGMANS, GREEN, AND CO.
1887

CONTENTS

OF

THE SECOND VOLUME.

CHAPTER V.

ENGLISH BISHOPS, 1714–60.

SECTION 1.—*George the First's Reign.*

	PAGE
Hoadly	1
Gibson	20
Potter	22
Chandler	25
Smalridge	26
Gastrell	29
Willis	30
Kennet	31
Smallbrooke	33
Bradford; Green; Long; Baker	34
Waddington; Boulter; Peploe, &c.	35

SECTION 2.—*George the Second's Reign.*

Herring	37
Secker	41
Gilbert	47
Sherlock	48
Butler	54
Hare	61
Benson	62
Pearce	63
Hildesley	66

Conybeare	67
Gooch; Fleming	68
Osbaldeston; Maddox	69
Mawson	70
Claggett; Lavington; Johnson	71
Hayter; Ashburnham; E. Willis	72
Trevor; Ellis; Tanner; Hume; Keene	73
The three Bishop Thomases	74
Harris; J. Cornwallis, &c.	76

CHAPTER VI.

THE ENGLISH CHURCH, 1760–1800.

Vice and irreligion	77
Signs of revival	78
Change of tone in religious, political, and literary questions	80
George III.'s personal character	82
Continued growth of philanthropy	83
Feelings as to religious differences	84
Widening of the gap between Churchmen and Nonconformists	85
The Test and Corporation Acts	86
Co-operation with Nonconformists	89
Ultra-Protestantism	91
Posture of Wesley and the Methodists towards Rome	92
English Roman Catholics and the temporal power	93
The Quebec Bill	95
The Lord George Gordon riots	96
Roman Catholic relief	97
The French immigrant clergy	98
Opinion during the century in regard of the relations between Church and State	100
In the reign of Anne	101
The Church and the Sovereign	103
Nonjuring opinion	104
Whigs and Low Churchmen on the authority of the State	105
Effect of the Toleration and Union Acts	107
The Essayists on Established Churches	109
Views held by Deist writers	110
Hoadly on Church and State	111
Butler; Watts; Doddridge	113
Warburton's 'Alliance of Church and State'	113
Secker; Hartley; J. Wesley	116
Dr. Johnson; J. Newton	117

	PAGE
Barbauld; Tucker; Balguy; Paley	118
Wilberforce; Hannah More	119
E. Burke on the National Church	120
Subscription to the Articles	122
The Feather Tavern petition	124
American form of subscription	125
Porteus's scheme of Church reform	126
Leland's History of Deism	127
Developments of English Deism in France	128
Paine's 'Age of Reason'	129
Secessions to Unitarianism	130
The Priestley riots	131
J. Wesley's Churchmanship	132
His consecration of Coke and Ashbury	133
Negotiations of Coke with White and Seabury	134
Methodists and the Eucharist	135
A possible opportunity of union	136
Methodism at the close of the century	137
The Evangelical movement	138
Fletcher of Madeley; Walker of Truro	139
H. Venn; J. Berridge	140
W. Romaine; Grimshaw	141
J. Hervey; A. Toplady	142
J. Newton; T. Scott	143
Other Evangelical clergymen	144
Cowper; Wilberforce; Hannah More	145
Relation of Evangelicalism to previous movements in the Church	146
Its growth and development	147
Its direct and indirect benefits to religion	148
Its deficiencies	150
The American war	152
The French revolution	153
Intense feeling excited by it	153
Enthusiasm in some circles	154
Violence of the reaction	155
The revolution and Christianity	156
Its influences on religion in England	158
And upon the English Church in particular	160
The Slave trade and abolition	163
Sunday schools and elementary education	166
Their rise and origin	166
Interest created by them	166
Peculiarity in their early character	168
Impulse given by them to general education	170
Dr. Bell and the Madras system	171

	PAGE
Religious and philanthropical societies	174
Episcopal Church of Scotland in the eighteenth century	175
In William III.'s reign	176
In Queen Anne's reign	179
The first Jacobite rising	180
The English Liturgy and the usages	181
Consequences of the insurrection of 1745	183
Bishop for America consecrated at Aberdeen	186
Debate on the Disabilities Bill	187
American Episcopal Church	188
Its position after the War of Independence	188
Bishops White and Provoost	189
Revised American Liturgy	190
Work of the S.P.G. in Canada	193
Christianity among the negroes	194
The Church in the colonies generally	195
India	196
The South Sea Islands	198
Africa; foundation of the Church Missionary Society	199
Moravian missions	200
Church fabrics and services	201
Sacred poetry of the century	201

CHAPTER VII.

ENGLISH BISHOPS, 1760-1800.

F. Cornwallis	205
Moore	207
Manners-Sutton	209
Drummond	209
Markham	210
Terrick	210
Lowth	211
Porteus	213
North	218
J. Egerton	219
Thurlow	220
Barrington	220
Hurd	223
Warburton	227
Newton	237
Halifax	240
Pretyman-Tomline	240
Shipley	241

	PAGE
Hinchcliffe	243
E. Law	245
Watson	251
Horne	257
Douglas	261
Horsley	263
J. Butler	269
Ross	269
Keppel; Butler; Courtenay	270
Moss; Green; Lyttleton	271
Vernon; Cornwell; Buckner	272
Cleaver; Squire; Warren	273
Yorke; Beadon; Randolph, &c.	274

CHAPTER VIII.

THE ENGLISH CHURCH IN IRELAND.

The old Church of the Pale	275
Effects of the Reformation	276
The Irish Church in the seventeenth century	277
The penal code	278
Its relaxation and removal	280
Proportion of Roman Catholics and Protestants	281
Ultra-Protestantism among Irish Protestants	283
Attempts to win Ireland to Protestantism	284
J. Wesley in Ireland	287
The Charter Schools	288
General neglect of the Roman Catholic peasantry	289
Absence of sympathy between the two races	290
Bishop Watson on co-establishment	290
Irish Presbyterianism	291
The Established Church of Ireland	294
Irish Church patronage	295
The bishops as political persons	295
The Irish primacy	296
The 'Irish' and 'English' interests	299
Effects on the Irish Church of Walpole's policy	301
Impoverished condition of the Established Church in the first half of the century	303
Spoliation of tithe	305
Pluralities and non-residence	306
'Non-cures'	307
General character of the Irish clergy	309

CONTENTS OF THE SECOND VOLUME

	PAGE
Their sufferings during the insurrection	310
Nonjuring and Jacobite controversies	311
The Irish Convocation	311
Deism; Arianism	312
Methodism; Mysticism; Evangelicalism; religious societies	313
The Irish bishops	313
Episcopal translations	314
The bishoprics and noble families	315
Boyle	315
Marsh	315
Lindsay	317
Boulter	317
Hoadly	321
Stone	321
Robinson	323
Newcome	325
King	325
Berkeley	329
P. Brown; Huntington	344
Pococke; Synge	345
Brief notes of Irish bishops	346
Bolton; Rundle	347
Clayton	348
Percy	349
Earl of Bristol	350
Barnard; O'Beirne, &c.	353
General character of Irish bishops in eighteenth century	354

APPENDIX.

LIST OF ENGLISH BISHOPS, 1700–1800	357
LIST OF AUTHORS QUOTED OR REFERRED TO	361
INDEX	371

CHAPTER V.

ENGLISH BISHOPS. 1714–1760.

Section 1.—*George the First's Reign.*

ALMOST the first bishop created under the new dynasty was one who, for good or evil, is more generally known, at all events by name, than any other bishop who belongs strictly to the eighteenth century—Benjamin Hoadly. Raised to the episcopate of Bangor in 1715, he was translated to Hereford in 1721, to Salisbury in 1723, to Winchester in 1734. He lived till 1761, and was thus a prominent figure in the English Church for forty-six years. Nor does this period comprise by any means the whole of his public life. He had held an important London lectureship as early as 1694; and in 1705 he had already entered into the full tide of controversy.

Gibbon well describes Hoadly as 'the object of Whig idolatry and Tory abhorrence.'[1] Perhaps there has never been any other English bishop whose opinions have been so extravagantly lauded by one party, so utterly detested by another. Akenside extolled him in an ode, from which the following words may be quoted:—

> We attend thy reverend length of days
> With benediction and with praise,
> And hail thee in our public ways,
> Like some great spirit famed in ages old.[2]

[1] Gibbon's *Autobiography*, p. 13. [2] Akenside's *Poems*, Ode vii.

'He lived,' said another author, 'to see the nation become his converts, and some have blushed to think their fathers were his foes.'[1] On the other hand, Hoadly himself says that he was inveighed against with every kind of opprobrious epithet. He was 'a Deist,' 'an Egyptian,'[2] a 'rebel against the Church,'[3] 'a vile republican,'[4] 'an apostate to his own order, the scorn and ridicule of a whole kingdom.'[5] He was 'preached and wrote against over all the nation.'[6] In later days the odium attached to his name has followed him more generally than the praise. One of his recent biographers exclaims that 'it is absolutely wonderful how so great a Dissenter could have retained, I will not say the episcopal, but even the priestly character;'[7] and the late Bishop Wilberforce considered that scarcely anything had done so much harm to religion in England as 'the deadly leaven of Hoadly's latitudinarianism.'[8]

However judgments may vary as to the good or evil of his opinions, no one, in our day, can fail to condemn severely his conduct as a bishop. There were numberless instances in the last century of disgraceful absenteeism, but Hoadly's offence in this respect was glaring even above others. For the whole six years he held the bishopric of Bangor he never once even set foot within his diocese. Even in later years his periods of non-residence were long and frequent. It might appear that he thought his pastoral duties the least important part of episcopal responsibility. Yet, with strange blindness to the contrast of his own neglect, he warmly praises his friend Samuel Clarke for residing so constantly upon his own cure. His personal infirmities must be taken into account: he was exceedingly lame, and

[1] Bowyer, in Nichols' *Lit. An.*, iii. 141.
[2] Hoadly's *Works*, i. 97.
[3] Calamy's *Life*, ii. 236.
[4] Hearne's *Reliquiæ*, iii. 159.
[5] The *Scourge*, June 3, 1717.
[6] *Id.*
[7] Cassan's *Bishops of Winchester*, p. 403.
[8] *Life of W. Wilberforce*, by his Son, p. 49.

in the pulpit was always obliged to preach in a kneeling posture. But in an age when roads were bad and travelling difficult, it was obviously inexcusable to accept a distant charge if physical weakness made him shrink from the lengthened journey.[1]

It is curiously characteristic of a century when such abuses were frequent that his contemporaries passed over this negligence with scarcely any comment. Hoadly's opponents were not at all likely to leave unnoticed what was evidently and greatly to his discredit, yet, with the exception of Whiston,[2] who was probably more alive than any one else to the evils which were undermining the Church, scarce any of those who declaimed against his views took any notice whatever of this blot upon his episcopal character.[3] As for those who looked up to him in admiration, there was perhaps not one who would not have held that he was better in London, upholding liberty and reason in the centre of the nation's life, than banished among the wild and savage[4] mountains of a Welsh diocese. And this, if any can be found, is Hoadly's only excuse. But this, a few years earlier, had not been the feeling of Beveridge and Bull.

As a preacher, where the subject was not one of a purely argumentative character, Hoadly was not successful. He said of his lectureship in the City, which he held between 1694 and 1704, that he preached it down to 30*l.* a year and

---

[1] It is said that the reason he himself alleged for not going into Wales was the 'party fury' that existed there (Chalmers' *Biog. D.*).

[2] Whiston's *Memoirs*, i. 205, and his *Life of Clarke*, p. 109.

[3] William Law, his most distinguished opponent, would certainly not have looked lightly upon such a breach of pastoral duty; but this good man had a great aversion to lowering the tone of controversy by anything which approached to a personal character.

[4] Readers need hardly be reminded that throughout the first half of the eighteenth century perception had not yet awakened to the beauties of mountainous country.

then resigned.[1] To stir the soul and warm the feelings was quite beyond his reach; and though, in his calm, dispassionate manner, he could reason with force upon the blessing of a life of Christian principle, this of itself can never sway the heart of a great congregation. Moreover, his style, though frequently rising into impressive dignity, was often diffuse and involved. Pope more than once ridiculed his 'periods of a mile,' and asked,—

> Which most conduce to soothe the soul in slumbers,
> My Hoadly's periods or my Blackmore's numbers?

Hoadly's fame rests entirely upon the power and unremitting energy with which he urged his ecclesiastical and political opinions. He was the typical Low Churchman of his age, and this in a manner far more decided than was the case with any of his contemporaries or predecessors. There were many Low Churchmen bishops in the two preceding reigns, but in all of these the distinctively Low Church element was modified either by some vein of thought which had a different character, or by the personal individuality of the man. But Hoadly was the principle personified, and developed both in its merits and defects to the utmost verge which the limits of the English Church allowed. The Low Churchmanship of that age was, it need hardly be observed, something widely different from what has gone by the same name since the rise of the Evangelical movement. They resemble one another in approximating more closely than their brethren in the English communion to the views commonly held by Protestant Dissenters, and in their comparative deficiency in what, for want of a more accurate name, may be called the Catholic turn of thought and sentiment. But whereas Evangelical feeling is apt to err in narrowness and intellectual timidity, the old Low

---

[1] Chalmers' *Biog. D.*

Churchmanship was prone to an excess of latitudinarianism, and to an over-exclusive confidence in reason. Piety, in the earlier Low Churchman, was apt to be too negligent of dogma; in the later it was apt, in appearance at least, to make faith too entirely a matter of believing. Both were capable of forming noble Christian characters; but the degeneracy of the one was a vague rationalism, that of the other an ungenial pietism. Hoadly, then, was essentially the Low Churchman of the earlier type, with very little to qualify, or divert the attention from it. He had, in a high degree, its distinctive virtues and its no less distinctive faults. He was a devoted lover of truth, and no less ardent in the cause of liberty. He believed in reason as a divine and heaven-sent power, and was not afraid to follow its leading. He was a true friend and champion of tolerance, hating not persecution only, but all unjust distinctions. Lastly, although too fond of controversy, he acquitted himself boldly and manfully in it; neither did he descend to the ignoble personalities which too often disfigured the polemics of his time.

These were his merits, and the enumeration of them is high praise. But they cannot be denied to him. They were enthusiastically acknowledged by his friends, and in the end not denied by his enemies; for though his views continued to be detested by a large body of Churchmen, he outlived personal animosity.

On the other hand, most English Churchmen will agree that his faults as a theologian were very great. He did not, in religious questions, set the current of the age, for it was already flowing fast; but he gave it a strong impetus in a direction which may have been guided ultimately to good results, but which, for a lengthened time, might be almost called disastrous. His opinions were grievously deficient in all that gives to worship fire, life, and unction. They neither had the High Churchman's reverence and appreciation of solemnity and beauty, nor the busy piety of the Evangelical, nor the earnest thoughtfulness of the Broad Churchman. And so, notwithstanding the valuable and admirable qualities which they did possess, his opinions, as they gained strength in the Church, had a depressing and even a deadening effect upon it. They seemed to lull its energies in a pleasant self-content of general philanthropy. The calm and dispassionate view of religion, however suitable it may be for philosophy, is too sluggish a thing to contend with powers of sin and cope with spiritual corruption. This was the great flaw in the Hoadleian divinity, or, as Secker called it, Christianity 'secundum usum Winton.'

Almost any theology is compatible in certain minds, and in certain periods, with dryness and want of fervour; and it is certain that if there had been more of the evangelist in Hoadly's temperament, there would have been nothing in his opinions which would have necessarily interfered with it. A High Churchman has no more right to attribute the coldness of the Hoadleian school to its Low Church theology, than the Low Churchman would be justified in assuming that its merits would have been incompatible with a High Church interpretation of disputed doctrines. At the same time, all who rejoice that the English Church, as a whole, has taken a position almost as far removed from that of a Dutch Arminian as from that of a Roman Catholic must feel that there was a baldness in his theological views which, so far as they prevailed, entered into a very unattractive combination with coldness of religious thought. Hoadly had no perception whatever of much which the great majority of Churchmen greatly value. There was nothing striking and imposing to his mind in the lengthened history of the Christian Church, its steady onward movement through varied periods and stages of civilisation, its continuous roll-call of saintly men and wise teachers. If he thought of it at all, it was rather to triumph in the hope that its manifold errors and corruptions might in his day melt away in a whiter light of truth and reason. Venerated names of primitive fathers and doctors of the faith had no weight for him. Never did he speak with such vehemence, such intensity of conviction, as when he felt that he was waging battle against authority, which seemed to him like a giant form overshadowing with a baleful influence the fair presence of truth. 'It is indeed the greatest and most irreconcilable enemy to truth and argument that this world ever furnished out since it was in being. . . . It is authority alone which keeps up the grossest errors in the countries around us. And where truth happens to be received for the sake of authority, there is just so much diminished from the love of truth, and the glory of reason, and the acceptableness of men to God, as there is attributed to authority. It was authority which crushed the noble sentiments of Socrates. . . . It was authority which hindered the voice of the Son of God Himself from being heard, and which alone stood in opposition to His powerful arguments and His divine authority. . . . It was the authority of Christians which, by degrees, not only laid waste the honour of Christianity, but well-nigh extinguished it from amongst men.'[1] It will be seen by such words that Hoadly, in his very genuine love of truth, was carried away into a very one-sided habit of thought. It is of course perfectly true that an exaggerated and indiscriminating respect for authority has been in every age the special adversary to the reception of new truth. Great reformers in particular periods may well be excused for repudiating with too little reservation all checks upon their full right of individual

[1] Hoadly's *Answer to the Repres. of the Com. of Convoc.*, pp. 312-14.

judgment. But even to them it is a loss not to feel reverence where reverence is due. To fail in this is sometimes almost as great an evil as to run into the opposite extreme. Religious thought in the eighteenth century was indeed passing through an invaluable training while it tried, with something of over-assurance, the powers of pure reason in matters of faith. But Christianity lost much of its depth and grandeur when thus viewed apart from the light it had shed upon seventeen centuries. Reason and Scripture together form strong ground upon which to rest, but even they cannot safely dispense with what may be further learnt from the experience and thought of ages. Hoadly, and those who after him thought like him, did dispense with it, and religion suffered thereby. We see it in many ways. He trusted so much to the judgment of individual reason, that, as judgments differ, he was driven to the conclusion that it is enough to be sincere, and that it is a matter of second importance what a man believes *if only he believes it truly.*[1] For a similar reason, self-sufficient in himself, he had little regard for words hallowed by sacred associations. The liturgical forms, which are so dear to most Churchmen, contained to his mind nothing that was particularly worth the keeping.[2] The same frame of mind, careless of all that does not appeal directly to the understanding, would strip worship of most of its comely and solemn accessories, and leave it bald and bare. It would be apt to go beyond this, and neglect those appeals to the feelings and affections without which religion inevitably grows cold,—further still yet, and disparage those spiritual faculties which are the chief life of the soul. Lastly, although it may not deny, or even doubt them, it will still incline to pass over and throw into the background doctrines which elude the full

---

[1] *Cf.*, however, his explanation, quoted i. 195.
[2] Al. Knox, *Remains*, i. 109.

comprehension of our reason; and where two interpretations are possible, it will at once prefer that which seems plainer and more simple, to another which may be at once more difficult to understand, but also far more full of deep and spiritual teaching.

In all these respects Hoadly's theology was deficient. While, therefore, he did service to his Church and age by those great merits of which mention has been already made—his ardent love of truth and justice, his hatred of tyranny and superstition, his tolerance, his fearlessness, and to a great extent his sound reason—it is no less certain that the popularity he deservedly won by such qualities increased also his power to depress in other respects the tone of religion by his small perception of much that is very requisite to it.

In forming an estimate of Hoadly's opinions and influence it should be borne in mind who was the special opponent against whom, in popular estimation, he was particularly matched. It was a man whom causes very slightly connected with religion had indeed raised to an extraordinary degree of fame, but whom no one, except such as were carried away by the enthusiasm or the clamour of the time, would dream of calling a wise and able representative of English High Churchmanship. Swift, in one of his letters to Stella, speaks of meeting 'Mr. Hoadly, the Whig clergyman, so famous for acting the contrary part to Sacheverell.'[1] Then, too, Hearne tells us of some doggerel verses Queen Anne found on her toilet-table, beginning—

> Among the High Churchmen I find there are several
> That stick to the doctrines of Harry Sacheverell;
> Among the Low Churchmen I find that, as oddly,
> Some pin all their faith upon Benjamin Hoadly.[2]

Religion was not likely, in any case, to benefit by con-

---

[1] Quoted in Cassan, p. 408.   [2] *Reliquiæ Hearnianæ*, i. 189.

troversies carried on, so to say, in the streets. So soon as the Sacheverell trial, and the ovation that followed it, had ceased to fill the news-letters and to excite the talkers of every coffee-house in the kingdom, the Bangorian controversy began, and, no less than the former one, 'seemed for a great while to engross the attention of the public.'[1] It may well be imagined by what personalities and by what coarse and gross misapprehensions of the points at issue such questions were adapted to the tastes of the populace. Doubtless some noble elements were, in a confused sort of way, mingled in the strife—liberty and Protestant zeal, loyalty and attachment to the Church. But in comparing the two controversies the first natural thought which arises in the mind is, what mischief would have befallen Christianity in England if either Sacheverell or Hoadly were to be the type on which the prevailing spirit of the Church was henceforth to be framed.

The reader shall not be wearied with a long account of the discussion in which Hoadly was engaged. A slight and general survey will be sufficient.

His early writings were all addressed to moderate Dissenters, with the object of winning them over to Conformity. From the first he utterly denounced any sort of pressure on the part of the civil power. But he hoped much from persuasion. He defended episcopal ordination, answered objections, urged the insignificance of the differences which separated them, and especially dwelt upon the argument that if Conformity were in itself lawful, it should be embraced from considerations of peace and unity.

His writings and speeches on occasional Conformity were on a kindred subject. He came into collision with many of his fellow-Churchmen by his strenuous advocacy

---

[1] Whiston's *Memoirs*, p. 205.

of the practice, as tending to Conformity, and in itself conducive to peace.

In 1705 his sermon before the Lord Mayor, on submission to civil magistrates, brought him into violent collision with an excited and very strong party who, on religious as well as on political grounds, upheld the theory of the divine right of kings, and in various degrees the duties of non-resistance and passive obedience. Foremost among his opponents was Atterbury, with whom he had already entered into controversy on two or three minor subjects. But the great majority of the clergy were deeply offended by his uncompromising denunciation of a doctrine which they had once held as altogether sacred, and which they had only departed from under the pressure of great necessity, with much doubt and many reservations. Their representatives in the Lower House of Convocation took up the question warmly, and condemned Hoadly's sermon as contradicting the Homilies, and savouring of wilful rebellion. Four years later, the House of Commons, in recognition of the power with which in his 'Measures of Obedience' he had maintained the new constitution, passed a vote of thanks to him, and represented in an address to the Queen the signal services he had done to the cause of civil and religious liberty.

Passing over various argumentative treatises which he published upon Fleetwood's work on miracles, upon Atterbury's sermon on the temporal rewards of goodness, upon the ancient prophets and the modern pretenders to inspiration, upon the Jacobite question, upon the Nonjurors, upon freethinking, and the extremes of implicit faith and infidelity, we come to the 'Bangorian' controversy. His 'Preservative against the Nonjurors,' published in 1716, had opened some disputed questions about the authority of the Church, and its relations to the civil government. But the controversy did not fully begin till the next year, when he preached before the king his famous sermon 'On the Kingdom of Christ.' Christ was the only lawgiver in matters relating to salvation; His kingdom was invisible and spiritual; no human authority had power to intrude upon the realm of conscience, and lay down judgments and decisions on points relating to the favour or displeasure of God; to apply to religious matters any motive of worldly force or worldly gain was opposed to the fundamental maxims of Christ's kingdom, and contrary, therefore, to its true interests.

There is a sense in which these positions cannot be successfully controverted; and Hoadly, well aware that he was on strong ground, maintained it with the power and prudence of a skilful dialectician. But, on the other hand, his words could be readily understood in a sense which, if carried out in practice, would act as a solvent to every kind of church constitution, and reduce the Christian body to a mere agglomerate of disconnected atoms. The argument, however true in itself, needs a good deal of careful definition before it can be fully accepted and practically worked. There was great need of its being discussed and defined, if it could be done without prejudice and passion. The Reformation had opened, but left wholly unsettled, the question as to the bounds of civil and ecclesiastical authority in matters relating to religion. Even those communions which had rejected most scornfully the claims of Rome had, in some notable instances, only replaced her authority by other no less absolute. In the Church of England it was quite time to come to a clearer understanding on this important subject; and now that the rights of reason were being everywhere vindicated, it was a subject the consideration of which could not long be deferred. Yet it was also a very unfavourable time for anything like a dispassionate investigation of such a theme. Minds, heated and embittered in the mixed political and ecclesiastical controversies which revolution had given birth to, were not likely to enter into discussion with any calmer spirit than that of partisans. Probably the first impression which Hoadly's sermon everywhere conveyed was that it was a terrible Whig manifesto.

No one can wonder that the Bangorian controversy which thus began was discursive and confused. The bounds of authority, the nature of the Church, its relations to the State, the rights of private judgment and its difficulties, the responsibilities of sincere inquiry, articles of communion, and in what sense they should be subscribed to, and by whom, the power of councils, the power of Convocation, the liberty of free thinking, how a church and how a state should act towards Atheists and towards Deists, questions of toleration, of tests, of Church establishments—there was not one of these and such other kindred subjects which a writer in this controversy might not enter upon fairly and without wandering from his subject; even an historian who should once enter upon it would scarcely know where to stop.

There is the less reason to enter upon it here, because what has been already said of Hoadly's cast of mind makes it almost superfluous to state his views on the various questions which the controversy brought under review. For it was essentially one of those discussions in which opinion depends more upon the tone of thought in spiritual and intellectual matters than upon weight of argument. In such cases it seems hopeless to expect even the fairest and most generous of controversialists to understand and be just to the position taken by his opponent. It was markedly so in the Bangorian dispute. There were numberless disputants on either side, and some of them very able; but looking back upon it from this lapse of time, the two figures which come prominently forward as representative

of contrasting theories and opposite forms of thought were
Hoadly and William Law.[1] What Hoadly was we have
already seen; William Law had not yet occupied the unique
and remarkable position which he afterwards held as leader
of a mystical school which had little in common with any other
theology of his age. As yet he was simply a High Churchman
and Nonjuror, profoundly religious, unworldly, and single-
minded, but with opinions formed in the somewhat narrow
groove of strictly High Church principles. Like Hoadly, he
was a powerful writer and a skilful controversialist. They
both kept close to whatever subject might be in dispute, and
both were far beyond their age in the temper and fairness
with which they argued. They did not come directly into
contact, for Hoadly left Law's published letters unanswered.
But their respective writings challenged the judgment of
their age on all the most material points at issue. Partisans
on either side held their own champion triumphantly superior. Rather it may be said that there was too entire an
absence of intellectual sympathy for one to understand the
other, and that each of them argued not so much upon
actual statements advanced on the other side, but upon his
own inferences and deductions from them. There are very
few principles of human thought or practice which allow of
being pushed to what might seem their ultimate logical
results. It was as certain that a great National Church
would refuse to be limited to the narrow bounds of High
Church orthodoxy, as that Hoadly's opinions, unless carefully guarded and largely supplemented, would be intolerable to many minds, and to some destructive of the very
idea of a church. But neither Hoadly would have consented

[1] There is a good analysis of Law's arguments against Hoadly in Overton's
Life of W. Law, pp. 18-30. An account of the controversy from the
point of view of one whose sympathies are with Hoadly rather than with
Law may be found in Hunt's *Relig. Thought in the Eighteenth Cent.*,
iii. 10 &c.

to much that was charged against him by Law, nor was Law, or any other reasonable High Churchman, so enslaved to authority, or so inimical to liberty of reason, as might be concluded from Hoadly's syllogisms.

In 1735, long after the Bangorian controversy had at last subsided, Law once more entered the lists against his old opponent. It was a question in which the religious feeling of English Churchmen was deeply concerned, as dealing with the highest act of Christian worship. There appears to be no doubt that ' A Plain Account of the Nature and End of the Sacrament of the Lord's Supper ' was by Hoadly, and that he wrote it from the most laudable motives; from a strong feeling of ' the gross superstitions which had sometimes gathered round it, and the severity and harshness which had deterred men from it.'[1] But the treatise bore throughout the marked stamp of his bald and utterly prosaic theology. ' Plain ' the account undoubtedly was, and simple in the extreme; but ' plain ' also in the sense of removing from the sacrament all its heights of sublimity, all its shades of mystical significance. Under his hands the eucharist became a bare memorial, an act of pious gratitude and obedience.'[2] The pamphlet attracted great notice. Not only did it elicit an immense number of replies, but it appears to have been a very frequent subject of general discourse. Although it fell in only too well with some prevailing tendencies of the age, yet even the abominable sacramental test had not seriously affected the deep reverence with which the hallowed ordinance was generally regarded. Opinion, therefore, was almost as much divided as it had been in the time of the former controversy. Those who did not miss what they did not find in Hoadly's works extolled with unbounded praise the genial spirit of universal kindliness and good-will which breathed through-

[1] Van Mildert's *Life of Waterland*, p. 208.   [2] *Id.*

out it. Archbishop Herring wrote of it, 'I see no reason
for such a prodigious outcry upon the "Plain Account." I
really think it a very good book, as orthodox as Archbishop
Tillotson. His prayers are very long, but in my opinion
some of the best compositions of the sort that ever I read;
and if I could bring my mind to that steady frame of thinking with regard to the Deity that is presented by him, I
believe I should be so far as happy as my nature is, perhaps,
capable of being.'[1] Fielding puts into the mouth of Parson
Adams a warm panegyric of 'that excellent book, "A Plain
Account," &c., a book written (if I may venture the expression) with the pen of an archangel, and calculated to restore
the true uses of Christianity and of that sacred institution.
For what could tend more to the noble purposes of religion
than frequent cheerful meetings among the members of a
society, in which they should in the presence of one another,
and in the service of the Supreme Being, make promises
of being good, friendly, and benevolent to each other?' The
tale then goes on to tell of the horror of his companion, who
felt himself present, 'for aught he knew, with the spirit of
evil himself, and expected to hear the Alcoran, the Levi-
athan, and Woolston commended if he stayed a few minutes
longer.'[2] Whiston spoke of it as 'that most injudicious
and unlearned treatise.'[3] Wheatley and Waterland charged
it with downright Socinianism. Others called it 'the worst
book that ever was written.'[4] Angeloni, an Italian who
remained for some years in London, wrote how 'the corrupted heart of a certain bishop of their nation has produced a book on the eucharist, with design to annihilate
all consideration of its being sacred. . . . He has done
more mischief to the cause of religion than all the Deistical

[1] Herring to Duncombe, Nov. 17, 1735, p. 28.
[2] Fielding's *Joseph Andrews*, chap. xvii.
[3] Whiston's *Memoirs*, p. 245.   [4] Overton's *Life of Law*, pp. 281-82.

writers of the world, and snapped the foundation of those principles which actuate more strongly than reason in producing happiness in man.'[1] It may be added, that the strong disapproval of the book which was so commonly felt was greatly reinforced by the praises both of the avowedly unorthodox and of the Deists. Of the former class was Middleton, who in a letter to Lord Hervey wrote to say how much 'he liked both the design and the doctrine, as he did every other design of reconciling religion with reason. Hoadly's enemies, he added, might insult him; but the candid would see that he sought only to destroy superstition by setting reason in its place.'[2] So, among the Deists, Chubb declaimed against 'the great and general opposition that has been made by the clergy to an attempt for restoring the institution of Christ commonly called the Lord's Supper to its original plainness and simplicity.'[3] Nor, when the readers of another Deist, Thomas Morgan, read what he said of our Lord 'following the usage of breaking a biscuit and distributing wine to those who were present, and asking His disciples, in reminiscence of Him, to do this, as they were to do all other things in His name,' could they fail to see that there was no very apparent difference between Morgan's doctrine in this particular and that of the English bishop. Another of Hoadly's controversies should be referred to here, as very characteristic of his singular insensibility to the emotional side of religion. He argued against Hare, Law, and others, that fervency and zeal were quite inappropriate to prayer, the manner of which ought, he said, to be wholly calm, rational, and dispassionate.

Hoadly's opinions, and the various feelings excited by

---

[1] Baptista Angeloni's *Letters on the English Nation*, i. 76.
[2] Nichols' *Lit. Anec.*, v. 421.
[3] Chubb, *On the Equity and Reasonableness*, &c., p. 69.

them among Churchmen and in the country generally, have been dwelt upon at some length, as being very illustrative of the currents and counter-currents of religious thought in the earlier and middle part of the last century. What remains may be said briefly.

The offence caused to a great number of the clergy by his sermon on Church authority, and the consequent resolution to proceed against him in Convocation, gave occasion to a prorogation of the ancient council of the Church which lasted so long into the present century. It would be unjust, however, to attribute this, as many of his contemporaries did, entirely to Hoadly. He defended himself against such an imputation. 'I had no other thought, desire, or resolution, but to answer in my place before the same house to which this accusation was designed to be brought. . . . The prorogation was not only without my seeking, but without so much as my knowledge, or even suspicion of any such design, till it was actually resolved and ordered.'[1] There can be no doubt the ministry were only too glad to find so good an opportunity for silencing, at all events for the time, what had become a somewhat unruly and turbulent assembly. Few things were more dreaded by a Whig government than a return of the frenzy which had pervaded the country and upset the existing ministry on occasion of the Sacheverell trial. And the fear existed so long as Tory and High Church passion was fanned by the organised efforts of excited clergymen in the Lower House of Convocation.

In regard of the prosecution of Atterbury, it is quite possible that in Hoadly's mind political duty and patriotic feeling overrode all personal considerations. Otherwise the active part[2] he took against his old opponent in controversy

[1] Quoted in Cassan's *Bishops of Salisbury*, p. 219.
[2] Williams' *Life of Atterbury*, i. 117.

accuses him of grave deficiency in the finer feelings of what was seemly and chivalrous.

When the Schism Bill was repealed, he was very desirous that the work of toleration should be further carried out by the removal of the sacramental test. It was not only, he said, impolitic and unreasonable to make it a qualification for civil and military employments, and to deprive the State thereby of the services of some of its best citizens; it was also exposing the most sacred institutions to be abused by profane and irreligious persons.[1]

There was one seeming exception to his uniform love of toleration. He insisted, in 1722, on the perfect justice of convicted Papists forfeiting two-thirds of their property. He was, however, very careful to make it understood that such an act would at once become persecution—'the most inhumane and unsociable of crimes'—if any consideration were introduced of differences in religion; 'the civil enmity must be the sole condition of such penalties.'[2]

Hoadly was a devoted friend to Dr. Samuel Clarke. He wrote his life, and looked up to him with an admiration which almost amounted to a passion. He asked, he said, for no greater distinction than to be remembered as the friend of so admirable a man. He was often charged, although no further ground could be alleged for it, with sharing in his friend's Arian opinions.

In private life he possessed a genial and happy temperament. Easy in manner and not wanting in humour, he was fond of society, but never so content as in the midst of his own family. Milner speaks of the 'incongruous association of emblems' on his tomb at Winchester—the pastoral crosier and the democratic pike and cap—the Scriptures and Magna Charta.[3] The pike, if it is indeed there, is incongruous

[1] *Parl. Hist.*, vii. 571. [2] Letters to 'Britannicus,' Hoadly's *Works*, iii. 52–72.
[3] Cassan's *Bishops of Salisbury*, p. 235.

enough; and the pastoral staff is suggestive of Hoadly's grossest defect. But the rest may well represent those elements in the bishop's character which make up for much that was wanting in it—his love of liberty, his love of justice, his reverence—exclusive to a fault—for the authority of Holy Writ.

Edmund Gibson succeeded Wake at Lincoln, 1716-23, and Robinson in the see of London, 1723-48. At Oxford, in the last ten years of the seventeenth century, he had gained repute by extensive reading in early English and its kindred languages, as also in topography and general antiquities. Archbishop Tenison made him his chaplain and Lambeth librarian. In 1703, when there was much contention between the Upper and Lower House of Convocation, he took an active part in asserting the authority of the former. 'We might,' he said, 'as well have no Episcopal Church, as have bishops under the awe and authority of presbyters, for, by their present measures, no. equality would scarce content them.'[1] In 1711 he wrote a comprehensive work on the legal rights and duties of the clergy. It was entitled 'Codex Juris Ecclesiastici Anglicani.' The book was one of some value and importance, and he was thenceforth often consulted on points relating to the constitutional position of the Church. But the nickname of Dr. Codex, which he obtained from it, hit a weaker side of his character. He was rather a stickler for rights and privileges, and somewhat cramped and legal in his ideas. Whiston, after granting that he was a pious and generous man, smiled at his deep respect for 'parliamentary laws and political injunctions,' and how he 'seemed to think the Church of England came down from heaven, as it just then happened to be established by laws and canons.'[2] Wake, on his

[1] Gibson to Thoresby, Thoresby's *Diary*, i. 435.
[2] Whiston's *Memoirs*, p. 252.

promotion from Lincoln to Canterbury, suggested Gibson as excellently adapted for the vacant see. The recommendation was acted upon, and fully justified by the assiduity with which he devoted himself to his office. When he became Bishop of London, for some time his influence with the Government was greater than that of any other Churchman of his day. The Archbishop of Canterbury had become very infirm, and Walpole, having a very high opinion of Gibson's ability and judgment, consulted him for some time on all Church matters. Some one declared to the minister that Gibson was his Pope. 'Yes,' said Walpole, ' and a very good Pope too.'[1] He was called heir apparent of Canterbury, and one of the triumvirate, the firm of three by whom England was governed—Townshend, Walpole, and Gibson. In 1736 Gibson annoyed Walpole by his opposition to the Quakers Bill, and the intimacy ceased.

Gibson was too emphatically a moderate man to be of any great service to his Church and time, although he was sometimes very highly praised. He worked well and preached well. He wrote some 'tracts against Papists,' a warning against enthusiasm, an 'earnest and affectionate address to the Methodists,'[2] whom he would gladly have encouraged if only they would fall in with established order. As regards Nonconformity, he endeavoured, with no great success, to steer a middle line between a great and a too little relaxation of the restrictive laws. He prevented Rundle, who was suspected of dangerous latitudinarianism, from being raised to the see of Gloucester,[3] but seems to have been content that he should go as bishop to Derry. He wrote against Tindal, and succeeded in stopping the publication

---

[1] Noble's *Grainger*, iii. 70. [2] Noble, iii. 70.
[3] Rundle to Duncombe in Hughes' *Correspondence*, ii. 35 ; *Gent.'s Magazine* for 1734, iv. 153, 196.

of one of his posthumous works. Some writings which he thought might be mischievous he bought up as they issued from the press, while he helped the authors to gain a livelihood by other means. He conscientiously refused the primacy, from a fear lest his health might prevent him from discharging its duties as he ought. He wrote a work of family devotion. He did not neglect his charge as bishop for the colonies. He offended George II. by inveighing against masquerades, an amusement of which the king was very fond. It should be said of him, lastly, that having received a bequest from Lord Crewe of £2,500, he at once handed it over to that bishop's relations on hearing that they were insufficiently provided for.[1]

The episcopate of John Potter was almost exactly contemporary with that of Gibson. He became Bishop of Oxford in 1715, was raised to the Primacy in 1737, and died in 1747. He was even more representative of his age than Gibson. For the latter, although too moderate and guarded to exert much beneficial power, was very free from the faults which most lowered the general estimate of episcopal character in that age. The same cannot be said of Potter. He had undoubtedly many merits, and well deserved promotion. But Whiston was probably quite right in saying that he was one of those whom promotion is apt to spoil. Born in humble station, he had raised himself first to the Regius Professorship of Divinity at Oxford, then to the Bench of Bishops, and at last to the very highest place in the English Church. This great position did not improve him as a man. When Canterbury was vacant, Queen Caroline asked Whiston what his opinion was of Potter. He replied that he could be highly recommended as a person of great piety, learning, and moderation; an excellent pastor, without pride or vanity. 'But,' says Whiston, 'when he became archbishop, not only

[1] Chalmers' *Biographies*, vol. xv.

did he assume a high and pontifical state—having, for instance, half a dozen bareheaded footmen by the side of his coach—but also became a courtier in his own ways, and fond of gross flattery from others.'[1] Nichols describes him as learned and in many ways exemplary, but not amiable, and somewhat haughty and severe. He disinherited his eldest son for marrying beneath his station.[2] His own writings prove that he was overmuch the courtier. He preached before the House of Lords at the accession of George I. and at the coronation of George II., and in either case did what Lord Mansfield said of a sermon soon after George III. was crowned—he 'bedaubed the king with praises.'[3] To judge from his words, each of the first two Georges might have been a Solomon or an Antonine, a Charles the Great or an Alfred. The former of the two was 'a prince of consummate prudence and invincible resolution, of strict justice tempered with equal clemency and mildness, and of great bravery and courage supported by the wisest conduct; one who hath been long experienced in the arts of governing, and hath never known any other rule or measure of his government but the happiness of his people.'[4] When at last this most noble and virtuous of sovereigns was gathered to his fathers, he was succeeded, as we find in the archbishop's writings, by a son of no less grandeur of soul than had distinguished his predecessor. They beheld 'a prince, lineally descended from a long race of great progenitors, who for many ages have swayed the same august sceptre, which, through the generous disposal of Providence, is now delivered into his sacred hands; . . . a prince whom the great Sovereign of heaven hath ordained to be a public

---

[1] Whiston's *Memoirs*, pp. 359–60. [2] Nichols' *Lit. Anec.*, i. 178.
[3] Warburton and Hurd's *Corresp.*, 319. On that occasion the young king expressed his offence publicly. 'He came to chapel,' he said, ' to hear the praises of God, not his own.'
[4] Potter's *Works*, i. 236.

blessing,' and wedded to a queen 'endowed with every Christian grace, every royal virtue.'[1]

Archbishop Potter also set an example of nepotism which deserved severer censure than it received in a time when opinion was far too easy on such matters. His son-in-law, Jeremiah Miller, was a good and learned man, and deserved advancement. But the following is the accumulation of good things which his fortunate marriage brought with it. 'His Grace obtained for him from the Crown the united rectories of St. Edmund the King and St. Nicholas Axon in Lombard Street, with that of Merstham, Surrey, and the sinecure of West Tarring in Sussex. From the chantorship of Exeter he was promoted to the deanery of that cathedral. All these preferments he held till his death, except that of West Tarring, which he resigned a few years before to his son.'[2]

Potter's orthodoxy, and his devotion to all the formularies of the English Church, were as strict and undeviating as Gibson's. But it was of a rather different kind. Gibson neither knew nor cared for patristic divinity, but was intimately versed in all that related to the constitution of the Church in this country, and would probably have thought it no whit the less perfect if it had differed ever so widely in all non-essentials from that of the first three centuries. Potter, on the other hand, was thoroughly well read in all the early fathers, and strove with laborious satisfaction to convince himself and others that the Anglican Church was shaped in close conformity with the primitive ecclesiastical type. His Discourse on Church Government is in its kind an excellent work, and is still frequently recommended to the study of candidates for Holy Orders. It was published before he became bishop. He also edited with great care the works of Clement of Alexandria.

[1] Potter's *Works*, i. 256.   [2] Nichols' *Lit. Ancc.*, iv. 171.

Earlier in the century, a Whig in politics was almost always more or less a liberal, or (as he would then have been called) latitudinarian, in his Church views. This was no longer the case when once the Brunswick dynasty was thoroughly established on the throne. But Potter, although he had never been a Tory, had always been strongly opposed to the old Low Church principles, and when he was archbishop was more than ever adverse either to concessions to Nonconformists or to increased latitude of subscription. His pastoral charges, however, are for the most part purely practical, and often contain excellent advice. One of the most interesting features in his archiepiscopate, and one which would hardly have been expected from him, is the disposition he more than once showed to look with favour upon Methodism, and his real active interest in the work of the Moravians. Like most writers and preachers of that period, he took a very dark view of the religion and morals of his day.[1]

Edward Chandler was raised to the Episcopate in the first year of George I.'s reign, and was Bishop of Lichfield and Coventry for sixteen years (1714-30), and of Durham from 1730 to 1750. He was a native of Ireland, had studied at Leyden at the same time with Secker, and with his distinguished Nonconformist namesake, Samuel Chandler.[2] His later intimacy with Lloyd, Bishop of Worcester, to whom he was for some time chaplain, tended no doubt to turn his theological studies in the direction of the prophecies. At all events, it was upon their elucidation that he expended his rich stores of Scriptural and Rabbinical learning. He was one of the studious prelates of the century, and little mention is found of him in any other capacity than as a writer. Browne Willis, however, his contemporary, speaks of him with much respect as 'our

[1] Potter's *Works*, i. 268.   [2] Nichols, v. 301.

present most worthy bishop,'[1] and during his long episcopate it does not appear that he ever had an enemy or disparager. But his repute rests entirely upon his valuable services in defence of orthodox Christianity against the Deists. Of the thirty-five answers or more which, within two years, were published, some of them by the ablest divines of the day, against Antony Collins' treatise on Prophecy, none were considered so powerful as the 'Defence of Christianity,' published in 1725, by Chandler.[2] Collins, without replying to the rest, put out all his strength to maintain his position against him, and the bishop met his arguments by a second work no less able than his former one. In each of these, Chandler's strength lay not only in his great learning, and in the thoroughness with which he covered the subject, but also in the discrimination with which he conceded points which many had maintained with no other effect than that of weakening the Christian argument. The dissatisfaction with which his work was read by some who were more zealous than well informed, only served to show his greater mastery of the controverted questions.

George Smalridge, who was Bishop of Bristol from 1714 to 1719, belongs in character and opinion more to the period of Queen Anne than to that of any of the Georges. In politics he was a thorough Tory, and as nearly a Jacobite as he could be consistently with the very lukewarm adherence he had given to the new constitution. His friendship with his old schoolfellow Atterbury, and their conjoint labours in editing Clarendon's works, had fostered[3] the regret with which he looked back to the loyalty and chivalry of which that author told. In a Thirtieth of January sermon before

---

[1] Browne Willis, *Survey of Cathedrals*, ii. 397.
[2] See Cairns' *Unbelief in the Eighteenth Century*, pp. 76-79; Hunt's *Rel. Thought in England*, ii. 378, &c.; and Overton's *Essay on Deists in the English Church*, &c.
[3] Lord Mahon has some remarks on this in his *History*, chap. xii.

the House of Commons in 1701, he had declared 'that whosoever does not abhor the execution of King Charles I. is so ill a person that no good man may converse with him.'[1] His pronounced views cost him in 1706 the Regius Professorship of Divinity at Oxford. In 1715 he incurred the displeasure of Parliament by refusing to sign a declaration which had been drawn up by the archbishop, expressing abhorrence of the Jacobite rebellion.[2] His High Almonership was taken from him on the pretext that he had exerted undue influence at the Bristol election. On the other hand, 'the Oxford Jacobites looked upon him thereupon as a brother.'[3] He was, however, wholly guiltless of anything like Jacobite intrigue. For his character was open and sincere, and he was held in high esteem by all who knew him, irrespectively of party. Queen Caroline paid him much attention,[4] and after his death procured a pension for his widow.[5] Addison wrote to Swift, 'The greatest pleasure I have met with for some months is the company of my old friend Dr. Smalridge, who is the most candid and agreeable of all bishops.'[6] He was much beloved by Robert Nelson, and was associated with him and Dr. Bray in almost all their works of Christian benevolence. Nelson bequeathed to him his Madonna by Correggio, ' as a small testimony of that great value and respect I bear to his lordship.'[7] The graceful Latin epitaph on that good man's monument in St. George's Chapel is Smalridge's composition.[8] Under the name of 'Favonius,' he is spoken of in the 'Tatler' in the warmest language of admiring respect as a very humane and good man, of well-tempered zeal and touching eloquence, and 'abounding in that sort of virtue

[1] Bincke's *Animadversions on Two Last Jan. 30 Sermons*.
[2] Noble's *Cont. of Grainger*, iii. 83.
[3] Wilkins to Nicolson, Jan. 171⁵⁄₆, Nicolson's *Letters*, p. 438.
[4] Lady Cowper's *Diary*, p. 18.   [5] Bishop Newton's *Life*, p. 10.
[6] Oct. 1718, *id.*, p. 8. [7] Secretan's *Life of Nelson*, p. 285. [8] *Id.* p. 116

and knowledge which makes religion beautiful.'[1] Bishop Newton has also spoken very highly of him, and adds that he was a man of much gravity and dignity, and of great sweetness of manner.[2] In reference to this last feature of his character, it was said of him when he succeeded Atterbury as Dean of Carlisle that he carried the bucket to extinguish the fires which the other had kindled. Whiston thought him 'one of the most learned and excellent persons in the kingdom,'[3] and said that if any one could have convinced him that he was in error, it would be he. He tried to flatter himself that he was convincing his friend instead, and argued that the small account in which Smalridge held the Athanasian Creed was a sign of Arian tendencies. This, however, Smalridge shortly before his death emphatically denied.[4] In fact, he was not at all the man to be discontented with the good old paths. His mind, cultured as it was, was not of a speculative turn; and once, when Whiston, a man of great ingenuity, had fairly puzzled him, he said with great earnestness, that even if it were as his companion had said, he had no wish to examine into it, and to find that the Church had been in error for so many hundred years.[5]

Smalridge published some sermons which Dr. Johnson thought were among the best of the century for style.[6] He also wrote the life of Grabe, a Prussian Lutheran, of great erudition in patristic literature, who had taken English orders. In company with him, Dr. Jablouski, and Archbishop Sharp, he took an active part in the efforts which were at one time made to bring the Prussian Lutheran Church into nearer conformity with the Anglican.[7]

Hearne tells a little anecdote about Smalridge, which is

[1] *Tatler*, Nos. 72 and 114.   [2] Bishop Newton's *Life and Works*, i. 7.
[3] Whiston's *Memoirs of Dr. Clarke*, p. 30.
[4] Newton's *Life*, p. 10.   [5] Whiston's *Life of Clarke*, p. 142.
[6] Boswell's *Johnson*, iii. 281.
[7] *Life of Archbishop Sharp*, i. 178; ii. 167.

illustrative both of the condition of the stage which made it generally indecorous for a clergyman to appear at a theatre, of the meritorious attempt of Addison in his 'Cato' to introduce a purer drama, and of that talking and smiling in churches which is so often alluded to in the essayists. Smalridge, he says, when Dean of Christ Church, being one night at the play to hear 'Cato' acted, there was great notice taken that a man of his order and dignity should be there. Some ladies laughed, as it seemed to him, and he said, 'Sure the ladies, by laughing so, think themselves to be at church.'[1]

Francis Gastrell was Bishop of Chester from 1714 to 1725. He is chiefly known by a useful little work he published in 1707, entitled 'Christian Institutes,' a well-arranged digest of parallel Scripture passages. It has been repeatedly printed, and 'may be very advantageously substituted for any of the subsequent larger and more expensive books.'[2] He was a man of some degree of mark, a Boyle Lecturer, and a writer of various controversial works against Collins, Clarke, and others. He seems to have taken a very frequent part in parliamentary debates, by no means confining himself to questions of religion or public morals. On some occasions he had strongly opposed Atterbury, but on occasion of his attainder pleaded earnestly for a remission of penalty, and did not spare his censures upon such of the bishops as had joined in the outcry against their Jacobite brother.[3]

Gastrell also came into notice by his contest with Archbishop Wake on the question of Lambeth degrees. He insisted that no degrees except such as had been conferred by the universities were valid qualifications for ecclesiastical

---

[1] *Reliq. Hearnianæ*, ii. 169.
[2] Horne, *On the Scriptures*, Part II. chap. vi. sect. 3.
[3] *Parliamentary Proceedings*, viii. 306.

preferment, and refused to admit Peploe (who was afterwards his successor at Chester) to the wardenship of the College at Manchester. He was not able to carry his point; but the University of Oxford, jealous of their rights, passed a vote of thanks to him in full Convocation.[1]

In his Boyle Lectures of 1697, Gastrell, like many other writers of that date,[2] had taken a very dark view of the condition of his age. It seemed to him, he said, that there was 'a public denial of religion, and all the obligations of it, with an attempt to despise the evidences brought for it, and to offer a more rational system of libertinism.'[3]

Richard Willis,[4] Gloucester 1714-21, Salisbury 1721-23, Winchester 1723-34, was a thorough Whig, and a consistent advocate of religious liberty. By those who disliked his opinions, and especially his liberal attitude toward Dissenters, it was commonly said that he owed his promotion to Winchester entirely to his vigorous speech against Atterbury. But he had other qualifications besides such as were connected with his political views. He was—what was not at all common among the clergy of that time—an excellent extempore preacher. He was much interested in charity schools, and in the proceedings of the Christian Knowledge Society, at whose first general meeting he preached the inaugural sermon. He appears also to have been liberal in his charities, as when he sent a generous donation to the distressed Salzburgers, and in the frequent help he gave to needy gentlemen in his diocese, towards sending their sons to school at his native town of Winchester.

[1] Ormerod's *Hist. of Cheshire*, i. 79.
[2] As Bentley (Bentley's *Corresp.*, i. 39); R. Nelson, Nichols' *Lit. Anec.*, iv. 207; Tillotson, *Works*, i. 54, 79; Swift, *Works*, viii. 66, &c.
[3] Quoted in Hunt's *Rel. Thought*, &c., pp. 3, 100.
[4] Cassan's *Bishops of Winchester*, pp. 216-21; Noble's *Cont. of Grainger*, iii. 76; *Parl. Hist.*, vol. vi. vii.

White Kennet, Bishop of Peterborough from 1718 to 1728, is most remembered as an historian and antiquarian. His work on 'Parochial Antiquities' will always remain a valuable contribution to English local history. The only other of his writings in general literature which need here be mentioned is the third volume in folio of 'The Complete History of England.' That period of the history for which he was responsible included the greater part of the seventeenth century. Although his accuracy has been much questioned, and though the book is now superseded, it was an important work in its time.

But Kennet also took a busy part in many of the leading movements of his day, not so much in active life, for he was a very studious man, but in the controversies occasioned by them. In early life, while yet a student at Oxford, he wrote, in 1680, so caustic a pamphlet against the Whigs, that notice was taken of it in the House of Commons,[1] and there was some thought of insisting upon his punishment. His change in later years into a decided Whig and Low Churchman was a sin which, in those days of excited party feeling, was not lightly to be forgiven. He was unmercifully lampooned and reviled, and was scarcely spoken of among Nonjurors and hot High Churchmen except as 'weathercock Kennet,' or 'the Dean the traytor.'[2] Welton, one of the most vehement of the Nonjurors, while he was yet rector of Whitechapel, put up an altar-piece in his church representing the Last Supper, in which Judas Iscariot was represented by Kennet. The likeness was beyond dispute. As a young man Kennet had met with a gun accident, which fractured the skull, and he always afterwards wore a black velvet patch on the injured place. The picture was quickly removed by order of the Bishop

---

[1] Nicolson's *Letters*, p. 642 (note).
[2] Noble's *Cont. of Grainger*, iii. 67; Nichols' *Anec.*, i. 401.

of London; but meanwhile none of the multitudes who went to see it could mistake the figure with the black scarf, white band, short wig, and black patch.¹ After all, as Kennet himself said, the times had moved away from him quite as much as he from his old opinions. He saw the most exemplary bishops and clergymen called Dissenters and Presbyterians in 1709, for expressing the very same views which in 1689 had been common in the mouths of the best High Churchmen.² For his own part, he wished the terms 'High' and 'Low' could be banished, and no distinction made but between good Churchmen and bad.³

As a contrast to the extraordinary instance of party virulence manifested in Welton's picture, it is pleasant to notice how similarity of literary tastes could bring together men who stood utterly apart in political and Church questions. We find Kennet entertaining in his house at Ambrosden the staunchest of Nonjurors, George Hicks, and receiving instruction from him in the Saxon and Northern languages.⁴

Kennet remembered something of the controversy with Romanists in King James's reign, and several of his early sermons had been on that subject. The memory of it clung to him, and he often seemed to be in fear lest the current of feeling should ever set toward Rome.⁵ For the same reason he always gave his hearty co-operation to everything that might lessen the gap between Churchmen and Dissenters, and bring the English Church into closer and more frequent communication with Protestants abroad. He was

¹ *Life of White Kennet*, by himself, pp. 141-42; Nichols, i. 398; Lathbury's *Nonjurors*, p. 256.
² *Life of Kennet*, p. 110.
³ Kennet's *Vindication of the Clergy*, p. 117.
⁴ Noble, i. 120. It was, however, almost impossible that there should be a long-continued intimacy between those who so vehemently differed in their most cherished convictions; nor was it so in this case.
⁵ Kennet's *Life*, p. 127.

of course a strenuous adherent of the House of Brunswick. Upon George I.'s accession he wrote to a friend, expressing not only his joy, but his fixed opinion that the king was 'one of the honestest of men, and one of the wisest princes in the world.'[1]

Kennet was much interested in the Colonial Church, wrote a history of the proceedings of the Society for the Propagation of the Gospel, and, in addition to much other valuable aid, presented to it every publication which he could find in any way bearing upon the colonies.[2] He did another good service to the Church of his time, in his 'Vindication of the Clergy' from various unjust imputations which had been brought against them.

None of the other bishops who were appointed in George I.'s time need be spoken of at any length.

Richard Smallbrook (St. David's 1723-30, Lichfield 1730-49) wrote a learned but somewhat over-long and diffuse work[3] against Woolston. The effect of a work which was not in itself so strong as many that were written against the Deists, did not gain further strength by his advocacy of their legal prosecution. Such reinforcement of controversial by temporal weapons[4] naturally gave a satirist of the day occasion to say of Woolston that—

Chains sure convinced him, though the prelate failed.[5]

Smallbrook seems to have been too obsequious in manner,[6] and too ready to give preferment to his own relations.[7] He

[1] Quoted in Stoughton's *Queen Anne*, p. 91.
[2] Anderson's *Church in the Colonies*, iii. 144.
[3] Hunt's *Rel. Th. in Eng.*, ii. 418-23.
[4] He was charged with defending religion by fire and sword. Waterland wrote in his defence (Van Mildert's *Life of Waterland*, p. 174).
[5] P. Whitehead's 'State Dunces,' *B. Poets*, x. 845.
[6] Horace Walpole (*Letters*, i. 67) refers to a caricature of this bishop bowing obsequiously as the ministerial coach passes.
[7] Nichols, i. 405.

showed partiality to his friends in a more exemplary way in the liberal help he gave to his old college, Magdalen, in the erection of their new buildings. His opinion on Methodism has been referred to in a preceding chapter. It may be added that Gibson thought highly of him, and was very anxious that he should be made Archbishop of Dublin.[1]

Samuel Bradford[2] (Carlisle 1718-23, Rochester 1723-31) was a man of considerable learning, Boyle Lecturer, a friend of Tillotson, and editor of his sermons. The northern gentry were generally much averse to him when he first went to Carlisle, on account of his opposition to Atterbury. But he won their respect and esteem.

Thomas Green[3] (Norwich 1721-23, Ely 1723-38) had been chaplain to Archbishop Tenison, and was strongly recommended by him. Bentham has little more to say of him than that he was 'an amiable man.'

He was succeeded at Norwich by John Leng[4] (1723-27), a distinguished Latin scholar. His Boyle Lectures were in some repute, and passed into a second edition. Whiston speaks of him as 'a good and learned man.' At college he had been a noted tutor, and in his diocese he is favourably described as a man of modesty and diligence, whose premature death by small-pox was much lamented throughout his diocese.

William Baker[5] (Bangor 1723-27, Norwich 1727-32) had been, like a great number of eighteenth-century bishops, master of a college. He was a good preacher; in opinion a thorough Whig and Low Churchman. A vehement High Tory writer—Dr. W. King—speaking of his appointment,

---

[1] Mant's *Irish Ch.*, ii. 504.
[2] Birch's *Tillotson*, i. 292; Jefferson's *Carlisle*, p. 236; Grainger, iii. 90.
[3] Bentham's *Ely*, p. 210; Blomfield's *Norfolk*, p. 593.
[4] Blomfield's *Norfolk*, p. 594; Nichols' *Lit. Ance.*, i. 401; Whiston's *Memoirs*, p. 547; Aug. Jessop's *Dioc. Hist. of Norwich*.
[5] Blomfield's *Norwich*, p. 596.

described him as one of those who 'for thirty pieces of silver
... preach up comprehension, moderation, occasional conformity, and all detestable doctrines of Forty-one.'[1]

Of Blackbourne mention has been made in a preceding chapter. His successor at Exeter was Stephen Weston[2] (1724–43). He was a friend of Sir R. Walpole, whose schoolfellow he had been at Eton. His sermons were edited and published by Sherlock.

Edward Waddington of Chichester (1724–31) appears to have been an excellent man, 'of the most endearing character, unaffected piety, primitive simplicity, and well-directed munificence.'[3]

Hugh Boulter was Bishop of Bristol from 1719 to 1724. He will be mentioned in another chapter in connection with Ireland, where he occupied a great political position, and where as Archbishop of Armagh his thoughtful munificence won him high popularity.

Samuel Peploe[4] (Chester 1727–52) apparently owed his elevation to his active loyalty to George I. when the rebel army advanced to Preston, where he was vicar. It is mentioned of him that he liberally gave £1,000 to the University of Dublin for a printing-house.[5]

Little of any kind worth mentioning is told of John Wynne (St. Asaph 1714–27, Bath and Wells 1727–43), William Bradshaw (Bristol 1724–32), John Waugh (Carlisle 1723–34), Richard Reynolds (Bangor 1721–23, Lincoln 1723–43), Joseph Wilcocks (Gloucester 1721–31, Rochester 1731–58), Robert Clavering (Llandaff 1724–28, Peterborough 1728–47), Henry Egerton (Hereford 1723–46), Thomas Bowers (Chichester 1722–24). Egerton must be distin-

---

[1] W. King's 'Vindication of Sacheverell,' *Works*, ii. 217.
[2] Polwhele's *Hist. of Devonshire*, p. 519; Noble's *Grainger*, iii. 93.
[3] Nicolson's *Letters*, p. 179, note. [4] Ormerod's *Cheshire*, p. 80.
[5] *Gent.'s Mag.* for Jan. 1734, p. 48.

guished from John Egerton who was afterwards Bishop of Durham; Wynne is spoken of by Hearne as a great student of Locke's philosophy; Doddridge mentions Reynolds as 'a valuable person'; Waugh is said to have been very acceptable at Carlisle, as being a native of that town; Clavering was a great Hebrew scholar.

Section 2.—*George the Second's Reign.*

When George II. became king, Archbishop Wake was the only one, except Atterbury, left of Queen Anne's bishops, although there were yet three survivors, Wilson, Hough, and Talbot, of those who dated their consecration from the seventeenth century. The remaining three-and-twenty had all been raised to the Episcopate in George I.'s reign. All the stir and energy, all the rancour and animosities which had characterised the Church of Queen Anne's time were past and gone. Religion in England had fully settled down into a long and somewhat indolent calm. The bishops who were appointed under the first two Georges were almost without exception men of their day, quite representatives of their Church and time. A great number of them were men of small note, estimable for the most part in their private capacity, and as bishops ready enough to perform their official duties with respectable conscientiousness, but still giving the idea that they mainly looked upon their sees as very comfortable promotions, out of which translation might lead them up to resting-places better still for themselves and theirs. The ablest and most celebrated among them were most of them men of very great worth, but sharing in the general characteristics, and marked by a sort of family likeness. Among those of whom sketches have already been given, there were Potter and Gibson, Chandler and Hoadly. Of those who in George II.'s reign were appointed to English sees, the most notable, or at all events the most well known, were Herring and Secker of Canterbury, Sherlock of London, Hare of Chichester, and a fifth, more illustrious than any of the preceding, Butler of Durham. He and Berkeley of Cloyne hold, so to say, a position of their own. The others, however much they differ individually, yet bear the impress of a common stamp which marks them one and all as bishops of the eighteenth century.

Thomas Herring was raised to Bangor in 1737, to York in 1743, and to Canterbury in 1747. He had been chaplain to Bishop Fleetwood, and in 1727 was a preacher of much repute at Lincoln's Inn. Neither then nor at any later time would his hearers gather from his sermons many suggestive thoughts to help them on the great questions which the Deists had brought generally into notice. For Herring had what might almost be called a morbid horror of controversy, and shunned statements of doctrine to an extent which must have taken much life and motive from his preaching. There were those who said he was an Arian.[1] He acknowledged that 'he abhorred every tendency to the Athanasian controversy.'[2] But his heresy, such as it was, was probably of a purely negative kind. His was no mind to appreciate the full bearings of even the most important theological distinctions. He did not seem to see their practical bearing, and what did not appear to him practical he impatiently thrust aside. For much the same reason, what he heard of the Methodist preaching inspired him with feelings of incredulity only and pity.[3] What had practical religion to do with all this show of emotional excitement? Those, however, who pressed to hear Herring preach, without looking either for impassioned appeal or

---

[1] Hunt, iii. 273.   [2] Chalmers' *Biog.*, vol. xviii.
[3] Nichols' *Lit. Ancc.*, v. 246; Duncombe's *Letters*, p. 171.

searching deductions from teachings of Christian theology, might depart well content with what they had heard. They would have listened to a man deeply impressed with the great love of God, inculcating with solidity and force the practical duties of a Christian life. Of his sermons, for instance, at Lincoln's Inn, none were so much admired as his course upon the Ten Commandments[1] and the Lord's Prayer. It must be added that his popularity in the pulpit was aided by the majesty of his person, his grace and gravity of manner, and the charm of his enunciation.[2]

Herring accepted a bishop's responsibilities with some reluctance. His natural temperament was somewhat indolent, and he looked forward with dread to new demands upon his industry. 'I fear,' he said, ' my friends will soon hear me repeating, "Vitæ me redde priori!"' He was not, however, the man to shrink from the not too immoderate labours which conscience and opinion required of him. He toiled over the Welsh mountains, thinking, as he shuddered at their rugged aspect, that they looked as if they had been made ' by the Father of creation, but in the wrath of power.'[3] And when he was transferred to York, he made long circuits round the diocese, and 'returned home with great satisfaction of heart for having done my duty, and acquired a sort of knowledge of my diocese which can be had by nothing but personal inspection.'[4] A hospitable and benevolent man, he was very much beloved in Yorkshire both by clergy and laymen. That his influence there was great is clear from the services he rendered at the time of the Jacobite invasion. He called the leading Yorkshiremen together, and spoke with such animation and vigour, that a contribution was quickly raised of 40,000*l*., and an example was set which spread throughout the nation.

[1] Hughes' *Correspondence*, ii. 206.   [2] Chalmers' *Biog.*, vol. xviii.
[3] Herring to Duncombe, Duncombe's *Letters*, p. 51.   [4] *Id.*, p. 63.

As primate, he was the same man he ever had been, kindly and generous, wholly tolerant, and careless to an excess of all that did not greatly affect the main fundamentals of religion. He was on the most friendly terms with Chandler and Doddridge and other leading Dissenters, and ideas of comprehensions which had long been dropped were once more seriously revived. An occasional interchange of pulpits would, he thought, make a very good beginning.[1] As for the Articles, they might properly be revised, and be restated in the words of Scripture.[2] His easy kindliness could extend to those freethinkers whom many would willingly have placed beyond the pale of tolerance. He, and Stone, the Irish primate, were almost the only exceptions, Hume tells us, to the clamour that was raised against him when his history was published. Both of these sent messages to him not to be discouraged.[3] So, also, he befriended the Jews at a time when 'such an abominable spirit,' he said, 'was raging against them, that I expect in a little time they will be massacred.'[4] His liberality, too, always free and open-handed, was given without distinction of denomination.[5] He, if all others were not, was thoroughly content with the religious prospects of his century. 'I think it happy,' he wrote to his brother, 'that I am called to this high station at a time when spite, and rancour, and narrowness of spirit are out of countenance, when we breathe the benign and comfortable air of liberty and toleration, and the teachers of our common religion make it their business to extend its essential influence, and join in supporting its true interest and honour.'[6]

Had Herring been of a more stirring character, and lived

[1] Hunt's *Rel. Thought in Eng.*, iii. 217.   [2] Perry's *Ch. Hist.*, iii. 376.
[3] D. Hume's *Essays*, ed. by Green and Grove, p. 5.
[4] *Maty's Rev.* for 1782, i. 241.   [5] Hughes' *Correspondence*, ii. 205.
[6] Quoted in Stoughton's *Relig. in Eng.*, &c., p. 261.

in more stirring times, his influence in the English Church might have been rather revolutionary. For though he was a good Christian man, full of beneficence and kindness, it is clear that his hold on specific doctrine was very slight, and that he would have seen the formularies of his Church broken down, and its Prayer Book neutralised, with very little feeling that any sacrifice had been made in the cause of liberality. But what he might have been quite willing to see, he was in no hurry to busy himself in bringing about. It quite suited his temper to let things be. Churchmen suspected heterodoxy in him, but thought it harmless, and could therefore love him for his general qualities. He had many friends and no enemies. Most men would have acquiesced in the praise pronounced upon him by his friend Dr. Jortin: 'He had piety without superstition, and moderation without meanness; an open and liberal way of thinking, and a constant attachment to the cause of sober and rational liberty, both civil and religious. Thus he lived and died; and few men ever passed through this malevolent world better beloved or less censured than he.'[1]

Herring was followed successively at Bangor (1743), York (1747), and Canterbury (1757–58) by Matthew Hutton. Mention of this prelate occurs much less frequently in the writings of the century than might have been expected of one who was in his time primate of either province. That he held very liberal opinions is evident from his promotion and warm approval of Blackburne,[2] than whom no Churchman of his day was a more thoroughgoing and prominent latitudinarian. He is spoken of by Nichols, briefly but favourably, as 'candid and generous,'[3] and by Horace Walpole as 'well-bred and devoted to the ministry.'[4]

---

[1] Jortin's *Tracts*, ii. 518.   [2] Perry's *Church Hist.*, iii. 375.
[3] Nichols' *Anec.*, iii. 16.
[4] Walpole's *Memoirs of the Reign of George II.*, p. 148.

Thomas Secker was Bishop of Bristol from 1734 to 1737, of Oxford from 1737 to 1758, and Archbishop of Canterbury from 1758 to 1768. He was the son of a Dissenter of small private means, who intended him for the Presbyterian ministry, and, with Dr. Watts's help, sent him to one of the best of the Nonconformist academies. It speaks well for the ability of his master, Mr. Jones of Gloucester and afterwards of Tewkesbury, that among his pupils at this time were three[1] who afterwards rose to great distinction— Secker, Butler, Bishop of Durham, the author of the 'Analogy,' and that very learned Nonconformist minister, Samuel Chandler. These three schoolfellows maintained their old friendship throughout life. As a young man, although not formally admitted into the ministry, he is said occasionally to have preached in some of the Derbyshire chapels.[2] It must have been about this time that, in the course of conversation, one of their preachers said, 'Ah, Secker, nothing will do for you but conformity!' 'No,' said Secker, earnestly, 'conform I never can.'[3] In fact, although he had closely studied the questions at issue between the English Church and Nonconformity, he was not satisfied, at this time, with either, but determined to go to Paris and study medicine. There he became intimate with Benson, who was afterwards one of the most exemplary bishops of the century. Partly through his influence, partly through that of Butler, who had taken English orders and kept up a frequent correspondence with him, and chiefly through that of Dr. Samuel Clarke, whom he had consulted on certain doubts and difficulties which perplexed him,[4] he was gradually drawn more into sympathy with the English Church than he had before thought possible. At last, when Bishop Talbot offered to ordain

[1] Bartlett's *Life of Butler*, p. 17.   [2] Nichols, iii. 752.
[3] Gilbert Wakefield's *Memoirs*, p. 166.   [4] Porteus's *Life of Secker*, xx.

him, he gave up medicine and returned to England. It was about the time when a remarkable number of leading Dissenters conformed to the National Church.[1] Nonconformity had been for some time on the wane, and after the Salter Hall controversy (1721), which greatly divided opinion, and made the terms of Dissenting communion much more rigorous than heretofore, a great many gladly turned to the greater liberty which conformity would give them. He graduated at Leyden, and afterwards, having entered as Gentleman Commoner at Exeter College, Oxford, received also, through special letters from the Chancellor, an English university degree. He was then ordained, and very soon afterwards became chaplain to Bishop Talbot. Thenceforward his well-known abilities and the powerful interest of the Talbots made advancement certain. He was made chaplain to the king, received an important living in Westminster, and was soon after raised to the Episcopate.

His preaching was thought very highly of. 'When Secker preaches the church is crowded.'[2] It was not only the matter, but the manner that was applauded:—

> Speak, look, and move with dignity and ease,
> Like mitred Secker, you'll be sure to please.[3]

His sermons are spoken of by Horace Walpole, who could not bear him, and never mentioned him without a sneer, in words which do not badly express their character from a hostile point of view. 'They were a kind of moral essays,' he said, 'but what they wanted of the gospel was made up by a tone of fanaticism that he still retained.'[4] Hurd gives

---

[1] The list is given in Calamy's *Life*, ii. 503. Among the number are three future bishops, Secker, Butler, and Maddox.
[2] Jas. Hervey's 'Theron and Aspasio,' *Works*, ii. 24.
[3] Chr. Pitt's 'Art of Preaching,' *B. Poets*, viii. 821.
[4] Walpole's *Memoirs of the Reign of George II.*, p. 66.

a somewhat similar idea of them. He speaks of their having 'a certain conciliating calmness, propriety, and decency of language, with no extraordinary reach of thought, vigour of sentiment, or beauty of composition. There is sometimes an air of cant in the expression, derived no doubt from his early breeding and education.'[1] The mention in these two criticisms of an ingredient of 'fanaticism' or 'cant' is curious, and characteristic of an age which was apt to look askance at anything like unction as if it were a suspicious and dangerous blemish in pulpit oratory. But there can be no doubt it was the element that was most deficient in the typical sermons of the time. Bishop Porteus gives Secker's preaching more unreserved praise. His sermons, he said, 'for argument, manly sense, useful directions, short, nervous, striking sentences, awakening questions, frequent and personal applications of Scripture, were very admired.'[2]

As a clergyman Secker had greatly won the attachment of his people. Whiston spoke of him 'as an indefatigable pastor,'[3] and Horace Walpole allows that he was 'incredibly popular'[4] in his parish. As a bishop he commanded for the most part respect and esteem rather than any warmer feeling. That he was generally thought very highly of is indeed very evident. Richard Newton, mentioning his recent death, speaks of him as 'that great and excellent prelate.'[5] 'Few bishops equal to him,' said Johnson of Connecticut.[6] But with many he was not at all popular. He was criticised as being rather haughty and

[1] Kilvert's *Life of Hurd*, p. 272.
[2] Porteus's *Life of Secker*, xx. Churton gives a somewhat similar account (Churton to Hurd on his *Strictures upon Secker*, p. 32).
[3] Whiston's *Memoirs*.
[4] Walpole, *Mem. George II.*, p. 66. Porteus says that when he preached his farewell sermon almost all the congregation were in tears.
[5] Newton's *Autobiography*, p. 119. [6] Johnson's *Life*, by Beardsley, p. 322.

imperious,[1] and of showing too much of an air of prelatical dignity.[2] That he was especially distant toward his old Nonconformist friends seems to be disproved by the undoubted cordiality of his relations towards Doddridge, Leland, Lardner, and Chandler. He was somewhat stiff, formal, and precise,[3] and often seemed reserved and cold. Porteus acknowledges this, but says that it generally arose from the bodily pain, depression, and fatigue to which he was subject, and that faults were often laid to his charge which did not really belong to his character.[4] Dr. Johnson did not much like him, and thought him prim. On one occasion in particular his spleen was raised at Secker's variation of the old toast 'Church and King.' 'The Archbishop of Canterbury,' said he (with an affected, smooth, smiling grimace), 'drinks "Constitution in Church and State."' Boswell, however, goes on to say that when Porteus's 'Life of Secker' came out, Johnson read it with avidity, and called it a life that deserved to be recorded.'[5]

The charge of sycophancy occasionally[6] brought against Secker was unjust, and appears to have arisen from his wish not to break with a court at which he was unpopular. George II., who had taken some offence with him, would not go to chapel when he was told he was to preach,[7] and for some years would not even speak to him, and both in that reign and the next he was less consulted than any archbishop had been for a long time before. On one rather flagrant occasion of this sort, some thought the archbishop ought to have shown resentment. But he answered that 'he had as sharp a sense of the indignity as any one could have, but he was very unwilling to break altogether with the

---

[1] Wakefield's *Memoirs*, p. 164.
[2] Nichols, iii. 752.
[3] Newton, p. 119.
[4] Porteus's *Life of Secker*.
[5] Boswell's *Johnson*, iii. 474.
[6] Grey and Mason's *Correspondence*, p. 229, and Walpole.
[7] Walpole, p. 66; Porteus, xx.

court, for then he was certain he could prevail in nothing;
he might now be able to carry some points for the good of
the Church.'[1]

Secker was very regular, methodical, and exact, and his
diocesan books, in which he kept accounts of each parish
and benefice, were probably better kept than those of any
other bishop of his time. He was skilled in Hebrew and
ecclesiastical history, and kept up a good knowledge of all
the best modern publications, but was not in any special
sense of the word a learned man. He administered patronage with care and judgment, and Bishop Newton speaks
with admiration of his extensive and liberal charities. While
Dean of St. Paul's he always attended service twice daily.
He was an early riser, and kept a plentiful, but plain and
simple table, never allowing any special delicacy to appear
upon it.

From what has been said, it will have been gathered
that Secker was a good, industrious, and conscientious man,
but of no striking ability, or much originating power.
There was, however, no wish at this time that a primate
should do more than execute the ordinary routine of his
office in an exemplary manner; and as Secker fulfilled
entirely to general satisfaction all that was required of him,
he obtained a somewhat higher repute than it may be
thought he was quite entitled to. 'Secker is decent,' said
Pope; and this perfect respectability (to use the word in its
fullest sense), this decent seemliness, this unimpeachable
moderation, pervaded all he said and did. His orthodoxy
could always be completely depended upon; in his staid
and dignified deportment there could be no tendency to
that bugbear of the age—enthusiasm; he was not latitudinarian, nor was he, on the whole, illiberal.[2] It was certain

[1] Newton, p. 119.
[2] The splenetic Wakefield called him, with very little reason, 'persecuting.'

that if the Church were animated by his safe and cautious spirit, it would be quite secure from undertaking any precipitate movement, or rushing into inconsiderate reforms. Also, in the House of Lords, it might always be confidently expected that the chief officer of the Church would express with sufficient earnestness and ease the sentiments most appropriate to a great spiritual peer, the primate of a National Church. Nor, indeed, was it a small merit that his voice should be so often raised on the right side. Such was the case in 1743, when he was foremost among the bishops in resisting the Spirituous Liquors Bill. Although he was mistaken[1] in his view of the Act about to be repealed, this did not affect the general character of his earnest appeal, not 'to sacrifice for ways and means the health, the industry, the lives of the people.'[2] He trusted that Parliament 'would not desist from endeavouring the recovery of the nation from its hateful vice.'[3] A little later he supported a bill for making provision for the widows and children of the Established Church of Scotland. In 1748, upon the bill for disarming the Highlands, he pleaded earnestly against the clause which excepted from toleration all Scotch episcopal orders as had not been given and endorsed by an English or Irish bishop.[4] In 1753 he spoke on the side of charity and moderation on the question of repealing the Jews' Naturalisation Bill.[5] In 1754, he brought upon himself much wrath from Nonconformists and New Englanders for urgently advocating the sending of one or more bishops to America.[6]

Secker's attitude toward Methodism has been referred to in a previous chapter. His too precise temperament was

---

[1] Lord Mahon's *History*, chap. xxv.
[2] *Parl. Hist.*, xii. 1204-7. [3] *Id.*, p. 1333.
[4] *Parl. Hist.*, xiv. 276. [5] *Id.*, xv. 117.
[6] Porteus's *Life of Secker*; S. Johnson's *Life and Correspondence*, pp. 179, 282.

greatly offended at its extravagances. He was not, however, blind to the work it was doing, and there was much in it which, in his charges, he brought before his clergy both for example and instruction. To foreign Protestants he was a kind friend. To many among them he gave pensions, and to some of their universities he was an annual benefactor.[1] With moderate Dissenters in England, of Doddridge's type, he was on very friendly terms, and was hopeful that the causes of separation might be removed. 'Indeed,' he wrote to Doddridge, 'it must be, and ought to be, acknowledged that the Dissenters have done excellently in late years in the service of Christianity; and I hope our common warfare will make us chiefly attentive to our common interest, and unite us in a closer alliance.'[2]

This worthy prelate suffered greatly in his later years from a carious thigh-bone, which at length caused his death. He left large bequests to charitable uses.

John Gilbert was Archbishop of York from 1757 to 1761, having been Bishop of Llandaff in 1740, and of Salisbury in 1747. He did no great honour to the Archiepiscopate. Horace Walpole speaks of him as arrogant and ignorant;[3] and though in this author's personal remarks a broad margin must always be allowed for his love of ill-natured slander, his remarks on character are generally not quite without foundation. Bishop Newton speaks of him as somewhat haughty;[4] and John Newton, the friend of Cowper, the leader of the Calvinist section of the Evangelicals, found him hard and inflexible when he vainly sought to obtain orders from him.[5] As for what Horace Walpole said of his ignorance, there is at all events no

---

[1] Bartlett's *Life of Butler*, p. 241.
[2] Doddridge's *Correspondence*, iii. 271.
[3] See *Qu. Review*, 27. p. 187.   [4] Bishop Newton's *Autobiog.*, p. 82.
[5] John Newton's *Letters*, ii. 57.

reason to suppose that he was in any sense a learned man. A story which is told of him at Salisbury represents him as passionate as well as imperious. He had a great dispute with the mayor about the separate jurisdiction of the city and cathedral, and would not allow the mace to be carried before him in the cathedral precincts. His orders not having been complied with, he had a personal scuffle with the mace-bearer. It was accordingly a joke with Baron Smythe, when the bishop was to dine with him at a circuit dinner, to send out orders to the cook that there was to be no mace in the soup, as his lordship did not like mace.[1]

Gilbert introduced at Confirmations a custom, which would seem now slovenly and unedifying, of simply laying his hand upon each candidate and pronouncing the words of prayer and dedication once only for all who knelt. But one generation cannot answer for another in matters of taste or feeling. The writer adds that clergy and laity thought that the practice Gilbert had adopted was solemn and impressive.[2]

Thomas Sherlock[3] (Bangor 1727, Salisbury 1734, London 1748-61) is one of the most conspicuous of eighteenth-century bishops. His mental power, which was much greater than that of Secker, was in part inherited from his father Dr. William Sherlock, a very eminent theologian both in controversial and practical divinity. He rose early into note, for in 1704, at the age of twenty-six, he was appointed Master of the Temple, in his father's room. The lawyers were somewhat prejudiced against him at first, on account of his youth; but his excellence and abilities

---

[1] Cassan's *Bishops of Salisbury*, p. 274. [2] Newton's *Autobiog.*, p. 77.
[3] My principal authorities for the sketch of this bishop are Mosse's *Charge* of 1764; Nichols' *Lit. Anec.*, iii. 216-17; Cassan's *Bishops of Salisbury*, pp. 241-66; Chalmers' *Biog. D.*, vol. vii.; and Sherlock's *Works*.

were soon recognised, and for the fifty years he held the mastership he was universally esteemed and honoured there. It was a post which he very highly valued, as bringing him into close intercourse with many of the ablest intellects of his day. His own knowledge of the laws and constitution of England was very extensive, and, when he was bishop, added very considerably to the weight of his speeches in the House of Lords.

Both at the Temple and elsewhere, Sherlock's preaching always commanded the attention of his hearers:

The Temple Church asks Sherlock's sense and skill.[1]

Mrs. Carter, one of the most accomplished women of the century, described his sermons as unequal, but often admirable as answers to the doubts and difficulties of the day. Sometimes, she said, he caught overmuch the spirit of those to whom he preached, and was too clever.[2] There is one very remarkable testimony alike to the memory of the hearer, and to the forcible impression caused by the preacher. When Sherlock published his occasional sermons in 1753, during the illness that preceded his death, Lord Chancellor Hardwicke had a copy of the first volume brought to him by Dr. Nichols. He asked him whether there was among them a sermon on John xx. 30–1; and on hearing that there was, bade him to turn to the end, and then beginning with the words, 'Go to your natural religion,'[3] recited from memory the whole passage contrasting Christ and Mahomet, with which the discourse had eloquently concluded. It was full thirty years since he had heard it preached.

At Cambridge, as Master of St. Catherine's, Sherlock had held a very commanding position. His great know-

[1] Dodsley's *Art of Preaching*, p. 114.
[2] *Life and Works of El. Carter*, p. 390.
[3] It ends the ninth discourse in Sherlock's *Works*.

ledge of the university, and his wisdom and policy in governing, made him looked up to as a sort of oracle, and Bentley nicknamed him 'Cardinal Alberoni.' It was murmured, however, that as Vice-Chancellor he let his political predilections get the better of his justice, and that being at that time strongly opposed to the Whigs, he connived at Tory disturbances among the young men.[1]

In the Bangorian controversy Sherlock took a leading part against Hoadly, and was often considered his most formidable antagonist. He was not only a principal contributor to its voluminous literature, but was prominent in the committee of Convocation which drew up the charge against the bishop. The part he had taken gave offence at court, and he was removed from the list of king's chaplains. Nichols says that in later life he disapproved of what he had written, and would not have it reprinted. Bishop Newton, however, says he had been assured by those who lived with Sherlock most, and knew him best, that this assertion was wholly groundless.[2] Sherlock was often matched against Hoadly in less serious encounters. They often met in that curious palæstra of theological controversy, Queen Caroline's drawing-room.[3]

Sherlock took an important part in the controversy with the Deists. His 'Trial of the Witnesses,' published in 1729, was quite the most popular work on the subject, and quickly passed through fourteen editions.[4] It is an answer to Woolston's attack upon the Gospel account of our Lord's resurrection, and is represented as arising out of an argument among some members of the Inns of Court upon the question which Woolston had raised. 'At length one of the company said pleasantly, "Gentlemen, you do

---

[1] *Life of Waterland*, p. 17.   [2] Newton's *Autobiog.*, p. 130.
[3] Fraser's *Life of Berkeley*, i. 109 ; Bartlett's *Life of Butler*, p. 40.
[4] Pattison, in *Essays and Reviews*, p. 303.

not argue like lawyers; if I were judge in this case I would hold you better to the point."[1] The idea pleased them, and on a fixed day the cause is regularly pleaded by counsel on either side before judge and jury. In the end, after the question is supposed to have been thoroughly argued, the judge sums up, and the jury after consultation give their verdict on the question whether the apostles are 'guilty of giving false evidence in the case of the resurrection, or not guilty.'[1] Sherlock carries out his design skilfully enough, but the whole form of it rather jars upon the feeling of a modern reader. It was characteristic of an age of which Dr. Johnson said, in allusion no doubt to this performance, that the apostles were once a year tried for forgery and acquitted.[2] The examination of 'the evidences' is necessary, and may perhaps be considered as the special task of theology in the eighteenth century. But though in theory law may be the perfection of judicial investigation, still, apart from the intimate connection of Christian evidence with moral and spiritual conceptions, which would not be tangible in a court of law, legal forms and subtleties of advocacy are more alien to the principles of theological inquiry than Sherlock and his contemporaries seem to have considered.

But this publication, useful though it was in its way, was by no means Sherlock's only contribution to evidential theology. In his treatise against Collins upon the use and intent of prophecy, and in many of his sermons at the Temple, he met the Deists on better and wiser ground than was sometimes the case. He was not so ready as many were to assume that every assertion of the Deists required to be condemned and refuted. Nor was he at all unwilling to allow that some of their positions were well deserving of

[1] Sherlock's *Works*, vol. iv. pp. 342-442.
[2] Quoted by Hunt, *Rel. Th. in Eng.*, iii. 81.

consideration, and only needed supplementing to be accepted as legitimate in thoroughly orthodox theology. He thought it, for instance, permissible to hold that the history of the Fall was an allegory of spiritual and moral truth. He conceded to Collins that specific prophecies had often had a too exclusive Messianic meaning ascribed to them. He thought that Tindal was right so far as he condemned dogmatism upon the nature of the atonement. On all these and such like points he of course stopped very far short of the Deistical conclusions; but to many minds (for some thought he granted overmuch [1]) it seemed that this concession did but strengthen his argument. It is a curious instance of the manner in which Deists often clung to the shreds of Christianity, after they stripped it of most of its essentials, to notice how eagerly Tindal and Chubb caught at Sherlock's acknowledgment that Christianity was a republication of the law of nature, while they minimised what he said of its being this and far more besides. Such additions, said Chubb, as the promises of life and immortality and spiritual help are not in their own nature constituent parts of religion, but means and helps to it.[2]

Sherlock's relations to Nonconformity are a mixture of liberality and its contrary. None defended more ably than he did the Test and Corporation Acts, and perhaps no one was so responsible as he was for the maintenance of these odious laws. On the other hand, he was desirous of such revision of the Liturgy as might reconcile the moderate Dissenters. He told Dr. Chandler that 'it seemed a very proper time for applying to the Government in behalf of a review, provided a competent number of the clergy and others should be found to forward so useful a design.'[3] His

[1] Warburton and Hurd's *Corresp.*, pp. 34–35.
[2] Chubb, 'On the Foundation of Religion,' *Works*, iv. 107.
[3] The conversation is reported by Jones of Welwyn, quoted in Cassan's *Bishops of Salisbury*, p. 262.

feeling of unity amid all wider differences is well expressed in a letter of his to Doddridge: 'Whatever other points of difference there are between us, yet I trust that we are united in a hearty zeal for spreading the knowledge of the gospel, and for reforming the lives and manners of the people according to it. . . . I have seen the true spirit and the comfortable hopes of religion lost in the abundance of speculation, and the vain pretences of setting up natural religion in opposition to revelation; and there will be little hopes of a reformation till we are humble enough to know Christ, and Him crucified.'[1]

John Wesley comments on 'a strange breach of charity' on Sherlock's part in his rejecting a request of the French prisoners that Fletcher of Madeley might preach to them.[2] But before it can be inferred that the bishop was actuated by any dislike of evangelical opinions it should be known whether the request was in any sense a general one. Otherwise he might, of course, very properly refuse to force upon Roman Catholics the ministrations of a Protestant clergyman.

During the alarm caused by the earthquake of 1750 Sherlock wrote a pastoral letter, which had an enormous circulation. Nichols relates that 100,000 copies of it were sold within a month.[3] It is remarkable for the very dark view which Sherlock takes in it of the wickedness of the times.[4]

Sherlock rarely spoke in Parliament, except on important questions of public morals, or where he thought essential interests of the Church or Constitution were involved. The Primacy was offered to him, but he refused it, as feeling symptoms of declining health. London was scarcely a

---
[1] Quoted by Chalmers, vol. xxvii.
[2] Wesley's *Life of Fletcher*, *Works*, xi. 290.
[3] *Lit. Anec.*, iii. 212.   [4] Sherlock's *Works*, vol. iv.

smaller responsibility, but he ventured to undertake it, as his business would be all near. He was, however, entirely incapacitated from work during the last eight years of his life. A writer who made a tour through Great Britain in 1738 spoke very highly of his activity and liberality at Salisbury, and of the good work he had done to the cathedral.[1]

Next comes one of the most eminent men whom the eighteenth century produced, whose name will be always familiar wherever systematic and philosophic thought is valued. Joseph Butler[2] (Bristol 1738–50, Durham 1750–1752) was born in 1692, the son of a substantial linen and woollen draper of Wantage. His father was a principal supporter of the old Presbyterian chapel there. The Nonconformist Academy, where he and Secker were at school together, seems to have been intended not for boys only, but for young men who were in training for the ministry. For it was while he was still there, at the age of twenty-one, that he entered anonymously into a correspondence with Dr. S. Clarke on some arguments in the 'Demonstration of the Being and Attributes of God,' which seemed to him unsatisfactory. The learned Doctor was so struck with the sound and ingenuous reasoning of his unknown correspondent, that he ultimately attached his letters to the treatise.

Butler soon after this decided against Nonconformity, and his father gave him reluctant permission to enter at Oriel College, Oxford, with a view to Anglican orders.[3] He was ordained about 1717, and the next year, through the influence of Dr. Clarke, then rector of St. James's, and of

---

[1] De Foe's *Tour through Great Britain*, i. 266.

[2] The facts in this sketch are chiefly taken from Bartlett's *Life of Butler*, Surtees' *Hist. of Durham*, a review of Bartlett's book in the sixty-fourth volume of the *Qu. Review*, and his own works.

[3] Madame d'Arblay's *Life*, iii. 232.

Bishop Talbot, with whose son he had been intimate at college, was appointed preacher of the Rolls. It was here he preached his published sermons, some of which are scarcely less known or less valuable than the 'Analogy' itself. Some of them, as he himself remarks in his preface, are abstruse, and must have severely taxed the attention even of his learned audience. They are more adapted to the study than the pulpit, and are philosophical rather than rhetorical. But as a study of human nature, and a system of Christian ethics, they have never been surpassed. It may be noticed that one memorable passage in the second sermon, on the jurisdiction of conscience, was soon after quoted with but little alteration where it might have been least expected—in Fielding's 'Tom Jones.'[1]

Meanwhile Secker, who was now chaplain to the Bishop of Durham, and Edward Talbot, two friends who were always zealous in his behalf, procured for him the wealthy living of Stanhope in Durham. There, in the quiet of his country living, he continued with deep attention his studies of all the theological and philosophical questions which for the previous fifty years had occupied so much attention, not only in the controversies between divines and sceptics, but also in the general literature and conversation of the age. He was impressed by a strong and perhaps exaggerated impression of the hold which irreligion and unbelief had gained upon the minds of the people. He thought that the objections raised by Deists and others called for a more thorough and searching answer than any that had yet been given, and he determined to devote the energies of his mind to a work which should show Christianity to be not only based upon the innermost grounds of human nature, but in close conformity with principles which seem to rule the natural order of the universe.

[1] *Tom Jones*, B. IV. chap. vi.

Even before the publication of the 'Analogy' he was fast rising into note. His sermons had proved him a man of no ordinary power of thought, and a wish began to be felt that he should not always be so far from London. In 1733 Lord Chancellor Talbot appointed him his chaplain. Queen Caroline asked where he was, or whether he was still living. 'He is not dead, madam,' answered Archbishop Blackbourne, 'but buried.' The queen soon made him her private chaplain, and thenceforward, during the part of the year which he spent in town, he was constantly called upon to be in attendance upon her, and to take a leading share in the theological discussions which she delighted in.

The 'Analogy' was published in 1736. It is creditable to the age that within the same year a book of such a nature, and requiring such close reading, should have come to a second edition. Bishop Wilson has well said of the 'Analogy' that probably no work in the compass of theology is so full of—to use Bacon's expression—'the seeds of things.' For few works have ever been written so suggestive of thought as this. Its author has condensed in it the reading and reflection of more than twenty years, during which time there was scarcely an objection or a difficulty which he had not noted and most carefully considered. The treatise is absolutely free from all personal allusion. He never mentions any one by name. Hence there is an occasional obscurity as to the exact drift and purpose of his argument, to those in whose minds some difficulty glanced at, some objection obviated, has never been felt. Some of his contemporaries complained [1] that he was not vigorous enough, that he did not confute the Deist or the sceptic with sufficient decisiveness. It was, indeed, at once his strength and his weakness that he never pretended to leave the field of probable reasoning. There were many who claimed for the

[1] Pattison, in *Essays and Reviews*, p. 305.

Christian evidences a position scarcely less than demonstrative. But such conclusions, however much they might satisfy and please a believer, only weakened the argument to a doubter, and left him more unconvinced than ever. He might read, on the other hand, a work like the 'Analogy,' and find the chain of probable reasoning so irresistibly closing around him as to leave him more open to receive those direct intuitions of spiritual truth which are alike stranger and more intangible than argument. This was its strength. For the same reason, its weakness lay in its limitation to the region of inference. It necessarily leaves untouched the evidence which appeals more directly to the consciousness, where the instinct of religion is even more deeply rooted than in the reason. If dwelt upon too exclusively, this mode of argument may even weaken the sense of religion by confining thought too much to the natural world, and seeming to imply that there is nothing in revelation which altogether transcends what is seen in nature. Revelation should throw light upon nature, and not only nature upon revelation. Yet, after all, however much we might dwell on the limitations of analogy, it is only saying that it is but one branch of evidence, and, until strengthened by accumulation, scarcely even a trustworthy one, for partial analogies might be pleaded in defence of almost any anomaly. Butler would no doubt have granted this. But it is wonderful with what accumulative power he has used his argument. The first careful reading of his 'Analogy' has been to many an era in their intellectual, if not in their spiritual, life also.

Several examples might be quoted of the respect paid to Butler in consequence of his great work. David Hume, sceptic as he was, much wished to be introduced to him, and to submit to his opinion, before they were published, the sheets of his 'Treatise on Human Nature.' If this might be, he was willing, he said, to excise such passages as might give offence, even though it might seem to himself a very mutilation. They did not, however, meet; neither would Butler comply with Lord Kame's urgent request that he would confer with him for the solution of certain doubts which had arisen in his mind. He would correspond with him, he answered, on the subject, but had great distrust of being able to do justice to his cause in a verbal discussion. Queen Caroline died the year after the 'Analogy' had been published, and had not the opportunity of bringing about his promotion in her lifetime. But on her death-bed she specially recommended him to the notice of the king, and the next year, 1738, he was made Bishop of Bristol. This bishopric being a very poor one, the deanery of St. Paul's was added.

It is a curious instance of the timidity with which, through fear of Rome, public opinion was at this time apt to regard the smallest approach to any High Church innovation, that a small marble cross placed by Butler in his private chapel at Bristol caused quite a storm of angry alarm. Even bishops, who should have known better, shook their heads. His old friend, the discreet Secker, thought it a thing to be regretted; and Bishop Halifax 'wished in prudence it had not been done.' It seemed as if this formidable offence against Protestantism could not be forgotten. When, some years later, he put into his private house some painted windows with Scriptural subjects, a cry was raised that they were a present from the Pope. As many as fifteen years after his death Secker thought it necessary to come forward in his defence against an absurd charge that he had died a Romanist. The grounds on which the accusation had been based were the old one that 'he had set up in his chapel the Popish insignia of the cross;' that in his Durham charge he had spoken of the unhappy neglect of the outward forms of religion, and that he had been accustomed to read lives of Romish saints, and other books of mystic piety. Where ignorant minds were thus filled with that anti-Popish panic which a few years later came to its climax in the Gordon riots, such considerations were quite enough to outweigh, not only Butler's condemnation of Romanism as 'the great corruption of Christianity,' but also a whole lifetime spent in that calm exercise of reason which would be the very last thing to lead a man to place his intellect in servitude to Rome.

When Archbishop Potter died in 1747, it is said that the Primacy was offered to Butler, and that he refused it from the gloomy view he took of the prevalent irreligion, and the feeling of his inability to grapple with it in that high position. He was raised to Durham in 1750. Horace Walpole's way of putting it is that he was 'wafted thither in a cloud of metaphysics.'[1] On the vacancy occurring, it had been intended to confer the Lord Lieutenancy of the county on Lord Barnard. But Butler, although no lover of state, and very quiet and reserved, declined to accept the see if it were shorn of an honour which had always been an appurtenance of the palatinate bishopric. The honour in which he was held, and the wishes of the king, who had not forgotten the request of Queen Caroline, prevailed, and the dignity which had belonged to his predecessors was continued to Butler. He went there with an earnest wish to make a worthy use of power, wealth, and patronage immensely greater than he had held at Bristol. 'Increase of fortune,' he said in answer to a friend's congratulations, ' is insignificant to one who had enough before; and I foresee many difficulties in the station I am coming into, and no advantage worth thinking of, except some greater power of being serviceable to others ; and whether this be an advantage entirely depends on the use one shall make of

[1] Walpole's *Memoirs of the Reign of George II.*, p. 118.

it: I pray God it may be a good one. . . . This right use of fortune and power is more difficult than the generality of even good people think, and requires both a guard upon oneself, and a strength of mind to withstand solicitations, greater, I wish I may not find it, than I am master of.'[1] In those days of unblushing nepotism, when men high in Church or State were almost expected to be fountains of promotion to relatives and dependents, it is mentioned, as specially honourable to Butler, that his large patronage was never given by any other rule than merit. 'I think, my lord, it is a misfortune to be related to you,' was the angry exclamation of a nephew, who, although an able man, was judged by the bishop not attentive enough to his work to deserve preferment. It is enough to add that his kind simplicity of nature, and his frank unstinting generosity, made him as much loved as he was respected, and that the last scene of his life was touching in its heartfelt humility. John Byrom, in his Memoirs, hits, perhaps, a slight defect in his character. He had been listening to an argument on the respective claims of reason and authority, in which Butler was maintaining the supremacy of the former. 'I wished,' said Byrom, 'I had Dr. Butler's temper and calmness; yet not quite, because I thought he was somewhat too little vigorous, which the others thought too.'[2] Theophilus Lindsey's criticism—a man who was more or less adverse to all Churchmen—was, that though his piety was great, it was of a gloomy cast, and that he always appeared dissatisfied with the public state of things.[3] There was some degree of truth in this, for certainly Butler was anything but an optimist. The times

---

[1] The letter is quoted in Surtees' *Hist. of Durham*, from the *Gent.'s Mag.* of 1780.

[2] Byrom's *Remains*, iii. 97.

[3] Belsham's *Memoirs of Lindsey*, quoted in *Q. Rev.*, viii. 432.

were far from what a good man could wish, and there was much that was unsatisfactory in the Church. But the age was not so dark as Butler's anxieties depicted it, neither, as he feared, was the English Church as yet tottering to its fall.

The bishop is described as patriarchal in aspect—his white hair hanging over his shoulders, and his pale face placid and reverend, lighted up during the ministrations of his office with a glow of animation.

Francis Hare[1] (St. Asaph 1727–31, Chichester 1731–40) was well known in his time, and a man of ability, but not the sort of bishop whom the Church of England needed. He had been chaplain to Marlborough, and had served with him throughout his campaign—a poor school for anything like depth and earnestness of character. In his work upon 'The Difficulties of Scripture' there was a flippancy and a covert irony which did discredit to the writer, and deserved the censure which it received from Convocation. Perhaps, however, he owed to it his mitre. A flavour of heterodoxy, if it were accompanied with learning, was irresistible to Queen Caroline, who was then the great dispenser of patronage. And doubtless he was learned, though it was not a learning which did much for the Church or age. His claims of having discovered the principles of Jewish poetry were confuted before long by a better Hebraist, Bishop Lowth. He edited Terence and Phædrus, and was much piqued at their being thrown into immediate obscurity by the far greater value of the editions which Bentley published. From about this time he became as warm an opponent of the great scholar as he had before been his admirer. Shortly before his death he was engaged in preparing an

---

[1] The facts are taken from Chalmers' *Biography*, vol. xviii.; Dallaway's *Sussex*, p. 95; Nichols' *Biog. Anec.*, iii. 57; v. 97-98; Whiston's *Memoirs*, pp. 116, 276; Hunt's *Rel. Thought*, &c., iii. 83.

edition of Plautus. He joined, though he did not contribute any work of importance, in the controversies against Hoadly and against Collins. He was a great encourager of learning, and is spoken of by Pope, in connection with Sherlock and Gibson, as an able preacher. During his episcopate he resided much on his private estate in Buckinghamshire. Probably his official duties sat as lightly upon him as upon many of his brethren at that time upon the bench. If, as was sometimes said, he was spoken of as a possible successor to the Primacy, it would show what very moderate qualifications could be thought sufficient for so great a post.

Martin Benson (Gloucester 1734-52) is never spoken of but in terms of the highest commendation. Though he was not a man who took any notable part in public life, nor yet one of profound learning or commanding ability, there is scarcely any bishop of the century who deserves more honourable record. The following is an account of him from one who knew him well, and if it is tinged by the partiality of a friend, it is borne out by all that is elsewhere told of him. 'He was from his youth to his latest age the delight of all who knew him. His manner of behaviour was the result of great natural humanity, polished by a thorough knowledge of the world, and the most perfect good breeding, mixed with a dignity which, on occasions that called for it, no one more properly supported. His piety, though awfully strict, was inexpressibly amiable. It diffused such a sweetness through his temper, and such a benevolence over his countenance, as none who were acquainted with him can ever forget. Bad nerves, bad health, and naturally bad spirits were so totally subdued by it, that he not only seemed, but in reality was, the happiest of men. He looked upon all that the world calls important— its pleasures, its riches, its various competitions—with a playful and good-humoured kind of contempt; and could make persons ashamed of their follies by a raillery that never gave pain to any human being. Of vice he always spoke with severity and detestation, but looked on the vicious with the tenderness of a pitying angel. His turn was highly sociable, and his acquaintance very extensive. Wherever he went, he carried cheerfulness and improvement along with him. As nothing but the interests of Christianity and virtue seemed considerable enough to give him any lasting anxiety, so, on the other hand, there was no accident so trifling from which he could not cause amusement and mirth.'[1] He is also favourably spoken of by Pope—'Manners and candour are to Benson given;'[2] and by Whiston, who mentions him by way of conspicuous contrast to others who he thought ill deserved their position in the Church.'[3] It may be added of him that he was a great friend of Secker and Berkeley, that he had a refined taste in painting and architecture, that he revived in his diocese the office of rural dean,[4] that he left a legacy for the support of bishops in America,[5] and lastly, that he took great interest in Whitefield's early labours, encouraged him in them, gave him money in his need, and offered to ordain him whenever he wished, even though he was under the age he preferred, and also to give him a cure.[6]

Zachary Pearce (Bangor 1748, Rochester 1756–74) was a very worthy bishop, and a theologian of considerable eminence. Dr. Johnson speaks of him as 'that excellent prelate,'[7] and Bishop Newton refers to him as a wise and religious man who had long deserved his bishopric.[8] Adam

[1] The account occurs in Porteus's *Life of Secker*, xxi–ii.
[2] Quoted in Fraser's *Life of Berkeley*, iv. 90.
[3] Whiston's *Memoirs*, p. 547.
[4] Porteus, as above.   [5] Bartlett's *Life of Butler*, p. 135.
[6] *Life of Whitefield*, p. 13.   [7] Boswell's *Johnson*, iii. p. 113.
[8] Bishop Newton's *Autobiography*, p. 57.

Clarke says of his 'Commentary on the Gospels,' that 'the learning and judgment displayed in these notes are really beyond all praise;'[1] and a modern writer praises his 'Vindication of the Miracles' as the best of all the answers to Woolston, and 'a perfect model of controversial writing.'[2] He was also well known in classical and general literature. He had published valuable editions of Longinus and parts of Cicero, had contributed papers to the 'Spectator' and 'Guardian,' &c., and did service in rescuing Milton from the hypercritical hands of Bentley. Without being latitudinarian in an objectionable sense of the word— for he was a zealous defender of the orthodox theology—he was a thorough and consistent liberal. In 1718 he joined with Boulter, afterwards Archbishop of Armagh, and some other clergymen in editing the 'Freethinker,' a well-written collection of essays, written after the manner of the 'Spectator,' which had for one of its special objects the design of vindicating freethinking, both in name and reality, from the opprobrium into which the Deists had brought it. 'He alone,' we read in one of the numbers, 'is properly a wise man, a philosopher, or lover of wisdom, who disdains to submit his reason to the prejudices of custom, of education, of authority, of interest, or of passion; who (to the utmost of his ability) examines into all things impartially before he determines either to approve or to reject them, and who is neither unwilling nor afraid to enlarge his understanding, and to exercise the faculties of his mind freely upon every kind of knowledge which he thinks worthy his notice, or his duty to learn, as a man. And yet, notwithstanding the elegancy, the dignity and significancy of this English expression, had I[3] not undertaken to rescue it

---

[1] Quoted in Horne *On the Scriptures*, ii. 308.
[2] Hunt's *Rel. Thought in the Eighteenth Cent.*, ii. 424.
[3] *I.e.* the *Freethinker*, impersonally, like the *Spectator*.

from the general clamour raised against it, through the rashness of some writers, the malice of others, and the bigotry of the ignorant, we had probably, in a few years more, thrown the name of Freethinking out of the language; which would have rendered it more practicable (in process of time) to banish out of the nation the manifold privileges arising out of the freedom of thought.'[1] The writers carry out their thesis to a point at which many who otherwise concur would strongly dissent. Ignoring altogether the blessedness of a faith which has never been seriously troubled with any doubts, they assert without qualification that no man of common reflection can be unblamable in his opinions who takes them upon trust, and never doubts of their validity. 'He doubts in order to be certain—removes his doubts by doubting.'[2] Apart from a few such passages, which seem to make a virtue of what is often far from a healthy condition of the soul, and as painful as it is for the time unsettling, the object of Pearce and his fellow-writers was an excellent one. The Deists had a great vantage-ground in their nearly successful attempt to claim that they were the special representatives of that liberty of the mind to which we owe the reception not of Protestantism only, but of Christianity itself.

In the gossiping autobiography which Bishop Newton wrote in his old age, he tells an incident of the promotion of Pearce to the deanery of Winchester, which is very illustrative of Sir R. Walpole's idea of making all his patronage useful to his own interests. Queen Caroline had recommended Pearce to the Minister for a deanery, and Walpole was quite willing to carry out her wish, and, if possible, to promote his own policy too. Pulteney accordingly came to Pearce, and added to his message, 'Though you may think that others, besides Sir Robert Walpole, have contributed

[1] The *Freethinker*, No. 159.   [2] *Id.*, No. 50.

to give you this dignity, yet you may depend upon it that he is all in all. Sir Robert may ask your assistance at the Winchester election.'[1] It may be doubted whether Walpole ever promoted any one in Church or State on principles wholly untainted with any thought of party. A somewhat similar instance of the paltry influences which were often brought to bear on Church questions occurred later in Pearce's life. When old age grew upon him he asked leave to resign, 'lest the Church suffer by my infirmities.' After much demur and delay permission was given, until it was found that George III., upon the suggestion of Lord Bath, had a successor to the bishopric in his mind. Upon this, the ministry, jealous of any influence but their own, withdrew their consent,[2] and the see of Rochester was consequently held for eleven more years by a bishop who had wished to be released from it as no longer able to fulfil its duties.

Pearce had been rector of St. Martin's-in-the-Fields. We hear of his Sunday evening conversations 'with the clergy of his parish and a few others on matters of religion and learning, wherein Dr. Pearce was excellently qualified to take the lead.'[3]

From his private fortune, which was large, he left some munificent bequests to public charities.

When Bishop Wilson at length passed away, after his long and honoured episcopate of nearly sixty years, he was succeeded in Sodor and Man (1755-72) by a man of whom it may be said in praise, that he was worthy of being Wilson's successor. When the Duke of Athol[4] appointed Mark Hildesley to the vacant see, Bishop Thomas, meeting

[1] Bishop Newton's *Autobiog.*, p. 59; Nichols' *Lit. Anec.*, iii. 109.
[2] *Life of Bishop Thomas of Rochester*, p. 74 ; also Walpole's *Journal in the Reign of George III.*, p. 382 (Doran's note). [3] Newton, p. 57.
[4] He was a sort of sovereign in the island. 'The Duke of Athol was received as king in Man by the inhabitants of that island, with firing of great guns, and expressions of great joy' (*Gent.'s Mag.*, Aug. 16, 1739).

the Duke, said 'My lord, you have done me an injury.' 'I am sorry to hear that; pray what is it?' 'You have deprived me,' answered Thomas, 'of the best vicar in my diocese!'[1] In the extensive parish of Hitchin, his activity and earnestness, no less than his many amiable and engaging qualities, had gained for him a very high degree of esteem. He went by the name of Father Hildesley, and, when he left, the streets were crowded with multitudes who turned out to pay him every mark of reverence.[2] In Man he followed[3] as far as practicable in the steps of Wilson, whom he cordially admired. He maintained the system of ecclesiastical discipline which he found there, did much for the enlargement of churches and schools, and without any pretensions to being the equal of the good patriarch whom he followed, inherited not a little of the attachment and regard which had been paid to him. His special work there was the translation of the Bible into Manx. It was a long work, and he was eager that it should be accomplished in his lifetime. 'If he could see it printed he should be happy, die when he would.' Through the active help of the Christian Knowledge Society his wish was carried out. He received the last sheets of it during his last illness, exclaimed very emphatically, 'Lord, now lettest Thou Thy servant depart in peace,' and died the next day.[4]

Like several other bishops of that time, he kept up a frequent correspondence with the eminent Nonconformist Doddridge. The Methodists he did not like, and at Hitchin refused Whitefield the use of his pulpit.

John Conybeare (Bristol 1750-58) was one of the most notable theologians of the century. For many years he

[1] Cassan's *Bishops of Salisbury*, p. 317.
[2] Quoted from Butler's *Memoirs of Hildesley*, in Nichols' *Lit. Anec.*, vi. 88. [3] Cruttesby's *Life of Wilson*, p. 322.
[4] Rivington's *Life of Hildesley*.

held a very prominent position at Oxford, first as Fellow of Exeter and Rector of St. Clement's, afterwards as head of Exeter College, and then as Dean of Christ Church. The reputation he early gained as a writer against the Deists was immensely enhanced by his 'Defence of Revealed Religion,' published in 1732 against Tindal. Warburton pronounced it to be one of the best reasoned books in the world; and Lechler, in his work on English Deism, speaks in the highest terms of its clear and luminous reasoning, its powerful arguments, its command of the subject, and its liberal and philosophic tone.[1] As a bishop he was unfortunately disabled, through almost all his episcopate, by severe illness. Otherwise he would have been a valuable accession to his bench. 'I rejoice,' said Berkeley, 'in his promotion. His writings and character raise him high in my esteem.'[2] He lived on terms of intimate friendship with James Foster and some other leading Nonconformists.[3]

Sir Thomas Gooch (Bristol 1737, Norwich 1738, Ely 1748-54) is described by Hayley as a man of extraordinary talent but not much learning, and not the sort of man who should have been a bishop. On the contrary, he says that he had, as Cardinal de Retz declared of himself, 'l'âme peut-être la moins ecclésiastique qui fût dans l'univers.[4] He was, however, a worthy man, as kind and charitable as he was witty and vivacious.[5] Although a High Churchman,[6] he was favourable to the plans which Sherlock and others were discussing for the comprehension of moderate Dissenters.[7]

Sir George Fleming (Carlisle 1734-47) is spoken of as 'a

---

[1] Quoted by Overton, *English Church*, &c., i. 198.
[2] Berkeley's *Works*, iv. 341.   [3] Parr's *Memoirs*, i. 134.
[4] On Hayley's *Life and Writings*, reviewed in *Qu. Rev.*, 31, 264.
[5] Bentham's *Ely*, p. 212. Among his benefactions was a valuable one for widows and orphans.   [6] Walpole's *Memoirs*, p. 148.
[7] Skeats's *Free Churches*, p. 452.

courteous gentleman and pious Christian,' receiving also the somewhat equivocal praise of 'the most consummate prudence.'[1]

Thomas Osbaldeston, his successor at Carlisle, 1747 was afterwards Bishop of London, 1762–64, appointed, says Hurd, rather ill-naturedly, 'to nobody's joy that I know of.'[2] But Archdeacon Moss, in a charge[3] delivered very soon after Osbaldeston's death, speaks with much respect of his strong sense of responsibility. He spoke also of his love of literature, his talent for business, and his hospitality. It may be further said of him that he had been one of George III.'s tutors, that he was a Liberal in his Church views, and that he was very vehement against the introduction of monumental statuary into St. Paul's.[4]

Isaac Madox (St. Asaph 1736, Worcester 1743–59) rose to a high position from a very humble one. His parents were small tradesmen, of a Dissenting communion. At their death he was placed by his aunt with a pastrycook, who would not keep him, because he paid more care to his books than to the business.[5] Meanwhile he did well at the charity school which he attended, and, by the help of an exhibition founded for Nonconformists, went to a Scotch university.[6] Bishop Gibson heard of him as a youth of much promise, and sent him to Queen's College, Cambridge. From that time his success was uninterrupted. He took orders, became chaplain to Bishop Waddington, Rector of St. Vedast, Clerk of the Closet to Queen Caroline, Dean of Wells, wrote in 1735, in answer to Neal's 'History of the Puritans,' a defence of the English Church and the leaders of the Reformation, and the next year was raised to the episcopate. The little we hear of him as bishop is to his credit.

---

[1] Note to Nicolson's *Letters*, p. 327. [2] Hurd's *Life*, p. 84.
[3] Moss's *Charge* of 1764. [4] Newton's *Autobiog.*, p. 145.
[5] *Parl. Hist.*, xi. 397 (note). [6] Nichols' *Lit. Anec.*, v. 170.

The historian of Worcester speaks of him as venerated and beloved, hospitable and open-hearted.¹ He seems to have taken a special interest in the improvement of poor benefices,² hospitals, and in the promotion of the British fisheries. When Doddridge was in his last illness he raised a fund to send him on a voyage to Lisbon, in the hope that it might recruit his health.³ About 1748, when considerable interest was felt in England on behalf of Zinzendorf and the Moravians, Madox warmly supported a bill which passed through both Houses for the more distinct recognition of their orders and of their position as a Church. 'It will be an edification,' he said, 'to the whole episcopal bench, and all true Protestants of England, if the British nation expresses itself in favour of the Brethren; for whatever benefit England confers upon the ancient confessor church must be an encouragement to all Evangelical Christians throughout the world to expect nothing but good from this country.'⁴

Matthew Mawson (Llandaff 1734, Chichester 1740, Ely 1754–70) is described as an awkward, absent man, with no ambition, and no desire to please; deserving, however, of much respect.⁵ He did not marry, and gained a reputation for parsimony in his private life, in order that he might be more munificent in his public benefactions. He spen great sums on the cathedral of Ely, was no less open-handed in the erection of municipal buildings, and of embankments and works of drainage, and bequeathed 9,000l. to the see of Chichester, and to Bene't College, Cambridge.⁶ He refused the bishopric of Gloucester in

---

¹ Val. Green's *Hist. of Worcester*, i. 216.
² Ph. Onslow's *Dioc. Hist. of Worcester*, p. 335.
³ Hunt, *Rel. Th. in Eng.*, iii. 248.
⁴ Stoughton's *Religion in England*, &c., p. 362.
⁵ Nichols' *Lit. Ance.*, iv. 459–60.
⁶ Bentham's *Ely*, p. 214.

1731, because he thought that Rundle had been injuriously set aside after being appointed.[1] There seems to be no other ground for his being suspected of sharing in Rundle's heterodox views.

Nicholas Claggett (St. Davids 1731, Exeter 1743-46) was a frequent and well-known preacher on special occasions. A passage may be quoted from one of his sermons on religious education. 'What pity it is that a mind capable of the sublime and heavenly pleasures of religion, of knowing and loving God, of being adorned with all the graces and virtues of a disciple of Christ—in a word, of becoming, ike other pious and holy souls, a temple for the great God of heaven and earth to delight in, and to reside and dwell n—what pity it is that such a mind as this, for a want of a little care and culture on our part, should be so far degraded as to wretchedly sink in vice and folly, should be the hold of every foul spirit, a cage of unclean birds, and the constant scene of impure and wicked imaginations!'[2]

Of George Lavington, his successor at Exeter, some account has been given in a previous chapter, in connection with his work on 'The Enthusiasm of Methodists and Papists compared.'[3]

James Johnson (Gloucester 1752, Worcester 1759-74) was a man of athletic figure, well informed, pleasant, popular, and hospitable, who by no means felt any anxious burden of episcopal responsibility. We are told that he kept a good table, beautified his palaces, and provided well for those who were fortunate enough to be related to him. He was ' notus in fratres animi paterni,' says Bishop Newton, 'a very father to his nephews and nieces.'[4] Rumour said

[1] Dallaway's *Hist. of Sussex*, i. 96.
[2] Claggett's Sermon at the meeting of the Charity Schools, p. 27.
[3] See p. 391, Vol. I.
[4] Newton's *Autobiog.*, p. 135.

of him that he was or had been a rank Jacobite.[1] He was killed by a fall from his horse.[2]

Thomas Hayter (Norwich 1749-61) is mentioned by Horace Walpole as 'a well-bred, sensible man,'[3] and by Dean Moss as 'one of the most respectable persons of his order.'[4] Hurd alludes with dislike to his 'oily smoothness,' and hints at intrigues in policy which he ought to have kept away from.[5] He was preceptor to George III. in his boyhood.

Sir William Ashburnham (Chichester 1754-97) doubtless owed his promotion to his name and family. This was constantly and avowedly the case in the eighteenth century. Some bishoprics, Mr. Greville said to Bishop Newton, are more properly given to men of ability and learning, and others to men of family and fashion.[6] If these qualifications were important, there seems to have been no reason why Sir William Ashburnham should not be a bishop, except that he was distinguished for nothing in particular but 'a fine voice and an impressive elocution.'[7]

Edward Willis (St. Davids 1743, Bath and Wells 1743-74) was famed for his skill in deciphering. Sir Robert Walpole said of him that he knew so many secrets, he might count on becoming archbishop.[8] Rowland Hill spoke of him gratefully for having ordained him without any condition whatever, when other bishops had refused on account of his Methodist proclivities.[9]

---

[1] H. Walpole's *Memoirs of George II.*, p. 304.
[2] Green's *Hist. of Worcester*, i. 216.
[3] H. Walpole's *Memoirs*, p. 87, who adds that he was a natural son of Archbishop Blackbourne. But a writer in the *Qu. Rev.*, 27, 187, shows from the register of Chagford that he was 'the son of George Hayter, rector of this parish, and Grace his wife.'
[4] Dean Moss, *Charge* of 1761.   [5] Hurd's *Life*, p. 84.
[6] Newton's *Autobiog.*, p. 113.   [7] *Qu. Rev.*, 31, 276.
[8] Doran's note to H. Walpole's *Memoirs*, p. 126.
[9] Charlesworth's *Life of R. Hill*, p. 26.

Richard Trevor, son of the first Lord Trevor, was Bishop of St. Davids (1743–52), and afterwards succeeded Butler at Durham (1752–71).[1] He possessed qualities which were considered by many quite as appropriate to the holder of the princely see as piety and learning. He was ' strikingly handsome, of noble and dignified manners, a sincere friend, a generous patron, a splendid and munificent prelate.'[2]

Anthony Ellys, his successor at St. Davids (1743–52), was a studious man of some learning. He wrote upon the Sacramental Test, upon Protestant Liberty, against Hume on Miracles,[3] and in defence of the Hutchinsonians, a temporary party in the Church, who numbered among them two or three men of some eminence, but who were generally more distinguished for piety than for sound reason.

Thomas Tanner[4] (St. Asaph 1731–36) was an antiquary of great note. His 'Notitia Monastica,' was published in 1695, when he was but twenty-one years old. His ' Bibliotheca Britannico-Hibernica,' published in 1748, had occupied him forty years. The Bodleian Library now possesses a collection of his archæological manuscripts. At the beginning of George II.'s reign he was prolocutor of Convocation, then little more than a nominal office.

John Hume (Bristol 1758, Oxford 1758–65, Salisbury 1765–82) owed his promotions rather to interest with the Duke of Newcastle than to any special merit. But as rector of Barnes he had been an exemplary parish priest, and as bishop fulfilled his duties with no less conscientiousness.[5]

Edmund Keene (Chester 1752, Ely 1771–81) was more notable for wealth and love of building than for any more episcopal qualities. He inherited a good fortune from his

[1] Surtees, *Durham*, i. 122.   [2] Nichols' *Lit. Ancc.*, iv. 481.
[3] Hunt, *Rel. Th. in Eng.*, iii. 317, 408.
[4] There are remarks on his life in the Notes to Nicolson's *Correspondence*, p. 57. See also Jessop's *Dioc. Hist. of Norwich*, p. 218.
[5] Cassan's *Bishops of Salisbury*, pp. 320-21.

brother, Sir B. Keene, ambassador to Spain; and through his interest with Sir Robert Walpole held various ecclesiastical appointments, which he did not scruple to hold together. The bishop's residences, at Chester, Ely, and Ely House, London, all attest the prodigality with which he indulged his favourite taste.[1] As Master of Peterhouse, Cambridge, he had been a very active vice-chancellor, and was in some odium with the younger members of the university on account of the great strictness of his discipline.[2]

It is rather curious that in the eighteenth century there were three English bishops distinguished (or undistinguished) by the name of John Thomas:[3]—

1. John Thomas, St. Asaph (elect) 1743, Lincoln 1743, Salisbury 1761–66.

2. John Thomas, Peterborough 1747, Salisbury 1757, Winchester 1761–81.

3. John Thomas, Rochester 1774–93.

All three had held livings in the City, the first at St. Vedast's, the second at Bene't's, the third at St. Bride's. The first and the third had both been royal chaplains, and the second had been preceptor to George III. Bishop Newton's story was that some one was speaking of Dr. Thomas. 'Which Dr. Thomas do you mean?' 'Dr. John Thomas.' 'They are both named John.' 'Dr. Thomas who has a living in the City.' 'They both have livings in the City.' 'Dr. Thomas who is chaplain to the king.' 'They are both chaplains to the king.' 'Dr. Thomas who is a very good preacher.' 'They are both very good preachers.' 'Dr. Thomas who squints.' 'They both squint.'[4]

[1] Newton's *Autobiog.*, p. 115; Nichols' *Lit. Ancc.*, iv. 324.
[2] Ormerod's *Cheshire*, i. 80.
[3] There was also a William Thomas, Bishop first of St. Davids, and then of Worcester, in the latter part of the seventeenth century.
[4] Quoted in Chalmers' *Biog. of Thomas of Rochester.*

Thomas of Salisbury and Winchester had gained much popularity as a preacher while yet a curate.[1] This brought him into repute, and he became rector of an important living, Boyle Lecturer, tutor to the Prince of Wales, and at length a bishop. George III. was very fond of him, and often visited him. He was a man of sound sense and strong independent feeling, a quality which for a time brought him into disgrace at court. Hurd speaks rather disparagingly of 'honest Tom's' ability.

Thomas of Lincoln and Salisbury[2] is spoken of as a worthy man, but too fond of the company of people of rank, and sadly forgetful of his promises. He squinted terribly and was very deaf; but his never-failing humour and facetiousness made him an amusing companion. George II. delighted in his society, and brought him over, with promises of promotion, from his chaplaincy at Hamburg. There were few Englishmen in his day so well versed in German.

Thomas of Rochester[3] may be mentioned here, though his episcopate was entirely in George III.'s reign. Everything we hear of him proves him a thoroughly conscientious man, well worthy of respect. He put off his ordination till the age of twenty-seven, that he might have more time for study and preparation; and when he was rector of Blechingley, he and his brother had worked very diligently among the poor. Zachary Pearce, a good judge of merit, was very anxious that he should be his successor at Rochester, as he ultimately was. He was an excellent

---

[1] Cassan's *Bishops of Winchester*, pp. 271-73; Cassan's *Salisbury*, p. 281; Kilvert's *Life of Hurd*, p. 119.

[2] Cassan's *Bishops of Salisbury*, pp. 316-18; Nichols' *Lit. Ancc.*, vi. 364; Newton's *Autobiog.*, p. 61; G. Wakefield's *Memoirs*, pp. 10-12.

[3] *Sermons and Charges of J. Thomas of Rochester, with Life*, by G. A. Thomas; Newton's *Autobiog.*, p. 110.

preacher, and scholarly and refined in his tastes, a lover of antiquities, and a skilled musician.

John Harris (Llandaff 1728-38) is said to have owed his see to a book which might be thought to have little enough to do with a bishop's work. He published when Prebendary of Canterbury an elaborate 'Treatise upon the Modes, or, a Farewell to French Kicks.' It had for the time a considerable circulation; and the Duke of Argyle, who was a patriotic reprobater of all French fashions, was reported to have used his interest to such purpose that Harris became a bishop.[1]

Cornwallis (Lichfield and Canterbury), Drummond (St. Asaph, Salisbury, and York), and Terrick (Peterborough and London) belong so entirely to the reign in which they held places of prominence, that they will be better spoken of among George III.'s prelates.

A few remain yet unnoticed—Robert Butler (Norwich 1732, Ely 1738-48), Elias Sydall[2] (St. Davids 1731, Gloucester 1731-34), Lord James Beauclerk (Hereford 1746-81), Edward Cresset (Llandaff 1748-54), Richard Newcombe (Llandaff 1754-61, St. Asaph 1761-69), Samuel Lisle (St. Asaph 1743-48, Norwich 1748-9), Charles Cecil (Bangor 1734-37), Philip Yonge[3] (Bristol 1758-61). All these seem to have lived quietly, with little comment favourable or otherwise.

[1] Noble's *Cont. of Grainger*, iii. 490.
[2] Sydall had been Dean of Canterbury. He is spoken of by A. Clarke as 'a man of real worth' (L. Sundon's *Diary*, ii. 193).
[3] Yonge had been Master of Jesus College, Cambridge. He is said to have owed his preferments to the favour of the Duke of Newcastle, whose duchess he escorted from Hanover to England (Jessop's *Dioc. Hist. of Norwich*, p. 223).

CHAPTER VI.

THE ENGLISH CHURCH. 1760–1800.

IT would be easy to accumulate passages in evidence that throughout the earlier part of George III.'s reign England was corrupt to the core. Massey, describing the state of manners in 1775, gives a dark picture of vice, brutality, and irreligion rampant throughout the country from the highest to the lowest. Venal politics, a dissolute stage, shameful laxity of morals, drunkenness a fashion, profane swearing a general habit, 'custom-house oaths' and such other perjury a byword and a jest, duelling an established usage of society, Tyburn horrors, roads garnished with gibbets, ruinous gambling, cruel amusements, might all afford material for a very dark estimate of the social condition of the age. Much might further be added of religion assailed with ribaldry and contempt, of a torpid Church, of indolent clergy and time-serving prelates, of enthusiasm regarded with horror even by esteemed divines, and, in fine, of Wesley and his fellow-workers struggling bravely but alone, amid insult and obloquy, to revive the power of Christianity amid a godless and perverse generation.

Warburton, writing to Hurd in 1771, quotes some words which Voltaire had written five years before. The French philosopher had been speaking of the Sacheverell commotion, and had cynically remarked that 'les Toris furent obligés d'avoir recours à la religion,' and then adds,—' Il n'y a guère aujourd'hui (1766), dans la Grande Bretagne, que le peu qu'il en faut pour distinguer les factions.'[1] 'The state of religion amongst us,' exclaims Warburton, 'though it be bad enough amongst us, is not quite so bad as this scoundrel represents it.' 'Miserable,' he continues, 'as the condition of it is at present, I am confident it will revive again; but as I am no prophet, but only a sincere believer, I will not pretend to say how soon. The present generation seems not to be worthy of this blessing, which believers only are indulged with a Pisgah sight of—just sufficient to support and confirm their faith, not sufficient to prevent their being laughed at by the profligate and even the sceptical.'[2]

This quotation conveniently serves a double purpose. It shows that an able and representative man like Warburton shared in the usual feeling that the general state of religion and of morals was bad. It shows also that he thought he saw some hopeful signs. Perhaps a modern writer may be justified in thinking that a somewhat brighter view might have been taken of the present, and a yet more hopeful one of the future. Irreligion, except in the grosser forms of atheism, was loud and outspoken, vice very devoid of shame and reticence. Voltaire, seeing little into the heart of English life, chiefly noticing what was conspicuous on its surface, might have been quite genuine in his belief that Christianity was almost effete among us. Nor is it at all surprising that more serious writers should have been shocked into the belief that the time in which they were living was very exceptionally bad. The truth seems rather to be that a comparatively slight depression in the general tone of religious and moral principle is abundantly sufficient to relax those bonds by which social opinion keeps vice under constraint. For in proportion as virtue is timid, vice increases in effrontery; and when religion is languid

---

[1] *Hist. de Louis Quatorze.*   [2] Warburton to Hurd, Letters, p. 231.

irreligion becomes emboldened. There can be no doubt that in the present age, notwithstanding the evils which swarm in our midst, public sentiment strongly reprobates, and that without any hypocrisy, what a century ago passed almost unreproved. But the most sanguine believers in moral progress will probably hesitate before they affirm decidedly that good is intrinsically stronger and evil weaker than in the days of our great-grandfathers. Let it be sufficient if we can fairly hope that, through the greater efficiency both of the National Church and of other religious organisations, Christianity is distinctly stronger than it was, and that goodness has more powerful aids for asserting itself and for repressing evil.

Religion was certainly at a low ebb at the accession of George III. Yet those who, like Warburton, thought they saw tokens of revival[1] were not mistaken. The Christian Church was beginning once more to see that moderation, however excellent in its kind, was not the sum and total of all Christian virtue. Even enthusiasm was beginning, though exceedingly slowly and cautiously, to be thought a thing that might under careful limits be sometimes tolerated. The actual word inspired, it is true, almost as much horror as heretofore. Up to the very end of the century the mystic writers, few though they were and far between, alone ventured to utter the word without a start of alarm. All besides them, of every school of thought, however good and zealous they might be—High Church or Broad Church, Evangelicals or (for the most part) Methodists—were all perfectly agreed[2] in speaking of enthusiasm as a thing to

[1] Thus Bishop Newton also, speaking of 'the gross immorality and irreligion of our people,' adds that there were 'still some vital signs, some symptoms of recovery' (Newton's *Autobiog.*, p. 179).

[2] *E.g.* 'No evil more to be feared than rancorous enthusiastic zeal' (Lyttelton's *Dial. of the D.*, Dial. 1). Langhorne's letters are 'unhappily a little tinctured with enthusiasm' (Johnson's *Lives of the Poets*, Langhorne).

be dreaded and deprecated. So deep was the impression left upon the English mind by what Wilberforce called 'the canting hypocrites and wild fanatics of the preceding century.'[1] Although, however, the word itself was too far tainted in general estimation by fanatical excesses to be as yet safely used, the fire and stir which it chiefly implies in its modern application was being here and there rekindled into life, not only among the Methodists, but in many and varied quarters. In poetry, the cold polish of Pope and his numberless imitators was beginning to lose admirers among those who could appreciate a simpler nature and a more earnest purpose in Gray and Cowper. Later in the century was to come a yet greater revolution in poetical thought. The spirit of ardent loyalty, long banished from British soil, or maintaining a feverish and unwholesome existence among the Jacobites, was to be found once more both in the court of the young king and in the hearts of many of his people. High Churchmanship, with its love of beauty, its clinging memories, its warmer imagination, although counted by many as 'a thing exploded,'[2] was yet slightly awaking from the chill into which German politics and Hoadly's theology had cast it. In religion, most thinking men who cared for its true interests were beginning to doubt whether pure reason were after all so potent for the discovery and realisation of truth as it

---

'Enthusiasm naturally leads to Antinomianism' (J. Wesley, on Christian Perfection, *Works*, xi. 431). 'The spirit of enthusiasm is ... a device of Satan to discredit the work of gospel truth' (Rev. J. Newton, *Memoirs*, p. 512). 'Doctrines of divine assistances disgraced by brain-sick enthusiasts' (Wilberforce, *Practical View*, p. 78). From Warburton and a crowd of other writers similar passages might be multiplied to any extent.

[1] Wilberforce, *Pract. View*, p. 73.

[2] I hope the High Church principles which formerly ... are now generally exploded' (J. Newton's 'Apologia' [1785], *Works*, p. 878). So Horsley, speaking, however, only of the theory of Divine Right, speaks of 'that exploded notion' of the old High Churchmen (Jan. 31, Serm. before H. of Lords, 1793).

had long been proclaimed to be. It might be that its empire was not so entirely supreme. The emotions must also be taken count of. Conscience might have other guides than reason. The Divine Spirit might chiefly hold communication with the soul of man through a spiritual faculty, which did not gather its highest intuitions from inferences which could be reduced to syllogisms. Even those who greatly disliked and mistrusted certain features in the Methodist revival were often led by it into grave thought. No fair-minded person could deny that its best results had been operated by some other power than that of reason. Souls awakening to a sense of sin, and longing for a higher life, would be likely to feel with Evander in Fellow's religious eclogue, rather than with Mezentius:—

> *Evander.* But when the waves of conscious terror roll,
> And dash tremendous on the affrighted soul;
> When the Most High descends with vengeful ire,
> When the earth shakes, air thunders, heaven's on fire,
> And the whole soul in tumult, fear, and grief,
> Reason's unable to afford relief.
> *Mezentius.* Nature's all-gracious Parent ne'er design'd
> Such strong dismay to seize the virtuous mind;
> Nor need you sink beneath these heavy woes,
> Would you regard the reason He bestows.
> *Evander.* This I must doubt, and certainly have cause.
> *Mezentius.* What, doubt the truth of reason's sacred laws?
> *Evander.* Yes; doubt if reason can my conscience clear,
> Or save me from the dreadful wrath I fear.[1]

Warburton insisted that Methodism had done more than anything else to retard the progress of a spiritual theology. In the last century people had rushed into cold moralities as a refuge from fanatical heats; and now, just when the balance was redressing itself, when faith was reassuming its rightful position, and 'the slighted doctrine of redemp-

[1] J. Fellow's *Grace Triumphant*, 1772, Dial. II.

tion was being reinstated in its ancient credit,' Methodists, by running 'to the old abusive extremes,' were creating a similar revulsion to that which had arisen out of Puritan rule.¹ This may have been the case sometimes, perhaps often. But, after all, the greater and more conspicuous effect was one of which Warburton took little note, and which was by no means reactionary—the Evangelical movement in the Church. In the first year of George III.'s reign, Evangelicalism, although as yet hardly visible on the surface, was rapidly growing into the vigorous life which it presently possessed.

Among the causes which tended to gradual improvement in the religious and moral life of the country, something must be attributed to the personal character of the king. The devout seriousness which marked his demeanour at his coronation [2] characterised him throughout his reign. He told Secker that he considered it his first and principal duty to support religion and virtue.[3] So also Sterne, writing from London on Christmas Day, 1760, said, 'The king seems resolved to bring all things back to their original principles, and to stop the current of corruption and laziness.'[4] It was far beyond the power of the worthy sovereign to carry out such a resolution very effectually. His example, however, and his influence were always exercised, sometimes in a mistaken and narrow-minded way, but with never-failing conscientiousness, in what he believed to be the way of right. The people knew this, and praised and loved him for it. Nor is it possible, in any country where the monarchical principle is still strong, for manners to remain wholly unaffected by a good or bad

---

[1] Warburton's 'Doctrine of Grace,' *Works*, iv. 712 16.
[2] Lord Mahon's *Hist.*, chap. xlii. v. 55.
[3] Stoughton's *Religion under the Georges*, ii. 5.
[4] Sterne's *Letters*, No. xiii.

example on the throne.[1] To it, no doubt, in some measure, although other causes more largely contributed to the improvement, was owing that great increase of religious feeling in the upper classes to which Hannah More, towards the close of her life, has borne strong testimony.[2]

Changes in religious thought and general morals are of course very gradual and imperceptible in their movement. Much that was said of the state of religion, of the Church, or of manners generally in a preceding chapter refers almost equally well to the first twenty years of George III.'s reign. What was there said of the effects upon religious thought of the subsidence of the Deist controversies belongs chiefly to the period immediately after 1760. In these years also, as in those directly preceding, the three most redeeming features in their religious history were the Methodist revival, the growth of philanthropy, and the growth of tolerance. Methodism extended its energies year by year. The benevolent agencies which had been taking root throughout the country multiplied, grew richer, extended their spheres of action, and sought out fresh fields for beneficence. Dr. Dodd, whose lamentable crime and miserable end must not wholly obscure his previous good deeds, by his own single exertions collected some thousands of pounds for charitable purposes.[3] Howard's unwearied labours in prisons and lazarettos have a world-wide reputation. Hanway and Raikes and Wilberforce and a multitude of other names might be added to

---

[1] In the end of the preceding century, Tillotson (Serm. xxvii.) quoted as still holding true,
 'Non sic inflectere sensus
 Humanos edicta valent, ut vita regentis.'
Whether, however, this could be said, without great qualification, of any period in English history is very questionable, certainly not for the last two hundred years.

[2] In 1813. H. More's *Memoirs*, ii. 199, 402.

[3] Malcolm's *London*, i. 84.

his in a roll of honour, and the zeal expended for the abolition of the slave trade worthily crowns the charitable work of the century. The growth of tolerance can only be spoken of, as in a former chapter, with many qualifications. It was partial and capricious, marred by some great inconsistencies, rudely and violently interrupted by the bursts of bigotry signalised in the Gordon and Priestley riots. Its merits were also, as was before observed, very equivocal, so far as it proceeded from no better cause than scepticism or indifference. In the last years of the century, when religious earnestness had greatly increased, it was a very common complaint that intolerant feeling was becoming more rife than it had been a generation before. Still, after making all deductions, there was both a real growth and a great gain. Throughout the more thoughtful and best educated classes, a sense alike of the justice and of the advantages of toleration was gradually becoming a steady, unmovable conviction. Such men did not always see their way to remove unjust disabilities. But if they continued to defend them, they defended them only as supposed necessities. Their minds were wholly free from the old spirit of religious persecution. It may be added that an argument was now to be sometimes heard which in former times was rarely if ever used among religious-minded Churchmen. Ever since the Reformation there had been many supporters of a free and generous toleration. They could have no more solid grounds than those upon which their conviction rested— namely, that liberty of conscience and of thought are inalienable rights, for the exercise of which a man is responsible only to his Maker; that no commonwealth has authority to dictate to its citizens what they shall believe; that the authority of the Church is not founded upon constraint, and that the solid interests of truth are forwarded by free inquiry. But, however strongly they might hold these opinions, and whatever might be the vehemence with which they denounced intolerance, there had been very few Churchmen in former days who did not hold that Nonconformity was in itself a very great evil, which could not be altogether avoided, yet which was altogether lamentable. Similarly there were, in all probability, very few Nonconformists of any sect who would not have exulted, as in the greatest of blessings, at a possibility that all their fellow-countrymen should come round to their way of thinking. Scarcely until the last century was drawing to its close was ever reasoned, although very rarely then, that great and manifold as are the blessings of unity, yet in this imperfect world there is no little compensation for its loss in the stimulus given by division, and in its discipline of candour and forbearance.[1] We may add that perhaps in some happier day means may be found of reconciling the two, and the Church learn to combine the advantages of both.

In speaking of the reigns of the first two Georges, some account was given of the great friendliness which subsisted between various bishops and other ecclesiastics in the English Church and the principal leaders of the Presbyterians, and, to a less extent, of the Congregationalist communions. But when Butler, and Herring, and Benson, and Waddington, and Conybeare, and others of similar views had passed away on the one side, and Doddridge, Watts, Chandler, George Benson, Farmer, Leland, Foster, and others on the Nonconformist side, there was very little of the same kind of intimacy afterwards. 'Oh, what a difference!' exclaimed Dr. Parr in 1778. 'How distressful! how disgustful!'[2] The English Presbyterians, who for a long time had not felt quite easy in their separation from the National Church, were fast declining. A gradual awakening of religious

[1] As in T. Somerville's *Life and Times*, 1741-1814, p. 88.
[2] Parr's *Works*, i. 134.

activity on either side awakened also the asperities of contrast. Then came the contentions which gradually led up to the American war, in which the Dissenters, as a body, favoured what they held to be the cause of liberty with no less warmth than Churchmen, for the most part, favoured the side which they considered to represent loyalty and order. Dissenters were charged with advocating republican principles, and with vexatious interference in opposing an American Episcopate.[1] These retorted with accusations of servility and oppressiveness. The attacks upon the National Church by Priestley in 1774 and many later occasions, as well as by Fleming and others, added further elements of strife. There was, therefore, for the most part much greater animosity in the seventh decade of the century between Churchmen and Dissenters than there had been in the fifth. Nevertheless, there was as yet no retrogression in the general advance of tolerance. In 1779 the Toleration Bill of 1689 received, after the long interval of ninety years, its first enlargement. Till that date, Dissenting ministers and schoolmasters had been required to subscribe to certain of the Articles. A declaration was now substituted of Protestantism and belief in the Holy Scriptures. On two previous occasions, in 1771 and 1773, a similar measure had been thrown out. Its rejection, however, had not been in any way an evidence of illiberal feeling. For Nonconformists had been by no means agreed as to its desirability. Terrick stated in Parliament that he had authority from Dissenters of high standing to say that the bill was disagreeable to them, and that they did not wish it to pass.[2] Many among them even formally petitioned against it, on the ground that religion generally would suffer from such a relaxation.[3] The sudden relinquishment of all opposition to

---

[1] Bishop Newton's *Autobiog.*, pp. 186, 200. [2] *Parl. Hist.*, xvii. 411.
[3] Skeats's *Hist. of the Free Churches*, p. 460.

it in 1779 is said to have been greatly owing to a sermon in favour of increased liberty to Dissenters, preached before the House of Lords by Bishop Ross.[1] In any case it passed through the Upper House without debate or division, as a measure, wrote Porteus, 'no less consonant to the principles of sound policy than to the genuine spirit of the gospel.'[2]

Ever since 1731 the operation of the Test had been to a great extent suspended by a series of Indemnity Acts.[3] In 1787, 1789, and 1790 three vigorous efforts were made to obtain the repeal both of it and the Corporation Act. All three were in vain. The bill was thrown out on the first occasion by 178 to 100; on the second by 192 to 102; on the third by the largely increased majority of 299 to 105.[4] After that, no further attempt was made for thirty-eight years. It is strange that a thing so utterly odious as a sacramental test should have thus held its ground. There was a general infatuation on the subject, from which few Churchmen were exempt. Many would have said that Lord Mansfield exactly expressed their opinion on the matter when he declared 'that he was not afraid of toleration, but that he thought the Test and Corporation Acts were bulwarks of the Constitution.'[5] 'A toleration and a test,' said Warburton, 'should always go together.'[6] The most liberal views were not altogether proof against this delusion. Even Dr. Parr, whose latitudinarianism was as nearly unlimited as the bounds of Christianity could by any means allow, was opposed to repeal on the first two occasions. In 1790, and afterwards, he opposed tests; but previously to that date he had actively exerted himself against any

---

[1] Skeats's *Hist. of the Free Churches*, p. 465.
[2] Bishop Porteus' *Life*, p. 57.   [3] Massey, iii. 432.
[4] This was, of course, owing to the strong Conservative reaction from the contagious excitement of the events going on in France.
[5] Seward's *Anecdotes*, ii. 340.
[6] Warburton's *Works*, iv. 684.

change being made.[1] Neither was the earnest piety of Wilberforce, nor his general readiness to co-operate with Dissenters, any bar to his falling in with the usual belief. He disliked, he said, the particular form of a sacramental test; but, not seeing how it could be replaced, he had voted in 1787 against the measure for repeal brought forward by his friend Mr. Beaufoy. In 1789 he did not vote, 'his mind not being made up.' Afterwards, on mature reflection, his 'reluctance to oppose the repeal of these laws had been overcome by a conviction of their present necessity.'[2] The king, as might be expected from his general opinions, was emphatically against an alteration of the law.[3] Among the bishops, Shipley and Watson appear to have been the only two who spoke and voted in favour of the motion. Cowper spoke of the test in a strain of worthy indignation:—

> Hast thou by statute shoved from its design
> The Saviour's feast, His own bless'd bread and wine,
> And made the symbols of atoning grace
> An office key, a picklock to a place?[4]

This seems the natural view to take of it. Yet certainly it was very rarely looked upon quite in this light, and there is some satisfaction in believing this, and that for the 150 years during which it lingered the Church and people were not in it offending against their own consciences. One is

[1] Parr's *Life*, i. 234.
[2] *Life of Wilberforce*, by his Son, p. 80. Jones of Nayland, that true worthy of the Church, expresses great alarm at the possibility of repeal (Stevens' *Life of Jones*, xxv.).
[3] Lord Russell's *Memorials of C. J. Fox*, iii. 251.
[4] Cowper's *Poems*, 'Expostulation.' Angeloni, writing of England in 1755, also speaks of the test with indignation, but not from the same point of view. To his mind, the scandal of it was that Hoadly's teaching as to the nature of the sacrament had so degraded it in English estimation, that instead of deeming it the most sacred of oaths, Presbyterian place-seekers resorted to it as to a mere ceremony. (Angeloni, *On the English Nation*, Letter IX.)

also glad to feel that actual intolerance [1] had no great part in it.

Except so far as the subject entered incidentally into the plans of the Revisionists of 1772 and 1777, there were no formal schemes for Church comprehension in the last forty years of the century. Broad Churchmen like Bishop Law and Bishop Watson, Paley [2] and Parr, frequently expressed a desire that it might be possible. But these were merely opinions and aspirations, which no one made any effort to carry out. Towards the latter part of the century many attempts were made to organise joint committees of Evangelical Churchmen, Methodists, and Dissenters, for the promotion of various religious objects.[3] Thus the 'Evangelical Magazine' was started in 1785, under the editorship of Eyre, a Churchman, and Boyne, a Congregationalist, to defend the common faith against disbelievers, and to maintain the general doctrines of the Reformation. A good many Churchmen as well as Dissenters supported this enterprise; and in 1795 they were strong enough to set afoot the London Missionary Society. This society, however, though in the first instance it invited Church co-operation, very soon became a purely Nonconformist organisation. There were similar attempts at

---

[1] Nevertheless, the violent reaction caused by the French Revolution, which often turned Liberals into Tories, and Tories into Retrogressionists, awakened into life whatever vestiges there were of the old intolerance. Early in the year 1800, Wilberforce said he was in the greatest alarm lest the privileges enjoyed under the Toleration Act should be materially abridged (Wilberforce, *Life*, p. 211).

[2] Referring to the closing words of Paley's tenth chapter of his *Moral and Political Philosophy*, Dr. Percival wrote, June 20, 1788, 'I am a Dissenter, but actuated by that same spirit of Catholicism which you possess. An Establishment I approve; the Church of England in many respects I honour; and I should think it my duty to come instantly into her communion, were the plan which you have proposed in your tenth chapter carried into execution' (Meadley's *Life of Paley*, p. 131).

[3] Stoughton, ii. 332, 351, 354; Skeats, 512, 519; Wilberforce, 223, &c.

united work in some of the village itinerancies, and to a still greater extent in the Religious Tract Society, started in 1799. No attempts at this kind of union were very successful. Many Dissenters disapproved of them. The Churchmen who joined them were almost exclusively of the Evangelical party; and even these, hearty Churchmen as they were, often felt themselves in a somewhat cramped and compromised position. The British and Foreign Bible Society, which was not formed until the present century (1802–4), afforded a more promising field for such combination; but even in it there were many difficulties, and much contention and controversy.

At the opening of George III.'s reign no one clause of the terrible penal statutes against Roman Catholics had yet been repealed. If the members of that communion did not feel their full weight, it was only because the worst penalties of the law were allowed to fall into abeyance, so long at least as Romanism remained very quiet and inactive. It retired, therefore, entirely into the background, and seemed to court the obscurity in which alone it safely rested. As Secker said in 1761, it harboured its strength and waited.[1] Its present conduct was unimpeachable, even to the most jealous eye. And so, for a time, it was almost unnoticed, attracting neither the tirades of the multitude, nor the kindlier attention which had been attracted to it in previous years by Wake and Courayer. Dr. Johnson, indeed, always cherished a respect almost amounting to a liking for the old Papal Church, and openly averred, to the astonishment and dismay of his faithful Boswell, that he preferred it to Presbyterianism.[2] But for the most part it was now only spoken of with aversion, mingled sometimes both with contempt and tacit dread, as if it were some fierce monster that lay maimed and inoffensive for the present, but might one day

[1] *Conc. ad Convoc.: Charges*, 3£1. [2] Boswell's *Johnson*, ii. 104–7, in 1769.

become formidable again. In 1768, Bishop Newton blazed into indignation at such a 'contemptuous defiance of all law' as the opening of 'a public mass-house' in Bristol, and quickly obtained the suppression of it.[1] A writer of 1765 spoke with much disgust of the publication by Phillips of the Life of Cardinal Pole. Such a work might be well for a few learned readers, but ought not to be 'too publicly regarded.'[2] Warburton apologises for seeming even for an instant to put Popery into comparison with Puritanism. 'As religions they can be no more compared together than a body irrecoverably corrupted with one but slightly tainted.'[3] Maclaine, editing Mosheim in 1768, is inclined to think that the connivance granted to it by the clemency of Government called for some modification.[4] Blackburne, in 1765, rushes into an absurd extravagance of ultra-Protestantism which at once discredits him as a writer on Church systems. He raves at the thought of there being in the English Church any 'one circumstance in her constitution borrowed from the creeds, rituals, or ordinances of Rome,' and imagines that 'every Papist is bound by his principles to destroy every Protestant, and to break the most solemn covenants he may enter into with people of that denomination, wherever and whenever he may do that with impunity.'[5] John Newton, one of the last men to make unmeaning apologies, thinks it desirable to excuse himself to his Evangelical readers for his firm belief in the true Christianity of 'such persons as Fénélon, Pascal, Quesnet, and Nicole, not to mention others.' 'Possibly some persons who may read these letters will form an unfavourable opinion of me for declaring that I have not the least doubt but the Lord has had, from age to age, a succession of chosen and faith-

[1] Newton's *Autobiog.*, p. 117. [2] Nichols, i. 636.
[3] Warburton, iv. 691. [4] Maclaine's *Mosheim*, v. 116.
[5] Blackburne's *Histor. View*, xx.

ful witnesses within the pale of that corrupt Church.'¹ John Wesley's opinions about Rome are a curious mixture of rational tolerance and vehement bigotry. But it must be acknowledged that the latter predominates. As an example of the former, a passage may be quoted from his 'Letter to a Roman Catholic, 1749': 'My dear friend, consider I am not persuading you to leave or change your religion, but to follow after that fear and love of God, without which all religion is vain. I say not a word to you about your opinions or outward manner of worship; but I say all worship is an abomination to the Lord unless you worship Him in spirit and in truth. . . . This, and this alone, is the old religion. This is the true primitive Christianity. . . We ought, without this endless jangling about opinions, to provoke one another to good works.'² What words could be better than these? So, in another work, speaking of members of the Church of Rome, he exclaims, 'How highly favoured many of them have been!'³ On the other hand, in 1780, the very year of the Gordon riots, he published a letter to the 'Public Advertiser' in which occur the following singularly unwise words: 'Let there be as boundless a freedom in religion as any man can conceive. . . . Yet I insist upon it that no Government not Roman Catholic ought to tolerate men of the Roman Catholic persuasion.'⁴ He grounds this on there being no security for their allegiance. But what a firebrand to cast among the excited fanatics of the Protestant Association! It would have been difficult for Wesley himself to reconcile the 'boundless freedom' and the absolute non-tolerance. How then was it possible for an ignorant and prejudiced multi-

¹ J. Newton's 'Apologia,' Newton's *Memoirs*, p. 885.
² Wesley's *Works*, x. 83–4.
³ *Journal*, 1768, quoted from Lecky's *England in the Eighteenth Century*, ii. 581. In his *Roman Catechism and Reply*, and elsewhere, Wesley shows a considerable study of Romish writers.
⁴ Wesley's *Works*, x. 160.

tude? They would naturally suppose that they were acting under the authority of one whom they venerated far more than any other living man, in holding that toleration of Papists was a national crime, and perhaps an individual sin. Can it, therefore, be wondered at that the Methodists, as Horace Walpole and Sir Samuel Romilly [1] both positively affirm, were in England the first and most eager to fan the flame of passion which led to the disgraceful scenes which in 1780 desolated London? But Wesley often spoke of Roman Catholics as if in religious belief they were practically pagans. For example: the principles of the Church of Rome 'have a natural tendency to hinder, if not utterly destroy, the love of God;'[2] 'The dregs of Rome, the worst idolatry;'[3] 'No Romanist can expect to be saved according to the terms of his covenant.'[4] Finally, a verse may be cited from one of his hymns:—

Heathens and Jews and Turks, may I,
And heretics, embrace;
Nor e'en to Rome the love deny
I owe to all the race.[5]

In 1774 the first gleams of an improved statutory condition dawned upon the Roman Catholics in a bill introduced into the Irish Parliament under Harcourt's viceroyalty, enabling them 'to testify their allegiance' by an oath which abjured the Pope's temporal power in this realm.[6] A further interest is attached to the measure in that it was the occasion of warm and lasting controversy among members of the Roman Church. For the question was

[1] Walpole's *Journal*, i. 376; Sir S. Romilly's *Memoirs*, i. 114. Walpole is speaking also and especially of their opposing any relief to the Roman Catholics of Quebec; Sir J. Romilly solely of the Gordon riots.
[2] 'Popery calmly considered,' *Works*, x. 157.   [3] *Works*, xi. 192.
[4] *Journal*, 1739, quoted in Lecky, ii. 582.
[5] Hymn III. in 'A Word to a Protestant,' c. 1745; Wesley's *Works*, xi. 195.
[6] Mant's *History of the Church of Ireland*, ii. 667.

put by some leading Roman Catholics in Ireland to the Doctors of the Sorbonne how far it was permissible to take such an oath. The Sorbonne was at this time greatly influenced by the ultra-Gallican opinions which about ten years before had been broached by Nicolas von Hontheim, Bishop of Treves, generally known as 'Febronius,' author of a celebrated Eirenicon,[1] and a powerful vindicator of the liberties of national churches. The answer, therefore, given to the querists was a favourable one, and stated that 'the doctrine of the right of the Popes to depose princes excommunicated is heretical "materialiter," that is, contrary to the very word of God.'[2] The matter did not end here. A few years later the English Roman Catholics, at the request of W. Pitt, for the purposes of the Roman Catholic Relief Act, put similar queries to the Faculties of Divinity in the Universities of Paris, Louvain, Douai, Salamanca, Alcala, and Valladolid. Febronian views prevailed in all; and, to the great indignation of some later Roman Catholic writers, to both the two questions—whether the Pope had any civil power in England, and whether he could release Englishmen from their allegiance—a negative answer was given, the Faculty of Paris, in particular, referring with approval to the previous answer of the Sorbonne. The English Roman Catholics, who have always been loyal-hearted subjects, welcomed the replies, and embodied them in a protestation which greatly contributed to their gaining the desired Relief Act. Nor is it probable that their sentiments on this point were very greatly altered by a rescript of the Cardinal Prefect of Propaganda in 1791, which strongly condemned 'the detestable opinions set forth with such pomp and circumstance by the six universities as Catholic doctrine.'[3]

---

[1] Condemned in 1764 by Clement XIII.
[2] E. S. Purcell, in Archbishop Manning's *Essays*, Series II., p. 118.
[3] Purcell, *ut supra*, 446-53.

In the same year as the Irish bill just referred to came the Quebec bill of 1774. As the French Roman Catholics in that province then numbered 150,000, while the Protestants were only 400,[1] it might have been thought that few could complain that the free exercise of their worship was thus conceded to the vast majority of the people. Nor was there so much general animosity to the bill as ministers had expected.[2] Still it was bitterly assailed by very considerable numbers both in Great Britain and in New England. Lord Chatham made a violent speech against it, and bitterly assailed the bishops for being, as he said, such traitors to their religion as to vote for it.

In 1778 came the first instalment of relief, and one of great importance to English Roman Catholics. This was in answer to a very loyal address presented by them. The bill passed almost unanimously. Henceforth, if they took the required oaths, priests and Jesuits might officiate in the services of their Church without incurring penalties of felony or high treason. Popish heirs, educated abroad, no longer forfeited their estates to the next Protestant heir; neither could the Protestant take possession of his father's property while its owner was alive.[3] It was surely time that these and such other fictitious crimes should be for ever erased from the statute-book.

But this was by no means the feeling of a large portion of the populace. The storm began in Scotland, and, if Somerville is correct, was, rather curiously, first set in motion, not by a Covenanter or a Cameronian, but by Abernethy, a Nonjuring bishop.[4] It presently raged there in full force. Tolerance could only be preached at risk of life. Dr. Robertson, the well-known historian, was in immi-

[1] *Parl. Hist.*, quoted in Mahon's *History of Engl.*, chap. li.
[2] Walpole's *Memoirs*, i. 375.   [3] Mahon, chap. lvii.
[4] Somerville, *My Own Life and Times*, p. 192.

nent danger of being torn in pieces by an infuriated mob.[1] The Protestant Associations, which had been formed in many of the North British towns, soon spread to England, and there rapidly arose among the lower classes an extraordinary ferment of anger and alarm. The Roman Catholics had given no new occasion for it. They had not augmented in numbers; they had not refused the oath; they had not attempted to proselytise; they had not made any ostentation of their increased liberty:[2] Such quiet behaviour was of no avail among the masses. The wildest rumours went abroad. 'I have heard,' wrote Sir Samuel Romilly, 'from three persons (all strangers to each other) who joined in conversation with the populace, that it was a current opinion that the king was a Papist. Some were sure of it; they pretended to know that he heard the mass privately, and that his confessor had the direction of all political concerns. A woman told a friend of mine that she hoped to see the streets stream with the blood of Papists.'[3] 'An Appeal to the People of Great Britain,' issued in 1779 by the Central Protestant Association, assured the people that 'to tolerate Popery is to be instruments to the perdition of millions of immortal souls now or yet to be, and is the direct way to provoke the vengeance of God, and to bring down destruction on our fleets and armies.'[4] All that follows belongs to the often told but ever strange and interesting story of the Lord George Gordon riots.

The attempt to intimidate Legislature had, as might be expected, a somewhat opposite effect to that which its promoters had proposed, and tended to hasten rather than delay the abrogation of persecuting laws. The possible results of the late measure were indeed carefully examined

---

[1] Somerville, p. 276.
[2] Romilly's *Memoirs*, i. 120; Bishop Porteus's *Life*, p. 61.
[3] Romilly's *Memoirs*, i. 128.   [4] Quoted in *id.*, p. 137.

into. Precautions were taken against any attempts on the part of Roman Catholic teachers to make proselytes; and inquiries were ordered to be made into the alleged increase of Romanism in England. But when this had been done, and when statistics [1] produced by Cornwallis, Porteus, Moss, and others had proved that the fears which had been expressed had no sufficient foundation, the feeling gained ground that other penal disabilities should be removed. A review published in 1782 fairly expressed what had now begun to be the prevailing opinion of educated society in regard of such relief—' that as the least penalty whatsoever was justifiable on no principle but that of absolute necessity, and as the behaviour of Roman Catholics both here and in France seemed to declare that necessity no longer existed, it was a scheme to be tried. So great an object justified some venture.' [2] Bishop Watson even argued, in 1783, that as in England Roman Catholics were so few, participation in civil rights might be safely given them. He thought also that in Ireland, although it was necessary rigorously to preclude them from civil power,[3] yet that their Church, as that of the vast majority, ought to be established side by side with the Protestant Church.[4] Public opinion was by no means ready to entertain any such ideas. But in 1791 the penal statutes were all of them practically repealed.[5] Probably this might have taken place a few years earlier had it not been for a difficulty about the oath of loyalty. A committee [6] of influential laymen of Roman Catholic opinions formed in 1782, with C. Butler, a friend of Dr. Parr, for their secretary, were willing, as we have

[1] *Parl. Hist.*, xxi. 760, 1378; Porteus's *Life*, p. 63; Walpole's *Journal*, ii. 420.   [2] Maty's *New Review*, 1782, i. 61.
[3] Watson's *Anecd. of his Life*, i. 216.   [4] *Id.*, pp. 251, 370.
[5] There was no absolute repeal, but it was provided that all who took the oath should not henceforward be liable to prosecution.
[6] Stoughton, ii. 35.

seen, to abjure in very decided terms the temporal power of the Pope in England. But the decision of Rome was opposed to that of the Roman Catholic universities; and it must be acknowledged that the oath which the English Government had proposed was worded in terms the very opposite of conciliatory. At last Pitt, Fox, and Horsley came to their aid. The proposed oath was expunged, and, with a few slight alterations, that was substituted which had been imposed on Irish Roman Catholics in 1774.[1]

If any violent exaggeration of antipathy towards the Roman Church still lingered anywhere among educated English Protestants, the French Revolution did very much to mitigate it. When Englishmen saw a pagan atheism rampant in the French capital, and blending itself with every kind of horror; when they felt also in every town, one might almost say in every village and hamlet, of their own country, some vibration of the shock under which thrones and altars had crumbled, it was impossible for thoughtful people with any sense of religion not to feel that the utmost differences which separated Roman Catholics and Protestants were almost insignificant as compared with the bond of a common Christianity. This feeling was greatly promoted, and associated with tenderer feelings of compassion, by the extensive immigration into England of French bishops and clergy. A remarkable and tolerably well-known passage of De Maistre, in which he speaks of the very favourable position which the English Church holds for advancing the reunion of Christendom, is prefaced and suggested by his observations on the circumstances under which, on this occasion, members of the two communions first came to a more personal knowledge one of the other. On account of the greater friendliness which henceforth existed between the prevailing forms of English and French

[1] Horsley's *Speeches*, p. 65.

Christianity, he says that this immigration of Gallican clergy may be said to form an epoch.¹ A writer of 1796, after speaking of the increased feeling of mutual kindliness and respect which was growing up about that time between English Episcopalians and Scotch Presbyterians, refers also to general improvement in the spirit of English Protestantism. We were wont, he says, to long for the destruction rather than for the amendment of Rome; what we now desire is not her total overthow, but rectification of error.² In the winter of 1792, Churchmen of all parties, and not Churchmen only, vied in providing shelter for their unusual guests. 'None,' said Horsley, 'are at this time more entitled to our offices of love than those with whom the difference is wide, in points of doctrine, discipline, and external rites—those venerable exiles, the prelates and clergy of the fallen Church of France.'³ Wordsworth wrote his sonnet of greeting to 'the Ministers of God,' who 'from altars threatened, levelled or defiled,' were seeking refuge among them.

> More welcome to no land
> The fugitives than to the British strand,
> Where priest and layman with the vigilance
> Of true compassion greet them.⁴

Wilberforce, upon whom, rather to his dismay, the National Convention had just conferred its gift of citizenship, was spurred by the ambiguous honour to exert himself all the more vigorously in behalf of the immigrant clergy.⁵ Again, three years later, he made a memorandum that, hearing of their distress, he 'kept awake at night, thought much of them, and formed a plan.'⁶ Hannah More

---

¹ Le Compte J. de Maistre, 'Considérations sur la France, chap. ii. p. 30.
² G. Bennett, On Eccles. Establishments, 1796, pp. 68, 72.
³ Horsley's Serm. before the H. of Lords, Jan. 31, 1793.
⁴ Wordsworth, sonnet 36.
⁵ Life of W. Wilberforce, p. 108.   ⁶ Id., p. 154.

published her 'Plea for the French Emigrant Clergy,' and found there were still those in whose nostrils it was an abomination. 'I have had the honour,' she writes, 'of being presented with three very severe answers. One accused me of opposing God's vengeance against Popery, by my wickedly writing that the French priests should not be starved, when it was God's will that they should; another declares that I am a favourer of the old Popish massacres.'[1] Prejudices such as these could be smiled at by all sensible people. There was, however, even among those who both respected the refugees and entirely approved the hospitality rendered to them, a natural fear lest these men should seek to win over their benefactors to the form of faith for which they were suffering.[2] In 1800 these fears were expressed in Parliament in a proposition to limit the period of their residence in England, and to put all places of education under a more rigorous supervision. It was, however, considered that the existing precautionary measures were sufficient. The feeling of security was further strengthened by an opinion not uncommonly held that the power of Romanism had permanently declined.[3]

Nothing was said in the previous chapters of this work, unless in some very incidental manner, of opinions held in the eighteenth century on the relations between Church and State. On this point it seems more convenient to take one general view of the century from its beginning to its end.

In the reign of William III. and in the early part of Queen Anne's reign, although there was much controversy as to the nature of the union subsisting between the Church and the State, there was none, or almost none, as to its desirability. Scarcely any one had yet disputed the general

---

[1] *Memoirs of H. More*, i. 531 (Sept. 13, 1793), and *Works*, xi. 195.
[2] *Considerations on the Present State of Religion*, 1801, p. 50.
[3] Horsley's *Speeches*, p. 358; Wyndham, quoted in *Quart. Rev.*, 89, 475.

prescription in its favour. 'It is true,' said a writer of 1680, 'that some enthusiasts have called it in question; but neither Presbyterians nor Independents, nor the hundredth part of Dissenters in England question it.'[1] In 1700 there were probably fewer still who did so. Recent dangers from an aggressive Romanism were still fresh in everybody's memory. There was scarcely a Protestant Englishman, Conformist or Nonconformist, who would not cordially have agreed with Tillotson's words : ' Is it not to every considerate man clear as the sun at noonday that nothing can maintain the Protestant religion among us, . . . nothing can be a bulwark of sufficient force to resist all the arts and attempts of Popery, but an established national religion, firmly united and compacted in all the parts of it?'[2] None doubted that in the great struggle which was then at its height the English Church headed ' the Protestant interest,' and that its strength was of great importance to all who, even if they disagreed in some particulars, were yet enlisted on the same side. Moreover, Dissenters were at this time well satisfied with their condition. They had no grievances of any consequence. The Toleration Bill had given them all they could venture to hope, and as much as they were yet ready to ask for. They were comparatively few in number, and their condition as separate denominations was not encouraging. English Presbyterians, if some concessions had been made, would gladly have joined the Established Church ; and most other Dissenters would have been quite content to enjoy toleration by its side. Dr. Watts wrote in 1705 a poem, which he retracted after the tumult of intolerance with which the reign of Anne closed, but which fairly expressed the feeling of most Dissenters when he wrote it.

[1] Dr. Collings' *Animadversions on a Sermon lately preached by Dr. Tillotson*, p. 5.
[2] Tillotson's Sermons, No. 20.

It is addressed to the Queen, and speaks of religion flourishing under her pious care : firstly in the National Church :—

> Here at thy side, and in thy kindest smiles,
> Blazing in ornamental gold she stands,
> To bless thy councils and assist thy hands,
> And crowds wait round her to receive commands.

Next among Protestant Dissenters :—

> There, at an humble distance from the throne,
> Beauteous she lies, her lustre all her own;
> Ungarnished, yet not blushing nor afraid,
> Nor knows suspicion, nor affects the shade.[1]

Thus Nonconformists, with very few exceptions, cordially acquiesced in a relation of the Church to the State which they could not aspire to themselves, but which they quite considered as a proper relation which religion should hold toward the civil government. It may be further added that Locke's arguments against secular interference with religious opinion had simply aimed at establishing universal tolerance; and that the early Deists, like Hobbes, were more inclined to merge the Church in the State than in any way to separate them.

Although thus far there was pretty general unanimity, opinions were a good deal tinged by varieties of politics or Churchmanship. The revolution which enthroned William and Mary in James's place, the Toleration Bill, the controversies about Church comprehension, had all brought into special prominence the relations between Church and State. Party feeling was hot, and far more inclined to exaggerate than to minimise all differences of thought on a subject which entered greatly into most questions of the day. There were still many who looked to the king in person as

[1] Watts's *Lyric Poems*, Book II.

the temporal ruler of the Church, the earthly head under which were blended and united the two bodies corporate, civil and spiritual. This opinion would have been far more common if, in the first place, the Romanism of James, and then the break in the succession, had not thrown doubt and confusion upon the sanctity which hedgeth round a king. But in Queen Anne's time the theory was not unfrequently revived of a real spiritual power inherent in or conferred upon sovereignty, after the example of the old kings of Israel and Judah. Thus Paterson, in 1714, speaks of St. James's Chapel as being out of episcopal jurisdiction, because it is under the immediate jurisdiction of her Majesty. And then he adds, 'Our king is a priest as well as a king; he is primogenitus Ecclesiæ.'[1] Apart from any dogma of this kind, it is certain that the royal prerogative in Church matters was often greatly exaggerated, by Whigs as well as by Tories. Swift speaks of many in his time, both clergy and others, understanding the king himself as the supreme magistrate, in whom legislative power was vested.[2] Much in the same way Archbishop Sharp says that people often seemed to suppose that a prelate was bound to obey the king's will with the same unquestioning fealty as a feudal baron would have followed his sovereign into the field. Some, he says, resented the opposition of eight of King William's bishops to the bill of attainder against Sir John Fenwick, 'as if it were unaccountable that they who eat of the king's bread should oppose measures necessary for his service.'[3]

The question, however, whether the State, in its relation to the Church, were mainly represented by the sovereign or by the Legislature was not practically one of much importance. It was a matter of far greater and more imme-

---

[1] Paterson's *Pietas Londinensis*, p. 110.
[2] In 1708. Swift's *Works*, viii. 269, 280.   [3] Sharp's *Life*, i. 295.

diate interest to know what were the claims of a National Church upon the obedience of the people, and what is the nature of the tie which links it with the State. On both these points—though the two are intimately connected—there was much discussion and much difference of opinion. High Churchmen, including the earlier Nonjurors, were generally inclined to consider the Church as wholly distinct from the State, and confederated to it, as Kettlewell said, by 'no more than a concordate.'[1] Such persons were, of course, very jealous in behalf of the independence of the Church, and loth to allow of interference with its powers. Nevertheless there was considerable difference between the extremer and the more moderate upholders of this view. Many of the Nonjurors—especially Dodwell, Brett, and Hickes—becoming more and more estranged from the national communion, and imbibing continually more of that true sectarian spirit which considers itself the orthodox remnant in the midst of a world of error, naturally pushed their High Church opinions to a further height, and became almost the first preachers in that century of an entire mutual independence of Church and State.[2] Others, such as Bishop Ken[3] and Leslie[4] among the Nonjurors, and many conforming High Churchmen, while they were by no means blind to the advantages of a National Church, always spoke of the Erastianism of Whigs and Low Churchmen with a tone of utter detestation, as if of all scandals to the Church it were the worst. A yet greater number of the same party exhibited their more moderate adherence to a similar opinion by their zeal in asserting the rights of the Lower House of Convocation.

[1] Nelson's *Life of Kettlewell*, § 51.
[2] Lathbury's *Hist. of the Nonjurors*, pp. 183, 258, 286; Brokesby's *Life of Dodwell*, p. 457. It does not, however, seem quite clear that Dodwell did not admit of some jurisdiction of the State in purely temporal matters.
[3] *Life of Ken*, by a Layman, p. 700, &c. [4] C. Leslie's *Works*, i. 412.

Those who were Whigs and Low[1] Churchmen held a view which, especially in a depressed state of religion, may become sadly debased, but which is in itself a noble and high-minded doctrine. 'Politics are from God; not only allowing and approving governments, but commanding them, for the better manifestation of His own glory, and men's greater good, temporal and spiritual. Hence it is evident that politics, both civil and ecclesiastical, belong unto theology, and are but a branch of the same.'[2] In other words, they held that the Church is not separate from the State, nor independent of it, but one with it; a Christian people being in a general sense of the word not only a Christian state, but a Christian Church, bound to make provision in common council for their spiritual as well as their secular interests. They held that the collective power of a commonwealth is able to do for the religious as well as for the material welfare of its citizens what would be far beyond the reach of individual effort. They acknowledged that, as the Church had its own revenues—protected and assured to it by the State—so also it had its separate council. They were not, however, anxious to see Convocation invested with any great powers, but distinctly preferred the jurisdiction of the Church being mainly in the hands of the national representatives.[3] To Government itself they were willing to entrust with all confidence a very wide power on all Church matters.

[1] In the old sense of the word, a sense which now nearly approaches to Broad Church.

[2] G. Lawson (end of seventeenth century), quoted as a motto to the third volume of Chr. Wordsworth's *Christian Institutes*.

[3] 'The Reformation,' said Calamy, 'had never been brought about, had it been left to a Convocation; nor will our breaches be ever healed but by a true English Parliament' (*Life of Calamy*, i. 205). It may be remarked that although Calamy's remark is true enough, yet no modern Parliament could hope to legislate successfully on any very important Church questions without the aid of a thoroughly representative body, fully competent to prepare such measures.

'Magistrates,' said Tillotson, 'are concerned to maintain the honour of religion, which doth not only tend to every man's future happiness, but is the best instrument of civil government and of the temporal prosperity of a nation; for the whole design of it is to procure the private and public happiness of mankind, and to restrain men from all those things which would make them guilty and miserable to themselves, and unpeaceable and troublesome to the world. Religion hath so great an influence upon the felicity of men, that it ought to be upheld and the veneration of it maintained, not only out of a just dread of the divine vengeance in another world, but out of regard to the temporal peace and prosperity of men. It will requite all the kindness and honour we can do it by the advantages it will bring to civil government, and by the blessings it will draw down upon it. God hath promised that those who honour Him He will honour, and in the common course of His providence He usually makes this good; so that the civil authority ought to be very tender of the honour of God and religion, if for no other reason, yet out of reasons of State.'[1] Tillotson's words have seemed worthy of quoting, both for their own sake, and because they well represent the opinion of a body of Churchmen than whom—whatever may have been their defects on some points of theology—none certainly have held a higher position in the general estimation of their times. His decided opinions on the power of the State in religious matters often gained him the repute of being an Erastian, if not a Hobbeist. The same charge was also brought against Archbishop Wake on account of his unwillingness to see Convocation established in a position of power and comparative independency.

Opinion as to the nature and authority of a National

[1] Tillotson's *Serm.*, iii.

Church had been greatly influenced by two events which, with the exception of the Revolution itself, may perhaps be called the most important ones which had occurred within the generation—the Toleration Bill and the union with Scotland. The Toleration Act, without being in advance of public opinion, could not fail to mark, as nothing else could, a change of thought which the Reformation had made inevitable, but which was none the less a gradual and silent growth. Although the Articles of 1562 had laid clearly down that every national and particular Church has authority to ordain change and abolish any ceremony or rite of human ordinance, the feeling had still been everywhere deeply rooted that—not in doctrine only, but in discipline also and government—there could be but one true orthodox form of Christianity. Although in stating their views they would have used some modified expressions, this was a long time practically held by Anglicans scarcely less than by Roman Catholics, and by Presbyterians and Independents and Quakers quite as much as by Anglicans. No doubt this opinion had a good deal given way; but the Toleration Act was something definite and palpable, which by its very nature, as well as by its declared object of uniting all Protestants in interest and affection, seemed to proclaim, as by the voice of the whole people, that the points of agreement among all Protestants were immeasurably greater than their differences. This was not a lesson which was very easy to learn, but the history of the years immediately succeeding show clearly that it was one which, at least for the time, was much taken to heart. Then came the union with Scotland; and the spectacle was beheld, which to many good men was a perplexing and almost unnatural one, of two forms of Protestant Christianity established in one dominion, under one royal sway. Among many Churchmen in England, and no doubt in Scotland too, the idea was received with something like reactionary aversion. Such persons set themselves with zeal invigorated by alarm to combat what they held to be the pernicious Erastianism of a belief that the government and surroundings of any Church can be modified by the civil Legislature. They were the more anxious because they imagined there was a danger of Presbyterianism invading England. There were some in whom the old feeling against Nonconformists revived in full force, and perhaps some who, if it were possible, would have revoked the Toleration.

But these represented the back eddy, not the advancing current. The majority, while they insisted strongly upon the benefits of an Established Church—while they eagerly desired that it should embrace within itself as large a proportion of the population as was possible, and reprobated separation from it for causes involving no essential principle—were yet disinclined to lay much stress on the intrinsic excellences of their Church. However much they might have considered it, as they generally did, the purest and best in Christendom, they were content to base its chief claim to allegiance on the simple fact of its being the chosen Church of the nation. They thought it very desirable that the terms of communion should be simple and comprehensive; they insisted that the fullest toleration should be conceded to all who refused to conform; they then used every argument in their power to show how unjustifiable they considered schism from a National Church to be, except on clear ground of strong conscientious feeling. In any case where it came to be a question whether it is better to obey God than man, there could plainly be no doubt as to Christian duty; but where there was merely difference in opinions not fundamental, the duty of believers would be to unite themselves with the National Church, and not separate into parties and several churches for that difference.¹ Some of these writers were apt—not so much on any special ground as by general temperament—to care too little for the definition and characteristic features which give to Church life so much of its force, attractiveness, and colour; but they were men highly esteemed among the most thoughtful of their fellow-countrymen, and of whom any Church might be proud.

After this general sketch of opinion as to Church establishments at the beginning of the century, it remains to review, in most cases very briefly, some remarks on the subject by various writers throughout the century.

The Essayists, or at all events the better known among them, often dwelt upon the benefits of an established form of religion. The following may be quoted from the 'Guardian' for August 10, 1713: 'The light in which these points should be exposed to the view of one who is prejudiced against the names religion, church, priest, and the like, is to consider the clergy as so many philosophers, the churches as schools, and their sermons as lectures for the information and improvement of the audience. How would the heart of Socrates or Tully have rejoiced, had they lived in a nation where the law had made provision for philosophers to read lectures of morality and theology every seventh day in several thousands of schools erected at the public charge throughout the whole country, at which lectures all ranks and sexes without distinction were to be present for their general improvement! ... Who would endeavour to defeat so divine an institution?'²

The Deists were some of them strongly against National Churches. Tindal said that churches were merely private

---

¹ Burnet's *Discourses to the Clergy of Sarum*, disc. iii. 258–60. Wall's *Hist. of Inf. Baptism*, Pt. II. chap. ii.; More, *Enthusiasmus Triumphatus*, Schol. to § 63; J. Scott's *Christian Life*, chap. iv.; Tillotson, *Sermons*, iii., 'On the Advantages of Religion to Societies.'

² *Guardian*, No. 130.

companies or clubs, and one had no right to any advantage over another.¹ Chubb held that a blending together of the Christian and civil societies was 'an unnatural coalition,' 'a deadly wound.'² Toland, on the other hand, spoke of 'those who aim at erecting the worst part of Popery here at home; I mean the independency of the Church upon the State.... This independency is what I call Protestant Popery.'³ Shaftesbury defended established forms of religion with the air of a perfect sceptic, and with a supercilious sneer at officious persons who are not content with the religion authorised by law.⁴ His idea was evidently that of Matthew Green—

> But, to avoid religious jars,
> The laws are my expositors,
> Which in my doubting mind create
> Conformity to Church and State.
> I go, pursuant to my plan,
> To Mecca with the caravan.⁵

Shaftesbury makes, however, one remark which is sensible enough: 'To take away a National Church is as mere enthusiasm as the notion which sets up persecution. For why should there not be public walks as well as private gardens? why not public libraries as well as private education and home tutors?'⁶

The Bangorian controversy, occasioned by Bishop Hoadly's writings, involved the question of relations between Church and State. It was charged against Hoadly that he impeached the legal supremacy in causes ecclesiastical, and denied the authority of the Legislature to interfere in matters of religion. His opponents constantly asserted that he was a Dissenter in lawn sleeves, and that

---

¹ Tindal's *Rights of the Christian Church*, quoted in Swift's remarks on it, *Works*, viii. 110, 360.   ² Chubb's *True Gospel*, p. 132.
³ Toland's *State Anatomy of Great Britain*, § 7.
⁴ Shaftesbury's *Characteristics*, Pt. III. § 3.
⁵ M. Green's *Poems*, 'The Spleen.'
⁶ Shaftesbury's *Characteristics*, Pt. I. § 2.

he wished to destroy the constitution of the Church in which he held high office. That his opinions in this respect were often spoken of in an exaggerated tone is certain enough. Some of his writings especially aimed at being persuasives to Conformity. As for the king's supremacy, he says that in the passages which were supposed to controvert it he 'never so much as once thought of it.' 'Nor,' said he, 'do I know of any greater benefit to the subject than the privilege of appealing to the civil power for what —under the cover of being called ecclesiastic or spiritual— in many cases very intimately concerns their civil and temporal concerns.'[1] He affirmed also that it was he, rather than those who differed from him, who 'most consulted the honour and interest of the Established Church.'[2] He considered that there were some points in its constitution which were contrary to the interests of true religion; but he saw no reason on that account for any one refusing to accept trust in it, and no bar to honest labour in it.[3]

There are many passages in Hoadly's works which, taken by themselves, might favour the belief that he desired a total separation of the Church from the State. The question never came before him in any distinct form. If it had done, it is probable, if not certain, that he would have prefered total separation to a union which required to be supported by tests and disabilities. Where ordinary toleration was not assured the case would be stronger still. 'For myself,' he said, 'I must presume to declare it as my judgment that an establishment without liberty and toleration, though at first the establishment of a method of worship, government, and discipline, very good and blameless in itself, yet would procure, and at last end in, just such a peace, stupidity, and lethargy as is not only seen but felt in

[1] Hoadly's *Answer to the Rep. of the Com. of Convoc.*, chap. ii. § 2.
[2] *Id.*, § 20.   [3] *Id.*, § 19.

too many other countries.'[1] But in England toleration was assured, and the test might yet be removed. His object was by no means to dispute the desirability of a National Church, so long as there was perfect tolerance, and no attempt on the part of the law to interfere between a man's conscience and his God. We have seen before how a horror of human authority in matters of religion was at once Hoadly's strength and his weakness. It added strength to his love of liberty and truth; it was one among other weak points in his mental character, when it made him almost a bigot against uniformity and order. Established or not established, a Church after Hoadly's liking would be a home of liberty unrestrained. The Easter Day of one congregation would be the mid-Lent of the next, and perhaps the Christmas Day of a third; and in every church some would kneel and some would stand, exactly as caprice and taste dictated.[2] Nevertheless, let it be added that in Hoadly's treatise on the Church he did, on the whole, a service to his age. The generation needed reminding, even though it might be in exaggerated terms, that whatever might be the law under which the external actions of the Church were guided, it was the kingdom of Christ alone, and subject, on all points of conscience, to no dominion but His.

Bishop Butler has several times spoken of the value of an Established Church, the neglect of religion in many places which its absence would create, the superstition and fanaticism which would be apt to spring up instead, the manner in which it keeps up in a nation's life the sense of religion, its regular instruction to the ignorant, its support

[1] Hoadly's *Answer to the Rep. of the Com. of Convoc.*, chap. ii. § 20.
[2] 'What harm 'if some congregations commemorate the nativity or resurrection of Christ, or the martyrdom or good actions of any saint, on a day different from others? or if some Christians kneel when others stand, or stand when others kneel?' (*id.*, iii. § 3).

of learning, its defence against Popery, and so forth. Yet there is something like an undertone of melancholy in his words. He saw it was not doing the work it should do, and was evidently contrasting in his thought the greater perfectness it might attain to.[1]

We have seen that at one time Dr. Watts spoke with favour of Established and Voluntary Churches side by side. After the intolerance of the Schism Bill had effected a change in this opinion he appears to have formed a singular theory, recommending the State to leave Christianity to itself, but for the sake of its own advantage to compel its citizens to be of some religion. It should also, he said, pay teachers of morality or natural religion, whose instruction could be further supplemented according to the choice of the individual.[2]

Doddridge, as might be expected from his close approximation to the English Church, his intimacy with distinguished Churchmen, and his desire for comprehension, was wholly favourable to the principle of a National Church. It was required, according to his opinion, in the interest alike of religion and of the State.[3] Those who, like himself, could not conscientiously conform must be satisfied with full liberty to adhere to their own views, undisturbed by others.

Warburton's 'Alliance of Church and State' was published in 1736. In a letter to a friend, and also in the dedication to the third edition, he has spoken of the circumstances which led him to write it. He saw the Church, he says, falling into a condition so depressed, that he feared lest religion might lose thereby its hold upon the minds of the people. He believed that the triumph of a narrow and

[1] Butler's fifth sermon, his sermon on the King's Accession, and that on Jan. 30, 1740-1.
[2] Hunt's *Rel. Th. in Eng.*, iii. 244.
[3] Doddridge's *Lectures*, quoted in Hunt, iii. 247.

encroaching form of High Churchmanship at the end of Queen Anne's reign had had a most pernicious influence. The party which came afterwards into power had, in their alarm, suppressed the Church so effectually, and had so deprived it of its rightful power, that it lay gagged and bound at their feet. At such a time, when immorality and irreligion were day by day increasing, and when the enemies of the Church were exultant at the overthrow which they supposed to be impending over it, he believed he should be doing good service if his arguments could put the Church in its relation to the State on a stronger and sounder footing.[1]

Warburton's theory is one of two independent powers allied together for mutual help. It may be stated as follows. The grounds and motives of religion are wholly different from those of civil society. The one has to do with spiritual things, with inward character, with soul, with sins, with truth; the other, with temporal things, with outward actions, with the body, with crimes, with utility. Thus their respective domains are in themselves independent and distinct; and though they have been often confused, such confusion is only to the detriment of both. Nevertheless, they can be of the greatest service to one another; and therefore, by a virtual though not a formal compact, they may properly conjoin their efforts. The wide field of morals is, from different points of view, common to both. Although the State has no jurisdiction over doctrines and opinions, it is vitally concerned with crimes which interfere with the temporal welfare of society. Neither can it subsist without the three fundamental principles of natural religion—the being of a God, His providence over human affairs, and the essential difference of moral good and evil. Therefore civil society, being of itself quite unable to supply adequate inducements to such right actions

[1] Watson's *Life of Warburton*, pp. 289, 485.

as are necessary for its uses, calls religion to aid. Religion, not being incorporate with the State as in Jewish times, but in its nature independent of civil government, is able to adapt itself by free alliance to the various kinds of human policy, and may receive thereby equal benefits with those which it confers. Religion, says Warburton, not only gains in protection, support, and influence, but in the furtherance of its own intrinsic qualities. For, after all, truth and utility coincide. A secluded religion, which estranges its best men from the world, from civil society and its rights and interests, becomes less useful, and therefore less true.

These general principles Warburton further develops. 'The greatest temporal good from religion is procured by becoming national; but national it cannot be but through alliance with the State.' The purer and truer that a religion is, the greater must be its civil use. It is impossible, however, for the State to constitute itself a judge of religious truth. The attempt would imply a spiritual authority which it manifestly has not, and would even authorise persecution for opinion. The State, therefore, leaving perfect toleration to every other, forms alliance with the religion of the majority. Religion loses thereby something of independence. There can be no 'imperium in imperio.' The supremacy of the ruling power must needs be submitted to in matters that do not touch the conscience. Yet it is no loss. If such moderate control adds to its usefulness, there must needs be gain. The allied Church, in return for the greater privileges and powers which it obtains, and which give it a greater capacity to carry out its own highest ends, benefits the civil objects of the State in many ways—chiefly by its work in checking immorality; but also by inspiring veneration for the ruling power, and by the services it can render to the civil as well as the religious welfare of the people.

Such seems to be a fair statement of Warburton's 'Alliance.' Notwithstanding what its author has said, it is liable to the obvious imputation that, after all, it remains a fiction. At all events, there is much that is fictitious and artificial in it. There is an air of unreality in a virtual compact between abstractions which represent the spiritual and temporal interests of the same individuals. Some questions also might be raised as to the place in his theory of those subjects of public care which lie on the borderland of the material and spiritual, such as art and education. Perhaps its chief fault is that he limits his view of national religion too much to that of a single Church. Yet, whatever may be its defects, it is a forcible and well-reasoned treatise, not unworthy of the fame of its author.

Archbishop Secker, while he felt strongly that ' the main support of piety and morals consists in the parochial labours of the clergy,' passed at once to the warning, that 'our legal Establishment will shake and sink under us if once it can be said we do the public little service.'[1]

Hartley, thoroughly dissatisfied with the state of the Church and with the moral condition of the country, looked forward to some happy restoration of happiness and true religion awaiting humanity, after present civil governments should be overturned and present forms of Church government dissolved. Meanwhile, he thought the variety of sects contributed to purify religion, and to show the practical importance of its various truths.[2]

John Wesley was profoundly attached to the doctrine and discipline of the English Church, but had no love for it as a Church Establishment.[3] Himself utterly indifferent

---

[1] Secker's *Charges*, pp. 239-40.
[2] Hartley's *Observ. on Man*, chap. iv. § 2.
[3] Overton, in *Ch. of Eng. in Eighteenth Cent.*, ii. 67.

to worldly considerations, and regarding mankind as his parish, he would have preferred a system such as that which he was founding to any other. Perhaps he would have seen without regret the complete breaking up of existing organisations, and the field left wholly open to labours such as his own. But so long as the city of God was built, he cared but little how; and his feeling towards the English Church in its relation to the civil power was not one of hostility but rather of indifference. In his answer to Toogood's 'Justification of Dissent' he unhesitatingly asserted the rights of the civil power in things indifferent, and added that allegiance to a National Church in no way affected allegiance to Christ.[1]

Dr. Johnson held stoutly to the patriarchal theory of the State, without any pretence of modification. 'The State has a right to regulate the religion of the people, who are the children of the State.'[2]

John Newton's high estimation of the Church of England, not only in its doctrine and order, but as an established form of religion, is the more valuable because it was an opinion which a man of very earnest piety gradually formed in the face of strong prepossessions against it. After the great crisis in his spiritual life, which was as truly a conversion as was that of the apostle Paul, he for some time associated almost exclusively with Dissenters, and speaks gratefully of the pleasure and benefit he derived from that intercourse. Among them he imbibed a strong prejudice against the Established Church, and he would then have thought it impossible that he could ever enter into its ministry. But, says he, 'reasons increased upon me which not only satisfied me that I might conform without sin, but that the preference was plainly on that side. Accordingly, in the Lord's own time, after several years' waiting to know His will, I sought

[1] In 1752. Wesley's *Works*, x. 503-6. [2] Boswell's *Johnson*, iii. 457.

and obtained episcopal ordination; . . . and though I took this step with a firm persuasion that it was right, I did not at that time see so many reasons to justify my choice, nor perhaps any one reason in so strong a light as I have since.'[1] He has expressed in strong terms his conviction of the great value of parcelling a country into parishes, and of the unspeakable good effected for religion and morality through the means of a national establishment.[2] He also contrasted favourably its liberty, as compared with that which he had found among Nonconformists, whose ministers were much at the mercy of their hearers, especially of the wealthier among them. 'So far as I am concerned, I have reason to acknowledge that the administration of our Church government is gentle and liberal. I have from the first preached my sentiments with the greatest freedom. I always acted in the parishes which I served according to my own judgment, and I have done some things which have not the sanction of general custom. But I have never met with the smallest check, interference, or mark of displeasure from any of my superiors in the Church to this hour.'[3] He spoke also with approbation of the variety of thought in the Church; and with high appreciation, mingled with some criticism, of its liturgy. Lastly, he spoke with deep satisfaction of a marked revival of true religion in the English Church.[4]

Mrs. Barbauld, in 1775, writing in a tone of somewhat cold impartiality of the comparative merit of Established and Sect Churches, thought that the fervour and strictness of a sect, without which it rapidly declines, is admirably fitted to some religious temperaments, but that there is a steadiness and stability in an Established Church better adapted for the more ordinary amelioration of the larger number.[5]

[1] Cecil's *Life and Works of J. Newton*, p. 882.
[2] *Id.*, p. 879.   [3] *Id.*, p. 890.   [4] *Id.*, p. 892.
[5] Aikin's *Works of A. L. Barbauld*, ii. 252-54.

Hurd, Tucker, and Balguy all wrote upon the subject, apparently against Priestley and Price. Paley sums up his argument with the following conclusion : ' That a comprehensive national religion—guarded by a few articles of peace and conformity, together with a legal provision for the clergy of that religion, and with a *complete* toleration of all Dissenters from the Established Church, without any other limitation or exception than what arises from the conjunction of dangerous political dispositions with certain religious tenets—appears to be not only the most just and liberal, but the wisest and safest system which a State can adopt, inasmuch as it unites the several perfections which a religious constitution ought to aim at—liberty of conscience with means of instruction ; the progress of truth with the peace of society ; the right of private judgment with the care of the public safety.'[1]

William Wilberforce, like others of the Evangelical party, was keenly alive to the benefits derived from an established form of religion. The heathenism about Cheddar, with which his correspondent Hannah More had made him fully acquainted, had supplied to some an argument that the National Church had grievously failed in these remote country districts. To his mind the inference was quite an opposite one. He remarked that the moral desolation he had found there was a striking illustration of what might often be if the parochial system were broken down. It was the absence of a resident clergyman (for none had resided there for forty years) which had brought the village into such deplorable ignorance.[2] So also thought Hannah More herself. In many of her publications she zealously opposed Paine's invectives upon Established Churches, as a part of his assault upon Christianity in general. That there were

[1] Paley's *Moral and Polit. Philos.*, chap. x.
[2] *Life of Wilberforce*, by his Son, p. 77.

many shortcomings in the National Church she was well aware, and rejoiced therefore in every new symptom of awakened life. It was to it she chiefly looked, and especially to the increase of an efficient clergy,[1] for the dispelling of the dangers which seemed to her to be gathering round the Christianity of the country.

The calamities which befell Christianity in France gave occasion to Burke's noble and eloquent defence of the association of religion with the State in England. Rejecting with dislike, as an idle and fanciful speculation, the idea of an alliance in a Christian commonwealth between Church and State, he regarded them, as Hooker had done before him, as several functions of one and the same community. So far from being out of the province or duty of Christian States, religion—as a great bond of human society, and having man's supreme good for its object—should be a principal thing in their care; society was indeed a contract, but 'not a partnership in things subservient only to the gross animal existence of a temporary and perishable nature. It is a partnership in all science; a partnership in all art; a partnership in every virtue.' 'Without civil society man could not by any possibility arrive at the perfection of which his nature is capable, nor even make a remote and faint approach to it.' A recognition of religion in a corporate as well as in an individual capacity is a part of the homage which civil society owes to the Institutor and Protector of it—a homage fitly performed 'with modest splendour, with unassuming state, with mild majesty and sober pomp.' 'The majority of the people of England . . . do not consider their Church establishment as convenient, but as essential to their State; not as a thing heterogeneous and separable, which they may either keep or lay aside, according to their temporary ideas of convenience.' If ever there

---

[1] H. More's *Memoirs*, ii. 558.

were need 'to remove its corruptions, to supply its defects, or to perfect its construction,' it would be done with reverence and love, as by those who 'know, and, what is better, feel inwardly, that religion is the basis of civil society, and the source of all good and of all comfort.' And 'it is from attachment to a Church establishment that the English nation did not think it wise to entrust that great fundamental interest to what they trust no part of their civil or military public service—that is, to the unsteady and precarious contributions of individuals. They go further. They certainly never have suffered, and never will suffer, the fixed estate of the Church to be converted into a pension, to depend on the Treasury, and to be delayed, withheld, or perhaps to be extinguished by fiscal difficulties. . . . The people of England think that they have constitutional motives, as well as religious, against any project of turning their independent clergy into ecclesiastical pensioners of State. They tremble for their liberty, from the influence of a clergy dependent on the Crown; they tremble for the public tranquillity, from the disorders of a factious clergy, if it were made to depend upon any other than the Crown. They therefore made their Church, like their king and their nobility, independent. . . . The Christian statesmen of this land would indeed provide first for the multitude; because it is the multitude, and is therefore, as such, the first object in the ecclesiastical institution, and in all institutions. They have been taught that the circumstance of the gospel's being preached to the poor was one of the great tests of its true mission. They think, therefore, that those do not believe it who do not take care it should be preached to the poor. . . . But whilst we provide first for the poor, and with a parental solicitude, we have not relegated religion (like something we were ashamed to show) to obscure municipalities or rustic villages. No! we will have her to

exalt her mitred front in courts and parliaments. We will
have her mixed throughout the whole mass of life, and
blended with all the classes of society. The people of
England will show that a free, a generous, an informed nation
honours the high magistrates of its Church; that it will
not suffer any species of proud pretension to look down
with scorn upon what they look up to with reverence, nor
presume to trample on that acquired personal nobility
which they intend always to be, and which often is, the
fruit of learning, piety, and virtue.'[1]

The question of subscription to the Articles had for
some time attracted a good deal of attention among English
Churchmen. In 1771 it came forward much more prominently. Archdeacon Blackburne was originally the prime
mover of it. He had felt some scruples on the subject at
his institution to a prebend in York Minster in 1750, but
had then satisfied himself that a broad and general interpretation of the Articles was warranted, both by the sixth
Article itself and by the allowed interpretation of the English
Church. When, however, some years later, he received the
offer of new preferment, his scruples revived, and he felt
that he must decline it rather than subscribe anew.[2] His
own opinions were not very heterodox. He was fanatic in
his detestation of the Church of Rome, and very discontented
that the English Church should retain any vestiges of a
pre-Reformation period.[3] In later years it was constantly
asserted that he held Unitarian views. This supposition
was not correct. His cousin, W. Comber, mentions in a
letter that Blackburne had more than once said in some of
his latest conversations, 'Cousin Comber, I firmly believe
in the divinity of Christ.'[4] But he was intimate with

---

[1] Burke's *Reflections on the Revolution in France.*
[2] Nichols, iii. 9-18.   [3] Blackburne's *Historical View*, &c., xx.
[4] *Gentleman's Mag.*, lxix. 915.

Lindsey, and others who adopted Unitarian views; and, for his own part—though he remained true to the general faith of the Church—he very strongly objected to abstruse definitions in theology which seemed to him to go beyond the simple words of Scripture. The result of his determination not again to subscribe was an anonymous work published in 1766, entitled 'The Confessional,' in which he denied the right of Protestant Churches to exact such laboured tests of orthodoxy as the Thirty-nine Articles. He then stated his objections to all theories of subscription which allowed a wide latitude of interpretation, and made the Articles mere symbols of a general unity and agreement.

At Cambridge [1] the subject was eagerly taken up. In the universities subscription was continually presented to the ey ein a preposterous form. Every lad who came up from school [2] was required to declare his assent to 'all and every' the theological and ecclesiastical formularies drawn up by the learned divines of the Reformation. It was easy to say in such cases, with Dr. Johnson, that it simply meant they would adhere to the Church of England.[3] Was it to be the same with grown-up men who were giving themselves to the service of the Church? If it were so, it was monstrous to retain a form of subscription which seemed to imply so much more; if it were not, it was an intolerable bondage to fetter down, if it were possible, the thought of educated men on subjects of the deepest interest to the exact formulas of a bygone age. Was every intelligent

---

[1] In one considerable college the Head and all the Fellows subscribed the petition (Nichols, i. 570; Wakefield's *Memoirs*, i. 165; Meadley's *Life of Paley*, p. 47).

[2] Walpole's *Memoirs*, i. 12; Dean Tucker's *Works*, i. 60. At Cambridge, however, subscription at matriculation appears to have been discontinued a little before this date (Nichols, iii. 10).

[3] Boswell's *Johnson*, ii. 155.

clergyman, who thought and reasoned for himself, to be liable to the taunt that he had entered into holy orders only by an evasion and a subterfuge?

The grievance was a very real one, and, once prominently brought forward, would, under most circumstances, have been removed or abated—if by no other means, at all events, as in 1865, by a relaxation of the precision and stringency of the declaration. But at this time there were both good and bad reasons to the contrary. The bad reason was the excessive reluctance, which had now for many years prevailed, to make any change whatever in the ecclesiastical *status quo*. Successive ministries had firmly made up their mind not to risk agitation in the Church by disturbing in any way the not very healthy calm which had settled upon it. The better reason was that the great majority both among clergy and laymen were satisfied that the relaxation asked for would at this time be attended with evil consequences to the Church. The association which met, under Blackburne's leadership, at the Feathers Tavern, and drew up their petition for relief, comprised some men of very ambiguous opinions. Among the 250 who signed it [1] there were many who disapproved of subscription to the Articles, but desired no change in the liturgy, doctrinal or otherwise.[2] Many, on the other hand, were known to entertain opinions of a distinctly Unitarian character, and were bent upon introducing into the public services of the Church expressions consonant to these sentiments. Causes similar to those which had encouraged Deism and the so-called Arianism of Dr. Clarke and others had promoted an active growth of the modern Unitarianism. English Presbyterians

---

[1] A few laymen, lawyers and physicians, signed the petition; but the subscribers were chiefly clergymen—beneficed clergy, Fellows of the University of Cambridge, and others.

[2] H. Walpole's account of the debate, *Memoirs*, i. 11. He says that Bishop Lowth was among those who at first favoured the subscribers (*id.* 9).

and General Baptists had largely adopted it, and in a milder form it was gradually advancing among some of the established clergy. When, therefore, in February 1772 the petition was presented by Sir W. Meredith, and the question debated, the petition was refused by a large majority of 217 to 71. Some of the petitioners—Jebb, Lindsey, Disney, and a few others—afterwards resigned their preferments, and seceded to the Unitarians. Thus the movement was more than ever discredited, as if it had been a mere attempt to give heterodoxy a legal standing-place in the Church. The question, however, continued for some time a subject of pamphlet controversy,[1] and if it bore no further result in England, it may have done so in America. When the independence of the States had been assured, and the Episcopalians there took occasion to revise their liturgy and constitution, a change was made in subscription. Candidates for ordination no longer signed the Articles, but simply the following form: 'I do believe the Holy Scriptures of the Old and New Testament to be the word of God, and to contain all things necessary to salvation; and I do solemnly engage to conform to the doctrines and worship of the Protestant Episcopal Church in the United States.'[2]

Subscription to the Articles was a weapon of attack frequently used by the Calvinistic section of the Evangelical party. Toplady, in the far too unbridled words which he permitted himself to use in controversy, charged Wesley with 'trickery' and laxity in his opinions and practice on this point.[3] So also when Bishop Tomline wrote his book on the Articles, while some praised the work, others brought serious charges against it. One writer dwelt at length

---

[1] As by Bishop Law, Watson, Parr, Paley, Balguy, &c.
[2] Baird's *Religion in America*, p. 502.
[3] Toplady's *Works*, vi. 102.

upon 'the deep Criminality of signing the Articles in any other than a Calvinistic sense.'[1]

The 'Free and Candid Disquisitions' of 1749 had been followed by a host[2] of ephemeral publications, many of them proposing a far less temperate revision of Church formularies than had been suggested by Jones of Alconbury. Many, therefore, who, like Archbishop Secker, had been well inclined for improvements in the liturgy and a re-translation of the Bible, were agreed that neither undertaking ought to be commenced until the 'rabies emendandi' had cooled down.[3] But at the close of the year 1772, after the failure of the Feathers Tavern petition, some eminent Churchmen—among whom was Porteus, afterwards Bishop of London; Percy, afterwards Bishop of Dromore; and Yorke, afterwards Bishop of Ely—thought that such schemes would best be counteracted by certain moderate reforms. They hoped also by such a measure to strengthen the Church, to render some of the Articles less open to objection, to improve Christian piety, and to bring over to the Church many moderate Nonconformists.[4] Introduced under such auspices, the project was for a few months very widely discussed. On the whole, opinions appeared to be against it. In particular the Evangelicals were averse; and their zeal was day by day deservedly raising them in influence. John Newton thought that so many dangers would beset the attempt, that although some changes were desirable, the remedy would be worse than the disease.[5] Horne said, in humorous satire, that 'if the intended reformation of our liturgy goes on, the reformers may hereafter bring us in a bill like that of the Cirencester painter:— Mr. C. Terebee to Joseph Cook, debtor: To mending the

[1] *The Church of England vindicated*, by a Presbyter, p. 35.
[2] Delany's *Correspondence*, iv. 13 (1763).
[3] Secker's *Concio ad Conv.* (1761), *Charges*, p. 363.
[4] *Life of Porteus*, pp. 39-40.   [5] J. Newton's *Memoirs*, p. 879.

Commandments, altering the Belief, and making a new Lord's Prayer, 21l. 1s.'[1] Toplady trembled for the seventeenth Article. 'What think you concerning the archiepiscopal scheme for "reforming" the liturgy and Articles? Such a plan is certainly on the carpet; and it as certainly originated at Lambeth. . . . The new Lambeth Articles (if Providence do not render the design abortive) will be of a very different cast from the old ones.'[2] In February 1773, Archbishop Cornwallis wrote to Porteus that he had consulted the bishops, and that the general opinion was that nothing could in prudence be done.[3] Porteus and his friends acquiesced, and the design was dropped. In 1789 and 1790, Bishop Watson tried to organise a fresh movement in favour of revision. But the Revolution had begun, and most Churchmen, whatever might be their views, had conceived an utter abhorrence of innovation.[4] As Hannah More put it in one of her popular political ballads,—

> Nor do I think our Church wants mending;
> But I *do* think it wants attending.[5]

An apposite saying, from quite another point of view, may be quoted from a correspondent of Dr. Parr. It may be one that has not yet quite lost its force. 'I hope, sir, you think that our Church established would not be the worse for a little republicanism.'[6]

Before 1760, the Deism, of which so much had been heard through all the earlier part of the century, was already a thing of the past. Leland, in his 'View of the Deistical Writers,' written about 1761, may be said to have written their epitaph. Already that was becoming true which Burke said of them a generation later: 'They repose in lasting oblivion. Who, born within the last forty years,

[1] Horne's *Works*, p. 286.   [2] Toplady's *Works*, vi. 161 (Feb. 4, 1773).
[3] *Life of Porteus*, p. 40.   [4] Watson's *Anecdotes*, i. 392.
[5] H. More's *Works*, xi. 101.   [6] Parr's *Works*, viii. 150.

has read one word of Collins, and Toland, and Tindal, and Chubb, and Morgan? Who now reads Bolingbroke? who ever read him through? Ask the booksellers of London what is become of all these lights of the world.'[1] Their special work, both its evil and its good, had been done, and the modes of thought which had inspired them had everywhere taken other forms. It was in France that their system of negation had generated its most destructive results. This was strikingly expressed in a saying of Diderot, prime leader of the wholly Antichristian and atheistic school. 'In the first visit,' said Sir Romilly in 1781, 'that I paid him, after he had talked a little of political topics, he turned the conversation to his favourite (materialistic) philosophy; he praised the English for having led the way to the true philosophy, but the adventurous genius of the French, he said, had pushed them on before their guides. 'Vous autres, vous mêlez la théologie avec la philosophie; c'est gâter tout: c'est mêler le mensonge avec la vérité. Il faut sabrer la théologie.'[2] Voltaire, whose stay in England had been contemporary with the full spring tide of Deism, had been strongly and directly influenced by it.[3] It had also largely aided to mould the mind of Rousseau; but in him it had taken that form of sentimental semi-Christianity which is so much more congenial to French than to English scepticism. Of him and Hume, the Earl of Charlemont tells the following story. 'When Hume and Rousseau arrived (in 1766) together from France, happening to meet with Hume in the park, I wished him joy of his pleasing companion, and particularly hinted that I was convinced he must be perfectly happy in his new friend, as their sentiments were,

---

[1] Burke's 'Reflections on the Revolution' (Wordsworth's *Christian Inst.*, iii. 98).   [2] Sir S. Romilly's *Memoirs*, i. 179.
[3] For further remarks on this, *cf.* Overton in *The Eng. Church*, &c., i. 240–11; also Cairns' *Unbelief in the Eighteenth Cent.*, pp. 123–43.

I believed, exactly similar. "Why, no," said he, "in that you are mistaken; Rousseau is not what you think him; he has a hankering after the Bible, and indeed is little better than a Christian in a way of his own."'[1] Hume himself, as is well known, was extravagantly flattered, not to say petted, in Paris society, where he found his own scepticism, thoroughgoing as it was in its kind, very far in the rear of the uncompromising unbelief he found there.[2] In England there was little or no professed atheism; but many were sceptics after the example of Hume and Gibbon; and later on, at the time of the Revolution, a flood of infidel literature was poured into England. This irruption caused the more alarm because Paine's 'Age of Reason,' written in a popular form, circulated among the humbler classes in a manner that no previous writings of the kind had ever done before. Bishop Watson's 'Apology for Christianity' was a useful answer to it; more good was done by the sensible little tracts in prose or verse written by Hannah More, and scattered in thousands through the country. But the chief preservative was the sound Christian feeling which, notwithstanding all influences to the contrary, lay deep in the English heart, and which had been awakened into greater activity by the Methodist and Evangelical revivals.

In more direct descent, alike from the Deism and from the Arianism of a preceding age, was the Unitarianism which, from about 1760, made great advances among certain classes in England and America, and which had a few distinguished men among its supporters. Its spirit differed widely from that of Deism. There was nothing in it of that cold and negative rationalism which fell like a blight upon all Christian feeling. Lardner and Priestley

---

[1] Hardy's *Life of the E. of Charlemont*, i. 230.
[2] Romilly, i. 179; Hardy, i. 236, &c.

had both fought in the foremost ranks of the late battle with the Deists. The transition, Lardner had said,[1] from Deism into atheism could only be prevented by holding fast to revelation. Such light as nature gives would never have sufficient influence upon the heart of the bulk of mankind to suffice even for common morality. The choice practically lay between revelation and no religion at all. So far also as theological opinions could be recommended by the lives of those who hold them, they had some powerful supporters. Priestley's private life is spoken of as 'radiant with goodness,'[2] and the characters of Lindsey[3] and Jebb and others are also described as highly exemplary.

But Unitarian views were quite unable to gain any popular standing. As Horsley said, the great majority had no relish whatever for their teaching.[4] Of the nature of their arguments the multitude could form no judgment. The religious-minded among the populace—and Unitarianism did not ask for the support of others—rejected, as if by instinct, a form of religion which was not strong enough for their needs. 'The utmost,' wrote Robert Hall, 'that the efforts of Lindsey, Priestley, and others effected was to convert the teachers of Arianism among the Dissenters into Socinians, who exerted themselves, with tolerable success, to disseminate their principles in their respective congregations. . . . Let the abettors of these opinions produce, if they can, a single instance of a person who, in consequence of embracing them, was reclaimed from a vicious to a virtuous life—from a neglect of serious piety to an exemplary discharge of its obligations and duties.'[5] Much

[1] Hunt, iii. 263.
[2] Aikin and Channing's *Correspondence*, p. 193; Parr's *Memoirs*, i. 295. Horsley also, in his *Charge* of 1783, spoke highly of the virtues of his opponent.
[3] *Quart. Review*, viii. 430. [4] Horsley's *Charges*, p. 192.
[5] R. Hall's *Works*, iv. 200; quoted in Bartlett's *Memoirs of Bishop Butler*, p. 179.

in the same way, Channing, notwithstanding his admiration of Priestley's personal character, and his acceptance of some of his opinions, yet 'cannot easily reconcile [his teaching] with clear moral perception or deep moral feeling. The terrible amount of physical and moral evil in the world never seems to have weighed upon or burdened his mind. He imagined he had got to the bottom of this mystery; he met it with an optimism more favourable to Epicurean tranquillity than to Christian sympathy and self-sacrifice.'[1] Coleridge and Southey are notable examples of men of strong religious feeling who accepted Unitarianism for a time,[2] but presently relinquished it as insufficient for their spiritual needs. When, in 1760, Lardner's essay on the Logos appeared, it was received, Dr. Parr says, with astonishment and horror, as if it were some altogether new form of heresy.[3] From ten to fifteen years later, when several clergymen seceded to it, Unitarianism seemed to be gaining alarming ground. But the mind of England generally remained unmoved by it. Gilbert Wakefield tells with great disgust that there was almost no demand for his publications, and that of his 'Enquiry into the Opinions of the First Three Centuries' there had been sold in eight years, notwithstanding its extraordinary cheapness, only 132 copies.[4] It would have been well if such opinions had been unpopular and nothing more. But the Priestley riots were a disgrace to the time. There might be some little palliation for the brutality of the mob, whose stupid ignorance accounted Priestley an atheist in religion and a traitor in politics; there could be no such excuse for the best educated of their leaders.

Of Methodism in its general aspects as much has been

[1] Channing and Aikin's *Corresp.*, p. 81.
[2] Gilman's *Life of S. Coleridge*, p. 54.   [3] Parr's *Works*, viii. 154.
[4] Wakefield's *Memoirs*, pp. 236 and 218.

said in a previous chapter as the limits of this work allow; a few remarks only need be added relating to its development in the later part of the century.

John Wesley, as most people know, remained, in thought and feeling, a true son of the Church of England up to the time of his death. 'I live and die,' he wrote in the 'Arminian Magazine' for 1790, 'a member of the Church of England; and none who regard my opinion or advice will ever separate from it.'[1] So also in the next year, nine months before his death, he implored his preachers, 'Be Churchmen still! Do not cast away the peculiar glory which God hath put upon you.'[2] Still the gap between the two communions—if in any sense they could yet be called two—was year by year widening, slowly but certainly, and perhaps inevitably. Wesley himself, however much he might struggle against the thought, could not be, and was not, blind to the possibility that Methodism might eventually be forced into Dissent. It was better to dissent than to be silent, yet it was part of his dying prayer that the necessity might not come. And here let it be said that the prayer has been in part fulfilled; the earnest desire of the saintly founder of Methodism has been in part accomplished. Methodism never has formally separated[3] from the Church, nor has it ever considered itself altogether a Dissenting body. There are to this day thousands of Methodists, and in some places whole communions of Methodists, who frequently attend the services of the National Church, not merely as friendly strangers, but as kinsmen, and claim in feeling, as well as by right, a share in her ministrations. If there are insuperable bars to any closer unity, it may at least be hoped that both Churchmen and Methodists will endeavour

---

[1] *Armin. Mag.* for April 1790; quoted in Curteis's *Dissent in Rel. to the Ch. of Eng.*, p. 384. [2] Wesley, *Serm.*, iii. 268; quoted in *id.*
[3] J. H. Rigg's *Churchmanship of J. Wesley*, pp. 103, 107.

to increase rather than to diminish whatever sense of close Church relationship has hitherto been able to survive.

A great step in the direction of separation was taken by J. Wesley himself, in 1784, by the ordination of Dr. Coke as 'superintendent,' or 'bishop,' over the brethren in America. He had for some time been convinced that, as a duly ordained presbyter, he had, in case of necessity, the power to ordain, and believed that the necessity had now come. Perhaps from his point of view it had. The position in America of our own Church, as yet unheaded by any bishop on that side the Atlantic, was becoming intolerable; and Wesley might well have thought that the Methodist community was in a more embarrassing condition still. Yet this was but ten weeks before Seabury was consecrated to Connecticut; and necessary, according to Wesley's views, or not, it could not but render precarious the tie which connected Methodists with a Church which had never allowed of any consecration of bishops except at the hands of bishops. His brother Charles exceedingly regretted such a step, and he himself felt doubtful about it. He spoke of Coke as 'superintendent,' not as 'bishop,' and not of 'ordaining' or of 'consecrating,' but of 'setting' him 'apart.'[1] Dr. Coke[2] himself, though he styled himself bishop, and in his turn set apart Ashbury, was inclined to distrust the authority he had received. Partly from this feeling, and partly from the same longing for continued unity with the English Church as that which actuated the Wesleys, he made in 1791 and 1792 overtures[3] to the Transatlantic bishops, which were very nearly accom-

---

[1] Stoughton's *Religion under Q. Anne and the Georges*, ii. 180-82.

[2] Dr. Coke was an Oxford man, a clergyman of the Church of England, and an able and excellent man; John Wesley's lieutenant after Charles Wesley's death, and his own immediate successor.

[3] Bishop White's *Memoirs*, quoted in Caswall's *American Church*, &c., pp. 214-16.

plishing in America what Wesley would have gladly welcomed in England. In letters and interviews between him and White and Seabury, it was proposed by Dr. Coke, and heartily agreed to by them, that he and Ashbury should receive episcopal consecration, and all the Methodist ministers in America episcopal ordination. The Methodist communities were to remain distinct and self-governed under Wesley's superintendents, and the Methodist preachers were to have authority to minister to congregations of the Church. Coke spoke with the utmost confidence of Wesley's entire approbation of his proposal, and when news came of his death the negotiations were continued. They unfortunately dropped through, not from any unwillingness on the part of the prime movers on either side, but because general opinion in America was not yet prepared for such a measure.

The second great step towards Nonconformity took place in 1787, when Wesley placed his chapels and ministers under the Act exempting Dissenters from penalties. It was forced upon him. Long before this, as early as 1767, some justices had refused to license his preachers except, greatly against their will, as Protestant Dissenters.[1] Similar refusals now came from some of the bishops; and Wesley, with a sad but indignant remonstrance at his people being thus driven, as he said, out of the Church,[2] felt obliged to adopt the measure which would give them legal toleration.

Before 1788 it was only in London and Bristol, elsewhere only in exceptional circumstances, that Wesley had given permission to his societies to hold their services in Church hours. In this year such permission was made universal, where the members did not generally object, except only on sacrament Sundays.

In the next Conference after Wesley's death in 1791,

[1] Wesley's Journal for 1767, *Works*, iii. 337.   [2] Rigg, p. 94.

England, Scotland, and Ireland were mapped out into 'circuits.' At the same time began an excited controversy among Methodists who entertained different views as to the administration of the sacrament. Wesley's immense personal influence had hitherto kept the question in the background; and many leading Methodists were very desirous of adhering as before to the practice of receiving the eucharist only from clergymen episcopally ordained. But the dissentients to this view daily increased in number and vehemence. At length, in the Conference of 1795,[1] it was agreed that although such a custom should not be encouraged, yet that where a majority of the stewards and leaders in any society, and also of the trustees of the chapel, desired it, the Lord's Supper might be administered by their own preachers. This resolution completed the separation from the English Church, so far as any has ever taken place. In 1797 began the first formal division of Methodists among themselves, the 'New Connexion' seceding on a question of lay rights.[2] In 1799 the Wesleyan Missionary Society was formed.

Thus gradually this great offshoot of the English Church was severed from the parent stem. There were not a few among English Churchmen who watched the process with regret. John Wesley himself, in his later years, had outlived for the most part all bitterness of opposition. Advancing years seem to have tempered some of the extreme opinions commented upon in a previous chapter; and the increased bitterness against the Church which had developed among a section of the Methodists threw into stronger relief the deep, unaffected Churchmanship of Wesley himself. The period from 1790 to 1795 was in some respects a more favourable time for a great and successful effort to retain Methodism within the Church

[1] Rigg, p. 107.   [2] Skeats, p. 544.

organisation than any previous date. The plan suggested by Coke was, in its general features, the only possible one by which union could then be effected; and then it might not have been too late. Moreover, it seems likely that Dr. Coke would have been better qualified to carry it out than his great predecessor could have been. He possessed Wesley's confidence, and would have been carrying out his views; and although far from being his equal—for, indeed, who was there that would be?—he was a man of zeal and sagacity, who probably did not greatly share in those exaggerated opinions in regard of human corruption which, far more than any other cause, had estranged from sympathy with Wesley the more cultivated of his countrymen. But the opportunity, if such there was, passed by. On the Anglican side there was probably not one man, unless it might have been Wilberforce,[1] who was qualified alike by temperament and influence to seize the occasion, and carry such a scheme successfully out. And so, to use the metaphor of one who in 1794 was pleading for continued union, the English Church, which for fifty years had 'been a sort of harbour to Methodism,'[2] where its bark had been secured from varying winds of doctrine,' was at length abandoned, and the vessel was launched upon 'the vast and boundless ocean of separation.'[3]

The varied feeling which might be found among Method-

[1] Wilberforce may have been too strait and rigorous a Churchman of the Evangelical type for what would practically have been a measure of comprehension. But he was much trusted in by the Methodists. It is to be added that J. Wesley, on the very day before he fell into the lethargy which preceded his death, wrote to Wilberforce on the subject of the slave trade, calling upon him to 'go on in his glorious enterprise, in the name of God and in the power of His might' (*Life of Wilberforce*, p. 80).

[2] *Cf.* a remark of J. Taylor on the immense advantage of the Methodi over earlier Nonconformists, that their zeal as evangelists was not divert by resistance to the Church (J. Taylor, *Wesley and Methodism*, p. 185).

[3] *Considerations on a Separation of the Methodists from the Estab. Church*, Bristol, 1794, p. 27.

ists at the close of the century as towards the English Church is expressed in the report of a convention of Lincolnshire clergy—a district where Methodism was strong—held in the autumn of 1799. A note appended to the report adds that it is probably applicable to a great part of the kingdom. Methodists, it says, might be ranked in this respect under three divisions. Some professed to be members of the Church of England, and regularly attended divine service at church, and partook of the holy sacrament; but had places set apart for additional exercises of devotion, at such hours as did not interfere with the Church service. These were 'frequently found useful and zealous auxiliaries in reforming and reclaiming many habitual sinners, both by their admonitions and examples.' The memorialists greatly regretted that such persons should register themselves as Protestant Dissenters. Others rarely, if ever, attended the Church services, took no note of the hours at which these were held, and had lately begun to administer the holy sacrament at their meetings. Many of them were persons of much piety; but they were very ready to set up rivalries and opposition to the clergy of the Church, and to foment divisions between them and their parishioners.[1] Especially it was regretted that these should appear to countenance and encourage a third division of so-called Methodists, who were commonly ignorant men, who held gross and extravagant views; and 'seemed to have no point of union except to calumniate the clergy and revile the Church, which they do with unrelenting violence.' The memorial further states that the Methodists did not generally consider themselves Dissenters; and that the real Dissenters were in their part

---

[1] Hannah More spoke of much opposition on the part of Methodis t to her schools in the neighbourhood of Cheddar (*Memoirs*, i. 501; ii 61).

of the country few in number, and in general by no means hostile towards the Church or its clergy.[1]

In the whole history of the English Church in the eighteenth century there is no feature more important or interesting than the rise and progress of the Evangelical revival. Here, however, it cannot be dwelt upon at any length. In the same preceding work [2] to which occasional reference has been already made, Canon Overton has treated the subject so far in detail, and with so much genial sympathy, that it will be sufficient to touch upon it with far greater brevity than would otherwise be proportionate to its interest. The reader will there be able not only to trace its connection with the Methodist movement, and to note some of the internal controversies which to some extent divided it; but also to see its influences illustrated in the pure Christian lives of its principal supporters. For it is a subject which fixes attention upon the men themselves— their doings, their example, their personal influence— rather than upon their modes of thought. We all know well, or think we know, the main features of the Evangelical theology, the strength and vividness with which it has realised certain cardinal doctrines of the Christian faith; the imperfections, on the other hand, and limitations which have cramped its power and hindered its success. But there is something exceedingly refreshing to come, after so much that is unsatisfactory in the religious history of the eighteenth century, upon a resuscitation of deep and fervent piety, no longer confined to individuals, but gradually arising in the heart of a great national Church, and quickening with the breath of new spiritual life a constantly increasing section of it. No doubt the Methodist revival was fully

---

[1] *Report from the Clergy of a District in the Diocese of Lincoln, convened, &c.*, 1800, pp. 9-12.

[2] Abbey and Overton's *Eng. Ch. in the Eighteenth Cent.*, II. chap. ii.

as important, and also more abounding in vivid and graphic incident. It contained, however, throughout, and from the beginning, so much which a sober and thoughtful Churchman, however much he might in some respects approve of it, could not conscientiously agree with, that such a one might welcome all the more gladly a movement to which he could accord a fuller sympathy. His points of disagreement will at all events be not so wide but that in reading or speaking of them he will feel himself to be among brothers, not only in the same Christian faith, but also in the very same church communion.

The worthies of the Evangelical revival were many, but a few were prominent among the rest; and to them some brief reference must be made.

There was Fletcher of Madeley, of whom Wesley said that he was all fire and love—'his writings, like his constant conversations, breathed nothing else;'[1] and of whom he elsewhere said that his life realised, in the highest degree, all he meant by Christian perfection.[2] Some said he was too severe;[3] others, that 'the Cardinal of Madeley' was over-confident in his opinions.[4] But never was a man whose whole soul was more intimately penetrated with the sense of a spiritual presence encompassing all the commonest surroundings of daily life. Wesley records that it was Fletcher's invariable rule to sit up two whole nights in every week, to spend them in reading, meditation, and prayer.[5] His seems to have been a saintliness which could never weary in anything that strengthened his communion with the divine. There was Walker of Truro, whom to know was to venerate. John Wesley could not bear with any satisfaction that the religious societies which

---

[1] Wesley's *Works*, xii. 333.
[2] Overton, ii. 115.
[3] Hill, in Wesley's *Works*, x. 376.
[4] Toplady's *Works*, vi. 208.
[5] Wesley's *Works*, xi. 283

this excellent clergyman had established around his neighbourhood should be so entirely independent of his own. But he added, with that tone of self-diffidence which one man of high Christian attainments may naturally use in speaking with admiration of another, that whatever comparison might be made as to gifts for the work of God and visible fruits of labour, 'yet am I clearly satisfied that you have far more faith, more love, and more of the mind of Christ than I have.'[1] There was Henry Venn of Huddersfield. He, too, was intimate with Wesley, as he was also with Whitefield, and was sometimes called a Methodist, and even an enemy of the Church.[2] Yet, said Wesley, he is one of those who 'love her Articles, her Homilies, her liturgy, her discipline; and unwillingly vary from it in any instance.'[3] He sometimes took a part in their itineracies. The establishment, however, of a Methodist society in Huddersfield was a very tender point with Venn. John Wesley had much conversation with him on the subject, and they came to a temporary compromise that preachers should come only once a month.[4] But soon the difficulty revived and increased; and Wesley was ready to suspend the preaching for a twelvemonth—anything rather than lose the alliance of so good a man. 'Let us make an offensive and defensive league. . . . Come and strengthen the hands of your affectionate brother, till you supply his place.'[5] Venn was the author of one of the best devotional books of the century— the 'Complete Duty of Man'—a work no less practical than the familiar 'Whole Duty of Man,' but imbued with the Puritan rather than the Anglican theology.[6] There was John Berridge of Everton, full of eccentricity and wit, a strong Calvinist and a Methodist, but one who viewed with

---

[1] Wesley's *Works*, xiii. 175.
[2] *Id.*, p. 503. [3] *Id.*, p. 350. [4] *Id.*, p. 174-75. [5] *Id.*, p. 209.
[6] Overton, ii. 187-89; Stoughton, ii. 95.

great misgiving and quick remonstrance every step which might have any tendency to lead Methodism into Dissent. His preaching was wont to excite intense emotion, and physical phenomena as strange and wild as any that are recorded in the journals of Wesley or of Whitefield. Few Churchmen could look for an unmixed gain to religion in 'the stifling crowd, the fainting, and the crying' in Everton Church, and 'people lying as dead in Mr. Berridge's garden,'[1] struck down by a terrible excitement. We can well understand that many Evangelical clergy were more pained than pleased by what they might call the fanaticism of Berridge's impassioned oratory. There was William Romaine, of St. George's, Hanover Square. His religious convictions appear to have been formed among the Hutchinsonians of Oxford, and he was a firm friend to Wesley. But he differed widely from him in opinion. His character, his form of expression, his preaching, his writing, were all much more nearly after the type of a sixteenth-century Puritan[2] than they were like the Methodists or Evangelicals of his own time. Wesley, though he had great respect for him, thought his teaching dangerous, and warned his hearers to keep away from it. He thought his theology had an Antinomian tendency, and that he quenched the hopes which a Christian should entertain of getting a perfect conquest over sin.[3] It may be added of Romaine that he strongly objected to the introduction into Church services of the hymns which were being composed in such prolific abundance. It was 'a preference,' he said, 'of men's poems to the good word of God.'[4] The Bible had inspired psalmody sufficient for all needs. There was Grimshaw of Haworth—'an Israelite indeed,' said Wesley of him; 'a

---

[1] Wesley's *Works*, xiii. 309-12; and a similar account, in some respects worded more strongly still, in ii. 485.   [2] Overton, ii. 179.

[3] Wesley's *Works*, xii. 343.

[4] Romaine's *Essay on Psalmody*, p. 106.

few such as he would make a nation tremble.'¹ He seems to have been much such a man as Latimer, and had just the gifts for a popular reformer—undaunted courage, earnest faith, and a power of preaching which was rendered all the more effective among the people by plentiful and racy humour.² His funeral in 1762 was attended by great multitudes.³ There was James Hervey of Weston-Favel. He had been one of the Oxford Methodists, but became a good deal estranged from them in later life. His sympathies were much more with the Church Puritans of a previous generation. Thus, in one of his letters we read, 'Is it Puritanical? Be not ashamed of the name. They (the Puritans) were the soundest preachers, and I believe the truest followers of Christ.'⁴ But although he was quite the Puritan in many of his ideas, nothing could be more unlike their style than the tricked and florid verbiage of his once popular 'Meditations.' A thorough Churchman himself, he was, like Venn, more inclined to fraternise with Dissenters⁵ than with Methodists. There was Augustus Toplady of Broad Hembury, author of 'Rock of Ages.' He died young; and the piety and diligence of his life is somewhat overshadowed by a personal virulence in controversy which more advanced years would probably have tempered. He spoke of what he supposed to be Wesley's theological errors as if they were so many unpardonable sins, the very thought of which almost drove him into frenzy. There was John Newton, curate of Olney, and afterwards rector of St. Mary Woolnoth, London. Once, to quote the words of his epitaph, he had been 'an infidel and libertine, a servant of slaves in Africa.'⁶ Out of the midst of such lawlessness and vice (though his conscience had never been altogether dulled) he emerged by what was

---

¹ Wesley's *Works*, xii. 175.   ² Overton, ii. 176.
³ Wesley's *Works*, iii. 86.   ⁴ Hervey's *Works*, vi. 24.
⁵ *Id.*, vi. 39.   ⁶ *Memoirs of Rev. J. Newton*, p. 65.

indeed a new birth unto holiness, so that the chief traces of his past history were width of experience, knowledge of the heart, and tenderness of sympathy. Such gifts made his power felt among all who knew him intimately. Whether his influence was favourable or not upon the poet Cowper is open to question, and not easily to be decided; but both William Wilberforce [1] and Thomas Scott [2] warmly acknowledge the debt of gratitude they owed him. We need not share in many of his views in order to acknowledge how instrumental he was for good, both to religion generally and especially in the English Church. His hymns, although as poetical compositions the bad vastly predominate over the good, have often been valued highly as expressions of spiritual needs. There was his successor at Olney, and afterwards rector of Aston Sandford, Thomas Scott. In earlier years he had so far adopted Antitrinitarian opinions, that unwillingness to subscribe to the Articles had disabled him from accepting preferment.[3] John Newton's influence and his own course of reading made him an Evangelical; nor were any of the good men of that party more blameless in their lives than he. William Wilberforce called him 'a rough diamond, and almost incapable of polish;'[4] but praised his strength of understanding, his unselfishness, and his perseverance. He is best known by his Commentary on the Bible. Those who know it well speak in high terms of this great undertaking. They see in every page of it the great diligence, the Scriptural knowledge, the deep religious feeling, and the independent thought of its author; and Dr. Horne adds that although his own views were often different, yet that he never consulted it in vain

---

[1] Colquhoun's *Life of Wilberforce*, pp. 70, 100.
[2] J. Newton's *Memoirs*, pp. 47-8.
[3] *Memoirs of J. Newton*, p. 47.
[4] *Life of Wilberforce*, by his Son, p. 200.

on any difficult passages of Scripture.[1] Scott lived on very friendly terms both with Methodists and Dissenters. In theology he was a moderate Calvinist, and from this standing-point was an antagonist of Bishop Tomline. There was Robert Cecil, 'perhaps the most cultured and refined of all the Evangelical leaders,'[2] and possessed of greater liberality of thought than was common in that school. There was Joseph Milner of North Ferriby, whose 'Church History,' though it has some grave defects, is yet a notable record of true Christian piety in every age of the Church. There was Isaac Milner, his brother, Dean of Carlisle, whose erudition and numerous sterling qualities contributed greatly to the position Evangelicalism held in Cambridge at the end of the last and the earlier part of the present century. Even Simeon partly belongs to the period under review, for his Sunday evening lectures at Cambridge began in 1792. There were many other Anglican clergymen who might be added to the list of well-known men who were more or less connected with the Evangelical school. Such, among others, were Haweis, rector of Oldwinkle, and Shirley, rector of Loughrea, both of them fellow-workers with the Countess of Huntingdon; Madan, and Adams, and Robinson, and Moses Brown, and John Venn, and lastly, Rowland Hill, as full of fervour as he was of humour, for a long time a Methodist Churchman, but at last a Dissenter, who counted himself almost a Churchman still. We might add Bishop Porteus, and also Bishop Horne, with Jones of Nayland, and others who, as well as the last two, belonged more or less to the school of Hutchinson.

All who have been hitherto mentioned were clergymen of the Church of England. But the influence of Cowper,

---

[1] Horne, *On the Scriptures*, ii. 259, and the Bishop of Calcutta's sermons quoted by him.   [2] Overton, ii. 107.

Wilberforce, and Hannah More was in many respects greater and more extended. Cowper's religious feeling, and also his theological opinions, were so intimately interwoven with the whole fabric of his poetry, that they could not fail to leave some impression upon the wide circle by whom his verses were read. Of William Wilberforce it is almost superfluous to speak. Evangelicalism was indeed fortunate in having as an exponent of its views among the higher and more cultivated classes a statesman whose piety was so genial, unaffected, and happy as was his. Still more fortunate was it in being able to connect itself so closely through him with the beneficent movements of which he was the prime leader. Among women, there were few in their generation who have been more useful than Hannah More. It was not only that she was as welcome in great men's houses and literary meetings as she was in the humble cottages of Cheddar; she also had the power and the tact to obtain a favourable ear for her writings both among the rich, when she lectured them on the sins and follies of fashionable society, and among the excited mechanics of the great towns, when she lectured them also in their turn in shrewd and homely terms, and bade them turn their thoughts from revolutionary schemes abroad to reforms of a better kind, more important and nearer home.

It is not easy to exaggerate the benefit to the English Church from the Evangelical revival. He who, from a Christian's point of view, surveys the course of English religious history throughout the eighteenth century may well feel the sense of a Providential government confirmed and deepened. Such a review does indeed point to the conclusion that the best interests of a Church at large are not always exactly coincident with those of the individuals who, at this or that period, may compose it. It is but correspondent to all analogy, that in spiritual, as well as in all other things, the welfare of the unit should in certain particulars be subordinated to that of the whole. If such involuntary sacrifice as the larger good requires involve no essential loss—if the postponement of certain opportunities and sources of religious refreshment cuts off no soul from sufficient grace, but simply withholds from it some elements of spiritual well-being, until a society or a church is ripe for their introduction, such considerations should surely be no stumbling-block to any one, and should strengthen rather than weaken faith. The religious life of England in many earlier years of the last century was not asleep when (to use the word without any suggestion of disparagement) the pietistic element was comparatively feeble. A great multitude of thoughts immediately connected with religion were working and fermenting in most classes of society. The influences of the Reformation—which had been greatly diverted to secondary and superficial questions, and which had been greatly interrupted by the civil wars, and by the social and political circumstances which followed them—were in full, active continuance. There was nothing in Christianity that was not being enquired into; scarcely any problem of natural or revealed religion which did not form a subject not only of learned discussion, but also of popular conversation. It is strange with what little enthusiasm these matters were debated. Everywhere there was only a grey cold light of reason and supposed common sense. Doubtless there was a purpose in this; doubtless it was designed that reason should have the field to herself more entirely than could possibly be the case when zeal was at a greater heat. Then came the great Methodist movement, ill adapted in many respects to win the sympathies of the educated and upper classes, and affecting, without interfering with, the controversies of the time, but sweeping on its way, like a flood of blessing, among the simpler and more ignorant: what was exaggerated and to some minds repulsive in it only adding fresh force and greater awakening power to all that was pure and noble and in the highest sense Christian in its character. Then, partly rising out of it, and in part simultaneous with and independent of it, the Evangelical movement began. Its special mission was different, though its general purpose was the same. From the first, and throughout its course, it flowed well within the ordinary channels of the English Church; and for the most part it discountenanced, rather than encouraged, the strong religious stimulants which were freely used in Methodism. In earnestness and piety it was its equal. It shared with it also in some of its weaker and more questionable characteristics. For many years it can scarcely be said to have had a separate existence of its own as a party or school of thought. Many sympathised, though in very varying degrees, with the Methodists, especially with the Calvinistic section of that body; some with the Countess of Huntingdon and her adherents; some with the followers of Hutchinson. Many were simply devout and active clergymen and laymen, who in no respect attached themselves to any leader, but in their several neighbourhoods were true examples of pure Christian living. The careless and the ignorant commonly called them 'Methodists,' without attempt at discrimination, however much some of them might be opposed to many distinctive features of those societies. But gradually, as Methodism began to show increased signs of drifting from full communion with the National Church, the Evangelicals began to assume more and more prominently a distinctive and important character of their own. Of their thorough Churchmanship there could be no question. They loved the English Church with a calm attachment, quite as deep and genuine as any that had been professed by clamorous partisans of Sacheverell in the old days. They were content with the machinery and means which the Church provided, and cared little for any other reform than that upon which their whole heart was bent—the revivification in themselves and others of a Christian life of faith. Therefore, throughout the last thirty years of the century, as they increased in numbers and collective force, they became a great power in the Church. Moreover, a gradual, but very important, change was taking place in their general theology. The earlier Evangelicals had been for the most part strong Calvinists. Those who succeeded them were also, oftener than not, Calvinists; but it was a far more tempered form of Calvinism, and one that adapted itself far more easily to the general tone of thought which prevails in the English Church. The change was probably favourable also in other ways to the influence of Evangelicalism. Calvinism is well adapted to give great intensity of character, but it is apt to be self-absorbed, and on several accounts less likely to spend itself in active philanthropic effort than a faith which, trusting none the less to Divine help, puts a fuller confidence in the unfettered power of human will. The piety of William Wilberforce and all who were of like mind with him was certainly not of a strong Calvinistic type.

It is not only among Evangelicals that we must look for the good work of Evangelicalism. Just as Methodism had been indirectly a gospel of blessing to many who were never Methodists, so also the Evangelical movement quickened the vital fire among multitudes who by no means adopted its characteristic modes of thought, and who certainly would not have called themselves by its name. Coleridge, for instance, and Wordsworth, and Southey, and those whose religious life they influenced, were in no sense of the word Evangelicals, but it may be greatly questioned whether they would have been what they were if Evangelicalism had never been. Or to take another example which happens to come to hand, but of which there were doubtless about the same time numerous similar instances. In 1799 we have the report of the meeting of a number of clergy in one district in Lincolnshire, convened, with the approbation of their bishop, 'for the purpose of considering the state of religion in the several parishes in the said district, as well as the best mode of promoting the belief and practice of it.' Nothing could be more natural and proper than this, and it might seem a trivial thing to refer to it. Yet, to a student of religion in the eighteenth century, there is a distinct air of novelty in it, as of an incident which would have been scarcely likely to occur a few years previously. The feeling is strengthened by words which come later in their report, in which they say: 'We declare our humble conviction and our unfeigned sorrow, that the frailties, omissions, and imperfections of the best of us have contributed in no inconsiderable proportion to lessen the utility of our Establishment; and that, though we reap some consolation from the evidence which has been given that the zeal and industry of the clergy in general have been increased, . . . yet with profound humility we acknowledge, and with deep contrition we lament, that these our efforts have by no means been adequate to the necessity.'[1] Probably some of these clergymen, perhaps a majority of them, were, in every sense of the word, members of the Evangelical party. It is not likely that all were. It may be taken, therefore, as a sample of much more that might be adduced in evidence of widespread beginnings of revival in the Church arising mainly out of the movement now being spoken of.

Before leaving this subject, it remains only to add a few remarks on the deficiencies of eighteenth-century Evangeli-

[1] *Report from the Clergy of a District in the Diocese of Lincoln, &c.* 2nd edit., 1800, p. 13.

calism. Mr. Gladstone has truly remarked of it, that so far as it was a party, 'however meritorious in its work, it presented, in the main, phenomena of transition, and laid but little hold on the higher intellect and cultivation of the country.'[1] As Dorner has said of a very similar movement in Germany: 'The morality to which their faith aspires is almost exclusively piety. It never attains, at least so far as earth is concerned, to the idea of a world animated in all its varied forms of life by the spirit of religion—a world whose task it is to bring to harmonious realisation all the powers and gifts of the first creation by the principles of the second. . . . To art and science especially but a very precarious and incidental position is conceded. . . . In their supreme motive of care for the salvation of a man's own soul, there is a loss of true unselfish Church feeling.'[2] In eighteenth-century Evangelicalism all such defects are strongly observable, and well-merited admiration of saintly-minded men need not blind us to the limitations of their creed. There were, indeed, men among them of such cultivated and sympathetic minds, that though they drew to the Evangelicals for love of the earnestness of their religion, they were yet very free from its special deficiencies. Such was Robert Cecil, and such, in perhaps a yet more eminent degree, was that noble-minded missionary Henry Martyn. He had been Senior Wrangler at Cambridge, and the fervent, self-sacrificing piety of his life never led him to disparage the full and free exercise of all gifts of intellect and reason. 'Since,' said he, 'I have known God in a saving manner, painting, poetry, and music have had charms unknown to me before.'[3] But this sort of spirit was somewhat exceptional among the Evangelicals, especially among the earlier

---

[1] W. E. Gladstone, *Chapter of Autobiography*, p. 50.
[2] Dorner's *Hist. of Prot. Theology*, ii. 218.
[3] Quoted in Stoughton, ii. 383.

ones. Examples might quickly be accumulated, as in J. Newton's faint admission that ' he would not have a man to be quite a stranger to the Belles-Lettres,' for it was some disadvantage to a man to be wholly uninformed, and they give ideas and variety of illustration, but how small ' their intrinsic value to creatures posting to eternity ! ' [1] Thus also James Hervey, although a man of cultivated mind, can hardly speak with patience of any literature which does not touch directly on sacred topics. It is not the presence of any irreligious element, but simply the absence of what is definitely religious which makes him exclaim, ' The poet shines ; but where is the Christian ? ' [2] Cowper did great services to the literature of his age as well as to its religion. It is the more regrettable that he should speak in a tone of such utter scorn of all labourers in history and science, as if their poor and mundane enquiries were wholly unworthy of a creature born for eternity.[3] A theology which teaches that they above all others are the

> bless'd inhabitants of earth,
> Partakers of a new and heavenly birth,

who banish themselves from the interests of the world,

> Their hopes, desires, and purposes estranged
> From things terrestrial,[4]

can never approach to the highest form of Christianity. Akin to this defect was the Puritanical spirit in many of the Evangelicals, though by no means in all, which repels the multitude and chills the young. Also there was the technical phraseology, which mars the simplicity of the gospel, and which to those who are not quite in earnest opens a ready door of self-deceit. John Wesley did good service in warning his hearers against the constant use of

---

[1] J. Newton's *Memoirs*, p. 899. [2] J. Hervey's *Works*, vi. 245, &c.
[3] Cowper's *Poems*, ' The Task,' Book III. [4] *Id.*, ' Conversation.'

such terms as 'imputed righteousness,' a doctrinal expression largely insisted upon by Hervey, Romaine, and others.

These and similar blemishes might easily be dwelt upon at much greater length. But in a Churchman writing upon the religious history of the eighteenth century it would seem downright ingratitude to dwell longer than is necessary upon the blemishes in a movement so prolific in good, and to which the English Church owes so great a debt. Dr. Arnold was keenly alive to what was commonly deficient in the Evangelical party, but seeing, as he did, so much of the true heart of religion in any worthy member of it, he added that if his special defects were remedied, if his views were enlarged, and an abundant knowledge supplied to him of men and things, 'he would then become a most complete specimen of a true Christian.'[1]

The two greatest events in the latter part of the century were the American War and the French Revolution. Of the first little need here be said. A small minority of Churchmen were strongly in favour of the American claims. They were headed by Bishop Shipley and Bishop Watson, and Hinchcliffe, after some hesitation, joined their side. Franklin had been for some time a guest at Shipley's house. Among other clerical opponents of the war the best known by name were Tucker, Jebb, Blackburne, Paley, and Parr. But the great majority both of bishops and clergy regarded it as a mere rebellion, the repression of which was necessary to the unity and interests of the kingdom. John Wesley was on the same side. He had no doubt whatever about the right to tax the colonies, and thought that independency would be not a blessing to the colonists, but a heavy curse.[2] One of his tracts on the subject was widely distributed by the English Government. Nonconformists, on the other hand, were generally

---

[1] Arnold's *Life and Corresp.*, i. 230.   [2] Wesley's *Works*, vii. 419.

in favour of American liberty, and were, in consequence, often charged with a growing spirit of republicanism. Difference of opinion on this great question certainly tended to weaken the understanding which throughout the middle of the century had subsisted between Churchmen and Dissenters. The principal effect upon the English Church of the jealousies which preceded the war, and the separation which followed it, was of course that which it had upon the Colonial Church, and this will be referred to later.

The French Revolution had many and important bearings upon religion in England, and therefore upon the English Church. Its gradual development was watched with an interest far deeper and far more general than is commonly excited by any political event. For some length of time the interest took the most opposite forms. 'Never,' says Dr. Parr, 'did the spirit of party rage more furiously among all ranks.'[1] No one had any doubt as to its vast significance. All felt, from the beginning, as by an instinct of which there could be no question, that movements so full of strange portent could not pass away without some convulsion which the whole civilised world would feel. A majority of the upper and middle classes looked upon it from the beginning with profound disquietude. Foreboding danger, they knew not how great or how unexpected in form, alike to their policy and to their religion, they began to feel a greater love than ever they had known before for all that was venerable and time-honoured in their constitution both in Church and State. No more thought of change; no more dallying with proposed reforms; they were well content with what they had, and would hold it fast. Others knew not what to think, or whether to hope most, or fear most, from the unknown birth of the approaching future. When the Earl of Mansfield was asked, some time after

[1] Parr's *Life*, by Field, i. 305.

the commencement of the Revolution, when he thought it would end, he said he feared it was not begun; and when his opinion was asked as to its ultimate issue, his reply was that 'it was an event without precedent, and therefore without prognostic.'[1] Many men of talent, especially among the young and ardent, were glowing with hot anticipation, as of blessings unheard of and unparalleled. They spoke and wrote as if the millennium were at hand, as if want and misery were about to be banished from the world, as if the corruptions of society and religion were about to be swept away, and Christianity to assume a new and more perfect phase, and brotherhood, and holy freedom, and a pure, simple, unsophisticated life were soon to flourish upon the earth. Most of all to the poets of the new school —Coleridge,[2] Wordsworth,[3] Southey,[4] Lamb,[5] Blake[6]—the prospect was one which filled them to the overflow with exultant enthusiasm. But other men of letters were not far behind them, such as Robertson,[7] Romilly,[8] Mason,[9] Campbell,[10] Hayley,[11] and Somerville.[12] Wyndham[13] was sanguine with hope and confidence, and those Churchmen who held strong Liberal opinions, such as Watson[14] and Parr, were promising themselves that human welfare would quickly make a great stride. At the universities all young men were eager on one side or the other.[15] 'The

[1] Seward's *Anecdotes*, ii. 437.
[2] Coleridge's *Relig. Musings*, pp. 85-94; Gilman's *Life of Coleridge*, pp. 46-48.
[3] Wordsworth's *Poems*, 'Ruth,' 'Prelude,' &c.; *Memoirs of*, by Chr. Wordsworth, p. 84.   [4] *Quar. Review*, 98, 465; Southey's pref. to *Joan of Arc*.
[5] B. Cornwall's *Memoirs of Lamb*, p. 67.
[6] Gilchrist's *Life of Blake*, i. 94.
[7] Lord Brougham's *Life and Times*, p. 27.
[8] Sir S. Romilly's *Memoirs*, i. 603; and Massey's *Hist.*, iii. 502.
[9] *Quar. Review*, 15, 380.   [10] Beattie's *Life of Campbell*, i. 6.
[11] *Quar. Review*, 36, 299.   [12] Somerville's *Life and Times*, p. 265.
[13] Massey, iii. 502.   [14] Watson's *Anecdotes*, ii. 23.
[15] Gilman's *Life of Coleridge*, p. 46.

French Revolution,' writes Sir S. Romilly in 1790, 'seems to be growing popular where one would least expect it, even in our universities. One of the questions proposed this year by the Vice-Chancellor of Cambridge for a Latin prize dissertation was " whether the French Revolution was likely to prove advantageous to this country " ; and the prize was given to a dissertation written in its favour.'[1] As for the English masses, it may be well understood what undefined expectations, what vague ideas of some wonderful improvement in their condition began to thrill among them.

The rainbow-tinted visions of enthusiasm were very rudely dispelled by the September massacres of 1792 and all the terrible scenes that followed. In most cases the revulsion was complete. A few still ventured to hope that out of the chaos which they beheld, and out of the horrors which accompanied it, good might arise not altogether disproportioned to its cost, and that even religion would be purer for the catastrophe out of which it would presently emerge. They had need to be bold who dared to express such hopes. General opinion hooted with contempt and execration such 'hypocritical professors of philanthropy,'[2] such ' footpads in the cloaks of philosophers.'[3] But for the most part, those whose expectations had been most sanguine were not content merely to deplore the collapse of their Utopia, and to search for such good as they might yet find in the fragments of it : they recoiled in utter dismay, acknowledged that their judgment had been wholly at fault, and ranked for the future among the ardent opposers of revolutionary ideas. At Cambridge, for instance, where in 1790 there had been a great many sympathisers with the Revolution, those principles had, in 1793, fallen so greatly

---

[1] Romilly's *Memoirs*, i. 404.
[2] Somerville, p. 265.
[3] R. Cumberland's *Plain Reasons*, &c., p. 43.

into discredit that even a Whig was scarcely to be found.[1] In place of the violent antagonism of parties which had been raging throughout the country, progress was being fast made to an unanimity of which it has been said that since the reign of Elizabeth it was unexampled in our history.[2]

The most ignorant could not fail to see how intimately religion was involved in the struggle which was distracting France and filling all Europe with apprehension. It seemed to not a few as if the last awful struggle had begun between the powers of good and evil which was to precede the consummation of all things. Tracts upon the Apocalypse were frequent,[3] and it was the opinion not merely of religious alarmists, but of such prelates as Horsley[4] and Porteus,[5] that the days of Antichrist, or of his precursors, were come, that the mystery of iniquity was at work, and that final judgment was approaching. Apart from any belief of this kind, no persons of the slightest pretension to any Christian feeling could witness unmoved the formal subversion of Christianity by the ruling government of France, or think without dismay what the consequences might be if the contagion of such impiety should spread. It could not be said with confidence that there was no fear of it. In the first place the conscience of the English people was by no means easy. We have had occasion more than once to refer to the dark and probably exaggerated tints in which the immorality and irreligion of the age were commonly depicted. Men who really believed in this great corruption of their times might well ask themselves what right they had to discard the fear that godlessness might reach a similar height in England. It must also be clearly under-

[1] Chr. Wordsworth's *Social Life of the English Universities*, p. 80.
[2] Gilman's *Life of Coleridge*, p. 86.   [3] G. Bennett's *Defence*, &c., p. 73.
[4] Horsley's *Charges*, pp. 84, 91.   [5] Porteus's *Works*, vi. 320.

stood that although the great bulk of educated opinion was now thoroughly hostile to the Revolution, yet that its principles were making no little advance among some classes of the population. It had many zealous emissaries who were leaving nothing undone to propagate their theories. The year 1792 especially was one which, both to Churchmen and statesmen, was full of grave alarm. If Burke's 'Reflections on the Revolution,' published the year before, had 'had a magic force,'[1] the pernicious influences of Paine's 'Rights of Man' had spread over a larger circle still. It was at this crisis that Hannah More did good service by her tract entitled 'Village Politics.' Many thousands of copies of it were sent out by Government to Scotland and Ireland, and hundreds of thousands of it are said to have been dispersed in London only.[2] 1794 was a somewhat similar year of scarcity and alarm. This fear gradually passed away. Methodism may have contributed, perhaps even largely, to this escape.[3] At all events religion and love of order were too firmly seated in the popular mind for the revolutionary leaven to take any violent form. Its more ordinary effect is fairly expressed in one of Wilberforce's letters: 'I am deeply hurt,' he wrote in 1801, 'by the apprehension, which is so strongly pressed upon me that I know not how to deny its solidity, that a rooted disaffection to the constitution and government has made some progress among the lower orders, and even a little higher; and when it is not quite so bad as this, there is often an abominable spirit of indifference as to our civil and ecclesiastical institutions, instead of that instinctive love and rooted attachment to all that is British which one used to witness. . . . I myself have observed a calculating, computing principle, considering what would be gained and

[1] Parr's *Memoirs*, i. 310.   [2] *Memoirs of H. More*, i. 524.
[3] Lecky, ii. 636.

what would be lost if there was to be a new order of things; confessing that our government was an old one, and had the vices and defects of age, and so forth.'[1]

The several ways in which the Revolution had a direct and contemporary influence upon religion in this country and upon the English Church in particular may now be briefly summed under different heads.

Such change of feeling as is spoken of by Wilberforce in the passage just quoted was plainly a combination of good and evil. So far as it was discontent and disaffection, so far as loyalty and patriotism were weakened, so far as the bonds were loosened both in religion and in politics which knit the present with whatever is most revered in the past—so far it was an evil. So far, on the other hand, as it inspired thoughts of progress, and a determination not to rest stupidly satisfied with forms which had become hurtful or effete, but to improve and reform the old, and adapt it to new conditions—so far, in Church questions, as well as in social and political ones, it was good.

Just as a wholly seditious spirit was to some extent propagated, so also, to a like limited extent, atheistic and anti-Christian teaching was more widely diffused. However, on the whole, this evil appears to have been more than balanced by counter energies for good.

Attacks upon Christianity often took the form, as they had done early in the century, of attacks upon the Church and the clergy. We hear much of the bitter tirades by which Jacobinical agitators endeavoured to estrange the people from religion in its established form.[2]

Meanwhile, among the vast proportion of the upper and middle, and very widely among all classes of Englishmen,

---

[1] Wilberforce to P. H., Aug. 1831, Chamberlain's *Select Letters*, p. 203.
[2] Horsley's *Charges*, p. 103; More's *Memoirs*, ii. 63, &c.

the crimes and excesses of the Revolution created feelings only of abhorrence and reaction.

Its greatest and best result was deeper seriousness. This was by no means confined to our country. It is illustrated quite as strongly in the tone of thought which pervades such writers as Schleiermacher, Madame Staël, Chateaubriand, as in the increased purpose and thoughtfulness of English writers, and in the spur it gave to philanthropic exertions.[1]

There was an extensive revival of attachment to the Church, less marked, but somewhat similar in cause and kind to that which arose when England headed the Protestant interest against Louis XIV. The contest had then been with France and Romanism; it was now with France and the new Paganism. But now, as then, it was felt that much depended on the strength and security of the English Church. Now also, as then, the cause of the Church was often vigorously advocated by those who were generally lukewarm and indifferent. As Bishop Horsley said, all the 'moralists' were for the time on the side of the Church.[2] Semi-Deists, who sixty years earlier would have taken in with relish those sarcasms against the Church in which the fashionable philosophers delighted, were now ranged among its defenders.

Such sort of support would not be a tower of strength to any church. Still, it had its value, and many who rallied round it were on the contrary animated by warm affection and deep conviction of the important place held by the English Church in this great crisis. These thoughts and feelings could have had no more eloquent exponent than Edmund Burke. But the main point in this gathering round the Church was far more vital than any which

---

[1] *Cf. Edinb. Review* for 1881, p. 308.
[2] Horsley's *Charges*, p. 56.

related to the strengthening of its position against outward foes. When the contest had been merely with Romanism there had been a great deal of mere policy and strategy with those who made their Church a rallying point in the fight. Not so now, or at least in a far less degree. The questions at issue were such as went to the very heart of religion. Churchmen looked to their Church, not as Anglicans, not as Protestants, but as Christians—who were chiefly concerned not for any forms and externals of religion, however much they might value these in themselves, but for the very core and kernel of their faith. They called upon the Church for a fuller discharge of its very highest functions; they appealed to it for defence, not against Papist or Puritan, not as a champion of the Reformation or of the Constitution, but against iniquity and infidelity—in a word, against the spiritual enemies of the human soul. These feelings are well expressed by Bishop Porteus in some of the concluding words of a Charge to the London clergy, after speaking of the 'portentous and alarming' events which were happening on the other side the Channel. 'There never was, I will venture to say, in the history of this island a single period in which the personal residence and personal exertions of the parochial clergy were ever more wanted, or more anxiously looked up to, and expected and *demanded* by the general voice of the whole nation, than at this moment; in order to fortify the faith, and to sanctify the manners, of the great mass of the people.'[1] Doubtless this tacit appeal, which Porteus thus put into words, met with only a partial and imperfect response. Still, it was not unresponded to. The Evangelical party in particular, who at this specific period were attracting into their ranks the greater share of whatever life and ardour was reawakening in the Church, were continually gaining in power both

[1] Porteus's *Works*, vi. 322.

among clergy and laity. Indeed, their influence at this period cannot be properly estimated without taking into account the impulse to serious religion which revulsion from the Revolution caused.

One special form of religious activity which was thus largely promoted was the cause of Christian education among the mass of the people. In the arguments commonly used in advocacy of the new institution of Sunday schools, now rapidly spreading through the country, we constantly find references to the anti-Christian spirit abroad. To quote again the words of Bishop Porteus: 'When we know that in other countries schools of irreligion have actually been established, and children regularly trained up, almost from their infancy, in the alphabet and grammar of infidelity: when we know, too, that the utmost efforts have been made, and are now making, here to shake the faith of the lower orders of the people, and to render Christianity an object of contempt and abhorrence to them: surely it behoves us to counteract and to guard against these attempts by every means in our power; and more especially by diffusing as widely as possible among the children of the poor the opportunities afforded by Sunday schools of acquiring the soundest principles and the earliest habits of morality and religion.'[1]

Mention has already been made of the sympathy excited by the sufferings of the immigrant clergy, and of the mitigation of old antipathies which naturally sprang out of these kindly feelings.

Nevertheless, the influence upon religion and the Church of reaction against revolutionary principles had some unfavourable aspects. It was a movement in which we may be glad to believe that the good decidedly pre-

[1] Porteus, vi. 294. The same arguments are used in the *Report of the Lincoln Clergy*, p. 31.

ponderated. Yet it had some alloy. In the first place, it impeded the carrying out of a more complete toleration. An opinion had got abroad, owing partly to Priestley and those who thought with him, and partly to the action of Dissenters in Ireland, that Nonconformists were on the whole inclined to republican principles. This supposed tendency was ill endured by those who were excited to passion by what they saw of republicanism in France. It is to be feared that a greater bitterness rose up at this period between Church and Dissent than had existed for many years before. A second fault was, that the movement in question discouraged reforms in the constitution of the Church no less than in that of the State. It created much anxiety that there should be a fuller and more refreshing stream of religious life in the Church, but would confine it rigorously to the old channels. There was to be no sort of revision, no sort of change, lest, perchance, change should become revolutionary. Thirdly, the artful way in which the French encyclopædists had set themselves to force science into the cause of infidelity had in many minds the baneful effect of creating distrust in physical discovery. A timidity to which the Evangelical school is perhaps prone was thus encouraged and exaggerated. Among the people generally there was a somewhat ominous outcry against 'the philosophers.' Lastly, it is quite possible, to judge from various allusions that may be met with in the histories of Coleridge and Wordsworth (though by no means true of either of them), that many who had at first entertained great hopes of what the Revolution might bring forth were really injured in temperament by the violent revulsion, so that they adopted despondent and depressing views as to any amelioration of mankind, and sank back into Epicurean selfishness.

On one great question of national morality—that which related to the slave trade—the influences in England of the

French Revolution acted in different ways. The traffic was condemned by all that was best and purest in the ideas of which the Revolution was the exaggerated and distorted expression. Its extinction, as an accursed thing, held a prominent place in the anticipation of all who were at first fascinated by the watchwords of the rising movement. When their hopes had ended in bitter disappointment, those who were still able to separate the gold from the dross amid which it was almost lost retained their firm hold of negro rights. Such men remained as staunch advocates for abolishing the slave trade as ever they had been. There were many, on the other hand, who seemed to think that what the Convention applauded sober Englishmen were bound to execrate. If Jacobins were bent on annihilating the traffic, there must needs be the elements of revolution in their projects, and Anti-Jacobins must resist. The king himself took this line. There had been a time when he had been wont to inquire graciously and with interest of Wilberforce 'how his black clients were getting on.'[1] After 1791 he was a determined opposer of the cause. Wyndham changed round in a manner still more marked. The failure of Abolition in 1792 was mainly caused by his fear of French principles.[2] It need hardly be said that the defenders of the slave trade did their utmost to attach the opprobrium of Jacobinism to its opponents. Meanwhile, above and beyond these temporary influences of fear, prejudice, and abhorrence was that more potent agency of which enough has been already said—that sense of the great preciousness of religion, not only to the individual but to the nation, which raised the ideal of duty, and strengthened the consciousness of responsibility. If this were at work, it could be but a question of a few years: the slave commerce of England was already doomed.

[1] *Life of Wilberforce*, p. 103.   [2] *Id.*, p. 250.

In a previous chapter it was remarked that till after the middle of the century scruples as to the perfect lawfulness of slavery were very exceptional. The only point on which religious people were at all anxious was, that slaves should not be left in utter spiritual ignorance. Whitefield had a number of slaves attached to his orphanage in Georgia. James Hervey, wishing in 1751 to make him an acceptable present, thought he could not do better than give him 30*l*. to buy another.[1] Bishop Warburton, much to his credit, appears to have been among the first to speak of the slave trade in tones of indignant remonstrance. ' " What then ? " say these zealous worshippers of mammon, " it is our own property ! " What ! property in your brethren, as in herds of cattle ? Your brethren both by nature and grace, creatures endued with all our faculties, possessing all our qualities but that of colour ? '[2] And so he continues in the same strain, eloquently and well; the more so, as there was no fear then of any such remarks on this subject becoming trite or commonplace. John Wesley seems to have shared for some time in the prevalent indifference on the subject. Later on, he was thoroughly alive to the enormities of such human traffic, and spoke of it with characteristic vehemence. In his journal for February 2, 1772, the entry occurs, ' Read of that execrable sum of all villainies, commonly called the slave trade.' About the same time, in 1776, we find Boswell recording—with some disgust, and with 'a solemn protest' against the doctrine on this point of his revered friend—Dr. Johnson's emphatic opinion of the essential unlawfulness of slave commerce.[3] Bishop Watson was an ardent abolitionist.[4] So was Paley.[5] Of Bishop

---

[1] Tyerman's *Early Methodists*, p. 277.
[2] Quoted in *Quar. Review*, vii. 403.   [3] Boswell's *Johnson*, iii. 206.
[4] Watson's *Autobiogr.*, ii. 63.
[5] Meadley's *Life of Paley*, p. 95.

Porteus his biographer writes: 'Next to the great and paramount concerns of religion, the Abolition was the object of all others nearest to his heart. He never spoke of it but with the utmost animation and enthusiasm. He spared no pains, no fatigue of body or mind, to further its accomplishment. . . . In short, the best years of his life and all his talents and powers were applied to it, and, I believe, the happiest day, beyond comparison, that he ever experienced was the day of its final triumph.'[1] Horsley was another distinguished bishop whose powers of eloquence were never wanting to the same good cause.[2] It may be added that, in the later years of the century, a whole chorus of poets—Cowper, Coleridge, Southey, Campbell, Hurdis, Barbauld, More, Montgomery—contributed their strains in support of negro liberty.

The foundation of Sunday schools in 1781 was a really important incident in the history both of religion and civilisation. That was no mere improvement in the minutiæ of education or parochial organisation, which could induce a cool-headed philosophical thinker like Adam Smith to say of it, that ' no plan has promised to effect a change of manners with equal ease and simplicity since the days of the apostles.'[3] Nothing could be more simple or unpretentious than what is generally spoken of as their beginning. Robert Raikes, the proprietor of a Gloucester newspaper, struck with the rude and noisy behaviour of the street boys on Sundays, determined to try if he could not get them to come tidy to school. He succeeded, and the example spread. That was all. It can scarcely be said even to have had the praise of novelty. Similar acts of unassuming usefulness of this kind had never been uncommon. For centuries past, it had been no unusual custom to collect

[1] Porteus's *Life*, pp. 222-23.   [2] Horsley's *Speeches*, pp. 195-258.
[3] Quoted in Mahon's *Hist. of Eng.*, chap. lxx.

children in the church, or into a house near it, or sometimes in a little room above the porch, and there to give them some instruction. Earlier efforts more exactly akin to that of Raikes are spoken of, and probably might have been instanced in considerable numbers if they had been thought worthy of permanent record. It might seem almost an accident that this experiment at Gloucester should have been so fruitful in consequences. But in truth the times were ripening for some more general extension than had hitherto existed in England of the means of elementary education. The State had done nothing. The Church, sleepy for the most part and inactive, had done but little, in comparison to what was left undone. It may be acknowledged, however, that, especially where there were no endowed schools, such education as there was among the poor was chiefly owing to the clergy. The more active among them had interested themselves in charity schools, had been diligent in catechising, and had probably taken pains in seeing that there should be some worthy dame more or less qualified to teach the first elements of knowledge to children whose parents might wish to send them. Perhaps the great majority of incumbents throughout the country were not altogether heedless whether the alphabet were accessible or not. But a little rudimentary instruction, badly attended, and indifferently given, passes for the most part almost utterly away. In many towns and most villages there were no charity schools, and the general ignorance was deplorable. Mrs. Trimmer says that when she and her fellow-workers began their Sunday teaching, the generality of children did not know their letters.[1] Her experience was probably not at all exceptional.

In 1780 any promising attempts to improve upon this state of things were sure to attract much attention.

[1] *Life and Writings of Mrs. Trimmer*, p. 166.

Methodism had not hitherto troubled itself much with schools or education; but the thousands whose hearts had been stirred by it, and who were living more thoughtful and serious lives than heretofore, were not likely to neglect anything which would help to keep their children steady, and give them the power of reading the Bible and joining with greater intelligence in the services of religion. Wesley himself greatly welcomed the Sunday schools. 'They are one of the best institutions,' he said, 'which have been seen in Europe for some centuries.'[1] The Evangelicals, and almost all earnest Churchmen, whatever their views might be, felt at once the importance of the movement. As early as 1782, Fletcher of Madeley was full of plans for their extension.[2] Rowland Hill opened the first in London.[3] Hannah More and her sister threw themselves most heartily into the work both of Sunday and day schools,[4] and Wilberforce and that excellent man John Thornton each sent them 400*l*. in aid.[5] Moore, Archbishop of Canterbury, warmly advocated the new Sunday schools.[6] Bishop Porteus wrote, in 1786, a long letter in recommendation of them to the clergy of his diocese.[7] He also drew out a careful scheme for their regulation. Bishop Tomline spoke with gratitude of 'that seasonable institution of Sunday schools, which seems mercifully designed as an antidote against the prevailing temper of the times.'[8] Horsley begged his clergy to promote their establishment by every means in their power.[9] Miss Burney enters in her diary that she had seen 'almost with reverence the man who had first suggested . . . an institution so admirable, so fraught with future

---

[1] March 24, 1790; Wesley's *Works*, xiv. 200.   [2] *Id.*, xi. 335.
[3] Charlesworth's *Life of R. Hill*, p. 55.
[4] H. More's *Memoirs*, i. 418, 453–56.
[5] *Life of Wilberforce*, by his Son, p. 195.
[6] Trimmer's *Life and Writings*, p. 66.   [7] Porteus's *Works*, vi. 234–58.
[8] Tomline's *Charge* of 1794, p. 18.   [9] Horsley's *Charges*, p. 111.

good and mercy to generations yet unborn.¹ Mrs. Trimmer, than whom few were more active in the promotion of the movement, spoke in 1786 with much enthusiasm of the rapid advance it was making, and of the visible good it was doing.² This latter opinion was strongly confirmed in the same year by Porteus. The good influence, he said, had been very apparent.³

It would be a misconception to suppose that these Sunday schools corresponded closely to those of the present day. We naturally think of them as gatherings of schoolchildren for about an hour in the morning and as much in the afternoon, for reading and Scripture, and general instruction on religious subjects. So also, in part, were those which were established in 1782 and succeeding years. But they were much more than this. In a vast number of cases these Sunday classes represented the entire school instruction of the children who attended them. The whole teaching gathered more or less round the religious element in it, but it included general instruction in reading, often from the alphabet upwards, and very often instruction in writing also. Much longer time, therefore, was taken from the Sunday. Porteus, writing to his clergy on the subject, spoke emphatically of the necessity for plenty of wholesome air and sunshine to children engaged during the week in trade and manufacture. Therefore, he continued, 'I should think that four, or at the most five hours, would be confinement fully sufficient for children so circumstanced. In villages, where they are, of course, more in the open air during the whole week, a little more time may be taken for instruction in the morning or evening.'⁴ He further added that rather than intrench too much on the ease and comfort and cheerfulness

---

¹ Mme. D'Arblay's *Diary*, iv. 129.
² Trimmer's *Life and Works*, i. 146.
³ Porteus's *Works*, vi. 245.   ⁴ *Id.*, p. 251.

of the Sunday, he would even give up the general learning, and be content with religious instruction only. Everybody knows that this limitation was eventually found to be necessary. Had it, however, been so from the beginning, the foundation of Sunday schools would not have been so considerable a movement as it was in the history of English education. As it was, it was a beginning of general elementary training, as contrasted with the very local and partial system which alone had hitherto prevailed. It gave an appetite for more. In towns and villages all over the country it set people talking about the desirability of all knowing, not only the elements of religion, but also how to read and write. Among other merits of the newly introduced system was that of economy. It was not expensive to secure a responsible teacher for one day in the week, especially where gratuitous help could be also given. The smallest parish could make some beginning. But, so far as general education went, it was soon found that it could only serve as a beginning. In the report, before quoted, of Lincolnshire clergymen, it is remarked that 'although many Sunday schools have been set on foot by the endeavours of the clergy, a great proportion of them at the sole expense of the ministers, and some taught by themselves, yet it is often with no small difficulty that the children are prevailed upon to attend, or the parents to send them.' They suggest, therefore, 'some systematic plan, such as the Legislature shall see fit and practicable, not only for the more regular instruction of poor children in their religious duties, but also for training them up in good habits.' [1]

Thus, Sunday schools gave an impulse to popular education which before long was productive of great results. Nevertheless, the progress of the movement was not altogether smooth. The violent and alarmed opposition

[1] *Report*, &c., pp. 7, 22.

which Hannah More met with in Somersetshire was but
the exaggeration and caricature of prejudices which were
not uncommon anywhere. Our own times are not altogether
unfamiliar with arguments that a little knowledge is a
dangerous thing, and that men and women were better
servants, and perhaps better Christians, in old days when
they were content to sign with an honest cross, and had
no more learning than enough to say by rote their duty
to God and their neighbour. In the latter years of the
eighteenth century such reasonings were infinitely more
common. The wide dissemination by agitators of seditious
and irreligious tracts added so much strength to this cry
as seriously to impede the progress of educational ideas.
Many persons who otherwise would have been favourable
to elementary schools were so scared by the insurrection
against established government in France, as to fear that
teaching the poor to read was putting a dangerous weapon
into their hands. It seems also that the agents of revolution were really endeavouring to turn to their own uses
some of the new schools. Horsley repeatedly asserted, as
what 'he knew to be the fact,' that Jacobinical schools of
atheism and disloyalty, 'schools in the shape of charity
schools and Sunday schools,' abounded throughout the
country.[1] To himself this seemed all the more reason for
promoting sound and religious education; not a few were
all the more confirmed in their opinion that the new-fangled
schools were one and all more mischievous than profitable.

Nevertheless such causes checked, rather than seriously
impeded, the cause of popular education. When Sunday
schools had begun to get general, industrial schools came into
notice. If, as was reported, they had succeeded in Ireland,
why not in England also? There seemed a hope that they
might be comparatively self-supporting; and, in any case,

[1] Horsley's *Charges*, iii.; also his *Speeches*.

they partly met the often-urged objection against withdrawing children from manual occupations. A society, formed in 1796, 'for Bettering the Condition of the Poor,' gave special attention to plans for promoting industrial schools. In 1797 a great impetus was given both to them and to elementary schools in general by Dr. Bell,[1] who arrived in that year from India, and began to lecture, with all the ardour of a fervent and impetuous temper, on the advantages of the so-called 'Madras System.' Dr. Bell had been a chaplain in India, and since 1789 superintendent of a school and orphanage near Madras. He had been singularly successful, and had proved to the full satisfaction of the India Company that half-caste children, who had been universally supposed to be a most unpromising material, could be trained into scholars who were not only quick in learning, but also diligent and truthful. It is certain Dr. Bell had been a very able schoolmaster. He had closely studied the principles of education, and never spared labour or was wanting in perseverance to carry them out. He was very thorough in his teaching, laying the utmost stress upon accuracy. He fully understood that the great purpose of the educator was the training of the intellect to assimilate its knowledge, the forming the mind, and not merely furnishing it. He combined admirable discipline with great brightness, and possessed the art both to interest his scholars in their work, and to engage their affections toward himself. He was always on the alert to observe and adopt any improvement in the method of teaching. Once, for instance, in the vestibule of a Malabar pagoda, he was much struck by a mode he saw of teaching children. One of the children repeated in a sort of chant a line of the lesson he had learnt, and at the same time traced it out on

[1] The facts relating to Dr. Bell are all taken from his *Life*, published by Southey in three volumes.

sand sprinkled on the floor. This done, the others chanted and wrote the same thing all together. And so the lesson continued. Bell at once adopted this mode of reading and writing together, and found it valuable.

But the essential feature of his system, and on which he was content that his fame should rest, was the plan of mutual instruction : tuition by the pupils themselves. He had found it impossible to procure schoolmasters of even a low average of competency, and also found that as soon as he had trained a master into his system, it was only to lose time again, as such a man was at once able to obtain a higher salary elsewhere. On this account he determined to try the experiment of conducting the school with no other help than that of the scholars themselves. Under his hands it succeeded admirably. A few years later, nearly at the end of the century, Pestalozzi tried the same method in Switzerland, not without fair success. But Pestalozzi adopted it only as a temporary practice. Dr. Bell made it permanently the keystone of his system. He maintained that the great economical gain was only a valuable accident, likely to enhance the popularity of his scheme and facilitate its extension. If, like Pestalozzi, he could have had a master to every five boys, or, like Fellenberg, one to every four, he would still have preferred his own means of instruction by the boys themselves. He thought it secured more effectual instruction, more cheerfulness, more unity of method, more stimulus of competition, more sense of responsibility, more moral training. 'Each class is paired off into tutors and pupils. Thus in a class of twelve boys, the six superior tutor the six inferior, each each.' 'When in their seats, each pupil sits by the side of his tutor.'

Such, in general terms, was Dr. Bell's system. It should be added that he was excessively opinionative, and that though he made himself much beloved by the young, his manner was offensive in the extreme to any adult teachers who might come under his superintendence. He was however, in all essentials, an excellent man. When he came to England, in 1797, his good report had preceded him. His intense belief in his own opinions gave all the more force to his enthusiasm, and his writings and lectures at once made a great impression on the public mind. He convinced many, as he had fully convinced himself, that a vast discovery had been made in the science of education. Sound teaching, religious and secular, was to be instilled far more universally, far more economically, far more effectually, than the world had ever known before. One of the first effects of his influence was to give a fresh impulse to industrial schools. The new teaching was to be so efficient an instrument, that there would be no need of the children of the poor being taken for more than quite a short time in the day from industrial labour. His system was at once adopted in various parts of the country, and the feeling in favour of general elementary education, which recent events had somewhat checked, was greatly revived.

The later history of the movement, its rivalry with the system of Joseph Lancaster—whose first school was opened in 1796, and whose system first came before the public in 1803—and its ultimate result in the foundation of the National Society, belongs entirely to the earlier part of the present century. The seed of new efforts for elementary education in England had been sown; it remained for the next age to show their progress and development.

Much in the same way as, in the latter part of the seventeenth century and in Queen Anne's time, active Churchmen had clubbed together for religious and philanthropical purposes, so, in a no less marked degree, was it in the revival which marked the later years of the century.

Societies of a purely devotional character, or for maintaining daily services, weekly lectures, and the like, were no longer among the ordinary outward signs of active religious feeling; but other societies were constantly being established. Such were those already alluded to, in which Wilberforce and Porteus greatly interested themselves, for 'Discountenancing of Vice,' and 'Reformation of Manners.' There was one started as early as 1750 for 'Promoting Religious Knowledge among the Poor,' which appears to have taken much the same ground as the Christian Knowledge Society, but to have been chiefly confined to Methodist and Evangelical Churchmen. There was one for the 'Support and Encouragement of Sunday Schools' established in 1785. The 'Naval and Military Society' for circulating the Scriptures among soldiers and sailors had its beginning in 1780. This also was a field in which the Christian Knowledge Society had not been inactive. Still, there was abundant room there for more than one religious agency of the sort. A worthy Methodist, who saw a good deal of the forces at the time of the Pretender's invasion, describes their profligacy and profaneness as utterly appalling.[1] Bisset, as early as Queen Anne's time, gave a similar account. He had heard, he said, of reformed officers, but he had never heard of reformers among them.[2] Soon after that date many good people showed concern for the spiritual and moral welfare of the troops. Among these was Queen Anne herself, by whose special desire every soldier and sailor was provided with useful little books, called respectively 'the Soldier's and Sailor's Monitor.'[3] In 1744 we find an entry in John Wesley's diary: 'About this time meetings began to be formed among the soldiers

---

[1] *Diary of N. Pidgeon*, p. 60.
[2] W. Bisset's *Plain English Sermon*, 1709, p. 38.
[3] J. Hervey's *Works*, vi. 283.

in the Low Countries.'[1] A little later than this we are frequently told of the earnest Methodism which might sometimes be found in the army,[2] and that officers would sometimes join in the meetings. Bishop Horne was among the most active promoters of the society of 1780. In the closing years of the century several associations busied themselves in circulating tracts by millions. There was one for dispersing the 'Cheap Repository Tracts,' of which Hannah More was the principal author;[3] there was a 'Philanthropical Society,' which might be supposed to be Jacobinical, but was not; there was the old 'Christian Knowledge Society'; and in 1799 Rowland Hill and others set on foot the 'Religious Tract Society.' The 'Church Missionary Society' was established in the same year. The 'Bible Society' was not founded till 1802. The 'London Missionary Society,' 1795, although joined by a few Churchmen, was chiefly a Nonconformist association.

As in the last fifteen years of the century the Episcopal Church of Scotland came once more into closer relations with the Church of England than it had done for a long time previously, this seems a proper place to give some short account of its history during the period embraced in this work.

Prelacy had been abolished, and Presbyterianism re-established, in 1690. The question, however, between the rival Churches had been by no means a simple one, and it is perfectly certain that if the wishes of the people only had been consulted, and the dynastic difficulty had not intervened, Episcopacy would have continued over a large part of Scotland as strong as ever. The relative strength of the two parties at the time is a point upon which very different opinions have been held, but it is clear from the evi-

[1] Wesley's *Works*, i. 450.
[2] *Id.*, i. 475; Pidgeon's *Diary*, pp. 210, 251. [3] H. More's *Memoirs*, i. 557.

dence of contemporary writers that they were not unequally matched. 'It is evident that the Cameronians, as distinguished from the moderate Presbyterians, formed the great majority in the south-western counties; that Episcopacy was generally unpopular in the south; that from the Forth to the Tay the adherents of Episcopacy and Presbyterianism were more equally divided, and that beyond the Tay the supporters of Episcopacy were much superior in number. If the opinion of the various classes of the people had been taken, it is certain that the nobility and gentry, the teachers in the universities, and the members of the College of Justice, would generally have adhered to Episcopacy, while Presbyterianism would have been supported by the majority of the burgesses and peasantry. It may, therefore, be reasonably inferred that the adherents of Episcopacy were the more powerful, wealthy, and educated party, and those of Presbyterianism the more numerous and also the more zealous.'[1] William himself was fully aware of the peculiar manner in which the two Churches were distributed over Scotland, and, though he had no personal preference for one or the other, would have preferred a tolerant uniformity throughout his kingdom. He directed Compton, Bishop of London, to inform the Bishop of Edinburgh that if Episcopalians would serve him in Scotland as he was served by them in England, he should prefer giving his chief support to them.[2] When, however, all the Scotch bishops refused to take the oath of allegiance, and a similar feeling was evident among the clergy and Episcopal laity, he consented to establish Presbyterianism over Scotland. He should leave it, he said, to the wishes

[1] G. Grub's *Eccles. Hist. of Scotland*, iii. 316. It is plain from the excellent authorities he gives that the estimate in the passage quoted in the text is in every way a moderate one.

[2] *Id.*, 297; Cunningham's *Church Hist. of Scotland*, ii. 266; Russell's *Hist. of Church of Scotland*, ii. 312-44.

of the people. This sufficiently decided the matter. However the case might stand as to mere numbers or material strength, there was an earnestness and a resolute fixity of purpose among the Presbyterians which might well turn the balance on their side.

Nevertheless, William used his best efforts to secure something more than toleration for all Episcopalians who would accept his claims, and to show much indulgence to those who would not. The bishops, indeed, were all of them wholly deprived, and for a period retired almost into obscurity. But otherwise Episcopalians were protected as far as possible. In the south-west, no prelatist could have held his ground for a moment against a people in whom the old Covenanting spirit was nearly, or quite, as strong as it had ever been. But in Edinburgh they were, even in 1705, in such force as to have fourteen separate congregations, in most of which the reigning sovereign was not prayed for.[1] In the north, Episcopacy for some time held even the churches and manses with a pertinacity which it would have needed the armed power of Government to resist. Some remarkable instances of this may be gathered from complaints made to the General Assembly. Thus, in 1711, when a Presbyterian minister ventured into a certain parish in Ross, with the intention of preaching, he was seized by armed men, kept in a cowshed on spare diet for four days, and dismissed with a warning that nothing but the Queen's forces should settle a Presbyterian preacher among them.[2] In a parish in Aberdeenshire, a Presbyterian minister, after labouring there for two years, petitioned the Assembly to remove him, on the ground that not a soul would come and hear him. Every man, woman, and child adhered to the Episcopalian curate.[3]

[1] Speech of Bishop Burnet, *Parl. Hist.*, vi. 692.
[2] Cunningham, ii. 351.   [3] *Id.*

Apart from such cases, which even in the northern half of the country might be considered more or less exceptional, the condition of Scotch Episcopalians throughout the reign of Queen Anne was not intolerable. Some, indeed, of the deprived bishops and clergy suffered from distressing poverty, which was only in part alleviated by the alms of their English brethren. Among such benefactors may be specially mentioned Archbishop Sharp,[1] and Bishop Ken, who, out of his slender means, helped them both with gifts in his life and with a legacy at his death.[2] But in most parts of Scotland Episcopalian congregations were not absolutely deprived of the ministrations they preferred. Those clergy only were formally tolerated who had both taken the oath of allegiance and had promised full submission to the Presbyterian discipline. These, rather more than a hundred in number, were left in possession of their churches and manses. King William had used all his influence to obtain this concession; and the Presbyterian rulers gave a reluctant consent, keeping, nevertheless, a very watchful eye upon them, and calling them sharply to account for any reported deficiencies in doctrine. Calamy, who was present as a guest at one of the meetings of the General Assembly, listened to one of these baitings of a 'protected' clergyman. The Moderator asked him in his ear what he thought of it. 'Why, we Englishmen,' said Calamy, 'should rather think it the Inquisition revived.' He smiled, and so did Lord Forbes who heard it. The Lord President asked what it was about; and from him the wholesome laugh passed on to the High Commissioner himself.[3] All other Episcopal clergymen were liable to be

---

[1] *Life of Abp. Sharp*, ii. 63.
[2] *Life of Ken*, by a Layman, pp. 664, 793. It should be added that Carstairs, most conspicuous among the Presbyterian leaders, was a generous friend to some of the deprived clergy.
[3] Calamy's *Autobiog.*, ii. 155.

silenced and prosecuted. Those, however, who had taken the oath of allegiance were, on the whole, protected by the civil government against Presbyterian interference; and even the Nonjurors, who formed the majority of the clergy, were usually connived at, especially if they confined their ministrations to private houses. Fortunately for them, the most ardent Presbyterians were, though on quite different grounds, almost equally opposed to the oaths of allegiance and abjuration. Although strongly hostile to the Stuart dynasty, they considered the oath a badge of Erastianism which could not be tolerated. The Nonjurors and the Nonjurants were about as opposite in their Church principles as could be conceived, but their common scruples on this one point were to the former a great gain. In Queen Anne's time the Episcopalian clergy even ventured to petition, that where a majority of the heritors and inhabitants were of the Episcopal persuasion, they might be enabled to hold benefices. This met with no response, and would, indeed, have been wholly contrary to the Act of Union. Full toleration, however, was now formally given to all Jurors.

Even in Queen Anne's time Presbyterianism increased in strength and numbers. The strong Jacobitism of the Episcopal Church in Scotland was its essential weakness. It was but natural that the opinions of the deprived bishops and clergy should become more pronounced, and that the more extreme among them should begin to feel that they and the most thorough of the English Nonjurors were become almost alien to the Church of the sister country, as well as to its king. Certainly when Bishop Rose was asked at Oxford whether he and the other Scottish prelates were in communion with the English Church, his answer was a very hesitating one.[1] Such principles, united with the hardships they had suffered, endeared them all the

[1] Grub's *Eccl. Hist. of Scotl.*, iii. 370.

more to the ardent Jacobites of the Highlands. But numbers who had hitherto held Episcopal opinions were either Hanoverian in politics, or at all events not strongly attached to the other side, and were, therefore, not inclined to cast in their lot with a Church whose principal pastors were generally all but hostile even to a semi-Jacobite Queen. There were also many, not very decided in their ecclesiastical views, who would at any time gravitate toward an Established Church.

After Queen Anne's death the Scotch Episcopalians became more than ever identified with the cause of the Pretender. Many who had acquiesced in the rule of King James's daughter were actively hostile to King George. When the insurrection began, 'the most distinguished of the Jacobite leaders were zealous supporters of Episcopacy; the sons of the Bishop of Edinburgh and Dunblane were among the ranks of the insurgents; and the public devotions of the army were conducted by the Episcopal clergy according to the ritual of the Common Prayer.'[1] They shared, therefore, in the disaster of their cause. As soon as the movement was quelled, orders were sent to Scotland that henceforward the limitations of the Toleration Act should be rigorously enforced. When, however, the alarm had abated, Episcopal congregations were not much worse off than they had been before. They numbered among their members so many gentlemen of great and hereditary influence that it was not thought desirable to molest them more than State necessities required. Moreover, the same cause which brought about the secession from the Presbyterian Church of the Erskines and the Associate Presbytery —departure from the old Covenanting rigour—largely increased the general spirit of tolerance. On the whole, the period that elapsed up to the rebellion of 1745 was one

[1] Grub's *Eccl. Hist. of Scotl.*, iii. 374.

of much external tranquillity to the Episcopalians. Beyond the Forth the bishops, clergy, and laity were generally very united, and warmly attached to the worship and doctrines of their Church. In the south there was more division, arising for the most part out of the dynastic question, in which points of Church government were much involved. In these counties many families which had hitherto been Episcopalian joined the Presbyterian communion, preferring it, now that moderation and culture were increasing in it, to a Church which had become closely mixed up with a proscribed political party. Some congregations procured the services of English clergymen, or clergymen in English orders, who were not recognised by the Scotch bishops, and who in return affected to be members of the English Church and not Scotch Episcopalians at all. On the other hand, there were many congregations in the south lowlands who, both in their ecclesiastical and political principles, were quite at one with their brethren in the north.

During the establishment of Episcopacy in Scotland between the Restoration and the Revolution, the English Liturgy had been rarely used, even in those congregations which were thoroughly attached to Episcopalian government. In Queen Anne's time its use gradually became general, being much favoured by Episcopalians of the upper classes, though it had at first to meet with much prejudice on the part of the less educated. Some of the 'protected' clergy endeavoured to use it in the Established churches. In this they were summarily stopped, sometimes by a mob, and sometimes by warning from the General Assembly. But the Assembly stepped beyond its right in endeavouring to stop its use in Episcopalian worship entirely outside the Establishment, and even by English chaplains in English regiments in Scotland.[1] This intolerance, which was

[1] Cunningham, ii. 346.

warmly seconded by De Foe,[1] was put an end to in 1711 by Greenshield's appeal to the House of Lords.

In a former chapter mention was made of the division which arose among Nonjurors as to the adoption of those sacramental usages which had been authorised in the first Liturgy of Edward VI., but had been omitted afterwards. Among Scotch Episcopalians this question occupied the foremost place of controversy during the peaceful interval between the two Jacobite risings. In addition to sympathies which, now that they were free to indulge them, attracted with equal force many English and many Scotch Nonjurors, the Scotch Episcopalians had a further reason for practically discussing the matter, because the 'usages' had been in the main embodied in the Prayer Book drawn up for Scotch use in 1637. In fact, after a time, the great point of debate, which was as keenly entered into by the laity as by the clergy, was whether the English Communion Office should be used, or the Scottish one. Those who advocated the special usages and the more distinctive office were at first few in number, but men of zeal and activity, who rapidly gained adherents. Those who resisted them did so partly from dislike at what might be called a more advanced ritual, but chiefly from anxiety not to do anything that might in any way widen the gap between themselves and Churchmen over the Border. The debate was complicated by what threatened for a time to be serious disagreement among the bishops. These were all Jacobite in feeling, but one party were anxious to continue the custom, which had lasted since the Revolution, of an Episcopal College, in which no member should hold any special see, until the hoped-for sovereign should be in a position to reinstate them. The other party held that such dependence on political contingencies was only injurious to their Church,

[1] Lathbury's *Hist. of the Nonjurors*, p. 253.

and that it was desirable to return at once to the principle of settled dioceses. For a time all the principal supporters of the eucharistic usages were members of the latter body. In the end their opinions, so far, at least, as related to the Scottish Communion Office, generally prevailed. In 1743 this office had become established in most of the congregations beyond the Forth. Those in the diocese of Edinburgh chiefly used the English form. Concord among the bishops being by this time perfectly restored, an harmonious understanding was arrived at, that either Liturgy could be used, but that antiquated usages not found in either should be prohibited. At the same time a declaration was made of full union and communion with the Church of England.

But the Jacobite insurrection of 1745 involved the whole Episcopal Church of Scotland not in disaster only, but in what seemed for the time to be hopeless ruin. The action of the Duke of Cumberland, after the battle of Culloden, in burning wherever he went all Episcopal chapels, was significant of what this hapless communion had to endure. The English Government proceeded deliberately to suppress it as a mere hotbed of disaffection. It was harsh treatment. The clergy especially seem to have been far less involved in the insurrection than they had been in that of 1715. Although Jacobite in their sympathies, they had not, as on that occasion, come publicly forward to promote the Pretender's cause. There were also severe clauses in the bill which were aimed directly at Scottish Episcopalianism in itself, and which would affect loyal, no less than disloyal, members of that body. Some of the English bishops—Secker, Sherlock, and Madox [1]—argued with so much force and justice against some clauses of the bill, that they were struck out—to be restored, however, the next day. Not only were all Nonjuror places of worship to be closed, under

[1] *Parl. Hist.*, xiv. 276-315.

heavy penalties upon all clerical and lay offenders, but toleration was for the future only to be granted to such Episcopal clergymen as had derived their orders from the English or Irish Church. All Scottish letters of orders were to be accounted null and void.

The blow fell with full force, and for nearly forty years the Episcopalian Church of Scotland seemed to the outer world almost lost. Legalised services under English clergymen, such as might be met with at Edinburgh and elsewhere, seemed little more than English colonies, and often had no connexion whatever with Scottish bishops. Elsewhere, Scottish Episcopalian clergymen did their duty faithfully, gathering the people to divine service at many different hours, and on different days of the week, in knots of four at a time, besides members of the household, so as to keep within the law.[1] Sometimes the statute would be evaded by arrangements which admitted only the statutory number into the room, but enabled others to listen. Occasionally greater numbers would be collected in secluded places out of doors. But the numbers of the laity fell rapidly away. Many, especially of the middle classes, conformed to Presbyterianism, and the gentry fell commonly into a habit of not attending any divine service. The clergy also became fewer, and more timid and desponding. After the accession of George III., although there was as yet no formal relaxation of the law, it became well understood that Episcopalian services would not be interfered with. In 1764 a revised edition of the Communion Office, which became the one generally recognised, was published under the superintendence of Bishop Falconer, the Primus. In 1766 the Chevalier died. He had been to the last acknowledged by the bishops and clergy as their rightful king, and they still continued their allegiance to his son. In

[1] Grub's *Eccl. Hist. of Scotl.*, iv. 40–44.

1777 an English Nonjuring bishop, John Gordon—the last bishop apparently of a race which must by this time have dwindled into the veriest fragment—wrote to the Scottish prelates to commend to their care, now in his advanced age, 'the poor orphans of the anti-Revolution Church of England, whom he should soon leave behind him.'[1]

In the eyes of most Englishmen the native Episcopal Church of Scotland was becoming almost as invisible as the 'anti-Revolution' Church existing unknown among themselves. Not that, even at its lowest ebb, it was ever inconsiderable in Aberdeenshire and the North Highlands. But regions that lay north of Edinburgh and Antonine's Wall were still, in general account, an unknown and barbarous land. It was not likely that English Churchmen, as a whole, should have much though tof a sister Church whose strength, such as it was, was chiefly centred there, and which was living on sufferance, impoverished, and under a ban.

But in 1784 this Church emerged from its obscurity, and came into relation with the English Church at home and abroad on an interesting and well known occasion. It has been already described how great a wrong had been done to English Churchmen in the American colonies by the deaf ear which the English Government had persistently turned to their repeated appeal for bishops. Some of the most eminent of our English bishops had pleaded their cause. But it was supposed that compliance with the request would increase the growing disaffection. That there was ground for this belief is true enough. The call for bishops came far less from the somewhat indolent Church of the South, than from that of the Northern States, which shortly before the war had begun to gain much ground. This progress was looked upon by American Congregationalists with aversion and distrust, partly from an ecclesiastical, but chiefly from a

[1] Grub's *Eccl. Hist. of Scotl.*, iv. 89.

political point of view. The general attachment of Episcopalians to the English constitution and the English connexion was notorious, and men in power were strongly opposed to anything which might tend to give them greater strength and influence. At the commencement of the war all of the Episcopal clergy north of Pennsylvania refused to join the majority; they were therefore roughly treated, and in many of the States all the churches were either destroyed or shut up.[1] When at last American independence was recognised, the difficulty about bishops revived with new force. Parliament made no demur in authorising Lowth, Bishop of London, to dispense with the oath of allegiance in ordaining American citizens. But when the Episcopal clergy of Connecticut elected Seabury for their bishop, and sent him to England for consecration, it seemed likely there might be much delay. Before the archbishop could perform this office an Act of Parliament had to be obtained; and the Ministry intimated that no further step could be taken until an official assurance had been received that the proceeding would not be offensive to the United States Government.

Seabury was not inclined to wait thus long. Before leaving America he had received distinct instructions[2] to suffer no unreasonable delay, but to apply, whenever he thought desirable, to the Scottish bishops. After consultation with Dr. Berkeley, son of the bishop, and Dr. Routh, late President of Magdalen, he determined to do this.[3] His consecration accordingly took place at Aberdeen in November 1784. On his return to Connecticut, his clergy met him with an address, at the close of which they warmly expressed

[1] Caswall's *America and the Am. Ch.*, p. 136.

[2] I am authorised to state this positively by Dr. Leighton Coleman, a thoroughly well-informed American Churchman, to whom I am also indebted for some other particulars relating to the American Protestant Episcopal Church.

[3] Caswall's *America and Am. Church*, p. 139; *American Church and the Am. Union*, p. 124.

their thanks to the venerable fathers from whom Seabury had received his commission. 'Wherever,' say they, in its last words, 'the American Episcopal Church shall be mentioned in the world, may this good deed which they have done for us be spoken for a memorial of them.'[1]

On January 31, 1788, Prince Charles Edward died. The Scottish bishops and their clergy, who, through good and ill report, had adhered tenaciously to their old political creed, were now quite prepared to render a willing and glad allegiance to the reigning king. To give a formal sanction to this resolve, a clerical and lay synod was convoked. One aged bishop and one presbyter were dissentient, and bated nothing of their old Jacobitism. With these two exceptions, all Scottish Episcopalian clergymen prayed publicly, on Sunday, May 25, for King George and the Royal Family. Next year, 1789, the Primus and two of the other bishops went up to London to see what could be done to remove the penal disabilities. Archbishop Moore gave them a friendly reception, and some of the bishops, as Horsley, Horne, Douglas, and Bagot, took up their cause with much interest.[2] Most Scottish members in both Houses gave them their assistance, as also did three principal members of the Established Church of Scotland—Principal Robertson of Edinburgh, and Principal Campbell, and Dr. Gerard of Aberdeen. There was no difficulty in the House of Commons. A bill, giving the desired relief, passed through it without any opposition. It met, however, in the House of Lords with formidable opposition in the person of Lord Chancellor Thurlow, who at first would not believe that there were such things as bishops in Scotland,[3] and, being assured by the English bishops that there really were, proceeded

[1] Grub, iv. 98.
[2] Horne's *Works*, pp. 150-57; Cassan's *Bishops of Salisbury*, p. 351; Horsley's *Speeches*, pp. 86-166. Bishop Warren appears to have acted a rather ungenerous part (Grub, iv. 106). [3] Bishop Horne's *Works*, p. 151.

to throw such obstacles in the way of the bill, that it was temporarily thrown out, and not brought up again for three years. In 1792 he was still unfavourable, though he no longer directly opposed it. If he had had his will, the same injury would have been done to Episcopalians in Scotland as that which English Churchmen had so long suffered in America. There was no need, he said, of bishops there; congregations could get their clergymen from England. Horsley had no difficulty in showing that, apart from the general question of what was just to a Church upon which there was no longer any imputation, and which had always been governed by its own bishops, it would also be quite impossible for English prelates to exercise pastoral care in districts far from their own dioceses, and where they could have no authority.[1] The bill was carried; though it still contained the illiberal clause, not mitigated until 1860, that no clergyman ordained by a Scottish bishop might on any occasion officiate in any English church or chapel where the Liturgy was used.

We are told that in Virginia, when the War of Independence was over, the material condition of the Protestant Episcopal Church was deplorable indeed. A large number of its churches had been destroyed or irreparably injured, twenty-three of the ninety-five parishes were extinct or forsaken, and thirty-five of the remainder were destitute of ministerial services.[2] If its condition elsewhere was not quite so bad as this, still it was everywhere in a state of great embarrassment and exhaustion. Its prevalent[3] political sympathies had for the time alienated the people; a great number of its clergy had been driven away; its churches were often in ruins; and it had no regular ecclesiastical

---

[1] Horsley's *Speeches*, pp. 86-160.
[2] Hawkes' *Episc. Ch. in Virg.*, p. 154; quoted by Baird, *Rel. in Amer.*, p. 248.
[3] Washington himself was an attached member of the Episcopal Church.

government as a centre of unity and organisation. The Society for the Propagation of the Gospel withdrew its help. Its committee, in their report for 1785, state that by the terms of their charter their assistance was limited to those who were under the dominion of the English Crown. They regret the unhappy event which would confine their labours to the colonies remaining under the king's sovereignty. Their affections were not alienated: they looked back with comfort to all that in past years had been done for the propagation of religion in the States; they earnestly hoped that their brethren in the Church would be zealous in all fruits of faith, and that, whatever their civil government might be, they would ever be kindly affectioned towards their fellow Churchmen in England.[1] Thus they wished the American Church God-speed, and left it to its own resources.

Seabury had sailed for England before yet the English troops had evacuated New York. The month after his return to America, a Convention of the Episcopalian Church was held, in which several of the States joined. In it certain changes in the Liturgy were proposed, and a request was forwarded to Canterbury through Mr. Adams, afterwards President, that the archbishop would consecrate bishops for the United States. After a few months' delay, arising from a wish felt among the English bishops to receive some further information as to the contemplated alterations in the Prayer Book, White and Provoost were consecrated at Lambeth in February 1787. Provoost was a man of pronounced democratic principles, who, it was felt, would on that account be the more acceptable to the people. White did an early and considerable service to his Church by the earnestness with which he advocated the admission of lay members into the General Convention. On this, and some other points, he was opposed to Seabury, who was also a strong contrast to Provoost in his

[1] *Abstract of S.P.G. Proceedings* for 1785, p. 55.

political views. Happily there was difference without dissension.[1] The Lambeth and Aberdeen prelates were not only in full communion, but were heartily anxious to work in concord. Seabury ceased to oppose the admission of laymen into ecclesiastical synods; and White and Provoost joined in recommending what Seabury was greatly bent upon,[2] the introduction into the American Liturgy of the characteristic features of the Scottish Eucharistic Office.

In the triennial Convention of 1789, the Liturgy question was thoroughly entered into, and many alterations made, though none of them sufficient to affect very materially the general character of the Church services. The preface attached to the book is an interesting one. It dwells on the liberty of adopting different forms and usages, provided the substance of the faith be kept entire—a liberty fully recognised by the Church of England, 'to which the Protestant Episcopal Church in these States is indebted, under God, for a long continuance of nursing care and protection.' It refers to the Commission for reviewing the Prayer Book, issued in 1689, as 'a great and good' design. The attention, it continues, of their own Church had been first drawn to the alterations made necessary through the change of civil rulers. 'But while these alterations were in review before the Convention, they could not but, with gratitude to God, embrace the happy occasion that was offered to them (uninfluenced and unrestrained by any worldly authority whatever) to take a further review of the Public Service, and to establish such other amendments as might be deemed

---

[1] On the part, however, of many American Churchmen the prejudice against Seabury was long and lasting. There were congregations who would not receive clergymen ordained by him.—(L.C.)

[2] The Scotch bishops had wanted Seabury to promise that the Scotch Communion Office should be introduced into the American Liturgy. But he neither would nor could do more than agree to use his best efforts to secure its introduction. (L.C.)

expedient.' They were 'far from intending to depart from the Church of England in any essential point of doctrine, discipline, or worship, or further than local circumstances require.' Finally, they entreat their readers to beseech the divine blessing on every endeavour for promulgating gospel truths 'in the clearest, plainest, and most affecting and majestic manner.'[1]

Among the omissions in the revised American Liturgy were the Athanasian Creed, the Absolution of the Sick, the Commination Service, parts of the ante-Communion exhortation, and (a loss which many must have deeply regretted) the 'Magnificat' and the 'Nunc Dimittis.'[2] In the place of these two canticles, the 92nd and 103rd psalms were substituted. The first words of 'Lighten our darkness' were altered into 'O Lord our Heavenly Father, by whose almighty power we have been preserved this day.' In the Collect for the Clergy, 'who alone workest great marvels' became 'from whom cometh every good and perfect gift.' 'Absolution' was changed into 'declaration of Absolution'; 'for the good estate of the Catholic Church,' into 'for the Holy Church universal'; 'verily and indeed,' in the Catechism, into 'spiritually,' and the word 'elect' omitted in the answer which speaks of the sanctifying work of the Holy Spirit. Several optional forms[3] were allowed, as, in the Apostles' Creed, 'went into the place of departed spirits,' instead of 'descended into hell.' The Nicene Creed, removed from the Communion Service, might be used at morning and evening prayers instead of the Apostles' Creed, and the Absolution in the Communion Office instead of that in the Daily Prayer. The 'Gloria' might or might not be used at the end of each psalm; at the end of the whole

---

[1] Preface to the American Book of Common Prayer.

[2] These are, however, used as anthems, and propositions have been made for restoring them to their own place.—(L.C.)

[3] Some of these optional forms have become perfectly obsolete in practice.—(L.C.)

portion of psalms either it or the 'Gloria in Excelsis' was to be said. Select psalms were chosen which might be used instead of those for the day. Certain specified portions of the Litany might be omitted. A bishop might use another form of words in the Ordination of Priests. A minister might, in the Baptism Service, omit, if desired, the sign of the cross, 'although,' it was added parenthetically, 'the Church knows no worthy cause of scruple.' Some well-chosen texts were added to the sentences with which morning and evening service begin. Second lessons were chosen for Sundays, and some changes made in the first lessons. Some of the prayers and thanksgivings for special occasions were rewritten, some transferred to that place from the Office for the Visitation of the Sick, and from that for Prayers at Sea. There were also some entirely new prayers, as for meetings of Convention, for persons in trouble, and for condemned malefactors. After the reading of the Commandments was added our Lord's summary of the duty of man to God and to his neighbour. Through the influence, already alluded to, of Seabury, the Communion Service proper was taken, as in the Scottish Episcopal Church, from the First Book of Edward VI. Some expressions in the latter part of the Funeral Service were altered or omitted. Forms were added for the Institution of Ministers, for the Visitation of Prisoners, for the Consecration of Churches; also a service of Family Prayer from Bishop Gibson, and a Thanksgiving[1] for the Fruits of the Earth. The State prayers were of course adapted to a republican government. Black-letter days were omitted from the Calendar, and many modifications made in the rubrics. Finally, various grammatical and verbal changes were made—including 'who' for 'which' in the Lord's Prayer—in compliance with the wishes of a

---

[1] One and the same day of thanksgiving is now observed throughout the country by the President's proclamation — (L.C.)

majority who disliked terms which had become quite or nearly obsolete in ordinary use, or, in some other cases, to suit somewhat exaggerated ideas about delicacy of language. The revision having been made, it was agreed that there should be no further change without at least three years' discussion, and after due consideration of the State Conventions. Subscription to the Articles was, as has been before mentioned,[1] not to be required of the clergy.

The work of the Society for the Propagation of the Gospel had been much cramped by want of means. It could show its best results in the Northern States. In them there had been throughout a fair degree of activity and life. The Church there, prior to the War of Independence, had fought an uphill battle, and had made much progress. Some considerable credit for this was due to the Society, which supported many of its clergy. In the South, on the other hand, the English Church, although sufficiently provided for, had been for some time in a deplorable state. It had been the great home and refuge of unworthy and incapable clergymen; and, though there had been many of a different sort, the Church established there was deservedly out of repute. After the war it took many years fully to recover itself, and cannot be said to have fully done so till the time of an active and excellent bishop in the early part of this century— Bishop Hobart. After the war, Canada and the Islands gave the Society abundant field for occupation. Inglis, the first Canadian bishop, went out to Nova Scotia in 1787. Four years later, in 1791, an Act of Parliament was passed, by which one seventh of all Crown lands was granted from that date to the 'Protestant clergy,' and for twenty-eight years this grant was limited to English Churchmen.

Before yet the slave trade had become a burning question, a certain amount of public interest had been felt in

[1] *Ante*, p. 125.

the moral and spiritual condition of slaves in British plantations. There were even some official enquiries as to the instruction given to them,[1] and it was strongly felt that some improvements were needed. Yet progress was slow; and throughout the middle of the century, and nearly to its close, perhaps somewhat less was done than at its beginning. A school for negroes at Charlestown, which for a time seemed to flourish, was gradually dropped.[2] The plantations in Barbadoes belonging to the Society for the Propagation of the Gospel were honourably distinguished by the kind consideration with which the 300 slaves were treated. But even there, although a catechist was maintained for their instruction, Christian and general moral teaching seems to have been given in a rather formal and perfunctory way; and the Society set aside, with very short discussion, the proposals submitted to them by Bishop Porteus for a supervision which would display a stronger sense of responsibility.[3] A little later, in 1788, circular instructions were sent by Lord Bathurst to the Governors of the Islands, urging them to provide both for better treatment of the blacks, and also for their religious teaching.[4] The Bishop of London took the same opportunity of also writing to the same effect to all the clergy there. There is a letter in 1786 from the Rector of Barbadoes, evidently a good and energetic man, deeply impressed with a feeling of duty towards the negroes in the island. There were schools, he says, in four provinces of the island, four also at Bermuda, and a large one in Philadelphia. Some few of the planters were quite in favour of his services and schools; but he met with opposition, and he much regretted the lack of countenance he had experienced from many of his fellow-clergymen.[5]

[1] Porteus's *Works*, vi. 159.   [2] *Id.*, p. 171.   [3] *Id.*, i. 90.
[4] *Id.*, p. 103.   [5] *Report of J. Bray's Associates*, 1787, pp. 36-43.

Methodist teaching was as attractive to the negroes in the West Indian Islands as it was in the Southern States. In many cases the Wesleyan ministers remained to the end of the century closely connected with the English Church. In Barbadoes the Chief Justice spoke of them as having greatly 'entitled themselves to the thanks of the Established Church, which they cannot, without being calumniated, be accused of undermining. . . . They had laid a strong foundation, upon which the fabric of the Church would be reared among the slaves in the West Indies.'[1] But except in Antigua, where the planters were so well pleased with the good political as well as religious results that they favoured their work, the Methodist preachers were often badly treated. In St. Vincent's an Act was passed against them, which was, however, disannulled by the king in council. Similar oppressive statutes were passed in Jamaica, and likewise cancelled by royal proclamation. Their missionaries were also mobbed, as 'Wilberforce men,' at St. Kitt's and Dominica. At Tortola, in 1794, they had a gratifying proof of their acknowledged ascendency over the blacks. The governor sent for their superintendent, and told him that the defences were adequate against the French, but that they were afraid to arm the negroes unless he would lead them, which he did.[2]

In regard of the colonies generally, it must be said of almost the whole of the last century, as well as of the earlier part of this, that the Church of England was far too heedless of the spiritual requirements of our colonists. In one of Southey's 'Colloquies,' Sir Thomas More, introduced as he might have been in Lyttelton's 'Dialogues of the Dead,' was with good reason represented as rebuking a generation which, in this respect at least, had degenerated from his own. 'In colonising, upon however small a scale, the vow

[1] Smith's *History of Missionary Societies*, i. 609. [2] *Id.*, p. 582.

should be remembered which David vowed unto the almighty "God of Jacob": "I will not suffer mine eyes to sleep, nor my eyelids to slumber, until I have found out a place for the temple of the Lord." The chief reason why men in later times have been worsened by colonisation (as they generally have been, from whatever nation they have been sent forth) is that they have not borne this in mind.'[1]

About India, also, the minds of some good men were not unreasonably troubled. It seemed shocking to them that the government of a great empire should be committed to a mercantile company bent only on acquiring riches.[2] Even Watson, whose somewhat secular mind was, perhaps, more interested in projects of civilisation than of religion, spoke with some dismay of the neglect of the great opportunities which the English possessed for promoting in India a knowledge of Christianity.[3] It is true that Schwartz, as we have seen, until his death in 1798, was doing, under the auspices of the Christian Knowledge Society, a noble work in Trichinopoly. But the splendid labours of the great missionary cannot disguise the general neglect. When Lord Macartney was in China in 1795, he said that the English had no desire to disturb or dispute the worship or tenets of others. 'They have no priests or chaplains with them, as other nations have.' Such words will bear a very defensible meaning; but put thus barely, they might well send a thrill through the heart and conscience of a man like Wilberforce.[4] It was a matter about which he was very anxious. In 1793, after long study of the subject, and much earnest consultation with the archbishop and other leading Churchmen, he brought the question forward in the House of Commons. He carried in committee his resolu-

[1] Southey's *Colloquies*, ii. 272; quoted in *Quar. Review*, 41, 25.
[2] See a paper on this subject in the *Mirror* for 1779, No. 28.
[3] Watson's *Life*, ii. 263.   [4] Wilberforce's *Life*, p. 120.

tion, in which, in general terms, the House acknowledged the duty of promoting, by all just and prudent means, the religious improvement of the native Indians. His specific proposals, however, were all thrown out.[1] They were strongly reprobated by the East India Directors; and, though Wilberforce argued as strongly as he could that they were not meant to force our faith upon the natives of India, it is probable that the Legislature had no other choice. It is obvious that distinct missionary work could not properly be undertaken by Government. It could not do more than facilitate voluntary agencies. Wilberforce may have been conscious of this. At all events, he turned with undiminished ardour to see what could be done by private enterprise. His journal in the last two or three years of the century records various consultations on this subject with Simeon, Venn, and others. About the same time, Bishop Porteus did a good work by insisting upon a practical exercise of his legal right of withholding approval to the appointment of Indian chaplains whom he might consider unfit for the office.[2] He was hotly opposed, and threatened with a mandamus from the Court of King's Bench. But he carried his point; and from that time more care was taken in recommendation of clergymen of approved principles. It was four years afterwards, in 1804, that Henry Martyn, Senior Wrangler in 1801, entered as a chaplain into their service, than whom no labourer in the gospel ever went to India with purer and saintlier resolves. Nor, in speaking of India at the close of the eighteenth century, must the name be omitted of a distinguished layman who was as eminent for piety and benevolence as he was for learning and varied accomplishments. Sir William Jones, in his studies of Brahminical theology, must have opened the eyes of many English divines to a truer

[1] Wilberforce's *Life*, p. 119.   [2] Porteus's *Life*, p. 146.

realisation of Eastern religious thought in the ancient creed with which their countrymen, in recent advances, had come into such close contact.

In 1775, the lion of the day in London society was a native of the South Sea Islands, who had come to England with Captain Cook, and was introduced into fashionable drawing-rooms by the Earl of Sandwich, First Lord of the Admiralty. His name was Omai, and he was spoken of as a man of importance in h s own country. Already no little interest, of a romantic and sentimental kind, had been awakened by the accounts brought home by Wallis, Carteret, and Cook. These idyllic pictures of emerald islands in Pacific seas, girt round with coral reefs, coroneted with waving palm trees, peopled by a simple race of kindly natives who garlanded their heads with flowers, aroused a sort of enthusiasm which the presence of Omai among them intensified.[1] He was feasted, and treated, astonished, and amused,

> And having seen our state,
> Our palaces, our ladies, and our pomp
> Of equipage, our gardens, and our sports,
> And heard our music—[2]

was sent back, none the better probably for his marvellous experiences, to his cocoas and bananas, his palms and yams. Still there were by this time many men of deep Christian feeling, in whom his visit, and the reports of the first circumnavigators, inspired other thoughts than those of curiosity and sentiment. These aspirations had no immediate result. But the first great missionary enterprise to people altogether out of English jurisdiction was to these islands. The London Missionary Society, founded in 1794, was neither wholly nor chiefly a Church organisa-

---

[1] J. Hutton's *Missionary Life in the South Seas*.
[2] Cowper's *The Task*, Bk. I.

tion. All Christian Protestants who practised infant baptism—the Baptists had started a missionary society of their own two years before—were invited to take part in it, and many Churchmen and laymen of Evangelical views took, in its early years, an active interest in it. A mission to Otaheite and the Friendly Islands attracted very wide sympathy. Contributions poured in. The East India Company promised a return cargo of tea from Canton. The Custom House relaxed ts stringency. In 1796 the 'Duff' sailed, with four principal missionaries and twenty-six selected artisans—its flag, three doves argent on a purple field, bearing green olive branches—and the expedition was further reinforced a few years later.[1] Its interesting history belongs of course to the present century.

In 1794, another impulse was given to missionary interest in England by Melville Horne's Letters from Sierra Leone. Wilberforce, Simeon, Venn, and other principal Evangelicals were moved with great desire to send the gospel there. The Society for the Propagation of the Gospel was fully occupied in the American and West India Colonies; the Christian Knowledge Society, so far as it had overstepped its more special sphere of work, was employed in South India. Hence rose, in the autumn of 1799, the Church Missionary Society, established in the first instance especially for Africa and the East. Wilberforce was very anxious that the archbishop should place himself at the head of it; but Moore, with provoking caution, regretted that he could not at once assume the offered post, and must be content 'to watch its proceedings with candour.'[2] Many Evangelical Churchmen also contributed to the missions set on foot by the London Society, in 1798, in Kaffraria and among the Hottentots. Several Churchmen

[1] Smith's *Hist. of Missions*, ii. 1-125.
[2] *Life of Wilberforce*, p. 210.

had also helped[1] to support the missions established in Bengal by the Baptist Missionary Society immediately after its foundation in 1792. Carey and Marshman, the two chief leaders of these missions, were admirable men for missionary work. Henry Martyn, himself a High Churchman rather than not, found them, when he arrived in India, most valuable coadjutors.[2]

The subject of missionary work must not be left without a brief allusion to the noble work of the Moravians: the more so as the friendly relations between the English Church and the Moravians in part of the last century have been more than once mentioned in this work. In Greenland, in the West Indies, in Georgia, on the Susquehanna, on the Oronoko, among the Caribbees, on the Surinam, in Labrador among the Esquimaux, in South Africa, among the Calmucks in Algiers, in Ceylon, on the Guinea Coast, in Persia among the Copts, in Nicobar—in every latitude of the known world their simple-hearted and devoted missionaries were found. Throughout a century, in which, until near upon its close, not the English Church only, but the whole body of Protestant Christians, were careless almost to apathy of the extension of the gospel to heathen countries, the Moravians were bravely toiling for Christ, alike amid Arctic ice and under tropical suns. When Fabricius had recounted some grave faults of the Roman Catholic missions, he spoke with the warmest admiration of their self-denying zeal. 'Hæc igitur libenter agnosco, admiror, amo, laudo.'[3] Who, even if he has fault in other respects to find, would not join in similar praise of the Moravians?

Most people have some idea of the general condition of Church fabrics, and the character of Church services,

---

[1] Smith, i. 324.   [2] H. Martyn's *Journal*, pp. 367, 379, 398, &c.
[3] J. A. Fabricius, *Salutaris Lux Evangelii*, p. 566.

in days now passed by, and before the feeling, now universal among Churchmen, had sprung up in favour of greater seemliness, order, and beauty in all that relates to public Christian worship. For more detailed information I may be permitted to refer to a previous publication, in which the subject is treated with some fulness.[1]

There is one other topic which has not been touched upon here, but to which an essay of some length was devoted in that work—the Sacred Poetry of the Eighteenth Century. As, however, this has been omitted in the later edition, I extract from the previous one the three concluding paragraphs :—

'It might' (I said) 'perhaps seem from the preceding sketch that the eighteenth century was, after all, rich, rather than not, in sacred poetry. Certainly, even without taking into account the Wesleyan hymns, it was not so barren in this respect as some have been apt to think. Throughout its course there was no period in which verse of a more or less religious kind failed either to be produced, or to find a very considerable number of readers. Yet it is equally certain that, until it began to draw near its close, the predominating influences of the age were essentially prosaic, and very unfavourable to any poetry which required for its due appreciation anything more than sound reason and ordinary practical sense. The state of feeling which existed among the cultivated classes in England encouraged poetry of a satirical, moral, or didactic character ; it applauded art, polish, and correctness ; it was willing to listen, not too intently, to the voice of its counsellors when they discoursed, either in verse or in prose, upon the wisdom of virtue and the folly of vice. But there was little intensity either of thought or feeling, little spiritual activity, little to stir

[1] Abbey and Overton's *English Church in the Eighteenth Cent.*, vol. ii. chap. v.

the soul and excite the imagination. Man cannot live with the mysteries of life around him, and that of death in front, without such reflections on time and eternity, and the meaning and object of existence, as cannot be altogether prosaic or commonplace. A Christian faith cannot, in all its leading features, be otherwise than sublime. Where Christianity, however depressed, is still a great power, there can be no age so wanting in depth of spiritual sentiment as to be altogether without materials for a religious poetry of a very high order. There were no influences in the eighteenth century so uncongenial to success that a truly great religious poet, if such a one had arisen, could not have triumphed over them. But, apart from the spiritual and moral grandeur inherent to it and inalienable, Christianity had, certainly, through various causes, come to be generally regarded from a lower and, so to say, a more worldly level than has been at all usual. It will be readily understood that when theology was in this condition, theological poetry was very apt to be either vague and impersonal, or frigid and deficient in warmth, or to have an air of being somewhat unreal and conventional. In the latter case, an attempt might probably be made to conceal the deficiency by a turgid declamatory style. All who have any knowledge of the poetical literature of the period under review will be well aware that the deficiencies here noted were very common. The solemn litany of sacred song was at all times far indeed from being silent, and its notes were often worthy of the greatness of its theme ; but throughout a great part of the century it certainly fell short in copiousness, richness, and fervour, both of a preceding and of a subsequent age.

'It will have been noticed that some of the best sacred poetry which the century produced had its origin in quarters which lay apart from the main current of popular thought.

Ken, deprived of his bishopric, and singing to his lute in the quiet seclusion of Longleat, belonged rather to the Churchmen of George Herbert's day. Norris was the last survivor of the noble school of Oxford and Cambridge Platonists. The sympathies of Hickes, and Hamilton, and Walter Harte, were all with the dispossessed adherents of the Stuart rule. Elizabeth Rowe, J. Byrom, and Blake, however much they might differ from one another, were all, in a greater or less degree, mystics, little understood by their own contemporaries. Among the hymn-writers, whose compositions form by far the most distinctive and prominent feature in the sacred poetry of the century, Watts, Doddridge, and several others were Dissenters. And though Methodism rose up in the very bosom of the English Church, it was too generally treated as an alien and an enemy; and the rich accompaniment of sacred song by which, through the talents of Charles Wesley, its rise and progress was attended, was for a long time neglected and discarded by the rulers of the National Church. Toplady, Newton, Cowper, and the other Evangelical hymn-writers might have shared the same fate, if Wesleyanism had not prepared the way for them, and created just that stir in the waters of which the spiritual life of the country stood so greatly in need. As it was, it cannot be said that Evangelicalism and its hymnody were in any way in discord with the prevalent development of popular religious thought towards the latter part of the century. And throughout the period, if a good deal of its graver poetry was not that which the age could best appreciate, there was also a very considerable residuum which fairly and generally represented the predominant style of thinking among educated people upon religious questions in which they were seriously interested.

'The last decade of the century stands in many respects on a very different footing from the rest. In none is this distinctiveness more marked than in the general character of its poetry. When so much that was old seemed rapidly passing away, and the new was so full of promise to some, so suggestive of fear and disquietude to others; when faith and hope, however much alloyed by visions of earth, were at all events vivid with life, and when religious doubts, on the other hand, were no longer mere speculative difficulties, benumbing action, rather than actively opposing it, but giants in the path with whom mortal combat was inevitable —when the foundations of society were in a state of upheaval and commotion, and all questions, divine and human, were being boldly canvassed—when great virtues and great wickedness came into strong collision—when brilliant promises were rudely checked, and when it seemed to others that glorious light might rise up suddenly out of utter darkness—at such a time it was not possible that great ideas should lose their strength through mere inactivity and torpor. To the partisans of the new, conceptions of Christian freedom, Christian brotherhood, and the like, had become pregnant with meanings they had never dreamt of before. The partisans of the old learned to treasure with a greater love blessings which, through familiar use, they had thought little of before—to appreciate the advantages they possessed, to overlook their deficiencies—to cling to all noble traditions of the past with a tenacity proportioned to their newly awakened fears. It was a time for revived enthusiasm and increased intensity of thought. . . . The eighteenth century had practically expired before its years had arrived at their natural term. Its latest portion belongs more to the present than the past; in nothing more so than in its poetry.'

CHAPTER VII.

ENGLISH BISHOPS. 1760–1800.

FREDERICK CORNWALLIS was George III.'s first Archbishop of Canterbury. He was a son of Baron Cornwallis; and as throughout the eighteenth century, and especially in its latter half, noble birth or high connexion, joined with conduct and fair average abilities, were a tolerably sure passport to promotion in the Church, it was almost a matter of course that he should become a dignitary. Granville told Bishop Newton with the most unblushing candour that there were some 'bishoprics of ease,' which ought specially to be reserved for 'men of family and fashion.'[1] Cornwallis, therefore, soon after taking orders was made Dean of St. Paul's, and in due course Bishop of Lichfield (1749–68), in which see he was succeeded thirteen years after by his nephew, a brother of the marquis of that name. Thence he succeeded to the Primacy, which he held for fifteen years (1768–83). Canterbury was not supposed to be opened by the key of birth, but by other and more fitting qualifications. Distinguished abilities and commanding character were not especially required, but dignity and moderation and a general aptitude for popularity and esteem. Cornwallis undoubtedly possessed these needful attributes. It has been said of him, with justice, that 'others had more shining talents, and more extensive learning; but in good solid sense and understanding, and right

[1] Newton's *Autobiog.*, p. 113.

discernment of men and things, in prudence, moderation, affability, candour, and benevolence, he was inferior to none.'¹ There were some who resented his elevation as of a man of not sufficiently high mark to fill so eminent a post.² But he seems to have amply satisfied all that the not too exacting opinion of his generation required of him. He laboured under a physical disability which might have been expected to impair his usefulness. As a young man at college he had a paralytic stroke on the right side, of which he never recovered the full use, and throughout life he was obliged to write with his left hand. 'But this notwithstanding, he has hitherto,' writes a contemporary, 'enjoyed uncommon good health, and never fails in his attendance upon the multifarious business of his station. He has greatly improved Lambeth House, he keeps an hospitable and elegant table, has not a grain of pride in his composition, is easy of access and receives every one with affability and good nature, is courteous, obliging, and condescending, and has not often been made an object of censure even in this censorious age.'³ Horace Walpole wipes the gall from his pen to give him a passing word of approval as 'an honest, good man.'⁴ Perhaps he was somewhat over-given to hospitality of a too indiscriminate kind. Lady Huntingdon made a formal complaint to George III. of the splendour of Mrs. Cornwallis's entertainments and of certain scandals which she said had been occasioned by them. The king took it up, and wrote a letter to the archbishop commenting on 'these improprieties,' and requesting that they should be suppressed immediately.⁵ He was a man of liberal views, and in the House of Lords always spoke

[1] Allen's *History of Lambeth*, p. 102.   [2] Hurd's *Life*, p. 532.
[3] Newton's *Autobiog.* p. 121.
[4] Walpole's *Journal of the Reign of George III.*, p. 226.
[5] *Life of the C. of Huntingdon*, quoted by Stoughton's *Q. Anne and the Georges*, ii. 16.

warmly in favour of toleration[1] both toward Dissenters and Roman Catholics. Though his views changed at a later date, he was at one time much in favour of a revision of Church formularies.[2] It is added of Cornwallis that he was very charitable, that he was an earnest peacemaker, and kind and generous in his superintendence of the clergy.[3]

The highest dignities of the Church are open to all ranks. Between Cornwallis and Manners-Sutton, nearly related the one to a marquis, the other to a duke, the Primacy was held by John Moore (1783-1805), the son, not indeed of a butcher, as some preferred to state it, but of a respectable grazier in Gloucestershire. In earlier life he had been tutor in the house of the Duke of Marlborough; and in the absence of very apparent qualification for an exalted position, rumour busied itself with ill-natured stories of the mode in which Woodstock influence had been exercised to secure his promotion. Doubtless it may have had some weight, for Marlborough was intimate with Shelburne, the Prime Minister of the day, and his recommendation would not be disregarded. Still, it was not necessary. When the Primacy was vacant, it was offered first to Hurd, the king's favourite prelate. When he declined it, as 'a charge not suited to his temper and his talents'[4]—unwilling also to leave the comparative ease of Worcester, and the engrossing interest of the magnificent library he was forming there—it was next offered to Lowth. But the offer was rather a tribute to the piety, learning, and amiable qualities of an excellent man, than one which could be really accepted: for Lowth was worn out with sickness, and almost dying.

---

[1] Walpole's *Journal*, ii. 419; *Parliamentary History*, xxi. 758, &c.
[2] Toplady to Dr. B. of Salisbury, Feb. 4, 1773, *Works*, vi. 161.
[3] E. Apthorp's sermon at Bishop Hallifax's consecration, p. 11.
[4] Kilvert's *Life of Hurd*, p. 146.

Both he, however, and Hurd recommended Moore, who was then made archbishop. It appears that, many years before, this honour had been anticipated for him. In 1774 he had been raised to Bangor (1774–83) from the Deanery of Canterbury. The year after, some verses were published relating to this promotion, in which the cathedral city is supposed to say—

> To me, you prophesy, our mitred Moore
> Revolving years may probably restore.[1]

If, however, much was ever expected of Moore, such expectations were disappointed. His archiepiscopate was far from being a notable one. He seems to have been a worthy, religious-minded man, of businesslike habits and kindly temper, but in no way remarkable. W. Hayley spoke of him in terms of cordial esteem, and said that he added to many other merits those of a gentleman and a scholar.[2] He took warm interest in the various religious and philanthropical movements which marked the close of the century. He was an earnest supporter of Sunday schools.[3] He zealously co-operated with Wilberforce in his efforts for association to promote a reformation of manners,[4] for improving the condition of the natives of India,[5] and for missionary work in general.[6] We read also of his actively interesting himself in behalf of the negroes in Barbadoes.[7] In the chapel at Lambeth in 1787 two bishops for America at last received consecration from the English Church. The only charge that seems to have been ever

---

[1] 'A Voice from Canterbury,' 1775 (Dean Moore made Bishop of Bangor), *Collection of Verses*, i. 237.
[2] *Memoirs of W. Hayley*, i. 375.
[3] *Life and Writings of Mrs. S. Trimmer*, p. 163.
[4] *Life of Wilberforce*, by his Son, p. 50.
[5] *Id.*, p. 119.
[6] *Id.*, p. 211.
[7] *An Account of Bray's Associates*, 1787, p. 36.

made against him was that he exercised undue influence over the king during his seasons of mental disorder.[1]

The primacy of Charles Manners-Sutton belongs to the nineteenth century; but he was Bishop of Norwich from 1792 to 1805. Jones of Nayland, who wrote the life of his predecessor in that see, speaks of him with great esteem.[2] His amiable manner and conciliatory ways seem indeed to have won for him a general regard. It is somewhat remarkable that while he was Primate of the English Church, his brother was at the head of the law in Ireland, and his son, as Speaker to the House of Commons, was First Commoner.

Robert Hay Drummond was Bishop of St. Asaph from 1748 to 1761, then, for a few months, of Salisbury, and Archbishop of York from 1761 to 1776.[3] He was a son of the Earl of Kinnoul. At the age of twenty-four he was made, by Queen Caroline's request, chaplain to the king, and went abroad with him. Then he became Bishop of St. Asaph, a diocese of which he always spoke with affection and delight. A man of warm feeling, he vindicated, in 1753, the character of two political friends, Stone and Murray, with such energy, that King George II. exclaimed, 'That is indeed a man to make a friend of!' He preached George III.'s coronation sermon in a spirit, as was said at the time, 'worthy of the excellent prelate and of the august assembly.' It is a severe reflection on some of his contemporary Churchmen that the words should be added, 'and free from fulsome panegyric.' We hear more of him as a statesman, a polished speaker, and a man of attractive and engaging manners, than as a bishop. He had a great

[1] J. Hunt, *Rel. in Eng.*, iii. 368, note.
[2] Jones's *Life of Horne*, p. 181.
[3] What is here said of Drummond is chiefly taken from Cassan's *Bishops of Salisbury*, pp. 284-303.

knowledge of history, of which he was very fond. In Church opinion he was strongly anti-Calvinistic; spoke with unusual freedom of what displeased him in the Articles or homilies, and expressed himself strongly against enthusiasm in religion. An admirer recorded of him with praise that he was

Pious, without enthusiastic flame.

William Markham was Bishop of Chester from 1771 to 1776, and Archbishop of York from 1776 to 1807. He had been head-master of Westminster, Dean of Christ Church, and tutor to the prince, and seems to have been something of the pedagogue throughout his episcopal life. He was very learned, very dignified, distinctly pompous, and apt to dwell over-much upon the claims of authority in political as well as in ecclesiastical matters. During the war he spoke of the American colonists much as if they were rebellious schoolboys.[1] In an angry altercation in the House of Lords the Duke of Grafton charged him with lauding up despotism, and betraying the principles of the Revolution.[2] He was unable, said he, even to pronounce 'liberty' without a qualification. The Prince of Wales, however, his old pupil, was much attached to him, and always spoke highly of him,[3] and Bishop Newton says of him that he was a generous-minded man with a noble way of thinking.[4]

Considering that Richard Terrick, who had previously been Bishop of Peterborough (1757–64), held for thirteen years (1764–77) the important see of London, less is heard of him than might have been expected. He must have been a man of some mark, for the Archbishopric of York was offered to him, and in Parliament he is said

[1] Walpole's *Journal*, ii. 119.
[2] *Parliam. Hist.*, xxix. 330, 350.
[3] Hurd's *Life*, p. 373.
[4] Newton's *Autobiog.*, p. 168.

to have been listened to with much attention.[1] But he was accused by some of being supple and artful,[2] and nothing that is told of him gives the idea of anything like power. Little can be said of a bishop who, so far as it appears, fulfilled the duties of his office with decent respectability, according to the standard of his age, but came in no way prominently forward as a leader of opinion or of action.

Few names of English bishops in the eighteenth century are so well remembered as that of Robert Lowth (St. David's 1766, Oxford 1766–77, London 1777–87). The pure and elegant Latin of his 'Prælectiones' permanently secured his fame as a scholar; his learning as a Hebraist is still more firmly established by his valuable works on the sacred poets of the Hebrews. An amiable and accomplished man, of deep unaffected piety, he would have been in any age an ornament to his Church. He was also an excellent preacher. Somerville speaks with much admiration of 'his manner, grave and solemn; his style, perspicuous, pure, and nervous.'[3] Another writer extolled him as an excellent judge of merit, and a liberal rewarder of it.[4] Warburton, fancying that some remarks in one of his works were directed against him fell upon him with all the ferocity with which he was accustomed to meet an adversary. No one could justly blame Lowth for the keen and polished sharpness of his retort. Yet it was regrettable that he should have allowed himself to be dragged into a war of words, and that a man who in all respects stood so deservedly high in repute should have given occasion for the sarcasm, that it was hard to say whether he or Warburton called names best.[5] It was

[1] *Parl. Hist.*, xxvii. 446.   [2] Walpole's *Memoirs*, i. 226.
[3] T. Somerville's *Life and Times*, p. 155.   [4] Nichols' *Lit. An.*, iv. 678.
[5] Dr. Johnson, in a conversation with the king (Boswell's *Life of Johnson*, ii. 49).

little merit to any to vie with Warburton in his worst characteristic.

Lowth was sometimes charged with weakness and inconsistency on the ground that he had first encouraged the revisionists and had then forsaken them.[1] That he did so seems to be certainly true. He was at one time inclined to think very favourably of the propositions made for reviewing Church formularies. In one of his visitation sermons he said that 'the light which arose upon the Christian world at the Reformation hath still continued to increase, and, we trust, will still shine more unto the perfect day. Much has been done in the great work of reformation, and much still remains to be done; and this work deserves our most earnest regard, the studies, assistance, and encouragement of all.'[2] The party for revision universally accepted such words as intimating approval of their purpose, and were proportionately disappointed when he refused to take any part in the 'Feathers Tavern' declaration. But there was good cause for holding back, or at least for being cautious. There were many liberal Churchmen engaged in the project with whom Lowth might have gladly co-operated, but there were others whose designs were of a much more doubtful kind. It was quite reasonable that the bishop, however willing he might be in the abstract to promote seasonable reforms, might shrink from acting with men who, in some instances, would have made revision an occasion for departing widely from the accustomed spirit and ancient doctrines of the English Church.

Lowth showed no inconsiderable poetical power. Indeed Cowper thought very highly of it.[3] There is much merit

[1] Walpole's *Journal of the Reign of George III.* i. 9.
[2] Quoted in the *Weekly Miscellany* for 1773, p. 615.
[3] Letter to Unwin, quoted in *Oxford Essays* for 1858, p. 143.

in some of his versions of the Psalms, and great spirit in a poetical address in 1745 'To the People of Great Britain,' beginning

> Did not high God of old ordain,
> When to thy grasp he gave the sceptre of the main,
> That empire in this favoured land
> Fixed on religion's solid base should stand ?[1]

Beilby Porteus (Chester 1777-87 ; London 1787-1809) was, as a principal leader of the Evangelical party, one of the most prominent among the bishops in the latter part of the eighteenth century. His father and mother were both natives of Virginia, and, though he himself was born after his parents had left the settlement and had returned to England, he naturally felt a special interest in the great questions afterwards at issue between the mother country and the colonies. Such family reminiscences gave force and pathos to his words when he pleaded for conciliatory efforts on either side, when he urged how contrary it was to the interests of America to separate, when he argued that there was yet time for both to see that they were in the wrong, and that surely it was not too late for fraternal affection to return.[2]

His poem on 'Death,' which took the Seatonian prize at Cambridge in 1758, is one of the best in that series. He wrote it with the more feeling from having lately lost his father, whom he had greatly loved and revered.[3]

Porteus was for several years domestic chaplain to

---

[1] Quoted in Southey's *Specimens of the later English Poets*, p. 290.
[2] *Parliam. Hist.*, xix. 866.
[3] Part of it may be read in Vicesimus Knox's *Elegant Extracts in Poetry*, p. 16. It contains some noticeable lines beginning—

> 'But chiefly, Thou
> Whom soft-eyed Pity once led down from heaven,
> To bleed for man, to teach him how to live,
> And, oh, still harder lesson ! how to die.'

Archbishop Secker. He was greatly attached to the primate, and, both in his 'Review of Secker's Life and Character,' and in various answers to some who were inclined to disparage him, spoke in the warmest terms of the talents, the learning, the beneficence, and the deep piety of the late prelate.

These were days when it was rare indeed for ecclesiastical pluralities to excite any misgivings even in the best of men. Porteus, before his elevation to the episcopate, was a very active parish priest; but he had no scruple in holding the two good livings of Lambeth and Hunton. Even as Bishop of Chester he only gave up the former, and was thought very conscientious in not availing himself of the permission to hold both. While Rector of Lambeth he published a letter on the universal neglect of Good Friday, which is said to have made a very marked impression both in London and Westminster. There never had been known such general observance of the day in closing of shops and in attendance on religious services as on the Good Friday subsequent to the publication of this letter.[1] It is curiously significant of the manner in which what might have been thought the most established Church observances were at this time becoming obsolete, that either on this or a later occasion he met with some rough usage in his attempt to revive some better keeping of the day, and that he was soundly abused for it in the leading journal of the day as nothing better than a Papist.[2] About this time, in 1772, while he was yet only a parish clergyman, his name came prominently forward on account of a petition to the bishops, in which he took a leading part, urging them to consider whether the Liturgy and Articles, especially the latter, might be advantageously revised. The petitioners spoke

---

[1] Hodgson's *Life and Works of Porteus*, i. 36.
[2] B. Hope's *Worship in the Ch. of Eng.*, p. 21.

particularly of the difficulty and offence caused by the 17th Article on election and predestination, and declared their belief that they were expressing the wishes of a large proportion both of the clergy and the laity.[1] A secondary purpose in this memorial was to meet by a more temperate scheme the principal objections of Blackburne and others who were bent on more fundamental changes.

Horace Walpole said, with a characteristic sneer, that 'Dr. Porteus succeeded to Chester on the merit of preaching a loyal pamphlet on the Fast.'[2] But in truth there could not have been a better promotion. The Evangelicals, who by this time were already beginning to represent, more than any other party in the Church, the vivid practical realities of Christian living, needed a worthy representative on the bishops' bench, and Porteus at once took this place, and occupied it well. How good a man he was may be gathered from the words of Hannah More, who knew him intimately and greatly esteemed him. 'As to the bishop,' she says, 'his life is a tissue of good actions. His industry is incredible; he still rises at five' (this was in 1795), 'and the end of one useful employment is only the beginning of another. His mind is always alive when any project of public good or private benevolence is on foot. His sweetness of temper, his playful wit, his innocent cheerfulness, embellish and delight our little society.'[3] Porteus was indeed an admirable episcopal leader of that active and beneficent section of the Evangelical party of which William Wilberforce and Hannah More were among the most conspicuous members. None were more diligent than they in all good works; but there was a brightness and a keenness

---

[1] *Life of Porteus*, p. 40.   [2] H. Walpole, *Journ.*, ii. 90.
[3] *Memoirs of Hannah More*, i. 561. She spoke of him with no less cordial admiration while recording her sorrow at his loss in 1808 (*id.*, ii. 147-53).

of enjoyment in their lives which was very far removed from that sort of depression, if not gloom, which rendered the society of many who held the same general opinions far from being attractive. The bishop's pleasant urbanity, his conversational power, and what people called, without any hint of foppery or affectation, the elegance of his manners, made his company delightful to that comfortable and generally well-to-do coterie who were at once men and women of the world, and true, simple-hearted Christian philanthropists. Hannah More, soon after the first beginning of her long acquaintance with him, while she spoke of him as 'perfectly to her taste,' expressed a hope, evidently not unmixed with fear, that popularity and high estimation might not spoil him.[1] Indeed it is a credit to him that he was not visibly the worse for all the incense of admiration with which he was received in the drawing-rooms and boudoirs of fashionable religious society. We catch a further glimpse of it in Miss Burney's diary, where she tells how 'Mrs. Streatfield talked of her darling Bishop of Chester with her usual warmth of passionate admiration, and Mr. Cambridge praised him very much also.'[2] He was popular also as a preacher. 'His sermon was admirable; rational, judicious, forcible, and truth-breathing; and delivered with a clearness, stillness, grace, and propriety that softened and bettered us all.'[3]

It will be enough to give a very brief, general sketch of Bishop Porteus's action in regard of various religious and ecclesiastical questions agitated in his time. He was in favour of the bill of 1779 for relieving Protestant Dissenters from subscription to the Articles, but urged the necessity of none being allowed to preach or teach without a formal acknowledgment of their being Christians and Protestants.

[1] H. More's *Life*, i. 173.
[2] *Diary and Letters of Madame d'Arblay*, ii. 233. [3] *Id.*, i. 334.

When the repeal of a most oppressive Act against Roman Catholics raised a storm of bigotry throughout the country, he steadily resisted the clamour of the 'Protestant Associations,' as full of exaggeration and unreason. On the other hand, he was opposed to the Catholic Emancipation Act of 1805. Although, like many other Evangelical Churchmen, he was often called a Methodist, he had little sympathy with Methodism, excepting esteem for the general piety he saw in it. It is not clear whether he regretted its severance by the close of the eighteenth century from the English Church. In any case he seems to have had no doubt that it was complete, and strongly objected to its clergy having anything to do with Methodist services or with those of the Countess of Huntingdon. He was very much in earnest on all points relating to the Sunday question. In 1781, alarmed at the sudden and rapid growth of Sunday debating societies, and Sunday promenades, both of which were becoming in different ways recognised places of amusement, where money was taken at the doors, he was mainly instrumental in bringing about the bill which stopped them. In 1798 he founded many voluntary associations for promoting a more religious observance of the Lord's Day; and in 1805 he exerted himself no less actively against a fashionable custom of Sunday concerts, in which hired professional performers took part, and which were attended by large assemblies. He was much interested in the condition of negroes; looked forward with hope to their final emancipation, and meanwhile laboured to get them Christian instruction, as he did also in measures for prohibiting the slave trade, and in forming societies for improving their general condition. Another work in which he took lively concern was that of organising the newly revived societies for the reformation of manners. The fierce outbreak of infidelity in France at the time of the Revolution filled him with anxiety lest the contagion of it might spread to England. He hoped much from the wide dissemination of cheap and sound publications, and, as his own contribution to the cause, delivered a series of Lent lectures on the Christian Evidences. Near the close of his life he became Vice-President of the newly founded British and Foreign Bible Society, and earnestly defended it against what he considered misapprehensions and misrepresentations. Finally, he took an active part in many matters relating to the wellbeing of the clergy, as in the subscriptions he set on foot for the relief of poor clergy and for the augmentation of some poverty-stricken London benefices, and in the measures he took for bringing about a more careful selection of chaplains for India, for encouraging residence, and for checking questionable contracts in regard of benefices. To these various labours may be added an effort to reform parochial psalmody.

It must be said of Brownlow North (Lichfield 1771–74; Worcester 1774–81; Winchester 1781–1820) that he was a bishop somewhat of the ornamental order. He entered upon the episcopate, by an easy road, at the early age of thirty,[1] his elder brother, Lord North, being then premier. Little more can be told of him than that he was an honourable English gentleman, dignified and courteous, amiable and generous.[2] He did not aspire at anything more than this. He took little or no part in political life, the more so as he was of a somewhat retiring and yielding disposition. It is said of him that he discharged with zeal the duties of his diocese[3]—a commendation, however, which must be taken with some reserve, as he appears to have been frequently absent for long intervals in continental

---

[1] Cassan's *Bishops of Winchester*, p. 279.
[2] *Id.* 'The Bishop (North) is charming' (Mme. d'Arblay's *Diary*, ii. 314).
[3] Cassan, p. 415.

travel.[1] He was a benefactor to charitable institutions, especially for the poorer clergy of his diocese.[2] We may add that he could well afford to be charitable, for beside his episcopal revenues and his private income he held also, at all events while he was Bishop of Lichfield, two livings *in commendam*.[3] In his bishop's office he certainly did not quite justify the high expectations of a very worthy man, his contemporary, who, soon after his appointment to Worcester, said that 'he rejoiced and blessed God that there was such a man in these abandoned times as Bishop North.'[4] Still, if he were not all that might be looked for in a bishop, he seems to have been a man who was generally loved and esteemed by those who came into relation with him. The majority of Churchmen in those days scarcely looked for more.

Henry Egerton has been briefly mentioned in a previous chapter as Bishop of Hereford. John Egerton (Lichfield 1768–71; Durham 1771–87) was of the type generally chosen in the eighteenth century for the palatinate see. While he was yet Bishop of Lichfield, Granville spoke of him as quite the man to be raised to Durham, if it should be vacant in his time.[5] What was wanted was a man of good presence, popular manners, and able by title of family,[6] wealth, and manners to hold the position of a benevolent, semi-feudal lord. Such was Egerton, who made his public entry in due state in 1771. We are told that he did much to conciliate parties, and to smooth over the fierce animosi-

[1] Stoughton's *Hist. of Relig.*, ii. 27.
[2] Green's *Hist. of Worcester*, p. 217. It was he who first set on foot the meetings of the three cathedral choirs, for the benefit of orphans of the choirs and others connected with the Church (Onslow's *Dioc. of Worcester*, p. 337).
[3] Fox remarked upon this in the House of Lords, Feb. 17, 1772—Walpole's *Journal*, i. 22.
[4] Dr. Johnson of Connecticut to Dr. Berkeley, Nov. 1, 1771, Hughes' *Letters*, ii. 301.   [5] Bishop Newton's *Autobiog.*, p. 113.
[6] Egerton was grandson to the Earl of Bridgwater.

ties which followed upon a contested election; that he won high favour there by concessions of timber rights, enfranchising copyholds, enclosing wastes, and repairing and enlarging bridges; that he was popular with all classes; and that few could have exercised the high privileges of that office with more liberal discretion or with less of blame or envy.[1]

Thomas Thurlow, his successor for four years at Durham (1787-91), had previously been Master of the Temple, Dean of St. Paul's, and Bishop of Lincoln (1779-87).[2] As brother of the Lord Chancellor, promotion had come rapidly to him. He was a man of some ability, but was in no way prominent in his public life.

After him came Shute Barrington, who was Bishop, first of Llandaff (1769-82), then of Salisbury (1782-91), and lastly of Durham (1791-1826), for the long space of fifty-six years. He was ninety-one when he died. There was considerable talent in his family. His father, the first Lord Barrington, had been, in Queen Anne's time, high in favour with Lord Somers, and, in addition to his legal and parliamentary services, had made a very useful contribution to theology in his 'Miscellanea Sacra,' published in 1725. His elder brother, William, who succeeded to the title, and whose biography was written by the bishop, spent the greater part of an honourable life in many high offices, as Lord of the Admiralty, Chancellor of the Exchequer, and Secretary for War. His brother Daines was king's counsel, and the author of some works of repute in law, natural history, Anglo-Saxon literature, and other general subjects. His other two brothers did good service to their country, the one in the navy, as vice-admiral, the other as

[1] Surtees' *Hist. of Durham*, p. 123.
[2] At the time of the Gordon Riots of 1780, Bishop Thurlow had a narrow escape from the mob, and got away over the leads of a house (Walpole's *Journal*, p. 419).

a general in the army. Bishop Barrington himself well deserved the general respect in which he was held. He did not write much or make many speeches, but what he did speak or write seems to have commanded attention. A carefully written treatise on the Roman question which he published in 1810 was spoken of with much praise;[1] and more than once it is evident that what he said in Parliament made some impression on his hearers. Thus we read on one occasion of the feeling and eloquence of his exordium;[2] at another time, when he was speaking of the principles of which Priestley was the principal exponent, and quoting from that writer, we have a picture of Lord Chatham listening with excitement, and interrupting with exclamations of 'Monstrous!' 'Horrible!' 'Shocking!'[3] Another incident in the House of Lords is of a different kind. In a debate relating to subscription in 1772, Lord Barrington declared that his brother believed the thirty-nine articles no more than he did himself, which made, says Horace Walpole, the bishop very angry.[4] In truth, the bishop, although it is likely enough that he would not have pinned his faith to all expressions in them, was among the last men to wander far away from acknowledged formularies. Although sensible and fairly tolerant, he was a strong Anti-Romanist,[5]

[1] 'The Bishop of Durham's very admirable, informing, and convincing pamphlet' (H. More's *Memoirs*, ii. 162). It is referred to in all notices of his life (Cassan's *Bishops of Salisbury*, p. 325; Surtees' *Durham*, i. 225, &c.).
[2] *Parliam. Hist.*, xx. 593. [3] *Id.*, xvii. 441.
[4] Walpole's *Journal in Reign of George III.*, i. 96.
[5] The vigour, however, of his hostility to Rome did not prevent his indulging an enthusiastic hope in the possibility of reunion. In 1810, he thought he saw such symptoms of moderated opinion in Roman Catholics as to justify the thought that there might yet be such dispassionate investigation into the causes of difference as might result in a healing of the schism. The time also seemed favourable for making common cause against the opponents of Christianity. 'If,' he exclaimed, 'I should live to see a foundation for such union well laid and happily begun; if Providence should but indulge me in even a dying prospect of that enlargement of the Messiah's kingdom which we have reason to hope is not very remote, with

belonged to the Evangelical school, and showed no inclination of deviating on any point from the ordinary modes of Protestant orthodoxy. As he had said in a sermon preached that same year, there were imperfections in all human institutions and formularies; but where the imperfections are slight, and the good great, our wisdom would be, let both go on together, lest while we intemperately strive to pluck out some fancied tares, we together with them root out the wheat also.[1]

Hannah More frequently speaks of Barrington, and in a manner which makes us feel that he must have been a very estimable man.[2] She often visited at his pleasant country house at Mongewell near Wallingford, where indeed he seems to have stayed rather more frequently than was consistent with a proper fulfilment of his duties at Durham. She tells of his deep[3] piety, his great sense, his polished manners; of his interest in the education of the poor, and of the earnest and devotional character of his addresses. One could not, she said, but be happy in such company.

It appears that from an architectural and archæological point of view, Barrington was a sad barbarian. In concert with his dean and architect, he lavished immense sums in more or less irreparable improvements, according to the taste of his age, in Durham Cathedral.[4] When, however, in 1799, the Chapter House was doomed to make place

what joy and consolation would it illumine the last hours of a long life! . . . May the gracious Saviour promote and prosper the blessed work of Catholic reunion; and for this purpose may He divest the minds of both Protestants and Papists of all prejudice and passion, of all indirect and uncandid views, and of every feeling contrary to the spirit of the gospel' (Charge of 1810, Barrington's *Sermons and Charges*, pp. 144-45).

[1] Sermon before the House of Lords, Jan. 30, 1772—Barrington's *Charges*, &c., p. 21.

[2] His published works give the same impression.

[3] H. More's *Memoirs*, i. 193, 199, 200, 267; ii. 42, 85, &c.

[4] M. Walcot's *Cathedral Customs*, &c., p. 50.

for 'a comfortable room,' the outcry of a distinguished antiquary happily intervened to avert the outrage.

Richard Hurd (Lichfield 1774-81; Worcester 1781-1808) was a bishop about whom opinions singularly differed. To judge from what is said of him by some of his contemporaries, he was an illustrious ornament of his Church and age. There are some, on the other hand, who represent him as among the most odious of mankind. Horace Walpole called him 'a servile pedant.'[1] He was much worse than that, according to Dr. Parr, who describes him, in terms of bitter hostility, as a mean and time-serving sycophant.[2] David Hume also has some very uncomplimentary remarks on what he calls his illiberal petulance and arrogance.[3] But if there were some truth in these imputations against him, it is evident that there was also a very different and far more honourable side of his character, which would lead to quite another estimate. He is constantly spoken of in terms of more than usual praise. Such praise might naturally be expected from Warburton, to whom Hurd had attached himself as a devoted friend and a hearty admirer. We find, therefore, Warburton extolling his 'candid manners, his generosity of mind, his warmth of heart,' and the ability with which, 'in a miserable time, he adorned letters, and supported religion.'[4] But, apart from the testimony of an intimate companion, it cannot be denied that he had won marked regard and esteem from many good men. He was George III.'s favourite bishop, reverenced by him as a clergyman and spiritual counsellor, and much valued by him as a friend. Porteus said of him, 'I always entertained high respect and veneration for the character of Bishop Hurd, whose piety, learning, taste, and genius rendered

[1] Walpole's *Journal*, ii. 457.
[2] W. Field's *Memoirs of Dr. Parr*, i. 276, 278.
[3] D. Hume's 'My Own Life,' *Essays*, &c., ed. by Green and Grose, i. 5.
[4] Warburton to Lyttelton, Kilvert's *Life of Hurd*, p. 59.

him the great ornament of literature and religion, and very justly gained him not only the esteem, but the affection, friendship, and confidence of his sovereign.'[1] Jones of Nayland, one of the best of men, says that he honoured his character no less than he admired his writings.[2] Miss Burney records the reverence she felt for him. 'I felt quite sorry,' says she, ' to lose sight of him. Piety and goodness are marked upon his countenance. . . . Indeed, n face, demeanour, and conversation, he seems precisely what a bishop should be, and who would make a looker-on, were he not a bishop, and a see vacant, call out, " Take Dr. Hurd; that is the man!"'[3]

Notwithstanding such wide diversity of opinion, it does not seem hard to form a tolerably fair judgment as to Bishop Hurd. A considerable deduction may at once be made from the aspersions cast upon him by his enemies. To be, in any conspicuous degree, 'the king's friend' was in those days a very invidious position; for though George III. was personally popular, faction, after a lull of some duration, was raging with virulence, and anyone high in favour at court was certain not to escape obloquy. In the case of Dr. Parr, there appears to have been not only strong political disagreement, but also offended personal feeling.[4] Furthermore, Hurd had adopted much of Warburton's literary arrogance, and those who had smarted under it were not likely to look very favourably on his words and actions.

Hurd did not deserve to be called either a hypocrite or a sycophant, or any of the other opprobrious names which those who disliked him were accustomed to use. But he had faults which made him very unattractive to many of those whom he did not care to please. He was stiff and

---

[1] Hodgson's *Life of Porteus*, i. 27. [2] Jones's *Life of Horne*, p. 34.
[3] *Diary and Letters of Mme. d'Arblay*, iii. 217, 232.
[4] *Quar. Review*, 39, 276.

precise, and always on his guard. He was also a great stickler for the external dignities of his office; so that, although very simple and temperate in all his personal habits, he seemed ostentatious, vain, and fond of state. He could not move from place to place without a certain pomp of retinue. A scholar alike by nature and use, of cultivated and very refined tastes, he was strongly tinged with literary pride, and could scarcely dissimulate a sort of disdain for unlearned people, or his aversion to anything that offended a too sensitive perception of what was correct. He was grave and placid in manner, intelligent and thoughtful, and in later life venerable in aspect. Those who knew him intimately praised his warmth and generosity of feeling, as we have seen; but there were few who could converse quite freely with him, or wholly escape the chill of his polished and courteous reserve. Ambition, in the ordinary sense of the word, was no part of his character, though many imputed it to him. He loved above all things the peaceful seclusion of Hartlebury, where, after fulfilling with such moderate diligence as would satisfy his own conscience what was ordinarily expected of a bishop, he would spend the full remainder of his leisure in literary pursuits and elegant hospitalities. When, therefore, the primacy was offered to him he had no hesitation in declining it. So great a charge, he said, was not suited to his temper or his talents.[1] It was far more congenial to read and write in his spacious library, whose ever increasing shelves bore witness to the delight with which he added to his collection each rare or valuable book. There he was most often to be found, as when Dibdin saw him in his eighty-first year, 'in full-bottomed wig and brocaded morning gown.'[2] The talent with which he wrote on subjects which interested him,

---

[1] Kilvert, p. 116.
[2] T. F. Dibdin, *Reminiscences of a Literary Life*, p. 165.

although it left no very lasting monument of itself, was very generally recognised both in England and on the Continent. Warburton speaks admiringly of 'the curious, the ornamental, and profound literature of Dr. Hurd,' and Wharton, who was no less able to give an opinion, calls him 'the most judicious and competent of modern critics.'[1] He was an excellent preacher, if the hearer were contented with a calm and judicious piety, thoughtfully reasoned out in finished and well-balanced periods. The popularity of his Warburtonian lectures in Lincoln's Inn Chapel was well attested by the crowded audiences which flocked to hear them.[2] But if any listener was unreasonable enough to expect that his feelings might be kindled, and the deeper emotions stirred, he would very certainly be disappointed. If there was one subject above all others on which Hurd would, in his sermons, most earnestly expatiate, it was the mischief and dangers of enthusiasm. There is little or nothing which can be actually objected to in what he says upon the subject; it is simply that he had no sympathy whatever with emotion as an element of religion. He does not deny that its influences may be valuable in minds of a certain complexion, but in general he doubted and suspected it.[3]

Hurd was the son of humble parents, of whom he was wont to speak in the warmest and most grateful manner, and whom he treated throughout their life with marked respect and reverence. They were 'very plain people, you may be sure,' he writes to Warburton, ' for they are farmers, but of a turn of mind that might have honoured any rank or any education. They never regarded any expense that was in their power, or almost out of it, in whatever regarded the

---

[1] Nichols' *Lit. An.*, vi. 471.   [2] *Id.*, p. 475.
[3] Hurd's *Assize Sermon on the Mischiefs of Enthusiasm*; also the remarks in his *Commonplace Book on the Controversy between Fenelon and Bossuet*; and frequent passages in his correspondence with Warburton.

welfare of their children.'[1] He went to Cambridge as 'a poor scholar.' He was afterwards Rector of Thurcastor, Preacher in Lincoln's Inn, Whitehall Preacher, and Archdeacon of Gloucester.

The great abilities and strongly marked character of William Warburton (Gloucester, 1760–69) makes his name very conspicuous in the ecclesiastical and theological history of the eighteenth century. Although not made a bishop till the year of George III.'s accession,[2] he was born in 1691, and had reached the height of his fame before becoming a dignitary in the Church. His father and grandfather had been solicitors, and for some little time he followed their profession. But he soon gladly exchanged a life of business for one of letters. As a boy at Oakham, he had been thought by his master to be ' the dullest of all dull scholars.'[3] His career singularly falsified this opinion. The pursuit of learning became, and continued to be throughout his life, an overpowering passion. Nothing came amiss to his insatiable greed for ever fresh learning. It may be mentioned, for instance, that in the midst of his multifarious studies of a deeper character, he did not hesitate to teach himself Spanish for the mere satisfaction of reading 'Don Quixote' in its own language.[4] But though his intellect was indeed omnivorous, Bentley scarcely did justice to it in his well-known saying of him that ' he had a monstrous appetite, but a very bad digestion.'[5] For not only was his reading very extensive, and his memory very retentive, but he also showed great aptitude in applying his vast stores of knowledge to any sub-

[1] Hurd to Warburton, July 2, 1754, *Correspond.*, p. 161.
[2] He might probably have received this promotion nearly thirty years earlier, if Queen Caroline had lived longer, to whom, shortly before her death, Hare had strongly recommended him when she enquired for ' a person of learning and ability to be with her at times and entertain her with reading and conversation ' (Watson's *Life of Warburton*, p. 57).
[3] Nichols' *Lit. An.*, v. 530.   [4] Bishop Newton's *Autobiog.*, p. 154.
[5] Nichols, v. 320; R. Cumberland's *Life*, i. 40, &c.

ject which he might have in hand. Neither did the weight of his erudition ever overpower the liveliness of his wit or the acuteness of his discernment. If he were somewhat overburdened with it, the evidence may be looked for chiefly in the fact that his greatest literary achievements were calculated rather to astound his contemporaries than to make much impression upon posterity. He could borrow instances, illustrations, arguments, from the obscurest and most recondite quarters, and use them with a dexterity and wealth of resource which made all men of letters wonder at him, as, in his kind, an intellectual giant. But he was wanting in some of the higher elements of genius, in those pregnant ideas which in the greatest writers bear fruit for all time. There was truth in the quaint epithet applied to him by Coleridge, 'thought-swarming, idealess Warburton.'[1] And therefore, notwithstanding the greatness of his fame, it is scarcely strange how little has been his permanent influence, how rarely he is quoted, how seldom any specific passage in his writings is now referred to. Every tiro in English literature knows his name, and something of his character; how few there probably are, even among the learned, who have read any one of his works.

It is evident on the surface that Warburton was much more the student than the Churchman, and adapted to fill with honour a university fellowship, or a professorial chair, rather than an episcopal throne. Even his friend and admirer, Hurd, doubted whether a private station would not have been best for him. Pitt gloried in his promotion[2]; and perhaps it was generally thought that the episcopate was not a little adorned by the attainments of so great a man. There were few in those days who doubted that great learning, combined with reasonable orthodoxy, amply qualified for

---

[1] Quoted by Purcell in Manning's *Essays on Religion*, p. 431.
[2] Nichols, iv. 732.

a bishopric. Moreover, Warburton always claimed to act as a bold champion of religion and the Church. None stepped forward with more confident ardour to counteract 'the madness of the times, whether shown in the ravings of impiety or fanaticism.'[1] 'Be not concerned,' he writes in another letter to Hurd, 'about my hand. I whose life is a warfare upon earth (that is to say, with bigots and libertines, against whom I have denounced eternal war) have reason to be thankful that the debility is not in my sword-hand.'[2]

But Warburton scarcely conceived of any more spiritual weapon to wield against the adversaries of Christianity than bare learning. This was what he specially urged upon his clergy as the great arm they needed wherewith to oppose fanaticism, bigotry, and infidelity.[3] This weapon he certainly did wield with masculine vigour; only it told but little as directed against some of his opponents. Reference has been made in a previous chapter[4] to a remark made by Jones of Nayland, that the Methodists spoke as contemptuously of Warburton's special merits as he of theirs. There was little Christianity, thought the Methodists, in the bishop's learning;[5] there was little learning, thought the bishop, in the Methodists' Christianity. Neither could appreciate nor understand the other; and therefore Warburton is never weaker in reality than when he is attacking either the Methodists, or William Law and the Mystics. His 'Doctrine of Grace' was thought by many of his time an overwhelming answer to Methodism. Hurd said of it in memorable words, that it was 'the singular merit of this discourse that it will be read when the sect that gave occasion to it is forgotten; or rather, the sect will find in it a

[1] Warburton to Hurd, Letter 232.   [2] *Id.*, Letter 161.
[3] First Charge: S. Watson's *Life of Warburton*, p. 593.   [4] Vol. I. 393.
[5] W. Law, in his *Confutation of Warburton's Defence of Christianity in the Divine Legation*, spoke in a very similar tone (Tighe's *Life, &c. of W. Law*, p. 66).

sort of immortality.'[1] Such a saying may take a high place in the long list of unfulfilled predictions. Yet Warburton's treatise was strong in its kind, in spite of Hurd's amazing over-estimate of its power. It is calm in tone, and truly and forcibly reasoned. He shows clearly enough that 'religion deprived of its foundation, natural religion, and of its best defence and ornament, human reason, lies a scorn to unbelievers, and a prey to fanatics and enthusiasts.'[2] His remarks upon the ordinary action of divine grace upon the soul are often as excellent as they are incontrovertible. It would be monstrous to say they were out of accord with the Christian spirit. But it is a maimed and imperfect Christianity none the less; just as, from a thoroughly opposite point of view, the religion of the more ignorant among the Methodist preachers, and, to some extent, of Wesley himself, might be held deficient in what many would feel to be real essentials. Still, Warburton's defect was the greater. He under-estimated the spiritual and emotional elements more seriously than they did the intellectual and the rational. His admirers thought he had gained a triumphant victory, but it may well be that, so far as it was a victory at all, it was one that did not cost his opponents the loss of a single follower.

Warburton's 'Alliance between Church and State,' published in 1736, was written in a manner characteristic of the deficiencies rather than of the merits both of Warburton and his age. It attracted much notice,[3] and he spoke of it with pride,[4] for he thought he had shown convincingly the value of a National Church at a time when it was visibly losing much of its ancient honour. His treatment, however, of his subject is somewhat disappointing. He might

[1] Watson's *Life of Warburton*, p. 538.
[2] Warburton's 'Doctrine of Grace,' *Works*, iv. 696.
[3] Nichols' *Lit. An.*, v. 517.
[4] Watson's *Life of Warburton*, pp. 289. 185.

have so illustrated it from his immense stores of information —so lighted it up with his wit and talent, as to make it very interesting. But he took a different line, and one which was not capable of kindling one spark of ardour in the very warmest supporters of the Church. It is all system and constitution-making, all expedience and mutual utility, never of any aspiring or exalted kind. In many of his observations there is much sound wisdom,[1] and well adapted to his times; but, in its general character, an artificial way of dealing with the matter, and his way of looking at religion in its purely human aspects and in its civil relations, must create a feeling that he is depressing a great subject to a needlessly low level.

The 'Divine Legation' is of course the work by which Warburton's power must be chiefly estimated. It is not within the scope of this work to enter into any detailed account of this remarkable literary performance. But no critic, however much he might dispute the main argument of its author, has ever denied the intellectual force which it exhibits. 'To the composition,' says one reviewer, 'of this prodigious performance, Hooker and Stillingfleet could have contributed the erudition, Chillingworth and Locke the acuteness, Taylor an imagination even more wild and copious, Swift, and perhaps Eachord, the sarcastic vein of wit; but what power of understanding, excepting that of Warburton, could first have amassed all these materials, and then compacted them into a bulky and elaborate work so consistent and harmonious.'[2] His arguments were directed mainly against the Deists, but also against the reasonings of Jews and Socinians.[3] In a spirit wholly consonant with his self-confident and combative genius, he

[1] Horsley praised it as 'one of the finest specimens that are to be found in any language of scientific reasoning applied to a political subject' (quoted by Watson, *Life of Warburton*, p. 57).   [2] *Quarterly Review*, vii. 398.
[3] J. Hunt's *Rel. Thought in the Eighteenth Cent.*, iii. 117.

built up his whole structure upon what was commonly held to be a paradox, and made admissions which terrified no small proportion among those whose cause he was advocating. The Deists of his age had dwelt much upon the great absence throughout the Hebrew Scriptures of intimations of belief in a future state. Warburton more than allowed all that they had thus urged, and proposed to demonstrate convincingly not only the necessity to the well-being of society of a belief in future rewards and punishments, not only the marvellous universality of this belief, but also that the Mosaic dispensation was wholly without it, and that this exception was in various manners a striking internal proof of the direct and special Providence which guided Jewish destinies. Upon this general thesis he lavished his treasures of learning, reason, and imagination, overflowing from time to time into episodes and digressions which were in themselves enough to furnish out many treatises, and which, in the judgment of many, were the most conspicuous adornments of his great work. Most prominent among these for their erudition and originality were his 'Investigation of the Pagan Mysteries,' and the 'Disquisition on Hieroglyphics and Picture Writing.' Of the work in general Lowth said, with sarcasm : ' It contains in it all knowledge, divine and human, ancient and modern ; it treats as of its proper subject "de omni scibili et de quolibet ente ; " it is a perfect cyclopædia ; it includes in itself all history, chronology, criticism, divinity. law, politics, from the Law of Moses down to the late Jews' Bill, and from Egyptian hieroglyphics to modern rebus writing, and to it we have resource, as to an infallible oracle, for the resolution of every question in literature. . . . He doth indeed in his pretensions bestride the narrow world of literature, and hath cast out his shoe over all the regions of science.' [1] Allowing for the satire,

[1] Lowth's *Letter to Warburton*, p. 13.

this might well describe the general impression which might be gained from a perusal of the 'Legation.' Its very cleverness encumbers it, and brought it, after a period of great fame, into ultimate neglect.[1] However great the ingenuity with which all kinds of material are woven into one web of argument, it would for all practical purposes have been more efficacious if it had been less paradoxical, less learned, and less clever.

One of the most interesting of Warburton's minor theological writings is his essay upon the defeat of the Emperor Julian's intention of rebuilding the Temple at Jerusalem. After stating in admirable words the qualifications of an unexceptional witness, he at all events showed conclusively that, to whatever cause the phenomena might be ascribed, the failure of the Emperor's effort was attended with very surprising incidents.

The great fault by which Warburton's writings are chiefly disfigured is notorious. 'His levity,' Mrs. Montagu said, 'shocks me, his *grossièreté* disgusts me.'[2] There was no measure to the arrogance of this inquisitor-general, to 'the pride and presumption with which he pronounced his infallible decrees,' or to the ferocity with which 'he lashed his antagonists without mercy or moderation.'[3] With a blindness to his own besetting fault, which would appear strange if it were less common, he has prefaced one of his works by remarking how grossly truth is abused, and its advocates dishonoured by the foolish use of scurrility in its defence.[4] Few writers equal to him in literary rank have been, even in an age in which such amenities were common, so great an offender in this respect as he himself was. All who encountered him in argument were, at the smallest

[1] *Cf. Quar. Review*, 38, 310.
[2] Doran's *A Lady of the Last Century*, p. 85.
[3] Gibbon's *Memoirs of my Life*, p. 92.
[4] Pref. to the *Doctrine of Grace*, iv. 510.

provocation, 'knaves' or 'hypocrites,' 'wretched fellows' or 'impudent calumniators,' 'flagitious wretches' or 'senseless and abandoned scribblers.' Even Lowth's gentle and refined temper was goaded into retaliation by his intemperate invective. There are few who, like a certain French writer, can answer with a quiet smile, 'My opponent calls me shuffler, renegade, apostate, coward, poltroon, liar, heretic, barterer of truth for gain, traitor, trimmer, and what not; it is his way of saying that he differs from me in opinion.'[1]

Warburton was, however, a placable enemy, and towards those whom he loved he is described as having been the very soul of friendship,[2] constant and zealous and full of impetuous warmth of heart. There is a particular charm in his intimacy with the eminent Nonconformist, Doddridge. In writing to him his habitual intolerance wholly disappears. 'Difference,' he says, at the beginning of this correspondence, 'of religious persuasion, among religious professors, never was, I thank God, any reason for restraining or abating my esteem for men of your character and learning.'[3] They remained excellent friends, and frequently exchanged letters, full of mutual respect and a reciprocal desire to please. In one Warburton has to thank Doddridge for sending him a delightful hymn; in another for one of his works in practical divinity. 'Before I left the country I had the pleasure of receiving your "Family Expositor." My mother and I took it by turns. She, who is superior to me in everything, aspired to the divine learning of the Improvements, while I kept grovelling in the human learning of the notes below.'[4] They corresponded freely on most religious and theological subjects of the day.

Warburton's close friendship with Pope was rather of a

---

[1] The quotation is taken from an old number of the *Scotch Eccles. Journal*. [2] Newton's *Autobiography*, p. 154. [3] Doddridge's *Correspondence*, iii. 319. [4] *Id.*, 362.

kind to exaggerate the defects of his character. It was the alliance, offensive and defensive, of one autocrat with another. Each was attended by a somewhat servile court of flatterers and admirers; each was looked up to in English literary society in general as supreme in his own domain; each was able to inspire a by no means groundless fear lest opposition might bring upon him a too presumptuous critic, some judgment that might gibbet him before posterity as a blockhead and a dunce. Confederate together, they therefore ruled too despotically the world of letters. Moreover, Pope, who, in the opinion of his time, was high above all emulation as a poet and a moralist, was himself deferential even to a fault towards Warburton. The overweening self-sufficiency of the latter had little need of being further aggravated by any such stimulus.

But Bishop Hurd was the most intimate of all his friends. He was a great admirer of Warburton, as indeed most were who were once drawn within the attraction of his genius, and he devoted no little time in defending the memory of his friend against all attacks, and in editing his works, or recording his life. To him we owe the publication of a series of letters which set before us with singular vividness the life, the thought, the feelings of the man, alike in his faults and in his merits. As usual, where intimate correspondence of this kind is thrown open to the world, a first thought is that no editor, even with the best intention, has a right to disclose the confidential utterances, with all the passing ebullitions of spleen, despondency, or impatience, which a man may unreservedly trust to the sympathies of a friend. Yet, although it is a severe trial, a character which has been distinguished alike for power and for warmth of feeling will not, on the whole, suffer from the ordeal. In the case of these letters of Warburton we see before us one who was at all events genuine and sincere.

The aspersions with which he was often assailed, as if he were playing a part and professing strong convictions in which he was not really a believer, are quickly seen to be unfair. We see in Warburton a man whose Christian faith was a strong reality to him, but in whom its intellectual element was disproportionately developed much to the prejudice of the deeper spiritual principle—a man too intemperate in words, too uncontrolled in passion, but truly anxious to do good in his generation, and to lessen the evil and unbelief which he lamented to see around him. He was an indifferent clergyman in regard of his pastoral duties, and an inactive bishop. His strenuous occupations in the library of Prior Park were clearly seen by his friends to be in decided contrast with his indolent labours at Gloucester.[1] But it is clear he was fully persuaded that his work for religion and the Church was to be a literary and intellectual one, and that he had no aptitude for any further mission. If he could labour in his own way he was well content. 'I hope the best, for I only aim at the honour of God, and good of man.'[2] 'I will tell you, my excellent friend,' he had said long before to another correspondent, 'what it is that supports me; it is the love of truth, and a mature conviction of the reality of revelation.'[3] John Wesley himself, though his whole temperament was utterly antagonistic to that of Warburton, though he would scarcely allow that there was religion in him, and spoke slightingly even of his acquirements,[4] yet, referring after his death to past controversies, spoke with a respect and tenderness by no means invariable in him, and trusted that he was resting in Abraham's bosom. The good old man had learnt to recognise that there was room for talents

---

[1] Hurd and Warburton's *Correspondence*, Letter 195.
[2] *Id.*, Letter 95.   [3] Nichols, v. 547.
[4] Wesley's *Works*, xii. 228.

very different from his own in the work of the heavenly vineyard.

Warburton was essentially a bishop of the eighteenth century. There could scarcely have been his counterpart in any preceding age, and he certainly could not have been what he was in our own. A somewhat similar remark may be made of another prelate, who, although utterly different from Warburton, belonged no less completely to that generation. Thomas Newton was Bishop of Bristol from 1761 to 1782. He was the son of a considerable spirit merchant at Lichfield, a worthy, religious man, who, after the laudable custom of good Churchmen in Queen Anne's time, had been accustomed to attend very constantly the daily service of the Church. His son, the bishop, was also a worthy man, but a worthy of that easy, satisfied, indulgent type, which can only flourish when a Church is in that relaxed and somnolent, but yet secure and respectable condition which was then generally prevalent. In his declining years it was a great pleasure to him to relate in a rambling and rather gossiping autobiography the principal reminiscences of his life. It may be that some who have written of personages and events of that age have formed their ideas of what the English Church then was too much from Bishop Newton's account. But, at all events, it does most truly represent that dull and torpid circulation in the body ecclesiastic, which, although sometimes exaggerated, was undoubtedly very characteristic of the period that preceded the Evangelical revival. A modern reader cannot fail to be struck with the artless revelation which it presents of a tone of sentiment distinctly lower than would now be possible in a Churchman who was Bishop Newton's equal in position and general worth. It was a world in which it might almost appear that place-seeking and preferment-hunting conveyed among the most part no sort of censure;

in which statesmen of high character would deliver themselves of maxims which might seem borrowed from a standard altogether lower than their own; and in which Churchmen who were ambitious of advancement felt no need of putting any curb whatever upon either their thoughts or words respecting it. There is no shadow of misgiving in the simple-hearted and rather garrulous tone in which Bishop Newton admits the world into his confidences, and narrates, to all who care to know, his various hopes or schemes in regard of patronage and promotions. They do not exactly give the idea of a worldly man, but rather leave an impression of wonder how a man who was not distinctly worldly should apparently think of high offices in the Church chiefly in the light of more or less comfortable resting-places. His ideal of life was far indeed from being a high one, but such as it was he fairly lived up to it. What he did was never wont to give occasion to censure. He fulfilled the expected round of duties conscientiously, untroubled by any thought that he might do more. He wrote a 'Dissertation on the Prophecies,' which deservedly did him credit, and gave him honourable rank in the list of learned prelates. It passed through several editions, and was translated into German and Danish.[1] His strict orthodoxy was wholly untainted with any dangerous 'enthusiasm.' He 'was always a friend of Government, and seldom opposed the measures of the Ministry.'[2] So far as was in the nature of a kindly hearted and easy man he utterly detested Levellers, Antinomians, and Republicans. He looked with horror at innovations; he was well content with the condition of his Church, and thought that those

---

[1] Bishop Newton's *Life and Works*, i. 72. J. Wesley bestows on it a very limited praise. It is 'well written,' he says, 'and shows a man of considerable learning. But there is no comparison, either as to sense learning, or piety, between Bishop Newton and Bengelius. The former is a mere child to the latter' (Wesley's *Works*, xii. 111). [2] *Id.*, p. 115.

who wanted reforms in it were only in search of a screen whereby to cover their own heresies.[1] He advocated perfect toleration, but held that those who enjoyed it should engage in return 'never upon any account to revile or disturb the religion established by law.'[2] He was a lover of art, and a patron of it. He was contented with his lot, and satisfied with himself—'he could not have been happier, and, by the good blessing of God, was able to make a competent provision for those who were to come after him, as well as to give something in charity.'[3] His religion, if not exacting in its calls, or exalted in its degree, seems to have been genuine in kind, resting chiefly upon cheering hopes in God's lovingkindness.[4] His life, judging from his own account of it, was very wanting in elements of real excellence, but he looked forward to its close with the most perfect peace. To use the words with which he ends the record of his life—'He hoped whether he lived, to live unto the Lord, or whether he died, to die unto the Lord. Living or dying he prayed to be the Lord's.'[5]

Bishop Newton's life is very characteristic of a Church which was sleepy, but not corrupt—inactive for the time, and comparatively inefficient, yet even then not unworthy of esteem. He, and men like him, beyond doubt, contributed much to keep the Church in its state of depressed vigour. But both in him and in his Church the life was present, although its circulation was slow. Under new influences and improved conditions there was no reason why it should not rise up into more fruitful activity.

[1] *Parl. Hist.*, xviii. 1276.
[2] Quoted in Maty's *New Review* for 1782, p. 344.
[3] Newton's *Life*, p. 148. Bishop Newton wrote all his Life in the third person.
[4] He warmly supported the belief in corrective punishments in a future state. Abstract of his arguments in the last sermon of his third volume in Maty, p. 384.
[5] *Life*, p. 180.

Samuel Hallifax (Gloucester 1781-89; St. Asaph 1789-90) was a respectable bishop of the learned type. He had been Professor at Cambridge, first of Arabic, and then of Civil Law, and was a fluent and elegant Latinist.[1] He left, however, little worthy of note, unless we except his 'Warburtonian Lectures,' and his 'Analytical Studies upon "Butler's Analogy."' In Church views he was a Liberal,[2] and, if he could have foreseen it, would probably have been much shocked that his friend Dr. Parr should have had to defend his memory from an ungrounded charge, brought against him by Dean Milner, of having died a Roman Catholic.[3] He was a friend of Hannah More, who spoke of his death with much regret as the loss of a good man.[4]

George Prettyman, afterwards Sir G. P. Tomline, was Bishop of Lincoln from 1787 to 1820, and of Winchester from 1820 to 1827. He had been tutor to William Pitt, was afterwards his secretary, and, after the death of the great statesman, published his memoirs. His friendship with the minister, who highly esteemed him, and endeavoured, though without success, to raise him to the primacy, though it gave him influence, exposed him also to much jealousy and disparagement.[5] His university distinction as Senior Wrangler, and his repute as a theological writer, give an air of absurdity to the representation that he was a man of contemptible abilities. For other aspersions to which he was from time to time subjected, there may be some slight foundation. William Wilberforce himself seems to have been of opinion that he was somewhat wanting in openness,[6] and he was certainly a little inclined to intoler-

---

[1] Nichols, vi. 449. To judge from an incident mentioned of him in Wakefield's *Memoirs*, he was apt to be curiously ignorant of current political events' (p. 96).   [2] Hurd's *Life*, p. 203.
[3] *Quar. Review*, 39, 304.   [4] H. More's *Memoirs*, i. 461.
[5] Wakefield's *Memoirs*, p. 127; *Asylum for Fugitive Pieces*, i. 97-105; ii. 190.   [6] W. Wilberforce's *Life*, p. 207.

ance, and to an over-straitlaced and precise orthodoxy. Also, like too many other prelates of his and the preceding age, he was a nepotist, whose first thought in dispensing patronage was to benefit his relatives and friends.[1] But he was a painstaking, hard-working bishop, who visited an extensive diocese with great regularity and care.[2] His well-known work, entitled 'A Refutation of Calvinism,' has been widely read. The chief criticism against it is one rarely escaped by those who strongly take that side in the great controversy—that of throwing too much into the background the workings of divine grace. Apart from this the book was one of considerable value, and showed much calm reasoning, great industry, and extensive learning.

Jonathan Shipley (Llandaff 1768-69, St. Asaph 1769-89) was a bishop of rather a secular type, but who was very highly esteemed in general society, and occupied quite deservedly an influential position. Dr. Johnson speaks of him as very intelligent and conversable, and as remembered with much respect even by those who belonged to quite a different party from his own.[3] His house in London was a sort of literary centre, where numbers of distinguished men used constantly to meet. Dr. Johnson would be there, with his satellite Boswell; Sir Joshua Reynolds, Garrick, Gibbon, Erskine, Bishop Percy, Dr. Burney; also Hannah More, and not a few other celebrities of the time.[4] Sometimes the Prince of Wales would be present. Shipley, 'a well-looking man, grave, quiet, and sensible,'[5] decided in his views, but always courteous and kindly, seems to have been a host whose company was greatly courted. One honoured guest, who on at least two occasions paid at his house visits

[1] W. Benham's *Diocese of Winchester*, p. 230.
[2] Cassan's *Bishops of Winchester*, p. 282.
[3] Boswell's *Johnson*, iv. 212.
[4] *Id.*, iii. 253; iv. 212; H. More's *Memoirs*, i. 186, 285.
[5] Madame d'Arblay's *Diary*, p. 144.

of some length, was Benjamin Franklin. When 'the good bishop,' as he was wont to call him, died in 1788, Dr. Franklin, in a letter of condolence to his daughter, spoke very highly of him. 'His departure,' he said, 'is a loss, not to his family and friends only, but to his nation and the world; for he was intent on doing good, had wisdom to devise the means, and talents to promote them.'[1] Shipley sided warmly against the Government on the question of the American war, and used his best powers and influence to stop the suicidal strife. 'If,' he argued, 'it was unjust to tax them, we ought to repeal the tax for their sakes; if it was unwise to tax them, we ought to repeal it for our own. A matter so trivial as the threepenny duty upon tea, but which has given cause of so much national hatred and reproach, ought not to be suffered to subsist one unnecessary day.'[2] His decided partisanship upon this subject brought upon him, however, much displeasure from some who thought differently. Hurd, who was no less warm in support of court and Government, seems to have had no patience with his episcopal brother. 'In good truth,' he exclaims, 'this "good man" is a very coxcomb.'[3] And when Shipley, in one of his charges, had expressed in earnest words his hope and prayer that the king might not continue to hold the opinion of which he was so tenacious, Hurd writes again, 'Have you seen the Bishop of Asaph's charge to the king, or rather his libel upon him, served up in the old Scotch form of a prayer? ... A grain of common sense (which, indeed, the coxcomb never possessed) might have taught him better!'[4]

It is to Shipley's credit that he voted[5] for the repeal of the Test and Corporation Acts, when a motion to this

---

[1] Franklin's *Autobiography*, II. Weld's edit., ii. 121.
[2] Shipley's *Works*, ii. 190.   [3] Kilvert's *Life of Hurd*, p. 115.
[4] *Id.*, p. 181.   [5] Bishop Watson's *Anecd. of his Life*, p. 262.

effect was for the first time tentatively brought forward in 1778. There were those who said that his thorough tolerance of spirit proceeded from laxity in his theology, and that he was not disinclined to the Unitarianism of Belsham.[1] There was no good ground for such a suspicion. A charge which might be brought upon him with greater probability would be that, like many other Welsh bishops of that age, he was somewhat remiss in the duties which his diocese demanded.

John Hinchcliffe (Peterborough 1769-94 [2]) was frequently associated with Shipley both in society and politics. Like him, he belonged to the Literary Club,[3] a society of wits, statesmen, and authors, to which none were admitted who were not in some way conspicuous in birth or talent. Hinchcliffe was not only ' a most pleasing preacher, with a clear and melodious elocution,'[4] but also a skilled and graceful orator.[5] It may be added that a bright, sociable [6] manner made him a welcome companion. He often spoke in Parliament, and, like Shipley, was exceedingly anxious that war in America should not be pushed to extremities.[7] In the earliest stage of the quarrel he had thought that although conciliation on the easiest terms should never be lost sight of, and though self-taxation might afterwards be conceded, yet that rights of legislature could not properly be surrendered to armed resistance. This was in 1774. But the next year, and so long as the war continued, he used all his admitted powers of eloquence in favour of peace. He earnestly deprecated warring for pre-eminence, or on a bare point of honour. He could not believe that absolute independence was the object of the colonies. If England

[1] *Quart. Review*, xiv. 48.
[2] He had previously been Master of Trinity College, Cambridge.
[3] Boswell's *Johnson*, i. 610. [4] Jones's *Memoir of Bishop Horne*, p. 144.
[5] Hansard's *Parliam. Deb.*, xviii. 290. [6] D'Arblay's *Memoirs*, i. 203.
[7] Hansard, xviii. 290, 715, 1277 ; xix. 332 ; xx. 9.

would give up all idea of exacting unconditional submission, it would not yet be too late to win back loyalty. But if loyalty should go, who would wish to rest on military force? In 1778 he asked permission to address the House, not as a statesman only, but as a Christian, and earnestly implored the Lords not to carry out a system of reprisals, nor encourage the tomahawk and the scalping-knife, and establish desolation as a system. If Great Britain had any hope in the justice of her cause, she did ill to defeat that hope. In these debates Hinchcliffe was anxious to make it clear that he had no thought of being a busy meddler in political matters. But surely, where right, justice, and mercy were at stake, and not only questions, however important, of political expedience, the Church did well to speak. It must be conceded with regret that some who sat with him on the episcopal bench were not of the same mind.

Hinchcliffe was a decided Whig, and is said to have declined the tuition of the Prince of Wales, on the ground that his political principles were not sufficiently in accord with those of the court.[1] Like most or all of his party, though a great advocate of tolerance in general, he was very jealous of any concession of further liberty to the Roman Catholics.

We hear little of him on purely Church questions and in his pastoral capacity, and may conclude that in these points he was neither more nor less than the average bishop of his age.

Hinchcliffe was followed at St. Asaph by Lewis Bagot (Bristol 1783-83, Norwich 1783-90, St. Asaph 1790-1802). This bishop is always spoken of in exceptionally high terms as a very estimable man. As Dean of Christ Church he had written in defence of Church subscription, and a series

[1] Note to Hansard, xviii. 290.

of Warburtonian lectures which were received with much approval at their time,[1] but are described by a modern critic as very ordinary.[2] His turn of thought was, in fact, somewhat narrow, and he was not very tolerant of difference of opinion.[3] But his thorough goodness, his mild manners, his placid benevolence, and his charitable kindness to those who needed help, made him very much respected.[4] The poet Cowper, who had little patience with the cultivated but rather worldly and careless type of prelate whom he saw in many of the sees around him, made a special exception in favour of Lowth and Bagot.[5] As a bishop he was an excellent patron to deserving clergymen; and one of his first acts after his promotion to St. Asaph was to rebuild the episcopal residence, and make it clear that he intended, as many of his predecessors had not done, to spend most of his time within his diocese. His health, however, was not good, and he is spoken of in his later years as wasted almost to a skeleton.

Edmund Law (Carlisle 1769–87) was a bishop who was most cordially disliked by most good Churchmen, but an eminent and remarkable man notwithstanding. He was born in 1702, and in middle life had occupied various important posts in the University of Cambridge, as Master of Peterhouse, Vice-Chancellor, principal librarian, and Professor of Casuistical Divinity. He had also been a Prebendary of Lichfield, and Archdeacon, first of Carlisle, and afterwards of Staffordshire.[6] His intellectual power was universally acknowledged, and he was accounted one of the

[1] Jessop's *Dioc. Hist. of Norwich*, p. 223.
[2] Hunt's *Relig. Thought in the Eighteenth Cent.*, iii. 337.
[3] H. More's *Memoirs*, i. 193.
[4] Nichols' *Lit. An.*, v. 631; H. More and Jessop as above; also Parr's *Life*, i. 371.
[5] Cowper's *Tirocinium*. But Cowper, from any point of view, might easily have found other exceptions.
[6] *Life*, by Paley, prefixed to his *Works*; and Jefferson's *Carlisle*, pp. 240-41.

best metaphysicians of the age.[1] As the greater part of his life had been spent in thought and study, and as he was not raised to the Episcopate till he was approaching the age of seventy, it could scarcely be expected that he should be very active in the pastoral duties of his office. But in those times few except Evangelicals and Methodists complained of a bishop who spent most of his time among his books and writings. If Law, mild and tranquil in temper as he was, had confined himself to theology and philosophy, he would have won abundant honour from his contemporaries. It was the part he took in the questions of revision of Church formularies, and subscription to articles, which brought upon him so much hot indignation.

It has been before observed that some even of the most moderate and cautious of the bishops were inclined, soon after the middle of the century, to look very favourably upon some project of revision. Edmund Law might therefore, without any offence, have fallen in with these opinions, or even have seconded, as he did,[2] the not unreasonable suggestions put forward, in 1749, by Jones of Alconbury in his 'Free and Candid Disquisitions.' But he wished to go considerably further than this. He was an ultra-Protestant, accustomed to speak with much animation of 'the imperfections of our first reformers and of their reformation.'[3] When, therefore, Archdeacon Blackburne published, in 1750, his 'Apology,' and the subsequent sermon, in both of which he advocated far more radical changes, and called for an utter extirpation of everything that had any affinity with Rome, Law wrote at once to Blackburne to congratulate him 'on the good work of reformation on which he was so happily engaged.'[4] In 1766, Blackburne began another movement, no less odious and dangerous in the eyes of all

[1] Watson's *Autobiog.*, p. 13. [2] Nichols' *Lit. An.*, iii. 25.
[3] Wakefield's *Memoirs*, p. 95. [4] Nichols, iii. 16.

who were content that the English Church should remain steady to the general course in which the Reformation had left it. In his 'Confessional,' published that year, and the petition to Parliament headed by him in 1772, Blackburne urged the abolition of subscription. Again Law sided with him. Many years before, in 1744, he had himself written a pamphlet entitled ' Considerations on the Propriety of requiring a Subscription to Articles of Faith '; and he now as a bishop approved of Blackburne's actions, wrote another pamphlet to enforce his arguments, and attended the committee at the Feathers Tavern when the petition in question was drawn up.[1] Law's action was the more liable to misrepresentation, as it was well known that several of the two hundred and fifty clergy who signed the petition had adopted Unitarian opinions. Blackburne himself declared in the most positive terms that 'he firmly believed in the divinity of Christ;'[2] and there seems no good reason whatever for supposing that Bishop Law was, as Belsham insinuated,[3] a Unitarian in thought. But the secession, upon the rejection of the petition, of Lindsey, Jebb, and others, brought suspicion upon all. The odium in which it involved Law is well expressed in an invective published under the title of 'Cambridge Triumphant':—

> But chief, O Law, to thee be honours paid.
> Well sits the mitre on thy hoary head:
> Wonder of bishops ! still pursue thy plan,
> Man to a brute, and God degrade to man.
> How can I count the labours of thy life ?
> With creeds and articles at constant strife ;
> With Blackburne leagued, in many a motley page,
> Immortal war with Mother Church to wage ;

[1] H. Walpole's *Memoirs of the Reign of George III.*, i. 9, 296; Lord Russell's *Memorials of C. J. Fox*, p. 71.
[2] Nichols, iii. 23.   [3] *Quart. Review.* xiv. 48.

Each fence that guards her altar to pull down,
And tack Geneva's cloak to prelate's gown ;

and so forth, in the same strain, concluding with a prophecy that ere long 'Humes and Gibbonses may wear lawn sleeves.'[1]

Although in these proceedings Edmund Law showed a courage and a firmness well worthy of respect, it was action to which very few Churchmen will accord more than a limited sympathy. It was especially an age in which full success to such endeavours would have been an unspeakable misfortune.

But on theological and philosophical subjects, and particularly on ground where the two intermix, Bishop Law has written much that is really valuable. In 1729 he published a translation, with notes, of Archbishop King's Latin treatise on the Origin of Evil, thus bringing into notice a work not then very accessible, but full of thought and learning. Horne says that when he was at Cambridge, between 1740 and 1765, this edition of King was in great request there, and extolled as a great repository of human science.[2] Referring to it in one of his later works, Law remarks that his leading thought in editing it was the hope that it would aid in 'justifying the ways of God to man.'[3] That his notes were thought highly of is sufficiently proved by Michaelis's translating them into German and lecturing upon them. In 1734 he wrote 'An Enquiry into the Ideas of Space, Time, Immensity, and Eternity'; and in 1745, 'Considerations on the Theory of Religion.' This last is a particularly interesting work, to be classed with Worthington's 'Essay on Redemption,' published about the same time, as a very favourable specimen of Broad Church theology in his time. It may be said, however, that its general tone is more like

---

[1] *Asylum for Fugitive Pieces*, 137–38.
[2] Jones's *Life of Bishop Horne*, p. 90.
[3] . Law's Advertisement to his *Considerations on Religion*.

that of the nineteenth than of the eighteenth century, and may be perused by modern readers with greater interest than most of the theological literature of that age. His main argument throughout is 'to show that arts and sciences, natural and revealed religion, have upon the whole been progressive from the creation of the world to the present time; as also that they have been suited to each other, as well as to the circumstances of mankind, during each eminent period of this their progress.'[1] He was convinced that such a persuasion would incline many to think that by waiting they would find their objections removed. It was agreeable to all analogy, to all the dispensations of Providence, to the whole constitution of things, that 'revelation should be propagated in a gradual, progressive, partial manner.'[2] He wishes it to be clearly understood that he does not speak of change in the primary essentials of Christianity. 'I desire, it may be observed once for all, that when I maintain improvements in religion, I do not intend a discovery of any new points, or improving upon the general doctrine of salvation, but only a more perfect comprehension of what was formerly delivered; a view of the extent and excellence of the great mystery concealed from former ages, and which was received but partially at least by the bulk of mankind, and soon adulterated to such a degree as may yet take more time to rectify it.' Especially in the exposition of Scripture, as something had already been done, so he hoped for much good yet to come 'by the help of a more sound philosophy, as well as by more sober rules of criticism, and more close, consistent methods of interpretation.'[3] He lamented the constant habit among his contemporaries of bemoaning the supposed degeneracy and increasing deterioration of the age. Such a supposition

---

[1] E. Law's Advertisement to his *Considerations on Religion*.
[2] *Id.*, p. 29.   [3] *Id.*, p. 299.

seemed to him to cast a cloud over the works of God, to confound our notions of His wisdom, power, and goodness, to raise distrust, if not disbelief, in His perfection, and thus also to deaden devotion and discourage effort.[1] Instead of ever looking back, and labouring to confine religion to the model of past times, we should learn rather, with the great apostle, to be 'reaching forward to those things that are before.' As regards the present he saw no reason for despondency. On the contrary, he believed (quoting Barrington) that the inhabitants of this country were, in the eighteenth century, far more virtuous than they had been in the thirteenth; and that, in particular, there was a spirit of benevolence, of toleration, and of liberty, to which no previous age could compare. 'Some partial fondness for the present times might be pardonable amid so much evident partiality against them.'[2] He granted that freedom of inquiry and debate had brought with it many errors and absurdities, and even libertinism and infidelity. But 'we have still reason to trust that, when truth and knowledge have got the better of error and superstition, the spirit of reformation will reform and rectify itself, and we shall have more of the new life and spirit of religion, as we draw nearer to those times wherein the word of prophecy has fixed its reign.'[3] He believed also that a good deal of the infidelity of the age proceeded from the very error which he wished to combat, that of being too confident that we wholly understand revelation, and that no serious misinterpretations of it have yet to be discovered.[4] He hoped much from a new and more correct version of the whole Bible.

To read this very noticeable work at once explains why Edmund Law was so opposed to subscription—which was

[1] *Considerations on Religion*, p. 283.   [2] *Id.*, p. 281.
[3] *Id.*, p. 208.   [4] *Id.*, p. 277.

more stringent than it is now—to precisely worded formularies. It was not so much that he was dissatisfied with them, or that they did not on the whole fairly express his own belief, as that he felt Christianity might be injuriously shackled in its gradual progress by a too rigid insistence on uniformity in those upon whom a special duty devolved of giving real thought to sacred subjects. There can be no doubt that his writings and action in this matter were greatly misconstrued at the time, and brought upon him much unjust suspicion.

Bishop Law also published an edition of Locke's works, with a life of the author, and several tracts, which attracted much greater popular attention than any of his more important works, on an Intermediate State between Death and Judgment.

His talent was inherited by his children. One of his sons was Baron Ellenborough; another, Bishop of Bath and Wells; and a third, Bishop of Elphin.[1]

Richard Watson was Bishop of Llandaff from 1782 to 1816. The English Church abounded throughout the eighteenth century in men who adorned an academical position, but were very indifferent prelates. Of this, Watson was a notorious example. It would have been better, perhaps, if he had never taken orders; it was certainly a misfortune to the Church that he should have been consecrated to episcopal responsibilities. To those who feel the value, in the high places of the Church, of sound practical sense, of freedom from mere ecclesiastical conventionalities, of liberality of thought and tolerance of feeling, of an aptitude in speaking or writing clear, forcible words, attractive to the popular ear, the character of Bishop Watson is especially a disappointing one. For he had all these qualities; and it must be added that on more than one occasion he employed

[1] Jefferson's *Carlisle*, p. 241.

his considerable talents to do good service in the Christian
cause. Yet, in spite of all his gifts, it is impossible not to
feel that he, and such as he, were depressing, to a calami-
tous extent, both the English Church and the estimation in
which it was held. All was spoilt in him by the absence
of some higher qualities, such as might be reasonably
looked for in any bishop. To speak of an utter secularity
in his tone of mind might give a wrong impression. One
or two essential truths of Christianity had undoubtedly a
firm hold upon his mind. But he would often acknowledge
that he had no particular regard for any one church more
than for another, or for any form of religion less wide than
Christianity in general. A belief thus vague and abstract
must at all events have an earnest spiritual element in it
if it is greatly to influence the life. In Watson there was
no appearance of this. To him faith was a teacher of good
morals and a good hope for the future. There it ended:
strong enough to preserve him from gross offence; strong
enough also to maintain in him a general good-will towards
mankind; but not strong enough to instil in him even a low
sense of responsibility in the great office he had accepted,
or to check his never-sated thirst for advancement and repute. He lived for a great part of his life exactly as a layman might, far away from his diocese, devoting his time to
politics, to economics, to agriculture, to science, digressing
occasionally from these more congenial interests to pen, in
the vigorous and popular style of which he was a master,
some short but telling answer to current attacks upon
Christianity. Such services are not to be undervalued, and
they brought him, not undeservedly, fame and repute. But
those who were acquainted with the author found no cause
in these writings for admiring him the more. A new success did but serve to feed his self-complacent vanity, and
to aggravate his querulous murmurs that preferment did

not swiftly follow upon what he considered his great and acknowledged merit.

Although he was infinitely inferior to Gilbert Burnet in all the higher qualifications of a prelate, he was much like him in other ways.[1] Like him, he was able, eloquent, and tolerant; like him, a strong Whig, and eager for reforms; like him, opinionative, interfering, and conceited. Perhaps he was conscious of a likeness which was real though it was too flattering to him; for he intended to write a History of his own Times, after the example of Burnet. He did not carry out this purpose; but he has left, written somewhat in the gossiping style of his illustrious predecessor, Anecdotes of his Life. These memoirs do not present a favourable picture of the man, and their candour would be more praiseworthy if it were not obvious that their author is usually, if not always, quite unconscious that many incidents which he relates are not by any means to his credit. No such suspicion crosses his mind. It is with singular complacency that he reviews his life, and admires both the ability which he had displayed during its progress, and the general success with which it had been crowned, until at last envy and faction had stepped in to arrest its further growth. He had come up to Cambridge a raw north country schoolboy, his manners awkward, his scholarship utterly devoid of that finish and refinement to which the public schools attached, as he thought, an absurd importance. What mattered it whether the Supreme Court at Athens were entitled Areopăgus or Areopāgus? But however weighted in the course, he had yet won his race. He had risen to a high place in the university—a polite and dignified college tutor, able at last to discourse in fluent Latin without a single false quantity. He had attained a confidence in himself which had almost the effect of genius.

[1] As remarked in an article in the *Quart. Review*, xviii. 235.

There was no sphere of learning, however new to him and untried, in which he was not prepared to hold the ground against all competitors. What was more important, he had seemed to have the power of inspiring into others a confidence in his ability no less unbounded. The chair of chemistry was vacant. Watson had never, he must confess, 'read a word of chemistry, or seen a single experiment;'[1] but why should he not stand for the professorship, especially as he was tired of mathematics? He did so; and though an eminent physician was an opponent, was yet unanimously elected, and was presently discoursing on chemistry[2] before full audiences. Presently a greater field, and one in which he was no less unversed, was opened to his ambition. Dr. Rutherforth, the learned Regius Professor of Divinity, died. Why should not he, Richard Watson, be appointed in his place? True, he said, 'my course of studies had been fully occupied in other pursuits; . . . with this "curta supellex" of theology, to take possession of the first theological chair in Europe seemed too daring an effort even for my intrepidity.'[3] But, amazing as such a thing might appear, this intrepidity was again successful; and the new Regius Professor, boldly vaunting his contemptuous disregard of fathers, councils, and the whole course of all ecclesiastical history, was wont to hold out the sacred volume in his hand, and to exclaim that he who had the Bible was a fully armed theologian, who had no need to trouble himself with any other encumbrances.

It must be acknowledged that Watson filled both his professorships with greater success than could have been expected. A theological professor who had never studied

[1] Watson's *Anecdotes, &c.,* i. 46.
[2] One singular result of his chemical studies was that in 1787, some years after he was made a bishop, a great improvement in the manufacture of gunpowder was carried out at his suggestion (*id.,* i. 263).
[3] *Id.,* p. 66.

theology, and a chemistry professor who had to learn the alphabet of the science, could not quickly become profound. But he had a great capacity of mastering with facility the main bearings of a subject and whatever details were needed for an immediate purpose, and great readiness and dexterity in argument served to fill up to outward appearance many a wide lacuna. Nor was he unaware of the advantages, even before an academical audience, of perfect self-assurance, a commanding figure, and a majestic voice.

In process of time he received his bishopric. It was given him on mere political grounds, and he accepted it on scarcely worthier grounds. He had, indeed, too honourable a spirit of independence to bind himself to the minister who had promoted him. But he evidently looked upon the bishopric of Llandaff as a sort of prize, very inadequate indeed to his merits, but still a seemly recognition of talent and intellectual industry. It scarcely occurred to him that any particular responsibilities were attached to the office. His health was not quite so good as it had been, and, moreover, there was no episcopal residence at Llandaff. Therefore, as a private fortune had been left to him, he settled quietly down to the life of a country gentleman in Westmoreland. In some of his writings he was not ashamed to dwell with truth and force on the good that may be done by a bishop who lives in his diocese, and devotes to it the best of his care and thought. But these were counsels for others, not for himself. Even his Regius professorship, which he continued to hold,[1] no longer gave him any concern, and its duties also were fulfilled only in such perfunctory manner as might be expected from a regular absentee. His very books were most of them left behind; for he betrayed, what otherwise would never have been suspected, that his studies had hitherto been carried on not so much

[1] Together with a number of other pluralities (*id.*, ii. 369).

from a generous love of learning as from a mere mercantile desire to turn them into means of advancement. The Ministry, he argued, were biassed against him; why then should he continue labours which would no longer bring him promotion? Forestry, therefore, and agriculture were henceforth the principal occupation of all his later years, varied, however, by the pamphleteering and speech-making of a busy politician.

It is difficult to read with patience the complacent pages in which he records all this gross abnegation of duty. Nor can it be doubted that, being, as he was, a man much before the world, he must have done much to lower the popular estimate of the Episcopate. Yet in the midst of this ignoble retirement he did some good work—work so useful, that though it employed the merest fraction of his time, even earnest Evangelical Churchmen seemed sometimes willing not only to condone all his negligence, but to raise him to a high rank among the principal living worthies of the Church. For his intellect retained all its facility of expressing argument in lucid and vigorous terms, well adapted to make impression on the popular mind. It cost him very little labour to send out a few sheets of pithy reasoning, which were read with delight, not only by cultivated men, but also by mechanics and small tradesmen. And when he did take this trouble, it was generally on a worthy subject. At one time it might be against the slave trade; at another, in favour of removing some odious remains of past intolerance; at another, to expose an abuse in the Church system, and to suggest a remedy. During the ferment of restless expectation excited among large classes by the French revolution a tract of his was widely circulated, and was thought to have done much good. But what earned him most gratitude from multitudes of religious people was his 'Apology for the Bible,' in answer to Paine's 'Age of Reason.'

It was not the first time he had been prominent among the defenders of Christianity. His answer to Gibbon, in 1776, had been one of the best replies to the offensive innuendos against Christian faith contained in the 'Decline and Fall of the Roman Empire.' Happily, when it appeared, it was not accompanied by a letter, written by him afterwards, which George III. might well call 'odd,'[1] containing as it did, in words of strangely exaggerated courtesy, a sort of excuse for the declaration of his belief, with a hope that the historian would pardon it. His answer to Paine was a more important work, and instantly passed through two large editions. Hannah More said, with justice, it was a pity a shilling poison should have a four-shilling antidote. Still, it appears to have been read largely by those to whom Paine had most addressed himself. In answer to the remark above, Watson was able to say that two butchers had been to his booksellers and bought one copy each, and the next day one of them had come and bought another.[2] It is too characteristic of its author to omit, that though he was gratified by its success, and by hope of good that it might effect, he appears to have been scarcely less gratified by the thought that it had taken him so little time. Admiration of the doer was generally an essential part of Watson's doings.

George Horne was a bishop for only two years (Norwich 1790-92), and for half of that time was disabled by weakness and ill-health. But he had long been well known in the Church as a man of much learning and great piety. For nearly thirty years he was to some extent a sort of religious leader at Oxford. He had entered at University College in 1745, at the age of fifteen. In 1750 he was elected to a Fellowship at Magdalen, and in 1768 to the Presidency of that college, which he held until his appoint-

[1] Watson's Anecdotes, &c., i. 108.   [2] H. More's Memoirs, i. 577.

ment to the Deanery of Canterbury in 1781. Throughout this period he was a principal member of a set of men, made up both of seniors and undergraduates of different colleges, who, from their adherence on many points to the religious and philosophical views of John Hutchinson, were called somewhat contemptuously 'Hutchinsonians.' They were limited in number, but thoroughly in earnest, strict in life, and strenuously opposed to the lax and latitudinarian principles around them. For their own part, with reactionary fervour, they went to an opposite extreme. To them, the Bible, rightly studied, was the sum of all human knowledge. Even the words and syllables of the sacred text, and all the imagery which it borrowed from natural objects, were, to their thoughts, pregnant with divine instruction.[1] They distrusted the Newtonian philosophy, as doubtful whether it were warranted in Scripture. The very name of 'natural religion' was an abhorrence to them, and Rationalism on spiritual subjects they held to be almost tantamount to infidelity. Especially they deplored the line which learned orthodox divines had taken for the last hundred years in their answers to Deistical objections. They would gladly see re-introduced the old Puritan mode of interpreting Scripture, freed only from what Puritans had overlaid it with.[2] In regard of the higher education, they could barely tolerate the existing university system. Its classics, its scholastic logic, its ethics and metaphysics, they held to be all but unchristian and irreligious. Such, in general terms, was the school of thought under which Horne's mind had been greatly formed. Nevertheless, he had in great measure maintained himself superior to its principal defects. His learning, his refinement of thought, his natural wit and humour, his constant association with men of culture, had preserved him from much of the narrowness and prejudice into which his opi-

[1] Jones's *Life of Horne*, p. 283, &c.   [2] *Id.*, p. 112.

nions might otherwise have led him. The Warburtonians sneered and disparaged; but there was the true salt of Christian living in him and in those who followed him. None could fail to respect the kindly, charitable, loving-hearted man, whose preaching [1] and example were so thoroughly full of simple and genuine devotion. It may be mentioned that when the notable highwayman Dumas was confined in Oxford gaol, prior to his execution, he would have no one but Horne to minister to him any spiritual counsel.[2] Some, after the manner of the time, called him a Methodist. This he was not; but he had a great esteem for Wesley, which the latter cordially reciprocated.[3]

Horne wrote various general and controversial treatises. Among the latter were an 'Answer to Clayton's Essay on Spirit,' 'Letters on Infidelity,' occasioned chiefly by Hume's publications, a 'Defence of the Divinity of Christ,' against Priestley, and various arguments against William Law and the mystics. But he is chiefly and best known by his devotional works. His Commentary on the Psalms passed quickly through many editions, and deserved its repute, not so much from its learning—though that is great—as by what Hannah More truly called its 'sweet and devout spirit.'[4] It originated in a conversation which he had in a stage-coach with a gentleman who, in a tone not unfrequent about that time, was declaring that the Psalms were 'nothing to us, and that other compositions more to the point should be substituted for them in our services.'[5] Horne spent twenty years over this work, which was published in 1776. His

[1] It may be mentioned here that Horne used to preach on St. John Baptist's Day from the stone pulpit in the quadrangle, which was decked round with green boughs in remembrance of the preaching in the wilderness. The custom had been discontinued (Jones's *Life of Horne*, p. 115).

[2] *Id.*, p. 75.

[3] Letter to Dr. Horne, 1762, Wesley's *Works*, ix. 117; and *cf.* Jones's *Life of Horne*, p. 162.

[4] H. More's *Memoirs*, ii. 107.   [5] Jones's *Life of Horne*, p. 112.

plan in it was first to give an analysis of the psalm, then a paraphrase of each verse, and then the substance of it digested into a prayer. To him it was truly a labour of love. 'Could the author,' said he, 'flatter himself that any one would take half the pleasure in reading the following exposition which he hath taken in writing it, he would not fear the loss of his labour. The employment detached him from the bustle and hurry of life, the din of politics, and the noise of folly—vanity and vexation flew away for a season—care and disquietude came not near his dwelling. He arose fresh as the morning to his task; the silence of the night invited him to pursue it; and he can truly say that food and rest were not preferred before it. Every psalm improved infinitely on his acquaintance with it, and no one gave him uneasiness but the last, for then he grieved that his work was done. Happier hours than those which have been spent on these meditations of the Songs of Sion he never expects to see in this world; very pleasantly did they pass, and moved smoothly and swiftly along; for when thus engaged he counted no time. They are gone, but have left a relish and fragrance upon the mind, and the remembrance of them is sweet.'[1]

Horne did a minor service to the devotional theology of his time by translating from the Greek Bishop Andrews' prayers, and so bringing them into notice and request.

It remains to mention his interest and sympathy in the affairs of the Scotch Episcopalian Church. He bestowed a panegyric on this communion which might well be valued as coming from the mouth of so good a man. 'He had,' he said, 'so high an opinion of it, as to think that if the great apostle of the Gentiles were on earth, and it were put to his choice with what denomination of Christians he would communicate, the preference would probably be given to the

[1] Preface to the *Paraphr. on the Psalms*.

Episcopalians of Scotland, as most like to the people he was used to.'[1]

John Douglas was Bishop of Carlisle from 1787 to 1791, and of Salisbury from 1791 to 1807. The 'Gentleman's Magazine' said of him at his death, 'The Church has lost one of its brightest ornaments, society one of its best friends, literary men in distress a generous patron, and the poor of all descriptions a father.'[2] No great exception can be taken to this praise, especially if it be understood from the point of view which might naturally be that of an English gentleman. Douglas was not particularly prominent as a bishop, and though estimable in that capacity, cannot be said to have represented it in anything approaching to its highest form. He was in a more thoroughly appropriate position as Dean of Windsor. Still, he would have adorned any society to which he belonged, being as he was a thoroughly upright and open-hearted man, generous and liberal in feeling, with an active intellect, highly cultivated tastes, and a bright, cheerful manner, which made his company universally attractive.

Douglas[3] was the grandson of an eminent clergyman in the Episcopal Church of Scotland, successor to Burnet in the living of Saltoun. It was the more natural, therefore, that in 1789 he should have shown much zeal in promoting the repeal of the disabilities under which that Church so long laboured. In early life he served for some time as an army chaplain in France and Ghent. At Fontenoy an officer invited him, as a Douglas, to join in the charge; but if he had had the wish, he could hardly have done so, laden as he was with watches and wills. Such reminiscences must have been revived in his memory thirty-five years later, in the time of

[1] Jones's *Life of Horne,* p. 157.
[2] Quoted in Cassan's *Bishops of Salisbury,* p. 360.
[3] This sketch is chiefly derived from Cassan's *Bishops of Salisbury* pp. 334-60.

the Gordon riots. He was then Canon of St. Paul's, and took an energetic part in providing for its security. He got within the building a detachment of guards, entertained them at his expense, and saved much from fire. About the middle of the century he travelled a good deal with Lord Pulteney. As a London clergyman, rector of St. Austin and St. Faith, while considered systematic and attentive in the business of his calling. he seems to have found time for multitudinous other employments. He was proctor for the diocese, President of Sion College, Vice-President of the Antiquarian Society, trustee of the British Museum, and a frequent writer on theological, political, and literary subjects. At the Literary Club, where most of the best known men of the day were wont to meet, his society was always welcome. For he was an excellent conversationalist, well able to make lively and interesting use of a strong memory, well stored both with general information, and especially with the secular and ecclesiastical history of his own and other countries. He was particularly noted among men of letters for his critical acumen, and for a lynx-eyed vigilance which seemed able to detect at once all attempts at literary fraud. Hence Goldsmith, in his 'Retaliation,' called him 'the scourge of impostors and terror of quacks.'[1] In theology he was much what might be expected from his general character. Thoroughly genuine and sincere on all religious subjects, he was in it, as in other matters, rather too much the man of the world[2] to understand much of the deeper spiritual feelings. Methodism he thoroughly distrusted, and thought little better of Romaine and the Evangelicals. He thought it was all 'enthusiasm'; and that 'although this might light up a false glare in the breasts of the credulous

---

[1] Cassan; cf. also Boswell's *Johnson*, i. 145, 182.

[2] Miss Burney speaks of him as more the easy-mannered man of the world than most other bishops (*Diary*, v. 393).

and the ignorant, it could never kindle in the mind of any sincere worshipper the pure flame of religion.' It was in this spirit that he wrote his 'Criterion,' a work which had considerable circulation among those who wondered with him that men should be 'so deficient in sense, and so mistaken in their ideas of religion, as to continue in their state of superstitious enchantment.'[1] Douglas might be, as Bishop Newton called him, 'a universal scholar, and one of the most knowing, intelligent men in the kingdom.'[2] He might also be, as he was, exemplary in his life, and beloved by many; but the greatest religious movement of his day was beyond his ken, and not known to his philosophy.

Mention yet remains to be made of a man of high distinction who adorned the episcopal bench at the close of the eighteenth century. Samuel Horsley (St. David's 1788-93, Rochester 1793-1802, St. Asaph 1802-6) is quite entitled to the name of a great bishop. Perhaps it may be even said that this title is more due to him than to any prelate who preceded him in that age. Others left behind them theological or philosophical works of far greater importance than anything which Horsley ever wrote. Others have a more universally recognised title to admiration and respect. Others have left a deeper stamp upon the history of their Church; but no English bishop of the eighteenth century was equal to him in those special characteristics which give to an ecclesiastical person dignity and power in his time. A wide range of theological and secular learning, great activity in his office, imposing eloquence, systematic business habits, skill in controversy, a deep interest in national and popular questions, a strong, uncompromising belief in the doctrines which he professed and the Church to which he was attached—such a combination of qualities could not but give him a weight and authority of no ordi-

[1] Douglas's *Criterion*, p. 179. [2] Newton's *Autobiog.*, p. 92.

nary kind. Even his faults were mostly those of a strong character. He was charged with being opinionative and peremptory, imperious and dictatorial, too fiery in his language, too impetuous in his assaults, too self-convinced of the excellence of each cause for which he was disputing to be always tolerant or just to those who differed from him. It was said of him that he was too dogmatic in his theology, and that he carried something of the same over-confident dogmatism into the realm of politics.

Horsley, like some others of the most eminent among English prelates, was of Nonconformist extraction. His grandfather had been a Dissenter, who afterwards conformed, and held an important London benefice. He was born in 1733. In 1759 he succeeded his father in the rectory of Newington; in 1767 he was elected Fellow of the Royal Society, and not long after, its secretary; in 1777 he became chaplain to Bishop Lowth; in 1781 he was appointed to the Archdeaconry of St. Albans. His vigour and energy in the controversy with Priestley was then attracting a widespread attention; and Lord Thurlow, saying of him that 'those who support the Church ought to be maintained by the Church,' made him, in 1783, Prebendary of Gloucester. His promotion to the Episcopate followed a few years later.

The diocese of St. David's, long accustomed either to mediocrities, or to bishops who, as it were, passed through it on their way to higher preferment, found in Horsley a ruler such as it had not had since Ottley. He did not, it is true, understand the language of the Welsh population. This was an accomplishment which, in the last century, might seem to have been considered a small matter by those who were appointed to Welsh bishoprics. But what he could do, he did. It was his special object to raise the level of the parochial clergy in his diocese, who were for

the most part very ignorant and poverty-stricken. There
were many who had cures worth no more than eight or
ten pounds a year,[1] and who were glad to eke out the
miserable pittance by the commonest servile labour. He
did much to improve their condition, and made himself
well and favourably known throughout the parishes by
continued travels among them, by frequent preaching in
the churches, by liberal kindness and useful counsels.[2]
His ordinations were vigilant; the reforms which he
instituted were regular and systematic. Ten years later
St. David's had such another chief pastor in Burgess. If
they had been more frequent throughout the Principality
in the last century the record of Church progress there
might have shown a very different character from that which
it actually wore. At Rochester and St. Asaph Horsley
was no less active; and his pastoral charges, always valuable in matter and forcible in style, were not the least
of his services to the Church.

He was by far the most powerful preacher of his day.
One instance of command over the feelings of an audience
is especially notable, though it probably owed more to the
circumstances of the time than to the eloquence of the
speaker. It was in Westminster Abbey, on the anniversary
of Charles I.'s execution, a few days only after the country
had thrilled with horror at that of Louis XVI. His congregation was the House of Lords, who attended divine
service there on that day according to custom, while the
Commons met at St. Margaret's Church. 'I perfectly
recollect,' says an eye-witness, 'his impressive manner,
and can fancy that the sound still vibrates in my ears,
when he burst into the peroration connecting together the
French and English regicides. So stirring were his words
that the whole assembly with one impulse rose to their feet,

[1] Nichols' *Lit. An.*, iv. 70.   [2] *Id.*; and Chalmers' *Biog.*

and remained standing till the sermon ended.[1] His renown, however, as a preacher was won not so much by bursts of eloquence or appeals to feeling—though these were not unfrequent—as by other merits. One was, that in an age which had been rather apt to undervalue specific theology, or at least to subordinate it in the pulpit to a general inculcation of Christian morality, Horsley, like the Evangelical clergy —with whom he otherwise had little in common—was wont to base his sermons clearly and conspicuously upon the distinctive truths of revelation. The other merit was an intellectual one. His was a thoroughly trained mind. He had gone deeply into mathematics, and into several of the abstruser branches of science. Well accustomed, therefore, to close and analytical reasoning, he often showed in his treatment of theological subjects an intellectual grasp which satisfied and delighted those highly educated audiences before whom he most loved to preach. He was never, indeed, tempted to stray beyond the limits of a strict orthodoxy. But at the end of the eighteenth century, when the reaction against Deism and all its allied forms had in England set in with full force, it was a great recommendation to a preacher to be at once so strong, and so wholly disinclined to tread in new paths. Under this condition, he rejoiced in grappling with difficult questions, and it was sometimes objected against his sermons that he was too fond of hard texts and disputed interpretations.

Horsley was a brilliant controversialist, though apt to be sometimes over-violent in language. Gibbon, who himself had had a passage of arms with Priestley, remarks with evident satisfaction of 'the dauntless philosopher of Birmingham,' how 'his Socinian shield has repeatedly been pierced by the mighty spear of Horsley.'[2] It is to the

---

[1] Nichols, iv. 685. It is quoted in Stanley's *Memorials of Westminster Abbey*, p. 535.   [2] Gibbon's *Memoirs*, p. 106.

bishop's credit that although he dissented with all his soul from his opponent's conclusions, he never condescended to the vulgar disparagement with which Priestley was commonly assailed, but willingly acknowledged not only his mental power, but also his personal piety. He met him fairly with solid argument. Samuel Coleridge, whose mind was at this time wavering in its transition from Unitarianism to orthodox Christianity, was evidently both interested in the discussion and influenced by it.[1]

Horsley's speeches in Parliament have been published in a separate form. A man of strong opinions both on civil and ecclesiastical matters, and having a ready power of expressing what he thought, he was not often content to give a silent vote on questions in which he thought the religious or other interests of the country were greatly concerned. This was especially the case during the period of the French Revolution. At that time more than ever, it seemed to him, as to many others, that the English constitution in Church and State was a palladium to be defended with all the enthusiasm of which men were capable. He saw in the French republic nothing less than 'the dreadful monster' of ancient Paganism 'beginning to rise in its ancient form out of the raging sea of anarchy and irreligion.'[2] The duty of resisting its aggressive progress appeared to him more sacred than any which in ordinary times would commend to Christians brotherhood and peace. When, in 1801, negotiations between the two countries were being discussed, Horsley did not hesitate to oppose them. He was ever, he said, the advocate of peace, 'but this was the mere counterfeit of peace, and germ of everlasting war.'[3] His horror of all approaches to Jacobinism sometimes led him into expressions which might give some colour to the

[1] Gilman's *Life of Coleridge*, pp. 157-60.
[2] Horsley's *Charges*, p. 93.   [3] Horsley's *Speeches*, p. 364.

charge of illiberal sentiment.[1] In 1795, Lord Lauderdale vehemently attacked him for an assertion that 'all the people had to do with the laws of the country was to obey them.' More, however, was made of this than was quite fair to the bishop. The context of his words, he replied, might sufficiently have shown he had simply meant, that where a law is clearly laid down, the subject, with every right to protest and petition against any grievance, has only to obey.[2] Among the subjects upon which Horsley spoke with much earnestness may be mentioned certain Bills relating to the observance of Sunday, the Bill for relief of the Scottish Episcopate, and those which on several occasions were brought forward, sometimes for new restrictions, sometimes for the removal of one or another of the stern penal laws which had been levelled against Roman Catholics. Although Horsley was opposed to opening high offices to them in Ireland, in all other respects he took the side of liberality and tolerance. On the slave trade he spoke with great energy and force upon ' the injustice and impolicy of that nefarious traffic; injustice which no considerations of policy could extenuate; impolicy equal in degree to the injustice.'[3]

Active as Horsley was in his pastoral duties as a bishop, and keen as was his interest in every religious, political, or social movement of the day, he contrived to find, almost to the end of his life, more or less time for his old scientific pursuits. His edition, with notes, of Sir Isaac Newton's works was published in five quarto volumes in 1788. In 1797 he contributed a paper on the achronycal rising of the Pleiades; in 1796, on the properties of the Greek and

---

[1] Although he declared intolerance was a thing to be abhorred (*Charges*, p. 175), he used expressions against Dissenters which they did not forgive, in reference to the ardour with which, for the most part, they for some time espoused the revolutionary cause in France.

[2] *Id.*, p. 176.   [3] *Id.*, p. 197.

Roman languages; in 1801, on the fundamental principles of mathematics. Other minor publications also exemplify the versatile activity of his mind. Amid controversies on Unitarianism or Calvinism, explanations of prophets, sermons, and thoughtful and elaborate charges to his clergy, we find him also writing in 1798 on the defence of the kingdom, and in 1796 on the scarcity of corn.

Personally he is described as somewhat irascible and dictatorial, but full of kindness and self-denying generosity, and very fond of children, in whose amusements he loved to join.[1]

With Horsley may end the list of the more notable among such English bishops as were created during the last forty years of the eighteenth century. Those who have yet to be mentioned may be spoken of more cursorily.

John Butler, Bishop of Oxford from 1777 to 1788, and afterwards of Hereford, is spoken of by Horace Walpole as 'a zealous courtier,' but a very sensible man, and the author of some able pamphlets. Indeed, the Letters of Junius were at one time ascribed to him. Hurd also seems to imply that he was too fond of great people, but also speaks of him with much affection and esteem. He describes him as 'a charming critic, and a lively, accomplished writer,' and in his sermons praises 'their constant vein of piety, good sense, and sound divinity.'

John Ross was Bishop of Exeter from 1778 to 1792. He was a very good man, plain and unimpressive in manner, a scholar who had published an excellent edition of Cicero's letters. Two pleasing incidents are mentioned of him. One is, that a sermon preached by him before the House of Lords in 1779, in which he expressed an earnest wish that toleration might be extended, and the fullest legal security given to Dissenters for the free exercise of

[1] Nichols, iv. 688

their worship, was instrumental in carrying out the Bill which authorised a declaration of Protestantism and belief in Scripture as a substitute for the subscription to the Articles before required from Nonconformist preachers.[1] The other is a little incident in the history of Methodism, contrasting favourably with the harsh treatment it sometimes met within the south-western counties. John Wesley, who had been receiving the holy sacrament in the cathedral, dined afterwards with the bishop. They parted well pleased with each other. Wesley, in his diary, commends Ross's 'genuine and unaffected courtesy,' and the furniture and equipments of the palace, 'nothing costly and showy, but just fit for a Christian bishop.'[2] The host, on the other hand, was no less pleasant with his guest, and with the fulness of information with which he conversed on a variety of literary topics. Some of the hot Churchmen of Exeter thought their bishop might have spared the compliment; 'but others considered it only another proof added to the many he had already given of his amiable courtesy, candour, and good sense.'[3]

Frederick Keppel, also Dean of Windsor, who preceded Ross at Exeter (1762–78), was one of those aristocratic dignitaries of whom it might be said—as of several others in that century—that he was a bishop because he was the son of an earl. He was in the political opposition, and strongly opposed to the American war.[4] In Exeter he was much esteemed.[5]

Ross was succeeded by William Buller (1792–97), Dean of Canterbury, and then by Henry Courtenay (1797–1803), who had previously been Bishop of Bristol (1794–97), of

[1] Skeat's *Hist. of the Free Churches*, p. 465.
[2] Wesley's *Works*, iv. 23 (*Diary*, July 18, 1782).
[3] *Gentleman's Magazine* for 1784, vol. liv. p. 280.
[4] Walpole's *Journal*, ii. 28.
[5] Polwhele's *Devon*, p. 324.

neither of whom there appears to be anything particular recorded.

Charles Moss (St. David's 1766-74, Bath and Wells 1774-1802) must be distinguished from his son of the same name who was made Bishop of Oxford in 1805. He had been chaplain to Sherlock. In 1800 Hannah More speaks of her venerable diocesan—he was then nearly ninety—as warmly supporting her in all good works.[1]

John Green (Lincoln 1761-79) had been Master of Corpus Christi College, Cambridge, Regius Professor of Divinity, and Dean of Lincoln. Archbishop Secker thought highly of his abilities; but he was of a rather indolent temperament, and did not make the use he might have done of them.[2] However, in those times a little supineness was not accounted much disparagement in a prelate of dignified and kindly manners, and Green was held in much esteem at Lincoln.[3] John Newton, the distinguished Evangelical leader, was ordained by him, and speaks warmly of his tenderness and candour.[4] He wrote against the Methodists, in letters to Berridge and Whitefield. The unblushing manner in which Church patronage was used in the Georgian era as a mere political instrument may be exemplified in a casual incident mentioned by Bishop Newton, who asked Green for a prebend for a friend. He would willingly, was the reply, bear his friend in memory, 'but at present he stood engaged eleven deep to the Duke of Newcastle, Lord Hardwick, and their friends.'[5]

Charles Lyttleton (Carlisle 1762-68) would doubtless, if he had lived longer, have been translated to a more important see. Being of noble family, brother of Lord Lyttleton, he was likely, Mr. Grenville said, to be raised to one of the

---

[1] H. More, *Works*, ii. 40. [2] Bishop Newton's *Life*, p. 27.
[3] *Id.*, p. 152. [4] John Newton's *Letters*, ii. 89.
[5] *Id.*, p. 151.

first appointments of this kind that fell vacant.[1] If he possessed no striking episcopal qualifications, he was, at all events, 'an affable, gentle, and benevolent man;'[2] moreover, a great antiquary, and President of the Antiquarian Society.[3] He had been a barrister, and afterwards Dean of Exeter.

Edward Vernon, afterwards Vernon Harcourt, son of Lord Vernon, was Bishop of Carlisle after Law, from 1791 to 1808, when he was raised to the Archbishopric of York. He was strongly opposed to the Roman Catholic claims.

Folliot Cornwell, previously Dean of Canterbury, was Bishop of Bristol from 1797 to 1803, then of Exeter, 1803 to 1809, and afterwards of Worcester, 1809 to 1831. He was an elegant scholar, of polished manners. But to Hurd's question, 'What has raised him to this dignity?'[4] the reply would be simple. He was nearly related to the Speaker, and he had been tutor to Lord Liverpool.[5]

Charles Buckner (Chichester 1798–1824) is spoken of in high terms as a zealous, urbane man, strongly attached to Protestant principles, and an active administrator of his diocese.[6] In his primary charge of 1799 he took a most desponding view alike of the Church and of the people in general. Religion was very evidently declining; there was more and more inattention to the ordinances of the Church; there was more rudeness of manners, more disorderly conduct, more profaneness and debauchery. He saw also, he said, great ministerial negligence, the fundamental cause of which was the frequent non-residence of clergymen.[7] We see in the general tone of his words a man who looked at

[1] Bp. Newton's *Life*, p. 115.   [2] Jefferson's *Carlisle*, p. 239.
[3] Nichols' *Lit. An.*, v. 380. He was a considerable benefactor to that Society, and got them their charter.
[4] Kilvert's *Hurd*, p. 324.   [5] *Public Characters*, 1823.
[6] Dallaway's *Chichester*, p. 97.
[7] *Gentleman's Mag.* for 1799, vol. lxix. p. 962.

things in a sombre aspect, but who was much in earnest to make them better.

William Cleaver,[1] Bishop of Chester from 1788 to 1800, and afterwards of Bangor, brother of the Archbishop of Dublin, was one of the 'Greek Play Bishops'; that is to say, he was best known among learned men by the extent and elegance of his erudition in Greek dramatic literature. At the same time he was also well informed on subjects more closely connected with his sacred profession. His 'Directions to the Younger Clergy on the Choice of Works in Divinity' was a useful digest, and one which implied considerable theological reading. He was also a good deal interested in the higher education of women.

Samuel Squire[2] (St. David's 1761-66) was a man of very considerable learning in early English, in constitutional history, and various branches of philology, and a frequent attendant at the Royal and Antiquarian Societies. He also wrote a treatise on the ancient history of the Hebrews, in answer to Morgan's Deistical work, 'The Moral Philosopher.' His elevation to the Episcopate, and various other preferments which he had previously held, were owing to the favour of the Duke of Newcastle, to whom he had been chaplain and private secretary.

John Warren was Bishop of St. David's from 1779 to 1783, and of Bangor from 1783 to 1800. Hurd says of his charges that they were like the man himself, 'plain, honest, and useful.'[3] He often spoke in Parliament, where the refined simplicity of his style and manner gained for him a favourable hearing.[4] He was quiet in temperament, a lover of tolerance, and, like most steady,

---

[1] Ormerod's *History of Cheshire*, p. 80; *Quart. Review*, iii. 210; xlv. 409; H. More's *Memoirs*, ii. 341.

[2] B. Jones and Freeman's *Hist. of St. David's*, p. 336; Kilvert's *Life of Hurd*, p. 82.

[3] Kilvert's *Hurd*, p. 156.   [4] Hansard, xxi. 761, note.

orthodox Churchmen of his day, had a great horror of 'wild enthusiasm.'[1]

The Hon. James Yorke (St. David's 1774-79, Gloucester 1779-81, Ely 1781-1808) is chiefly known as an ardent advocate for a revision of the Articles.[2] Richard Beadon (Gloucester 1789-1802), 'the worthy and learned orator of the University'[3] of Cambridge, was a good man, who was much interested in the Sunday school movement.[4] We hear of John Ewer (Llandaff 1761-68, Bangor 1768-74) in connection with the renewed agitation for bishops in America.[5] John Randolph, previously Regius Professor of Divinity, and afterwards Bishop of London, was an able administrator, a good scholar, and a well-known theologian; but he was made a bishop only in the last year of the century (Oxford 1799-1806, London 1807-23), and his episcopal life in no way belongs to that period. In Sodor and Man we find Richard Richmond (1773-80) vainly striving to stem the torrent of Methodism[6] which, after good Hildesley's death, invaded the island and for a time carried all before it.[7] His successors were George Mason (1780-94) and Claudius Crigan (1784-1813). The remaining English bishops of the last forty years of the century, whose names only need be given, are Edward Smallwell (St. David's 1783-88, Oxford 1788-99), William Stuart (St. David's 1794-1800), Robert Lambe (Peterborough 1764-69), Spencer Madan (Bristol 1792-94,[8] Peterborough 1794-1813), and Hon. John Harley, Dean of Windsor (Hereford 1781-88).

[1] Warren's *Sermon* of Jan. 31, 1781, p. 25.
[2] Porteus's *Life*, i. 39; Parr's *Life*, p. 117.   [3] Nichols, i. 564.
[4] H. More's *Memoirs*, ii. 54-73, 103.
[5] Beardsley's *Johnson*, p. 311.
[6] Wesley's *Works*, iv. 100.   [7] Keble's *Life of Wilson*, p. 970
[8] According to some accounts, Madan had gained an unenviable popularity, before he was a bishop, by taking an active part against Priestley in the Birmingham riots (Skeats' *Free Churches*, p. 506).

CHAPTER VIII.

THE ENGLISH CHURCH IN IRELAND, 1700-1800.

ALL Irish history in the eighteenth century is but the sad continuation of a dreary past. All through the long record of years which had elapsed since Adrian bestowed his Papal blessing on the arms of Henry II., there had been no one period in which the relations between the two islands had been even tolerably harmonious. It had been 'the miserable history of a half-subdued dependency.'[1] The English settlers had maintained their position and their ascendency, but had done little or nothing more. Wars and insurrections, savage feuds, wild retribution, penalties and confiscation, had repeated themselves through a series of ages. Henry VIII. did as little to create permanent peace as John or Edward II. Elizabeth, James I., and Cromwell were all in their several ways sincerely desirous to see Ireland tranquil and prosperous; but in each case, when the bitter process of reconquering had been concluded, some unhappy destiny seemed to prohibit the steady continuance of any tranquillising and statesmanlike policy. In Church matters, even before the Reformation, the discord had been proportionally great. The old Irish Church, proud of its insular independence, and of the splendour of its ancient annals, was very disinclined under any circumstances to surrender its distinguishing peculiarities, and to become merged in the uni-

[1] Goldwin Smith's *Irish History and Irish Character*, p. 1.

form system of the great Papal organisation. Still greater became such aversion when these ecclesiastical changes were proposed for their acceptance by the intruders of the English pale. Apart from the common basis of Christian truth, there could be nothing winning in a Church into which the stern temper of their victors had engrafted all the worst abuses of feudalism. For almost four centuries the National Church of Ireland and the Papal Church of the pale remained distinct and antagonistic. The Reformation did indeed unite the two, and that so strongly that nowhere else did the new Ultramontanism so thoroughly establish itself. But the old differences were succeeded by others which were deeper, and more productive than ever of bitterness and hate. Henceforth the war which raged upon the Continent between the rival creeds was superadded to the old hostility between the two races in Ireland. Those who wielded the secular power did not indeed go to the same length as in France or Spain. Protestantism could be excessively intolerant, yet not so utterly blind to the essential conditions of its existence as to push intolerance to its logical limit of extermination. If there had been no such check, yet the most relentless of inquisitors could not have entertained the thought of crushing out by fire and sword the convictions of an entire people. The English, therefore, never dreamt of practising in Ireland the persecutions under which their co-religionists were suffering abroad. Even the intolerance which stopped short of inflicting the extreme penalty was wont to veil itself under the specious name of political necessity. But within these bounds the Church of the recusant Irish was treated with a severity well adapted to leave such indignant resentment as scarcely a long lapse of years could obliterate. For some seventy years after the Reformation the Roman Catholic worship was entirely proscribed. 'The religious houses were gone, and the prohibition of the mass had closed the churches except in districts which were in armed and open rebellion. For many years, over the greater part of Ireland public worship was at an end. The Protestant clergy could not venture beyond the coast towns, and there they were far from welcome. The priests continued to confess and administer the sacraments, but it was in the chiefs' castles, or at stations in the mountain glens, to scanty and scattered families, and the single restraint on the passions of the people was fast disappearing.'[1] It must have been a melancholy spectacle to a traveller passing through the land to see the parish churches, as Bishop Bedall wrote of them in 1630, 'all, in a manner, ruined, and unroofed, and unrepaired.'[2] The fierce rebellion of 1641, its stern suppression by Cromwell, and the later commotions which disturbed the unhappy country, all added to the havoc. If, therefore, Swift could speak of churches in England at the opening of the eighteenth century as bearing such marks of defacement and ill-usage, as if Turks and heathens had invaded the country, he might well go on to speak of Ireland in much stronger terms, as though in not a few districts the tokens of Christianity had been utterly destroyed.[3]

It is impossible for us not to sympathise in the justly indignant words of an Irish Nationalist of 1799, when he exclaims, ' Even the Reformation itself, by which so many other countries were illustrated and improved, was made an instrument for brutalising Ireland. Without consulting the opinion of the Irish, without compassionately endeavouring by reason to dispel their errors, without affording means of improvement, or time for those means to operate, their religion was regulated by Act of Parliament

[1] Froude's *History of England*, x. 534; quoted in Godkin's *Ireland and her Churches*, p. 44. Lingard, however, speaks as if this proscription were less complete (*English Hist.*, vii. 86).
[2] In a letter to Laud, Godkin, p. 63.
[3] Serm. vi.; Swift's *Works*, vii. 482.

to the exact standard of English faith.'[1] Unhappily, as time went on, things did not improve. The reign of William III., mild and tolerant though he was by nature, is sadly disgraced by those provisions of the Penal Code which, in successive sessions of Parliament during the last years of the seventeenth century, were levelled one after another against the Roman Catholics of Ireland. It is needless here to repeat in detail the well-known list of regulations by which, as Roman Catholicism could not be trampled out, the attempt was made so to discourage and degrade it, that possibly it might die away, or at least be rendered powerless for mischief. This last was undoubtedly the main object, for in all the articles of the code the political and social effect is that which was mainly aimed at. The Irish people might remain Papists, if so it must be, provided all could be reduced to the level of ignorant squireens, small struggling farmers, and a sordid, poverty-stricken peasantry. For this they were precluded from the franchise, from the liberal professions, from holding freehold property; for this, estates were to be broken up by gavelkind, and parents were prohibited from educating their children at home or abroad. Protestant sons were permitted to disinherit, so to say, a Roman Catholic father, and intermarriage with Protestants was forbidden. A lame and partial excuse for such laws might have been alleged from the necessity of anticipating insurrection by studiously weakening the sources of influence and power. But no excuse was asked for. Even Dean Swift, whose active compassion for some of the wrongs which he beheld won from Irishmen enthusiastic honour, had yet nothing but admiration for the Penal Code. 'The Papists, God be praised, are, by the wisdom of our laws, put out of all visible possibility of hurting us; besides, their religion is so

---

[1] T. A. Emmet's 'Essay on the History of Ireland,' in W. J. Macniven's *Pieces of Irish History*, p. 3.

generally abhorred, that they have no advocates or abettors among Protestants to assist them.'[1] He elsewhere expresses an expectation that, under the late strong Acts against Popery in Ireland, it will daily crumble away, 'and in the meantime the common people, without leaders, without discipline or natural courage, ... are out of all capacity of doing any mischief if they were ever so well inclined.'[2] Instead of thinking the law too harsh, Englishmen were generally inclined to compare it complacently with what had been decreed against the Huguenots of France or the Lutherans of the Palatinate, and, above all, to point to the indulgent laxity with which the penal provisions were commonly administered. On this point Bishop King of Derry wrote, in 1697, more sensibly than most of his contemporaries. 'If,' said he, 'we should measure our temper by our laws, I think we are little short of the Inquisition; but if by the execution of them, I doubt we shall seem as indifferent in matters of religion as our neighbours in Holland: whereas soft laws and strict execution are what wisdom and interest would recommend us.'[3] But no doubt a certain laxity in administering it made the statute itself more permanent. Oppressive and degrading as it was, it yet did not shock the humanity of careless and superficial observers. People argued rather sophistically that it was unreasonable to describe as a penal code directed against Romanists laws which were in reality a protective code framed to defend the Protestants.[4] In fact, said others, they promote the benefit of the Papist,[5] they preserve him from restless agitation, and from the domineering presence of foreign ecclesiastics, and guard his industry from the pernicious influence of superabundant festivals.

[1] Serm. v.; Swift's *Works*, vii. 463.
[2] *Id.*, 'Letter on the Test;' *Works*, viii. 367.
[3] Bishop Mant's *Hist. of the Church of Ireland*, ii. 81.
[4] Mant, p. 75.   [5] *Id.*, p. 123

The code, therefore, remained in credit, and was even reinforced in 1703 by new measures, directed as before against all Papist recusants. It was not until more than seventy years of the eighteenth century had passed that any change of feeling set in. Many circumstances then combined to incline English statesmen toward juster and more generous counsels. Irish 'patriots' argued naturally but unfairly that all concessions were wrung from English fears, and that it was merely the rebellion of American colonists, anxiety about French advances, and afterwards the destruction of tyranny in the French Revolution, which at last extorted from Government a reluctant and partial redress of long-standing oppression.[1] It may be granted that England's experiences in America, and the European movement which came to its crisis in 1793, were favourable to greater liberty in Ireland. But, in any case, it would have been quite impossible for the Penal Code to have withstood the deep and ever-growing sentiment in favour of religious tolerance which already in the early years of George III.'s reign had gained hold upon the nation. Moreover, it was only to a very minor extent that these statutes had ever been directed against a particular religious creed. They had taken rise almost entirely from a conviction that a Romanist, and still more an Irish Romanist, could not be a loyal citizen, and that severe enactments were necessary for the public security. Now that Jacobitism was practically extinct, and even the most timid could not fear an interruption of the Protestant succession, the relaxation and ultimate removal of the code became inevitable. The Revolution itself did but check a movement which was already making fast and favourable progress. Pitt, in his purposes of giving to Ireland free trade, parliamentary reform, and a liberal education to the Romanist clergy,

[1] Macniven, Introd., xii.

was doing what her best friends could wish. 'But the liberal policy of Mr. Pitt, like the liberal policy of Continental reformers, was fatally arrested, and the world was flung into dismay, despair of liberty, and absolute reaction by the tremendous eruption of absurdity, cruelty, and ultimately of military vanity and rapacity which Frenchmen imagine to be the greatest and most beneficent event in history.'[1]

At the very beginning of the eighteenth century the majority of Roman Catholics over Protestants was not so overwhelming as at a later date. In 1672 the population of Ireland was reckoned to be 1,100,000, of whom 300,000 were Protestants, and 800,000 Roman Catholics.[2] For a time war prevented any great increase in the aggregate number, and the proportions may on the whole have remained nearly the same; but before long they greatly altered. The two Churches dwelt side by side alien and distinct, and members of the one rarely passed into the ranks of the other. The one, however, rapidly multiplied, while the other gradually dwindled. The native Irish, too destitute to have any idea of thrift, married early, and their hovels swarmed with children. The English and Scotch settlers, on the other hand, often found that, in spite of their political and social privileges, Ireland was no fit soil for making a livelihood. When population was yet thin they had obtained leases on favourable terms, and became prosperous with little trouble. When their leases expired circumstances had become altered. A ragged host thirsting for land were always ready to outbid them with offers which the landlords eagerly accepted. Then, also, England, with a policy as short-sighted as it was selfish,

[1] Goldwin Smith's *Irish History*, &c., p. 165.
[2] According to Sir W. Petty, the best authority of that time (R Murray's *Ireland and her Church*, p. 314).

had by high duties closed to them the woollen market; consequently for one reason or another they emigrated in numbers. The last-mentioned cause especially affected members of the Established Church, for the encouragement of linen manufactures gave full employment to the Presbyterians of Ulster. There were large emigrations of Protestants engaged in the wool trade in 1698–1700.[1] The difficulty of getting farms on advantageous terms drove out still greater numbers in 1717–20.[2] In 1728, Archbishop Boulter speaks of 'a phrenzy among Irish Protestants for the West Indies;' in the last summer, considerably more than three thousand had sailed.[3] Hundreds of families also, all Protestants, had removed out of the north to America.[4] The Irish Primate considered that at this time there were at least five Romanists to one Protestant.[5] This was taking the general average of the whole country. In some large districts the contrast of numbers was vastly greater. When Bishop Downes went in.1820 to his diocese of Elphin, on the Shannon, he wrote to a friend that for every Protestant there were fifty Papists.[6] Perhaps in this part of Connaught, and in the neighbouring counties of Mayo and Sligo, Roman Catholics were more immensely in the majority than elsewhere; but there were many parts of Ireland in which they outnumbered the Protestants by as many as twenty to one. There was, doubtless, many a beneficed clergyman who, like Dean Swift at Loracor, rarely ministered to more than half a score in all, 'most gentle, and all simple.' Sometimes, according to Lord Orrery, the Dean's congregation simply consisted of Roger the clerk.[7]

As the force of circumstances made Irish Romanists more ultramontane than any Italians, so, on the other side,

[1] Mant, ii. 121.   [2] Id., p. 330.
[3] Primate Boulter's *Letters*, i. 261.   [4] Id., p. 250.
[5] Id., pp. 123, 206.   [6] Mant, ii. 368.
[7] H. Craik's *Life of Swift*, p. 98.

Irish Protestants, Episcopalians no less than Presbyterians, were equally extravagant in their opposition to Rome. Had it not been so, they could have hardly defended the anomaly of their position. It is scarcely too much to say that, until somewhat better relations began to arise, they considered, or affected to consider, the mass of their fellow-countrymen in Ireland something in the same light as they would heathen savages. 'I am sure,' says Boulter, writing to the Bishop of London about the Charter Schools, 'your lordship will be glad of advancing the glory of God, and promoting His service among those who at present are ignorant of it.'[1] Thus, also, a memorial to the king, signed in 1730 by the Primate, the Lord Chancellor, the archbishops, and a number of earls, bishops, barons, judges, gentlemen, and beneficed clergymen, speaks of the means proper 'for the converting and civilising of these poor deluded people.'[2] Much after the same kind are the words of the Earl of Chesterfield on the need of some educational measures for Kerry and Connaught. 'Let us make them know,' says he, 'that there is a God, a king, and a Government, three things to which they are at present utter strangers.'[3] After all, there was some good foundation for such words. If dismal poverty, brutal ignorance, gross superstition, can degrade Christian men into heathens and savages, such agencies were not wanting in Ireland. Yet, perhaps, in spite of superstition and ignorance, their Christianity was more genuine and deep than that of the grasping and secular-minded men who were to be found in numbers among the ruling class. Their priests were, for the most part, illiterate in the extreme, but there is sufficient testimony of the unremitting zeal with which they often worked among

---

[1] Mant, ii. 518.   [2] *Id.*, p. 512.
[3] To Bishop Chenevix, Oct. 8, 1755; quoted in Mahon's *History*, iv. 131.

their people.¹ Their influence was by no means all that could be wished, but among other merits which may be justly ascribed to them, not the least was their great success in inculcating upon a passionate race the sacred duty of family purity.

If the mass of native Irishmen were indeed, as English Protestants were apt to assume, little better than idolatrous barbarians, it might be supposed that great efforts would at all events be made to convert them from their errors, no less than to elevate their general condition. The letter and memorial referred to in the last paragraph show that this duty was not altogether forgotten. But all such efforts were more or less transient and spasmodic, and were gradually blighted either by apathy or mismanagement. In 1703 the Irish House of Convocation passed various resolutions as to the need of preachers in the Irish tongue. 'The endeavouring,' it added, 'the speedy conversion of the Papists of this kingdom is a work of great piety and charity.'² At this time no very practical results followed. A little later, in 1709, the question was again moved in Convocation as a matter of great concern, which required the united application of all Protestants, and their most serious thoughts. Resolutions were agreed upon for printing in Irish the Bible and Liturgy, for providing and encouraging Irish preachers and catechists, for applying to Parliament for some provision for their maintenance, and lastly for establishing a charitable corporation to receive and manage moneys contributed for the purpose. At the same time the Dublin University, at the instance of the Archbishop, and with the consent of the Provost and Fellows,

---

¹ O'Beirne, an excellent bishop of the Established Church towards the end of the century, speaks of their activity in warm terms of admiration (Mant, ii. 738).
² Mant, ii. 164.

established an Irish professorship and private teacher of the language. In the next year a new impulse was given to the movement from a great number of Irish priests declining the oath of abjuration, and either leaving the kingdom, or withdrawing from all religious offices. Several zealous clergymen of the Established communion stepped into the gap, offered to baptise the children, and prayed and preached with the people. They met, we are told, in many cases with great and unexpected success. Many attended and warmly declared their preference of Irish to Latin prayers. Some even bought primers and learnt to spell out Scripture. Meanwhile the Committee of Convocation, headed by Archdeacon Parnell, the well-known author of 'The Hermit' and other poems, pressed the movement further. A memorial, signed by many of the nobility and clergy, was submitted to Queen Anne by the Duke of Ormond, Lord Lieutenant, and the Archbishop of York. The queen received it with much favour, and desired that the Irish Convocation and Parliament should at once discuss the question and draw up a Bill. Thus far it seemed likely that a movement would be inaugurated on some considerable scale for the religious and educational advantage of the Irish. Yet all ended in nothing. Although a certain number of noblemen in the Upper House felt real interest in the matter, this was by no means the case generally. The great majority of Protestant Irish laymen throughout the eighteenth century were distinguished for anything but zeal for religion. They detested Romanism, but valued their Protestantism chiefly, it would appear, as a means of upholding their political superiority, and were jealously anxious not to see their Church reinforced from the ranks of Irishmen. Nothing was further from their wishes than a national Protestant Church, strong in Irish support. 'They would have the natives made Protestant,' wrote a contemporary, but were 'deadly afraid of their coming into the Church.'[1] Others strongly objected to preaching or printing in Irish, lest it should tend to perpetuate a language which they hoped would gradually die out.

Among the clergymen who, in Queen Anne's reign, distinguished themselves for the truly evangelistic zeal with which they laboured among the Irish poor may be mentioned Nicholas Brown, rector of Dromore, and Walter Atkins, vicar of Middleton. It is certain that both these two won to a great extent the affections of their warm-hearted native hearers, and that threats and admonitions of the priests were quite ineffectual to prevent many of their people joining the Established communion. Mant records as one anecdote of Brown's preaching that a priest, troubled to see a number of native Irish listening with much attention to some prayers translated from the English Liturgy, told them aloud that all they heard had been stolen from the Church of Rome. 'Yes,' said one of the bystanders, 'but they have stolen the best, as thieves generally do.'[2] John Richardson, a clergyman of some literary distinction, should also be mentioned in connection with this movement, as devoting great labour, and most of his property, to printing religious works in Irish.

The Established Church of Ireland was at this time too scanty, too poverty-stricken, and too occupied with its own pressing needs, to be able to provide out of its own resources anything like a regular missionary organisation. Probably, also, the will was wanting too; for in Ireland, as well as in England, the stronger religious life which, on the whole, characterised the early years of the century, was followed by an ever-increasing apathy. Genuine self-denying zeal,

---

[1] Richardson to Swift, July 28, 1711; Mant, p. 224.
[2] Mant, ii. 166.

never too common, became less frequent than ever,[1] and it is not likely that anything short of this would make much impression on the Irish peasantry. Indeed, it was only under special circumstances that any effort whatever on the part of Protestants could make much ground against the deep-rooted prejudices of the people. Even Methodism, although better suited than many forms of Protestantism to an untaught and emotional people, was quite unable to make any advance among them. John Wesley spoke gratefully of the personal kindness he sometimes received from Irish cottars, and at Athlone and some other places they flocked to hear him,[2] but very few from among their ranks were numbered among his proselytes.

Schools for the young might offer a more promising field for Protestant enterprise. Much certainly might have been done for the general improvement of the poor if some scheme of national education had been carried out such as Swift suggested. 'It is indeed in the power of the lawgivers to found a school in every parish of the kingdom, for teaching the meaner and poorer sort to speak and to read the English tongue, and to provide a reasonable maintenance for the teachers.... And considering how small a tax would suffice for such a work, it is a public scandal that such a thing should never have been endeavoured, or perhaps so much as thought on.'[3] Some years later, chiefly between 1730 and 1737, were founded the Charter Schools, to which some allusion has already been made. The project had been set on foot by Maule, Bishop of Cloyne, and was taken up with great ardour by Primate Boulter. The correspondence of this somewhat secular-minded prelate

---

[1] We find Bishop Berkeley deploring the absence of missionary zeal among the Irish clergy (Mahon, iv. 131).
[2] Wesley's Journal, June 1748; *Works*, ii. 60.
[3] Serm. on the condition of Ireland, Swift's *Works*, viii. 7.

shows him to advantage whenever he touches upon this subject. Although it thoroughly fell in with the fixed policy, of which his letters are full, that of strengthening the English interest in Ireland, he also, in pleading for these schools, shows a real warmth of concern for the best welfare of the people which is scarcely to be traced in his other writings. While he urges the political wisdom of establishing a great system of English schools, he dwells with still greater emphasis on the hope of gradually bringing over the general multitudes to a purer faith. This was also put prominently forward in the charter obtained in 1733, at the urgent request of many of the principal men in Ireland, for the incorporation of 'a Society to promote English Protestant Schools in Ireland.' A number of these schools were established, and some of them no doubt did good. The successive viceroys, in their speeches at opening of parliaments, used very commonly to speak of them in terms of praise, as institutions founded in wisdom and humanity, and eminently entitled to public regard.[1] A specially valuable feature in them was the industrial element.[2] Nevertheless, they were often far indeed from being all that could be desired. The spirit of venality and corruption, which, bad as it was in England, was far worse in Ireland, found its way into the management of these schools, and turned, not unfrequently, almost into easy sinecures what had been designed for a great public benefit. Even where they were conducted honestly and well there was something essentially demoralising in a system which, by offering free maintenance, bribed parents to consent to the proselytising of their children.[3] A better and more really national system was submitted to the Irish Parliament in 1786. It was an

---

[1] Mant, ii. 698.
[2] Sermon by Wilcox, Bishop of Rochester, *On the Irish Working Schools*, 1739, p. 16.   [3] Godkin, p. 434.

excellent working scheme, carefully thought out, and there seemed a great likelihood that it would be carried into effect. But the unexpected death of the Duke of Rutland, then Lord Lieutenant, postponed the full consideration of the measure. Two or three months afterwards Parliament was prorogued, and the question of general education was not resumed.

On the whole, it must be acknowledged, with great regret, that the great mass of the Roman Catholic peasantry were, throughout the last century, disgracefully neglected. There were many exceptions; and, notwithstanding the bar of language, those who did show a genuine care for the people among whom they lived were sometimes loved with an affectionate gratitude greater than they would easily have found elsewhere. Two Protestant Bishops of Kilmore, one in the seventeenth and one in the eighteenth century, could have equally testified to this. Not even the fury of the terrible insurrection of 1641 could shake the love felt for good Bishop Bedell. A hundred years later, when Bishop Cumberland was buried by Bedell's side, we are told by his son that the Roman Catholic poor, 'who almost adored him while living, howled over his grave and rent the air with their lamentations.'[1] Irish history would have worn a very different hue if such examples had been more common. As Mr. Godkin says, with only too much truth, 'there are few things more astonishing in history than the way in which the mass of the Irish population, constituting so large a majority, were ignored even by the most fiery patriots who complained loudest of English misgovernment.'[2] The two races lived side by side, unlinked by any bond of union, the law doing, for the most part, all within its power to exaggerate the complete absence of all sympathy. If there

[1] Cumberland's *Memoirs*, quoted in Mant, ii. 655.
[2] Godkin's *Ireland and her Churches*, p. 574.

were not open animosities, or those never-ending bickerings which have made Kilkenny¹ a household proverb, there was apt to be avowed contempt on the one side and patient hatred on the other. They were seeds that ripened into a terrible harvest in the atrocities of 1798, horrors for which either party must equally divide the blame.² Although from about 1770 to the date of the outbreak a far better feeling had begun to grow up, both in regard of general opinion and in friendly relations between the two races, no gradual change such as this, however favourable, could lightly remedy the sins of the past.

Before leaving this part of the subject it may be added that Bishop Watson of Llandaff, with a few other Liberals of that date, were quite alive to the very anomalous position of their Church in Ireland. 'Co-establishment,' he said in 1789, 'ought to have been long ago set on foot there.'³ It might not, he remarked at a later date, be politically expedient, but it would be none the less right, just, and lawful.⁴

The contrasted terms 'Papist' and 'Protestant' occur

---

¹ The constant contentions of the two populations, who were separated by a narrow stream, gave rise to the saying about Kilkenny cats (Craik's *Life of Swift*, p. 11).

² *Cf.* the words of Sir Jonah Barrington : 'I was myself in the midst of the tumult, a zealous loyalist, an officer in the corps of barristers, an active partisan, in a word, a strong adherent of government – but not a blind one. I could not shut my eyes, I could not close my ears ; I would not pervert my reason ; and the full use of those faculties at that time enables me to state as an historic fact—which some will deny, and many will discredit — that the barbarities of that period (though not precisely) were pretty nearly balanced between the conflicting parties' (*Personal Sketches of his own Times*, ii. 345). The frightful vindictiveness which inflamed both parties is equally evident in the correspondence of Lord Cornwallis, Lord Lieutenant and Commander-in-Chief at the time of the rebellion. He declares it made his office complete misery to him (*Correspondence*, ii. 355, 369, &c.). His own temper was admirable, and so were the instructions under which he acted ; but many of the principal men about him would have hailed with delight a religious crusade and a war of extirpation (pp. 356, 372, 415). And hatred on the other hand was no less intense.

³ Watson's *Anecdotes of his Life*, i. 395.   ⁴ *Id.*, ii. 74.

so continually in Irish history of the eighteenth century, that a casual and uninformed reader might well suppose that the religion of the minority presented one uniform front against what was spoken of as the common enemy. In reality there was very little amity between Episcopalians and Presbyterians. The latter formed an important section of the community. After the unsuccessful rebellion of Tyrconnell and Tyrone in the reign of James I., the confiscated lands, scantily peopled by a mere remnant of the once turbulent men of Ulster, were portioned out into six new counties, and planted partly with English Puritans, but chiefly with settlers from Scotland. Under Strafford the Presbyterians were discountenanced and harassed; in the insurrection of 1641 they were involved in the ban which had gone forth against all Protestants in Ireland. After Cromwell had crushed the rebellion they were strongly reinforced by new Scottish immigrants, and were for some years the dominant power. At the Restoration their clergy were evicted, and Episcopacy became once more supreme. But Presbyterians could not afford to resent their loss of influence. Both Churches felt themselves in the presence of a resentful and watchful foe, who was beginning to gain not strength only, but also the royal favour. Englishmen and Scotchmen, Churchmen and Dissenters, were ready for a time almost to sink their difference rather than let their disunion give advantage to Roman Catholics. After the final repulse of James II. the Established Church in Ireland was placed in a position of complete ascendency. Presbyterianism fell into a very depressed condition. Many of its chief members conformed; the transition being all the easier because a strong Puritan element had combined with hostility towards Rome to make the English settlers much more favourable to Low Church views than their kinsmen across the Channel. 'The highest Tories,' said Swift, 'in

Ireland would make tolerable Whigs in England.'[1] Archbishop King said in 1706 that although the Presbyterians were stronger in the diocese of Derry than in any other part of Ireland, yet that even in it there were but nine of their congregations, as compared with forty-two of Churchmen. He added that they had become very lax in religious worship, only one Presbyterian out of ten attending any divine worship; while their celebrations of the Lord's Supper were so rare that for the whole of seven years there had only been nine throughout the diocese.[2] It is possible that King, although a thoroughly honest and good man, might not have been perfectly accurate in his statistics, but they show, at any rate, that Presbyterianism was not flourishing. The archbishop adds that during his visitation they everywhere crowded to his preaching, and that he was accustomed to 'entertain them with a discourse generally showing the non-necessity of separation on their own principles.'[3] At Dublin, on the other hand, about the same time, a correspondent of Thoresby deplores the violent animosities which he found raging between the two communions.[4] There were some who even attempted to raise a foolish 'Church in danger' cry, and who professed to fear that Presbyterians, being so active and industrious a body, might once again reign and oppress them with a grievous yoke. About 1731, Swift declared there were many hot-headed men among them who, however much they might hate the Roman Catholics, were more alienated still from the Established clergy.[5] Whether, however, they were formidable or not, there was no inclination to relax the law in their favour. Year after year, between the beginning of the century and 1733, the Presbyterians

---

[1] Swift, 'On the Test,' 1708; *Works*, viii. 364.   [2] Mant, ii. 22.
[3] *Id.*, p. 105.   [4] Thoresby's *Diary*, April 1709, ii. 157.
[5] 'The Presbyterian Plea,' Swift's *Works*, viii. 417.

strove in vain to be relieved from the vexatious burden of the test. After that date they for some time gave up the attempt as useless. The concession was, however, made in 1780—a good example which was not followed in England until almost another half-century had expired. Throughout the middle of the century the Irish Presbyterians seem to have shared in the disintegration which was at that time affecting their communion in England. Many of the more moderate among them conformed, many joined the Methodist bodies, many others adopted views scarcely to be distinguished from those of Deists. Towards the end of the century they had very generally adopted strong republican principles. Hence arose a remarkable coalition. Hitherto they had detested Popery and all that belonged to it as much as Knox himself; but the spirit of the Commonwealth appeared to have survived in them more visibly than anywhere else throughout the king's dominions, and the revolutionary movement in France awoke in them a great longing for an Irish republic. The barrier of religious prejudice was for the time swept away by what had become a stronger passion still. In 1791 and the following years they eagerly [1] joined the associations of the 'United Irishmen'; and though they nominally affected only to support the demand for reform of Parliament and Roman Catholic emancipation,[2] there were many who were fully at one with their colleagues of the Roman creed in the ulterior objects which their more advanced members chiefly cared for. Some of the Presbyterian clergy of Belfast were even bold enough to pray openly in their pulpits for the success of the republican arms. This lasted for some four or five

---

[1] Even strict Covenantors pressed into the secret clubs (Macniven, p. 49).
[2] How far the Presbyterians desired Roman Catholic emancipation is not quite clear. Emmet says it was one of their dearest objects (Macniven, p. 31). The editor of the *Cornwallis Correspondence* (ii. 342) asserts that they did not at any time advocate it.

years, and then there came a change. The atrocities and the rampant atheism which had been witnessed in Paris dismayed the Presbyterians, and made them recoil. They shrank also from being drawn into open rebellion against English rule. Neither were they content to find themselves no longer prime agents in the movement, but a weak minority, likely to be borne down the stream by the influx into the ranks of the United Irishmen of new multitudes from the eastern and western counties.[1] Happily, therefore, they were not nearly so implicated as might have seemed at one time probable in the rising of 1698. Early in the present century their condition again improved, and they shared in that revival of religious life which began gradually to quicken the energies of their neighbours in the Established Church.

As for the Established Church itself, its history in Ireland all through the century is one which no Churchman can follow with any satisfaction. It continued the old record of a Church calling itself national with no valid title to the name. Still, as before, it was a Church imposed by conquerors on a reluctant people, stamped as before with the defects inherent to such a state. The political motives and secular objects which had preyed upon its life for so many long generations, if abated in some respects, were in others aggravated. Until near the end of the century the country was in peace. The faults, therefore, of the dominant Church were not, as in some old days, those of a warlike period; but the misgovernment, the abuses, the political corruption, under which the province suffered in its civil relations, extended also to its ecclesiastical state.

English statesmen scarcely thought of the Established Church of Ireland as a spiritual organisation. They knew,

[1] *Cornwallis Correspondence*, ii. 363.

of course, that the Protestantism of the country mainly depended upon it for its services of religion. But being also well aware that Irish Churchmen were but a small section of the whole population, and that this proportion was largely made up, except in some of the coast towns, of scattered gentry who were apt to be lax in their religious views, careless of church attendance, and not over-particular about their bishops or their clergy, they thought, therefore, that for such spiritual duties as were required, one clergyman would do about as well as another. They felt, therefore, free to dispense patronage almost exclusively by political and party considerations. From these points of view Irish Church patronage was both valuable and important. Ever since Christianity had been established in Ireland bishops had been comparatively more numerous there than in any other part of the world. It had been a peculiarity of the Keltic Church in that country, and in mediæval times had been cherished all the more because it was not conformable to Romish usage. At and since the Reformation a number of sees had lapsed and been merged into others. But in the eighteenth century they would still have been numerous even if the country in general had acknowledged their ecclesiastical authority. In proportion merely to the number of square miles, there were about thirteen in Ireland to every eight in England. In proportion to the whole population there were about two in the smaller country to one in the larger. In proportion, however, to the number of Protestant Churchmen, the ratio of the Irish Episcopate to that of England must have been more than twenty to one. All the bishops were appointed by the Crown, and the patronage of far more than half the benefices was vested in the bishops. The Crown also had many livings at its disposal. Thus, in one way or another, directly or indirectly, the English Government could fill almost all places of importance in the Irish Church with occupants whose views were agreeable to their own. Where the ruling race were comparatively so few in number, this was a matter of real political importance. The bishops in particular were not only, in such a body, men of much social importance, but also had their seats and votes in the Irish Parliament, and, not being over-burdened with work, had much leisure to attend its sittings. It was matter for very reasonable and not unfrequent complaints among the temporal lords, that as there were twenty-two bishops in Parliament, and seldom so many of their own number, they were always liable to be outvoted.[1] The English Government, on the other hand, whose main object on all Irish questions was to govern the country with as little trouble as possible, and who looked with much distrust on many of the nobility, were very well content to see so much power in the hand of their own nominees. Above all, it was considered a matter of great State concern that the Primate should be a man who was thoroughly competent to take a leading place in the politics and administration of the island, and one who could be quite trusted to support English interests. This was the more urgent, as it was part of the slack and corrupt system for the Lord Lieutenant to be a constant absentee, coming into residence in the castle at intervals, and at other times doing his work by deputy, and receiving his salary with little corresponding expense. This was particularly the case, and almost as a matter of course, in the second year of each lieutenancy.[2] At such times the functions of the absent viceroy devolved partly upon his Cabinet and the Chief Secretary, and partly, at least on many occasions, on the Archbishop of Armagh. Indeed, there was no time in which he was not expected to be a

[1] Mant, ii. 285.   [2] Mahon, iv. 127.

very responsible State personage.¹ When the Irish Primacy was offered to Bishop Newton, Mr. Grenville told him that 'he should expect him always to be one of the Lords Justices, constantly to correspond with him, and to give him constant intelligence of everything material; he should rely upon his advice as upon a friend on whom he should repose the greatest trust and confidence.'² Such, in a pre-eminent degree, was Archbishop Boulter, Primate from 1724 to 1742; but his predecessors, and those who came after him, held a very similar position. In accordance also with this policy, every Primate throughout the century, after Boyle, who died in 1702, was by birth an Englishman. In the more distinguished Irish ecclesiastics of the eighteenth century there was a strange resuscitation of mediæval precedents. There was much in common between Boulter or Robinson and the feudal prelates imposed by the early Norman kings upon some half-conquered English province. At the beginning of the century, Primate Marsh, although very careful and diligent as a great officer of State, was more the bishop than the politician, and had little taste for the public business to which he was compelled to devote no little of his time. Newcombe, at the end of the century, was appointed by the special wish of George III., who, unlike some of his Cabinet, cared much more for episcopal and theological qualifications in an Irish archbishop than for what might be his business talents. Lindsay was generally considered a weak man for so high an office. Stone, even if he had been a statesman only, and not also a bishop, would be considered ambitious and worldly-minded. Boulter, John Hoadly, and Robinson (afterwards Lord Rokeby) were too secular in tone. But apart from all question as to the desirability of combining civil with eccle-

¹ King speaks of the Primate as being officially at the head of the Council (Mant, ii. 411). ² Newton's *Autobiography*, p. 113.

siastical offices, if Government simply required men of ability and judgment, who, holding an influential and independent position, should reside permanently in Ireland and act as their responsible agents, to give trustworthy information and conscientious advice, they might well have made a worse choice than the Primates. The Protestant nobility —and none others were admissible to office—were often non-resident, often steeped in prejudices, and often bent on turning all administration to the exclusive benefit of an Irish[1] clique. It would be the fault of those who had the patronage if the bishops, headed by their Primate, were not comparatively free from any of these objections. Of course they would be strong upholders of their own Church, and perhaps obnoxious on this account both to Roman Catholics and Presbyterians. This, however, would be a recommendation rather than not, for it was a thoroughly established principle of Irish Government that no countenance should be given to any other creed. English opinion had nothing to say upon the matter. It would not for an instant have brooked any approach to ecclesiastical predominance in English councils. So far, on the other hand, as it felt concern at all in Irish matters, it would doubtless have been very well content that in a land where Papists swarmed, English bishops should be largely admitted into the confidence of its Protestant rulers.

The bishops fulfilled without reproach their share in civil duties. No breach of trust nor offence against integrity and honour appears to have been imputed against any of them. Their presence was a distinct gain to the general character of the Irish House of Lords; and as they were not responsible for the intolerance of the system under which they acted, it is some praise that it was not aggravated by

[1] 'Irish' in the sense spoken of in the next page.

intolerant words or acts on their part, and that they generally used their influence in the direction of lenity and moderation. On the other hand, not one of them, unless Marsh be partly excepted, was ever wise enough or bold enough—for such action would have met with the most vehement and passionate opposition—to expose the fundamental causes of misgovernment in Ireland, and to make a firm stand for the just rights of its people. Many qualities of heart and intellect were needed to produce a man thus superior to the rooted prejudices of his time. Still, a great opportunity was lost, worthy no less of a Churchman than of a statesman, for an eighteenth-century bishop to have come prominently forward as the Stephen Langton of an oppressed nationality. If, in particular, Primate Boulter had used his intimate relations with Government, and his very considerable powers of administration, with as much zeal in behalf of the whole Irish people as he exhibited in support of what was called the English interest, he might have won for himself much gratitude and a great name.

Readers of Irish history, in this period, hear more than enough of ' Irish and English interest.' The former term has a much smaller meaning than might naturally be expected. It did not the least mean the interests of the Irish people, but simply those of a limited party of native Protestants who considered that all ruling power, and all promotion both in Church and State in Ireland, should be their exclusive property. To be independent, or nearly so, of England, and to rule the Irish as once they were ruled by the oligarchs of the pale, was their great ambition. The English interest, on the other hand, aimed at placing all posts of high office, both secular and ecclesiastical, into the hands of Englishmen, and ruling the island as altogether an English dependency. It was a favourite scheme of Walpole, and one which he determined largely to promote, by using all his

Church patronage in Ireland in such manner as thoroughly to infuse the whole body of the bishops and clergy not only with decided Hanoverian principles, but also with strong English sympathies. He determined to fill secular offices in the same manner; and his plan had the further recommendation that it would greatly help him in rewarding trusty supporters. Moreover, it would be occasionally convenient to give preferment in these remoter and more secluded parts to men whose promotion might not give general satisfaction at home. He carried out his design, but not without much resistance. The Irish Protestants, and some even of the Roman Catholics, forgot for a time their older differences, to combine against this new invasion of men and ideas from England. 'We consist,' said Swift, 'of two parties. I do not mean Popish and Protestant, High and Low, Episcopalian and sectarian, Whig and Tory; but those of English extraction who happen to be born in this kingdom, and the gentlemen sent from the other side to possess most of the chief employments here. The latter party is very much enlarged by the whole power in the Church, the law, the army, the revenue, and the civil administration deposited in their hands, although, for political ends, and to save appearances, some employments are still distributed to persons born here.'[1] Primate Boulter, on the 'English' side, threw himself heartily into Walpole's policy, and was strongly impressed with its importance. His letters to the home Government are full of it. As soon as he anticipates that a bishopric may soon be vacant, he emphatically urges the importance of filling up the appointment, when it occurs, with careful regard to the English interest.[2] Thus, when Cashel was vacant, he writes both to Carteret and the Duke of Newcastle, ' My Lord Chancellor and I have been comput-

[1] 'Advice to the Freemen of Dublin,' Swift's *Works*, vii. 362.
[2] Boulter's *Letters, passim.*

ing that if some person be not brought over from England to the bench, there will be thirteen Irish to nine English bishops here, which we think will be a dangerous situation.'[1] So, again, of Dublin : ' I am satisfied there will be a good deal of murmuring here to see the archbishopric filled with an Englishman, but I think it is a post of that consequence as to be worth filling aright, though it should occasion murmuring.'[2] In dignity and true worth Archbishop King was at the head of the 'Irish interest,' but Dean Swift was its most able and impetuous champion, and it may be well understood how unsparingly he discharged the vials of his wrath upon these imported Englishmen. Of course he was the idol of his party, who looked upon the new-comers with the extremest jealousy as ' foreigners ' and ' intruders.'[3] Any one, said Boulter, alluding to Swift, can grow popular by setting up for the Irish interest.[4] At the same time Swift had more title to such popularity than many ; for the limits of his Irish patriotism, narrow as they were, were yet somewhat larger and more comprehensive of the country as a whole than was the case with most of his partisans.

It is plain, upon the face of it, that this wholesale introduction of political motives in the dispensing of Irish ecclesiastical patronage was very pernicious to the spiritual well-being of the Church. As for the appointments themselves, many were quite unobjectionable, or distinctly good. This might well be the case, for there was necessarily a much larger choice of deserving men in England than in the small Irish community. But some were bad. Primate Boulter was well aware that the Ministry was apt to be not too particular when Irish preferment was in the question ; we

[1] Feb. 18, 1726-27 ; i. 141, 139. [2] *Id.*, p. 135.
[3] Downes to Nicolson, in Nicolson's *Letters*, Feb. 20, 1719-20, p. 569 ; also Boulter's *Letters*, p. 1.   [4] Boulter, ii. 54.

find him repeatedly begging that a good man be sent, and not one who is mainly recommended by being 'troublesome or uneasy elsewhere.'[1] There were instances, also, where heterodoxy, which would not have been tolerated in preferring to an English bishopric, seems to have been thought no bar to one in Ireland.

In the system of patronage, a clergyman's zeal and efficiency in his calling was made a very secondary consideration. Swift declared in 1733, that 'from the highest prelate to the lowest vicar . . . there were hardly ten clergymen throughout the whole kingdom for more than nineteen years who had not been either preferred entirely upon account of their declared affection to the Hanover line, or higher promoted as the due reward of the same merit.'[2] This was bad enough, but the regular preferment-hunting which the policy involved and encouraged was worse still. The deserving men stopped at home and worked in their parishes, unregarded by those who had the power of placing them in a larger sphere. The self-seekers went up to London, paraded their devotion to the ruling powers, and competed with one another for the favour of Ministers. As early as 1696, King writes to Bishop Lloyd, begging him to use his best, in behalf of the Irish Church, to stop such canvassing.[3] He elsewhere, in 1714, deplores the loss of heart and the loss of ground which his Church had suffered through this cause.[4] Even the preferments which were in his own gift were no longer his own. When there were deserving men in his own diocese, for whom, in the then impoverished state of the Church, he could barely find a livelihood of some 50*l.* a year by uniting several parishes together, directions would come from England calling upon him to give promo-

---

[1] Boulter, ii. 274, 117, 139, &c. So also Abp. King to Gibson, Mant, ii. 289.   [2] Quoted in Mant, ii. 568.
[3] Mant, ii. 68.   [4] *Id.*, p. 269.

tion to the amount of 200*l*. per annum—'in many dioceses near a fifth part of the maintenance of the clergy of the whole diocese'—to some 'cast clergyman whom you are not willing to prefer in England.'[1] He attributed it partly to the prevailing ignorance of Irish affairs in the sister country, but it was none the less a cruel wrong.

The passage just referred to does not exaggerate the impoverished condition of the Established Church of Ireland in the earlier years of the eighteenth century. Privileged though it was, and propped up, chiefly for political reasons, by a whole code of exclusive and intolerant laws, it was yet in a state of miserable destitution. From a mere temporal, as well as from most other points of view, Archbishop Marsh might well speak of 'this poor distressed Church,' and Archbishop King of its 'crazy and languishing condition.' The lot of many an Irish vicar was for many years a very unenviable one. Scowled at by the mass of his nominal parishioners as a heretic and alien, eyed with jealousy and disparagement by his Presbyterian neighbours, if there were any near him, defrauded by rapacious proprietors who had long fattened upon the spoils of the Church, he often had to bear at one and the same time the reproach of rank pluralism and the cares of pinching poverty. For ecclesiastical property had become very ruined and dilapidated. Churches in tolerable repair were few. Great numbers had been levelled to the ground; many were half burnt or unroofed ruins.[2] In parish after parish there was no house, no glebe.[3] Laymen had everywhere taken advantage of the unsettled and neglected state of the country to seize and impropriate tithes and church land. The tithes, where they did exist, were very precarious. Archbishop King wrote in 1707 that among his clergy there were not more than five who had 100*l*. per annum. 'Above a dozen have

[1] Mant, ii. 289, 274.   [2] *Id.*, ii. 17, &c.   [3] Boulter, i. 211, &c.

not 40*l.* per annum; several have nothing at all certain; and some have but 10*l.* or 16*l.* per annum.'[1] In a majority of cases a bare pittance was, as we have already seen, only obtainable by massing a number of parishes together, a custom constantly alluded to as an absolute necessity of the time. The bishoprics, even when the revenues of the Church were at the lowest, were, with few exceptions, provided for. They were too important politically to be allowed to fall into the same decay. But in Connaught, if not elsewhere, a great part of their revenues were obtained in a manner which told a tale of great poverty elsewhere. 'In most parishes,' says Sir James Ware, writing about 1734, 'the impropriator has half the tithe, the bishop the quarter.'[2] An improvement set in with the earlier years of the century. All the best of the bishops set themselves with commendable vigour to leave their Church less needy than they found it, and many made legacies for the same purpose. 'I have made shift,' wrote King, 'since I came to this diocese, which is about ten years, to get seventeen churches built and rebuilt, and as many repaired.'[3] The restoration of the firstfruits by Queen Anne was even a greater boon to the Irish than to the English Church. Various Acts of Parliament were also passed to facilitate the building of parsonages, to encourage the building of churches, and to secure to clergymen their tithes. Moreover, the value of land greatly increased on account of a large development in the cattle trade, through an outbreak of murrain on the Continent.

But in 1734 the Established Church was again plunged into poverty almost greater than before by the act of the Protestant landowners. That same eager competition for land on any terms which had lately driven out of the country numbers of English and Scotch farmers, had raised

[1] Mant, ii. 204.
[2] Sir Jas. Ware, *History of the Bishops of Ireland*, p. 619.
[3] Mant, ii. 205.

rent so high that it was scarcely possible to pay it. The owners solved their difficulty for the time being at the expense of their Church. There had always been a greater uncertainty about the law of tithe in Ireland than elsewhere. They took advantage of this, conspired together, boldly proclaimed that pasture was not subject to a rent-charge,[1] and having almost all legislative power in their own hands, got their claim ratified by an Act of the Irish Parliament. Thus by one sweeping measure they transferred to their own credit the whole amount, retaining with little or no intermission the old system of rack-rents. The greater part of their demesnes were exempted from charge, and the support of the Protestant clergy was thrown almost entirely upon the oat and potato land of the smaller cottars. No redress could be obtained for this violent and arbitrary act. The Court of Exchequer was fairly intimidated, and the English Government, however disapproving,[2] did not venture to oppose so great a mass of Protestant landowners. One of the greatest ensuing evils was that the system of fagoting a number of benefices together, which, under more favourable influences, was gradually disappearing, again became as necessary as before. After the middle of the century the outward circumstances of the Church again improved. This was brought about partly by the exertions of all who were concerned in its welfare, and partly through advances in the trade and agriculture of the country. Hampered though Ireland was by vexatious commercial restrictions, it could not but share to some extent in the

[1] The technical name of the rent-charge thus unscrupulously confiscated was 'tithe of agistment,' agistment being the pasturage of all animals not in use for the yoke or the pail, and therefore not paying other tithe, but simply quartered and 'couchant' upon the ground, the Norman term being 'gister,' Latin 'jacere.'

[2] Bishop Benson writes to Berkeley (May 13, 1735) that the affair was 'making a good deal of noise in London, as the injustice of the case is very notorious' (Fraser's *Life and Letters of Berkeley*, p. 238).

great development of material prosperity which in England was a marked characteristic of the century. It was in Munster and Connaught that poverty pressed hardest upon the clergy and for the longest time.

It is obvious that pluralities and non-residence, great as the evil was, were, to a great extent, unavoidable. In many cases it was by no means that scandal and reproach to the Church which it might at first appear, that an Irish clergyman should be rector or vicar of half a dozen parishes or more. It might well be that his subsistence was smaller than that of most curates. Also, in a very great number of parishes there was no residence, and no house where the most ordinary comforts of life could possibly be obtained. Although ecclesiastical law gave every facility and encouragement for building, and although every year witnessed some progress made, the remedy was necessarily one which could only be accomplished by degrees.

Where several parishes were united, a clergyman could not do more than reside on one of them, and manage others either by a curate, if that were possible—as often it was not—or else by frequent and periodical visits. But in Ireland, as in England, non-residence without cause was much too common. Archbishop King spoke with just severity of 'that humour of clergymen living near Dublin, and declining remote and barbarous countries, as they call them.'[1] The bishops themselves were many of them apt to set an example of the same culpable neglect. We find, for example, from King's correspondence, that the dioceses Kilmore, Killaloe, Clogher, Raphoe, and Elphin, were in a condition of almost simultaneous neglect. Bishop Pooley, he said, 'during the eleven years he was bishop, hardly resided eighteen months, and seemed to design making as many non-residents as he could.'[2] To Ashe

[1] Mant, ii. 155. [2] *Id.*, p. 282.

of Clogher he wrote as his metropolitan, 'I assure you there is great exception taken at your long absence. Your friends murmur at your deserting them, and your enemies excuse their negligence by your absence; and the common enemies of the Church conclude that bishops are not necessary, since they can be so long spared.'[1] If it be asked what Ashe was doing all this time, and where he was lingering, an answer may be found in Swift's journal to Stella. At this date he was in London, with half a dozen other bishops from Ireland. He was dining constantly in the best society, playing at ombre for threepence, and seeing 'Cato' at the theatre, but privately in a gallery.[2] Meanwhile he was not by any means neglecting his temporal interests. By good introductions and fascinating manners he had gained the favour of men of great influence, so that after refusing the Archbishopric of Tuam, as more honourable, indeed, but less profitable than his own see, he was transferred in 1717 to the wealthy see of Derry. Addison, who knew him simply as an intellectual and cultivated companion, lamented his death in 1718, as that of an 'excellent man, who has scarce left behind him his equal in humanity, agreeable conversation, and all kinds of learning.'[3] Sometimes it was not the English, but the Irish capital. 'If,' said Bishop Downes, in 1720, of some of his episcopal brethren, 'they take the course, that is too much in practice, to fix in Dublin, and only make an excursion once a year into their diocese, I am afraid the gentry and people of the country will not easily find out of what use they are.'[4]

There was one form of non-residence of a specially odious kind, and peculiar to the Irish Church. There

[1] Sept. 23, 1714, Mant, p. 283
[2] Swift's *Journal*, quoted in Fraser's *Life of Berkeley*, p. 55.
[3] Mant, ii. 316.   [4] *Id.*, p. 367.

were benefices which went under the name of 'non-cures.' In these there was neither glebe, house, nor church. Men, grievously wanting in all feeling of responsibility, would get instituted to such livings, and consider themselves dispensed from all care of the souls committed to their charge. Such a false pastor would leave his people, as Bishop O'Beirne indignantly expressed it, 'to whatever casual instruction they could gather from others, to pick up the word by the wayside; to beg even for baptism for their children from some charitable hand, often from ministers of another faith; while he, standing on the mere privilege of an accommodating conscience, sets every other consideration at defiance.'[1]

But, as a rule, the Established Church of Ireland was served by unobjectionable, respectable men. Neither more can be fairly said of them than this, nor less. Bishop Rundle, describing his diocese to an English friend, writes, 'I have but thirty-five beneficed clergymen under my care; and they are regular, decent, and neighbourly; each hath considerable and commendable general learning, but not one is eminent for any particular branch of knowledge.'[2] There were rather a greater number of curates, and he had had to discard five during the five years he had been in the diocese. Rundle's account may fairly represent what was generally to be found elsewhere. The current of Church life was everywhere flowing languidly; in Ireland more so than elsewhere, and perhaps with more excuse. Berkeley, in a charge to his clergy, expressed his regret that they 'too often look on Papistry within their parishes as having no relation to them, nor being at all entitled to any share of their pains and concern.'[3] The good bishop himself set an excellent example of kindly and thoughtful interest in

[1] Mant, p. 737. [2] Hughes' *Letters of Eminent Persons*, ii. 91.
[3] Berkeley's *Works*, ed. by Fraser, iv. 650.

the well-being of the Roman Catholics as well as of the Protestants around him. But there were not many who followed in his steps; and if the clergy confined their care to those of their own communion, they would be apt, when not spurred by any special zeal, to lead somewhat indolent lives. In most parts of Ireland their poorer parishioners would be but few, and the Protestant laity were not all of a sort who would encourage much pastoral activity among their clergy. Many were exceedingly jealous of the faintest approach to ecclesiastical influence, and, as a rule, they were far more anxious that their clerical neighbours should be pleasant companions in the field or at the table, than that they should be adorned with qualities more distinctive of their office. Their sequestered life, far distant, in most cases, from any centre of thought and movement, the dearth of intelligence, and the difficulty of getting books, the smallness of their church, and the lack of corporate life in it, all tended to disincline them to exertion. Those who were studious or literary could enrich their own minds; but it was madness for a man of small means to think of publishing in Ireland. As Archbishop Boulter said to Dr. Woodward, 'if a man's thoughts should put him on anything that might deserve the press, he must pay for the printing, and distribute it gratis. . . . We are less given to buy books here than can be imagined.'[1] There were a few learned men among the bishops—Berkeley, pre-eminently the first, Percy, King, Newcombe, Peter Browne, Synge, Nicolson, Pococke, Huntington. Such also, among other Irish Churchmen in that century, were Leslie, Skelton, Delany, and Graves. As a rule, the names of Irish clergymen are conspicuously absent from the lists of theology and literature. Skelton was also a man of great zeal in all good

[1] Mant, ii. 552-54.

and pious works; as also was Dean Graves, and his father before him.

During the last thirty or forty years of the century the Established clergy often suffered severely from armed gangs of Irish peasantry, who bitterly resented the payment of tithes to an alien Church. In 1787 the lawless violence of Rapparees and White-boys made it necessary for the Irish Legislature to pass an Act to prevent clergy from being maimed, persecuted, or despoiled, churches from being burnt, injured, or fastened up, and services from being obstructed.[1] When the long excitement culminated at last in open insurrection, several clergymen lost their lives, sometimes with the most deplorable aggravations.

On most matters of general religious and ecclesiastical interest, common alike to England and to Ireland, it need only be said that the questions and controversies which were discussed in the larger Church were reflected in the lesser one with a faintness correspondent to the more circumscribed sphere. Thus the Nonjuring controversy was represented in Ireland by one bishop and by one distinguished writer. The bishop was Richard Sheridan,[2] of Kilmore, who, in 1692, was deprived for his resolute allegiance to James. He then lived in London, relieved from utter penury only by subscriptions from his late English and Irish colleagues, and died about 1716. Among the few Irish clergy who declined the new oaths was Charles Leslie, son of a Bishop of Clogher, and one of the principal theological writers of the eighteenth century. He wrote

---

[1] Mant, ii. 754; Barrington, ii. 452.

[2] His brother Patrick was Bishop of Cloyne. Another of the same Irish family, Dr. Sheridan, the friend and instructor of Swift, and father of the distinguished humorist, was said to have lost his court chaplaincy for selecting, by accident or otherwise, for a sermon preached on the anniversary of George I. before the Lord Lieutenant, the text 'Sufficient for the day is the evil thereof' (*Life of R. B. Sheridan*, by R. G. Sheridan, p. 8).

against Deists, Socinians, Jews, Romanists, Quakers, Presbyterians, and not only voluminously, but well. His earnestness of purpose, his clear, incisive reasoning, his literary style and keen wit, were improved rather than not, in the opinion of his contemporaries, by the vigour of his invective, and an intolerance which often transcended the bounds of common justice. Dr. Johnson had a very high opinion of his argumentative powers. 'He *was* a reasoner,' he once said to Henderson, ' and a reasoner not to be reasoned against.'[1]—Nonjurors there might be in the Established Church of Ireland, for a man's conscience might not release him from his former oath ; but real Jacobitism there scarcely could be. An outbreak in favour of the Stuarts might mean to any Irish Protestant ruin, if not death. Still, the sentimental Jacobitism, once so common among the gentry and clergy of England, was not altogether wanting in Ireland. The evidence for this may excite a smile. A discussion was carried on with perfect gravity, and some little heat, between two excellent bishops, Synge and Brown, on the question whether it were permissible to drink toasts in remembrance of the dead. If there were not in Ireland many toasts in memory of the royal martyr, those, on the other hand, which were drunk in honour of 'the immortal memory' of William III. were numerous enough to move the indignant spleen of those who loved to cherish in their Toryism some little flavour of the Jacobite.—The Irish Convocation, which had not met since 1661, was once more summoned in 1703. Its proceedings contrasted favourably, rather than not, with that of England. There was not the same contention between the two Houses, and there was less disposition to wander from practical subjects into thorny paths of controversy. In these sittings the Lower House showed to more advantage than the Upper, discuss-

[1] Boswell's *Johnson*, iv. 256, note.

ing some important questions with an apparent earnestness which may well inspire regret that this means of exchanging ideas and arranging measures of usefulness was not longer continued. The Upper House, much to Archbishop King's dissatisfaction, were somewhat inclined to be lukewarm and obstructive.[1] After 1711, Convocation was prorogued, and did not meet again throughout the century. There was some idea of reviving it in 1727, but the Lord Lieutenant and the Ministry were not in favour of it. 'Neither,' said Primate Boulter, 'do I desire it, except they had some useful business to do, and I was thoroughly certain they would confine themselves to that.'[2]—The Deistical controversy, of course, found its way to Ireland. If the Deists met with an able antagonist in Leslie, they found in Berkeley one who was far more formidable still. His thoroughly religious and deeply spiritual philosophy was, to those who could appreciate it, a very powerful antidote to the cold-and hard rationalism to which it was opposed. Another Irish writer against the Deists of considerable eminence was Peter Browne. His writings were specially aimed at Toland, who used to boast in jest that he had made him Bishop of Cork. Archbishop King's once celebrated book on the Origin of Evil was also directed to the investigation of some important subjects collaterally raised in the course of the great controversy. A fourth Irish bishop, Robert Clayton, gained a more questionable renown by espousing opinions which, though not Deistical, were very unquestionably Arian.—Methodism was received by Churchmen in Ireland much the same as in England, but on the whole more favourably than there. John Wesley was opposed by many, and regarded with very doubtful and divided minds by others; but some of the clergy diligently attended his preaching, and gladly admitted him

[1] Mant, ii. 176.   [2] Boulter's *Letters*, i. 206.

into their pulpits.[1]—Mystical theology had one noble-hearted representative, whose life and opinions have already been touched upon, in Henry Brooke, a man in whom the graces of an accomplished gentleman were combined with the piety and virtues of a true saint. His father was an Irish rector. —The Evangelical party in the Church during the latter part of the century had no prominent leaders in Ireland. But the views of devout men like Dean Graves assimilated with theirs more naturally than those of Churchmen of equal piety in England. Irish Protestantism, having from old times a strong infusion of Puritan and Presbyterian elements, had not much sympathy with a more Anglican type of devotional thought.—Of religious societies such as those which in Queen Anne's time were entered into with much enthusiasm by religious people in England, in Ireland we hear but little until near the end of the century. Soon after 1790, numbers of influential people, both lay and clerical, joined the 'Associations for Discouraging Vice and Promoting the Practice of Religion and Virtue.'[2]

It remains to give some brief account of the principal Irish bishops of that age. Appointed, as they very generally were, on scarcely any other principle than that of supporting a policy or rewarding a partisan, there were many among them who looked upon a bishopric as a mere place of influence, or a prize given to them to enjoy. No Irish bishop could be overburdened with pastoral duties, however conscientiously he might wish to fulfil them. An idle man had every opportunity of indulging his indolence to the full, or might even, without incurring any severe censure, be almost as much an absentee as if he were an ordinary Irish landowner. A learned divine might give up his time to theology; a man of literary or artistic tastes had abundant leisure and means wherewith to gratify them;

[1] Mant, ii. 696.   [2] *Ib.* p. 740 ; Dean Grave's *Works*, i. 35.

another, of strong political tendencies, might devote most of his days with the consciousness of doing what his patrons most expected of him to the promotion of the English or Irish interest at Dublin. A bad custom, quite on a par with that which guided the dispensing of patronage, made it usual to translate bishops who enjoyed the favour of Government, by easy and gradual successions, from the sees which were less esteemed to the more lucrative or influential ones. Thus, to take one instance among many, Henry Downes was three years bishop at Killala, four years at Elphin, three at Meath, eight at Derry, and, had he lived longer, might have hoped, without any very special qualification, to rise to Cashel or Dublin, or even to the supreme height of Armagh. Few minds could resist the unsettling and injurious effects of this constant anticipation of new preferment. In this respect, as in most others, Bishop Berkeley was well worthy of imitation. Though very doubtful what he should do, he might have accepted the primacy. A man so full of activity, so fertile in ideas, so rich in intellectual power, would have had no right to say positively, either to himself or to others, that he would under all circumstances decline a post in which he could do service. But with this possible exception he made up his mind never to change his see. 'He had very early in life got the world under his feet, and he hoped to trample on it to the last.'[1] He saw, as he could not but see, and as we can plainly see in the letters of some of Bishop Nicolson's correspondents, that the surmises and expectations which every new series of promotions gave birth to, opened too ready a path, even in men of much general worth, to the aspirations of ambition and worldliness. In fact, almost everything relating to the appointment had a tendency to encourage the very characteristics which are

[1] Berkeley's *Works*, iv. 302.

least to be desired in the leaders of a Christian church. The wonder is not that there were several among them of a very decided secular type, but rather that there were not more. Many of them were excellent men; and for the most part, if they were too easy, and if care for their few sheep in the wilderness rested too lightly upon them, they were also generally respected, kindly and hospitable, and not so far engrossed with the interests of their families as not to be fairly liberal in aiding public charities and private needs. In the latter part of the century, and in the earlier years of the present one, ministers evidently considered that Irish bishoprics were admirably adapted to help them to keep on good terms with the Irish aristocracy. Thus, at Clogher, Lord J. G. Beresford was succeeded by the Hon. Percy Jocelyn, and he by Lord R. P. Tottenham; at Derry, the Hon. F. H. Hervey by the Hon. W. Knox, and he by the Hon. R. Ponsonby; at Cork, the Hon. T. Stopford was followed by Lord J. G. Beresford, he by the Hon. T. St. Lawrence; at Tuam, the Hon. J. D. Bourke was followed by the Hon. W. Beresford, and he by the Hon. P. Trench. It was all the same principle of political convenience which had governed the Irish Church for centuries.

At the opening of the century Michael Boyle was primate. He had been an Irish bishop ever since the Restoration, and now, his memory gone, deaf, and almost blind, was a mere wreck of the past. In 1702 he died, at the age of ninety three, and was succeeded by Narcissus Marsh, a very good man, who had deservedly held in succession the Provostship of Trinity College, Dublin, the see of Leighlin, and the Archbishoprics of Cashel and Dublin. During the troubles in King James's reign he had fled for a time to England, after narrowly escaping from a party of soldiers who beset his house at midnight in search of him; and he speaks with much gratitude of the kindness he then received from

Sancroft, Compton, Burnet, Lloyd of St. Asaph, and other English bishops. 'The Lord,' he exclaims, 'remember them for all their kindness to the distressed.' His diary gives quite the impression of a pious and conscientious man, and contains many such ejaculations. Thus after drawing up, in concert with some other prelates, a scheme for the reformation of certain abuses in the Church, he writes an entry, very much in the spirit of Ezra, 'O God, remember me for good, and cause the abuses to be reformed, and put it into the hearts of those concerned to do it.'[1] At another time, in reference to an appointment which he thought an improper one, he writes, 'In which consecration I had no hand, the Lord's name be praised for it, nor may I ever be concerned in bringing unworthy men to the Church.'[2] So, again, speaking of dissensions and scandals in religion, he adds, 'I pray God to preserve our Church from her secret as well as open enemies, and that holiness of life and purity of doctrine may be still countenanced, and shine gloriously among us.'[3] He was very diligent and careful in his visitations and in the general management of his diocese, did much for the building and repairing of churches, and was deeply interested in the new missionary undertakings which the great English societies had set on foot.[4] As primate, he had much to do both with ecclesiastical legislation and with the routine of political administration. The urgency of the former is expressed in a letter to a friend: 'The continued weighty business of our Parliament —wherein I am more deeply concerned than any one man to provide for the necessities of the Church, which lacks many good laws here that you have in England—hath hindered me hitherto from writing to you.'[5] Of the latter he wrote, 'Worldly business is that which above all things I do hate.'

[1] Mant, ii. 51. [2] Id., p. 27. [3] Id., p. 132.
[4] Sir J. Ware's *Irish Bishops*, p. 362. [5] Mant, p. 107.

Nevertheless, as a privy councillor, sometimes a Lord Justice, and sometimes a first commissioner, he had much to do, and did it with his accustomed diligence. Among his benefactions one of the most useful was the gift to Dublin of a library, ' the only useful one,' said Sir James Ware, ' in the kingdom.'[1] He built, stocked, and endowed it, and got an Act of Parliament to secure it. It mainly consisted of Stillingfleet's library, which he bought at great expense in 1707. The worst thing recorded of him must be attributed to the times rather than to the man. He took an active part, not indeed in the severer statutes against Roman Catholics, but in the imposition of some unfair disabilities. But with allowance for the imperfections of our nature, he deserved the praise recorded of him on his tomb in St. Patrick's Cathedral, as ' a high and noble soul, . . . dear, worthy, and useful to all.'

His successor, Thomas Lindsay (1714–24), was a man of too little vigour to leave any mark upon the history of his times. The cathedral of Armagh was indebted to him for the provision he made that its choral services should be henceforth celebrated in a manner more worthy than before of the first of Irish sees. But the greatness of his position in the Church and State was more visible in the grandeur of his obsequies than in the events of his life. We are told of the stately procession moving through the streets of Dublin, with crosier and pastoral staff, and King-at-Arms wearing the royal tabard, and carrying the mitre on a velvet cushion.[2]

Hugh Boulter,[3] on the other hand, held throughout his primacy (1724–42) a position of very great influence, so

[1] Ware, p. 362. [2] Mant, ii. 402.
[3] The authorities for the facts in this sketch are Mant's *Irish Church*; Sir J. Ware's *Irish Bishops*, p. 133; Boulter's *Letters*; Craik's *Life of Swift*, pp. 386-87; and *Gentleman's Magazine*, vol. xii., for 1742, p. 547.

much so that for some years he was practically the ruler of Ireland. In earlier days he had been well known in England. As a Demy of Magdalen College, Oxford, where he had been elected at the same time as Addison, he had been a student in whom Hough had taken especial pride. There he remained for a time as Fellow, then became rector of an important London parish, Archdeacon of Surrey, chaplain to George I., preceptor to Prince Frederick, Dean of Christ Church, and Bishop of Bristol. He was very unwilling to leave England, and declined the Irish primacy when it was offered to him. But the king or his ministers evidently knew him to be the man they wanted, and the royal command was so pressed upon him that he could not refuse to obey. Henceforward he fulfilled with indefatigable zeal the office imposed upon him of supporter of 'the English interest' in Ireland, and confidential adviser to the home Government. His assiduity in these functions detracts from his character as a bishop. In England, both as rector of a populous parish and bishop in a great city, he had been distinguished for the zeal with which he had thrown himself into his work. This energy now took a new line, for although it could not at any time be said of him that he was inactive in his episcopal duties, the whole force of his character was concentred on political interests. The vast power of patronage which he wielded was all primarily directed to this object. He was in no respect an ambitious or self-seeking man. There was, therefore, nothing ignoble in his aims, though they were not such as might best become a bishop. He believed it to be of the utmost consequence, not only to English interest in Ireland, but also to that country itself, that it should be ruled not by a small native oligarchy, but by those who would loyally carry out the principle of English predominance. Parties were evenly balanced, and there were very few whom he felt he could wholly trust.

He knew that influences counter to his own were actively at work. Whenever, therefore, any great appointment was vacant either in Church or State, he urged with a vehemence of entreaty that it might be so filled up as to strengthen the policy which he believed the prosperity of the land required. In the Church, although he was always anxious to have good and strong men, it is painful to read in his letters how piety and learning are yet subordinated to the necessary political qualifications. And yet, after all, it is quite possible that much injustice has been done to Boulter in supposing that he was actuated by motives, disinterested indeed, but still far from the noblest. His action may have been more worthy of a true Christian prelate than might at first appear. A frequent saying of his is related that 'he would do all the good to Ireland he could, though they did not suffer him to do all he would.' This purpose is quite borne out in the large schemes he entertained for the extension of Protestantism, the improvement of popular education, and the development of agriculture. If in all such projects he never for an instant loses sight of their bearing on the English interest, it is quite reasonable to believe that this was, in his opinion, essential to all the best plans which his heart or mind could frame. Supposing him to be convinced that the rule of the native Protestant landowners meant degradation to the country at large, he would be right, even from the very highest point of view, in making such a consideration supreme. Even in the appointment of bishops he might be right in holding that, so long as unworthy men were not preferred, no considerations were, under the peculiar circumstances of the island, of such great consequence as the maintenance of a cause which he held to be for the time synonymous with that of the welfare, the civilisation, and, to a great extent, the Christianity of the country. Boulter's character would so be vindicated from the reproach of unworthy secularity. There are more types than one of Christian-like high-mindedness; and though Boulter may have been mistaken in the opinion which he espoused with so much ardour, yet if he truly held it, he was fulfilling with faithfulness the peculiar and important duties which circumstances had allotted to him. As it happened, the Primate's efforts had no very sensible 'effect in raising the condition of the Irish people. But we must judge by motive rather than by result. If, therefore, as is not improbable, he was consistently influenced by noble intentions, he deserves to be estimated much more highly than he often has been. A pure wish to better their country is certainly, in those who are specially called to it, not the lowest form of duty to God and their neighbour.

Boulter is described by a contemporary as a man of grave and venerable aspect, and temper genial and sweet, wholly devoid of all pride and affectation. In periods of dearth, by which Ireland was from time to time afflicted, he spent his income on the poor with princely generosity. In 1729, and again in 1740–41, he maintained almost wholly at his own expense all the distressed poor of Dublin, until another harvest brought relief. In the later of the two famines more than 2,500 were thus fed twice a day. He was not only very active in establishing Charter schools, but also founded hospitals both at Drogheda and Armagh for clergymen's widows, built a market-house at Armagh, and was always ready to use both his purse and his interest in promoting canals, coal mines, and other useful works. His various benefactions for augmenting small livings and buying glebes amounted altogether to more than 30,000*l.*

In earlier life Boulter was a frequent contributor to the pages of the 'Freethinker,' a series of essays which proposed to combat the Deists with their own weapons, and to show that Christianity need never be afraid of exercising its right of free thought. The fulness and hardiness with which this principle was enunciated alarmed many, and the work had not an altogether favourable reception.

The Primate after Boulter from 1742 to 1747 was John Hoadly, brother of the Bishop of Winchester, and previously Bishop of Ferns and Leighlin, and Archbishop of Dublin. His character is not an engaging one. He held Boulter's political principles without his earnestness; his Church views were of the same bare and cold latitudinarian type as those of his more distinguished brother, but with little of his single-minded devotion to truth and liberty. His chief merit, if it may be so called, was the very nonepiscopal one of 'indefatigably promoting the improvement of agriculture by his skill, his purse, and his example.'[1] The characteristic subject of one of his five published sermons is 'The Nature and Excellence of Moderation.' He also wrote a defence of Burnet on the Articles, and an account of the theological works of a venerable divine, which must have been an extraordinary production indeed, for it is entitled 'A View of Bishop Beveridge's Writings in a Humorous Way.'

The secularity which had begun to attach itself to the Irish Primacy reached its height in George Stone (1747-65). He came into Ireland supported by great political interest, being brother of the English Secretary of State, and high in favour with the Viceroy, the Earl of Dorset, to whom he was probably chaplain. Pushed, therefore, along the path of preferment, Dean of Ferns, Dean of Derry, Bishop of Ferns, Bishop of Kildare, Bishop of Derry, he arrived at the Primacy at the early age of forty.[2] Almost immediately

---

[1] Quoted in Mant, ii. 597.
[2] Horace Walpole spoke indignantly of his being hurried up 'unwarrantably young, and without any pretensions in the world, . . . through two or

after, in the absence of the Lord Lieutenant, he was placed at the head of the Commission, in company with the Lord Chancellor and the Speaker. What he henceforth was is well described in the words of one who had excellent opportunities of knowing. 'Government,' says Hardy, 'was led on by Primate Stone, a man of unbounded ambition. Lord Charlemont, who knew him perfectly, often assured me that the temper and genius of the English people and English constitution, averse to all ecclesiastical interference or domination (which the Primate was well aware of), alone prevented him from aspiring to a distinguished place in the councils of Great Britain.[1] . . . In another country, the chicane of negotiations, the subserviency of foreign cabinets, the tumults of wars, the friendship or the overthrow of princes, would alone have completely filled up every part of his mind. He at first captivated all who approached him by the uncommon beauty of his person, his address, and the vivacity of his conversation. He had in some respects far juster views of Ireland than many of his contemporaries; but his own aggrandisement predominated over every other consideration. Whilst in the more early part of his political life he affected no other character than that of a statesman,[2] he was, though unpopular, dignified and imposing; when, towards the close of it, he thought proper occasionally to assume the lowliness of an ecclesiastic, satiated with the bustle and splendour of the world, the artful statesman still glared so over every part of his behaviour as to render it in some measure revolting. He

three bishoprics, up to the very Primacy of the kingdom' (Walpole's *Memoirs*, an. 1752, p. 280).

[1] F. Hardy's *Life of the Earl of Charlemont*, i. 158.

[2] Bishop Newton said of the two brothers, that 'if Andrew Stone had been Primate of Ireland instead of his brother, and his brother Secretary of State in his stead, the change might have been suitable to either' (Newton's *Autobiog.*, p. 131).

quickly perceived this effect of his newly adopted manner, and reassumed his old one, in which not the least trace of a Churchman was visible.[1]' His intriguing and aspiring temper at one time gave so much umbrage, that there was some thought of hinting that he had better reside upon his diocese. But other counsels prevailed, for though he does not appear to have been much liked by the Whig Government, it was thought that his power would be the best security of English rule in Ireland.[2] Nor was his genius merely that of the subtle politician. In the abortive rising of 1763 he appears to have acted alike with judgment and humanity.[3]

Such was Primate Stone. There were several instances in Ireland where, as Cumberland said, the gravity of character maintained by English dignitaries was laid aside, and the mitre freely mingled with the cockade;[4] but its extremest example was in Stone, a scholar, a politician, and a gentleman, as the same author adds, but anything rather than a bishop. Whether there is truth in the story that he encouraged or permitted any kind of excess among his guests rather than lose the support of the young Irish aristocracy,[5] cannot be certainly known. It may have been only one of the libels of which his position and his temper made him the constant object.[6] Finally, it may be said to his credit that his attention and kindness as a landlord made him greatly beloved among his tenantry.

Next came Richard Robinson, afterwards Baron Rokeby, who had been Bishop, first of Killala, next of Ferns and Leighlin, and then of Kildare. He was Primate for nearly thirty years, from 1765 to 1794. He had some excellent

---

[1] Hardy's *Life of the Earl of Charlemont*, i. 201-2.   [2] *Id.*, p. 87.
[3] *Id.*, p. 190.   [4] R. Cumberland's *Memoirs*, i. 229.
[5] Goldwin Smith, *Irish History and Character*, p. 139.
[6] Mant, ii. 602.

qualities; but in him also there was thus much of the secularity of some of his predecessors, that his virtues were for the most part those of a great nobleman rather than of a prelate. He was not conspicuous either for eloquence in the pulpit, or for learning, or for power of skilfully organising and directing the work of the Church. But he used his great revenues, private and official, in such manner as might well become a bishop palatine. He spent large sums in creating new parochial cures, and in building houses for the clergy. He erected several parish churches, did much to repair and beautify his cathedral, founded a public school, a public infirmary, a public library, an observatory; and provided on a vast scale employment for the industrious and food for the hungry. He was unmarried, he gave few entertainments, and administered his affairs with care and system, or he could not have done so much. Nevertheless, he considered it incumbent on his office to keep up in his personal surroundings a great deal of the pomp of state. 'I accompanied him,' says Cumberland, 'on the Sunday forenoon to the cathedral. We went in his chariot with six horses, attended by three footmen behind. . . . At our approach the great western door was thrown open, and my friend (in person one of the finest men that could be seen) entered, like another Archbishop Laud, in high prelatical state, preceded by his officers and ministers of the Church, conducting him in files to the robing chamber and back again to the throne.'[1] He cared little for popularity, though among the people generally he was very popular, and to strangers he seemed somewhat reserved. Those who knew him better found him full of kindness and benevolence. He was very well known at Bath, whither he often went for his health.

[1] R. Cumberland's *Memoirs*, ii. 355.

The last Irish primate of the century was William Newcome (1795–1800), who had previously been Bishop of Dromore, of Ossory, and of Waterford. No political considerations entered this time into the appointment. His elevation was chiefly owing, no doubt, to Charles James Fox, whose tutor he had been; but the king himself is said to have wished it. At any rate, he was a deserving man. Lord Charlemont, then a great leader of opinion in Ireland, spoke of him with great praise, as recommended to high office only by 'unassuming virtue, conduct, principles, and erudition.'[1] The new primate proved an active bishop and an industrious theologian. He is best known in the latter capacity. His 'Harmony of the Gospels,' with commentary, maps, and indexes; his annotated translations of the Gospels, and parts of the Old Testament, together with his 'History of Biblical Translations,' all testified to his judgment, thought, and learning.[2] His primacy lasted only five years, but he held it with universal respect.

One of the best and most distinguished of Irish bishops in the eighteenth century was William King, Bishop of Derry from 1691 to 1703, and Archbishop of Dublin from 1703 to 1729. No one can read what is told of him by his contemporaries, or the history of his thoughts and doings as we find it in his own correspondence, without seeing that he was a very good and able man and a thoroughly efficient prelate. He lived in times most trying to an Irish Churchman who was alive to the evils with which he had to contend. But he struggled against those difficulties very indefatigably. There is a charm in all that relates to Berkeley, which will always in general opinion rank him first of Irish bishops in that century. Regarded, however, simply as a bishop, King must take the foremost place;

---

[1] Hardy, ii. 734.
[2] Horne's *Sacred Philology,* pp. 133, 189, 290, 293, 304.

nor is it at all certain that any English bishop of the same century could take precedence of him. Swift was generally far more lavish of his censure than of his praise; but of King, whom he respected and feared more than any other person with whom he corresponded, he spoke in terms of the highest admiration. After telling of his great sufferings (he had twice been thrown into prison in the time of James II.), and of his eminent services, he goes on to say how the Ulster Presbyterians, against whose opinions he was perpetually writing or speaking, yet thought so highly of him that 'upon his removal to Dublin they parted from him with tears in their eyes, and universal acknowledgments of his wisdom and goodness. For the rest, he does not busy himself by entering deep into any party; but spends his time in acts of hospitality and charity, in building of churches, . . . in introducing and preferring the worthiest persons he can find; . . . in short, in the practice of all virtues that can become a public or private life. This, and more if possible, is due to so excellent a person, who may be justly reckoned among the greatest and most learned prelates of his age.'[1] This was written in 1708. In 1729, just after his death, Sir James Ware spoke in terms of equally unreserved praise. 'He appears in the tendency of his actions and endeavours to have had the advancement of religion, virtue, and learning entirely at heart. . . . His capacity and spirit to govern the Church was visible in his avowed enmity to pluralities and non-residence; in his strict and regular visitations, both annual, biennial, and parochial; in his constant duty of confirmation and preaching; and in the many excellent admonitions and charges he gave his clergy upon these occasions; in his pastoral care and diligence in admitting none into the sacred ministry but persons well qualified for their learning and

[1] Quoted in Mant, ii. 198.

good morals. . . . His hospitality was suitable to the
dignity of his station and character, and the whole course
of his conversation innocent, cheerful, and improving; for
he lived in the constant practice of every Christian virtue
and grace that could adorn a public or a private life.' He
tells of him how versed he was in Popish controversies;
how greatly consulted by the Protestants in difficult cases;
how, in Dublin alone, he got nineteen new churches, seven
rebuilt, fourteen repaired, and how greatly the Protestants
there multiplied under his charge; how he was four times
Lord Justice, and enjoyed the unreserved confidence of
George I., and of his great anxiety in all ways to promote
the public good and the king's interest. All this is very
high praise, but is quite borne out by other accounts.
Mant gives a number of his letters, which are preserved
in Trinity College, Dublin. There is often a trace of melancholy and almost despondency in them, yet never sufficient
to overshadow the true-hearted determination of a brave
man to do his best. It seemed to him that 'the faith of
religion was very weak amongst all, and the sense of it
almost lost;' that hearty effort was chilled, discountenanced,
and opposed. Even among the bishops and clergy—
although he had high commendation for some—there was
much time-serving and much obstruction to salutary reforms. The interests of religion and the Church were
being lamentably sacrificed to the unworthy end of conferring promotion for mere political services. Sometimes,
again, he was afraid that his Church was about to be
handed over to the domination of Presbyterianism. Amidst
all his cares for the Church, he had further to regret that
' he had not one friend near him whom he could with re-
liance and necessary freedom consult in these matters.'
But ' I thank God I am willing to be at any pains and to
venture anything for Christ's sake, and do find a comfort

and satisfaction in doing so.'¹ 'I cannot,' he said, shortly before his death, 'sit down and rest from my labours. St. Paul has set me a better example. There is no stopping in this course till God call us from it by death. . . . I am ashamed, every time that I think of the course he ran, when I compare it with my own. I was consecrated on the day we celebrate for his conversion, and proposed him to myself for a pattern. But God knows how short the copy comes of the original.'²

King himself says that he was often charged with being positive, arbitrary, and wedded to his own opinions. But, says he, he saw little good from ways of easiness and compliance. His critics all acknowledged that he was useful and serviceable to the Church. 'Assure yourself that if ever I was so in anything, it was by doing those very things that got me the censure of being opinionative and singular.'³ Perhaps, judging by modern standards, he might be called a little intolerant. He opposed certain Bills brought forward in 1719 for the greater relief of Presbyterians and other Dissenters, and fell therefore into disfavour with the Government. He would not, however, grant that he failed in tolerance. 'I am for making all mankind easy,' he said, 'especially in matters of religion;'⁴ but he strongly objected to having one law in England and another in Ireland, when the Constitution, as he considered, required that they should be the same.

Archbishop King, though descended from a very ancient family, was born in a humble condition, his father, to whom in his old age he paid the most dutiful attention, being a miller.⁵ His manner was discreet and dignified, and he was noted for his power of conversation, flavoured with a

¹ Mant, ii. 95. ² *Id.*, p. 495.
³ *Id.*, pp. 327. ⁴ *Id.*, pp. 339 40.
⁵ Noble, ii. 103.

keen and pungent wit, which remained undiminished to the last. 'He is really a prodigy,' wrote Lady Carteret, 'in wit and spirit, considering he is eighty years old.' [1]

His Latin work on the 'Origin of Evil' showed much thought and reading, and attracted great notice both when it was first published, and when, later in the century, it was translated, with notes, by Bishop Law.

No eighteenth-century ecclesiastic of any country has been held in more universal or deserved honour than George Berkeley,[2] Bishop of Cloyne from 1734 to 1753. Admirable alike in heart and intellect, in thought and action, his name suffices by itself to shed a kind of lustre upon the unsatisfactory and feeble Church of which he was so distinguished an ornament. In Ireland, England, and America, and among leading men in Church and State of very varied views, he was widely known, and all who knew him could not but value and esteem him. Few men, equal to him in energy and talent, ever passed through the world so free from envy, odium, and disparagement. Fortunately his temperament suggested a kind of vent by which the jealousy could easily evaporate which is aroused in too many of mankind by superior merit. There was apt to be both in his thought and action a strain of unworldly idealism, which, while it made his character, his writings, and his conversation infinitely more attractive than they would have been without it, yet made it easy for any one, especially in that age, to shrug the shoulder with a feeling of superiority, and to say, in good-humoured disparagement, that this excellent bishop was mad. It was so with the cynical wits of Walpole's time, the fine gentlemen and town-bred ladies who saw him at Queen Caroline's court, his 'handsome face beaming with

---

[1] Lady Sundon's *Diary*, Dec. 19, 1724, p. 124.
[2] See, especially, the *Life and Works of Bishop Berkeley*, by Prof. A. C. Fraser, in four volumes.

intelligence and goodness,'[1] pleading with utmost earnestness that a way might be opened for him to give up his bishopric, and carry out in the remote Bermudas his darling scheme for carrying civilisation and Christianity to the Indians of America. They could not help but love and admire; but, said they, a man possessed with such extraordinary crotchets must needs be a little affected in the brain. So also with his speculations on mind and matter. Full though they are of beauty, and teeming with suggestive thought, nevertheless half of polite society were ready to exclaim that it needed no reasoner to see that the author of such extravagant paradoxes must surely be well-nigh crazed. His theories on matter, apart from its sensible properties, set many of the deepest minds in Europe thinking. But to many nothing seemed easier than to 'vanquish Berkeley with a grin,'[2] or to answer his doctrine as Dr. Johnson did, 'striking his foot with mighty force against a large stone till he rebounded from it, "I refute it thus;"'[3] or, like Warburton, to exclaim in half-contemptuous praise, and in reference to his work in Ireland, that 'he is indeed a great man, but the only visionary I ever knew that was.'[4] Berkeley was indeed a great man, not, in most particulars, cast in an eighteenth-century mould, yet not one who ever felt himself out of harmony with his age. In whatever period his lot had been cast, his versatile energy and active interest in the welfare of his contemporaries, and in all questions that might be stirring the intellect of the time, could never have failed to bring him into some degree of prominence.

Berkeley was born in 1684, of an English family who had suffered for their loyalty to Charles I., and had settled

[1] Lady Sundon's *Diary*, p. 172.
[2] 'And coxcombs vanquish Berkeley with a grin.'—Dr. J. Brown's *Essay on Satire*, ii. 224.
[3] Boswell's *Johnson*, i. 143.   [4] Warburton to Hurd, p. 45.

in Ireland soon after the Restoration. He passed from Kilkenny School into Trinity College, Dublin, at the age of fifteen. As a youth, his tutors and companions hardly knew what to make of him, or whether he were the greatest dunce or the greatest genius in college. His eager, inquisitive ways made him seem eccentric, while flashes of brilliancy contrasted with what seemed a heavy indifference to much of his routine studies. But in three or four years those who knew him got to admire him for the promise of great learning no less than they loved him for his simple-hearted goodness. He had grasped with avidity the new ideas which in the philosophy of Newton, Locke, and Boyle were slowly but surely superseding the old scholastic teaching. Berkeley worked with all the fresh enthusiasm of his character. At the age of twenty he had written a Latin treatise, published three years later, which showed the originality and independence with which he studied mathematical subjects. Especially he delighted in the metaphysical aspects of abstract mathematics, but most of all in the wide field of thought which philosophy opened out to him. The notes and jottings of his commonplace-book clearly indicate with what deep interest he was pondering manifold thoughts about matter and its qualities, space and time, existence, soul, God, and duty. In 1709 and 1710, earlier in life than any eminent writer who has preceded or followed him in the same field of reasoning, he launched into the world his philosophical speculations. In the first of these dates he published his 'Theory of Vision,' and in the second his 'Principles of Human Knowledge.' Of these two treatises, illuminated as they are by a singular beauty of thought and style, it must be sufficient here to remark that, however much they may doubt his conclusions, few thoughtful readers can rise from their perusal without deeper and, so to say, sublimer thoughts of the supremacy, in the midst of material phenomena, of the greater universe of mind and spirit. It must be added, however, that all Berkeley's thoughts on philosophy were penetrated and suffused with a profound sense of their important bearing on practice and religion. 'After all,' he says in his ' Theory of Vision,' ' what deserves the first place in our studies is the consideration of God and our duty; which to promote, as it was the main drift and design of my labours, so shall I esteem them altogether useless and ineffectual if, by what I have said, I cannot inspire my readers with a pious sense of the presence of God.'[1]

Remembering the zeal with which Berkeley had studied the works of Locke and the newer forms of thought, it is remarkable that in 1712 he should have come forward as an uncompromising vindicator of the now exploded doctrine of passive obedience. But the treatise admirably shows in what spirit this theory had been held over and over again by noble-minded men in whom there was not the faintest trace of servility. It was Berkeley's conviction that non-resistance to a supreme power in the State was a primary moral principle, like in kind to the great commands of the decalogue, implanted by the Creator in the hearts of men in order to save them from the anarchy which is the worst of social evils. Resting, therefore, on first principles of law and order, it was essentially divine right, which men have no more authority to transgress in hope that some temporary good might come, than they have permission, upon a similar argument, to violate the eternal statutes against murder or adultery. When such principles were involved, fluctuating circumstances had no longer any weight. Such being Berkeley's views, than whom no man was less likely to preach and not practise, he would certainly have been a Nonjuror had he lived a little earlier. As it

[1] *Theory of Vision*, § 156.

was, the powers that be were already established in the new line; and though for a time this discourse brought upon Berkeley some suspicion of Jacobitism, he was always perfectly loyal to the House of Hanover.

In 1713, Berkeley, hitherto engaged in literary and tutorial work at college, was introduced by Swift at Queen Anne's court, and became well acquainted with Addison, Steele, and other celebrities of the day. During this stay in London he contributed to the 'Guardian' fourteen short essays, chiefly directed against Collins and the other Deists. In the same year he published his 'Dialogue of Hylas and Philonous.' 'He emerged in provincial Ireland the most elegant writer of the English language for philosophical purposes who had then or has since appeared, at a time too when Ireland, like Scotland, was in a state of provincial barbarism.'[1]

That autumn he was, at Swift's recommendation, appointed secretary and chaplain to the Earl of Peterborough, Ambassador Extraordinary to the King of Sicily. He spent five years abroad, chiefly in Italy and France. His foreign journal graphically portrays the lively interest with which he made use of these travels to study men and manners, art and nature, religious customs, and antiquities. It is said that Berkeley had an interview with Malebranche, and that it had a lamentable issue; inasmuch as the Frenchman, not being well at the time, became so excited by conversation with the brother philosopher, that the heat of it brought on a relapse, by which he died a few days after.

In 1721, Berkeley was again in England, and after staying in London long enough to become intimate with Pope and Atterbury, to cement his friendship with good Bishop Benson, and to form an acquaintance with Secker and Butler, returned to Ireland as chaplain to the Duke of

[1] Fraser, iv. 62.

Grafton, the Lord Lieutenant. He was also Lecturer in Greek, Lecturer in Hebrew, University Preacher, and Senior Proctor in Dublin University. About this time Esther Vanhomrigh, Swift's 'Vanessa,' very unexpectedly left him the greater part of her considerable fortune.

In 1724 he was presented to the Deanery of Derry, one of the richest preferments in the Irish Church. But this gave him no satisfaction, for his mind was now bent on quite a different sphere of work. When he returned from his travels in 1721, he had been most painfully impressed with the state of things he found in London. His essay, published that year, 'Towards Preventing the Ruin of Great Britain,' shows with what gloomy forebodings he surveyed the vice, the irreligion, the recklessness, the flippancy which he everywhere beheld. He knew not, he said in the opening of this essay, whether it was the flush of material prosperity which had preceded the South Sea project, or whether it was the ruin which followed, which had brought things to such a pitch. But he was sure that unless old-fashioned maxims of religion, industry, frugality, and public spirit were once more revived, England would be undone. On his return to Ireland the press of university employments appears for a while to have somewhat distracted him from these thoughts. But they returned upon his impressible mind with such force, that an ardent longing possessed him to be an agent in establishing a new and purer civilisation beyond the Atlantic. The legacy which had been left him had placed him in a position in which he would be more competent than he had been before to carry out such a design. He proposed, therefore, to resign his deanery,[1] and found a college

[1] 'His heart will break,' wrote Swift to Lord Carteret, 'if his deanery be not taken from him, and he allowed to carry out his project' (Fraser, iv. 103).

at the Bermudas, wherein to train up the colonial and native youth of America and the Indies as scholars and missionaries. A vision as of Utopia floated before his mind as he thought of such a home for piety, learning, and all pure and refining influence, diffusing its blessings throughout the continent of the future, and where a kind and genial nature would co-operate with the frugal simplicity of Christian scholars.

So persuasive was Berkeley's eloquence, so contagious the example of his enthusiasm, that he induced three Fellows of Trinity College to relinquish the prospects which were opening to them, and to join him on salaries of forty pounds a year in the college which he hoped to found. He then went to London to raise funds for his university, and to procure a charter for it. His success there was marvellous. The glowing ardour with which he urged his cause was irresistible. He gained the assent and favour of George I. Bishops, peers, members of Parliament, and other leading men promised their support. From Sir Robert Walpole himself, than whom no man in England had less of the spirit of romance, he obtained the promise of a contribution of 200*l*. The wits and politicians of the Scriblerus Club met him at dinner at Lord Bathurst's, and began to rally him on his scheme; but he met them with such eloquence, such vivacity, such enthusiasm, as not only to silence jesting, but to turn it into warm support. Much as he disliked the empty theological disputes in which Queen Caroline delighted, he attended them rather than lose a chance of furthering his all-engrossing plan. He next set himself to obtain for it a public grant; and by indefatigable exertions won so many members to his side, that, to the amazement of Walpole and Townshend, the House of Commons moved an address to the king in favour of a grant for the purpose of 20,000*l*. from the lands of St.

Christopher.[1] The grant was assented to; the charter had been obtained; and at length, in 1728, Berkeley sailed for America, full of noble thoughts and philanthropic aspirations, to prepare for carrying out this scheme so soon as the promised grant could be made.

He stopped at Rhode Island, wishing both to invest in land for the benefit of the future college, and also to engage the interest of the New England colonists. But it was not the mere halting-place he had intended it to be. He remained there three years, heartsick with deferred hope, and never reached Bermuda, for the promise on which he had depended was never fulfilled. When Walpole was no longer under the spell of Berkeley's fascinating eloquence, he was too skilled a master of evasion not to find excuse for escaping from an inconvenient promise. Berkeley, meanwhile, was not the man to be made idle by delay and disappointment. He pursued his philosophical and theological studies, and wrote there one of his best known treatises; he gathered around him all the most cultivated of the settlers, and formed a very prosperous literary and philosophical society; he made his house a central resort for all who were engaged in missionary enterprise; he made himself acquainted with the adjacent Indian tribes; he interested himself in the negroes, not sparing his indignant remonstrances at the 'irrational contempt of the blacks as creatures of another species, who had no claim to be instructed or admitted to the sacraments;' he set himself with all his sympathetic earnestness to create good feeling between Churchmen and other sects; he often

---

[1] By the treaty of Utrecht in 1713, certain territories in this island had been ceded by the French; the proceeds of which, to the amount of 80,000*l.*, had been intended for the endowment of four bishoprics in America. As there now seemed no likelihood of carrying out this design, it was from this fund that Berkeley's grant was to be made. (Beardsley's *Life of Johnson*, p. 69.)

preached, and all denominations delighted to hear him—
'even the Quakers with their broad-brimmed hats came and
stood in the aisles.'

At length suspense became certainty; and early in
1732, Berkeley, bitterly disappointed, arrived again in
London. He left, however, to America a substantial monument of his care, for he handed over to Yale College at
Newhaven [1] not only the best collection of books which had
hitherto reached that continent; but also his Rhode Island
farm, to endow a scholarship for the advancement of
classical learning.

However unfairly Walpole had acted to Berkeley in the
matter of the promised grant, it was creditable to him that
at a time when Church preferment in Ireland was ordinarily given with sole reference to the support of 'the
English interest,' he should have appointed Berkeley to
the Bishopric of Cloyne.

This was in January 1734. In the short interval before
his consecration he published on a subject which recalled
his early Dublin studies. It was entitled 'The Analyst,
or a Discourse addressed to an Infidel Mathematician,' and
was followed in 1734 by his 'Defence of Freethinking in
Mathematics.' They contain an interesting application of
an analogy derived from the incomprehensibilities upon
which mathematical fluxions are founded, as applied to
corresponding mysteries in theology.

The quiet seclusion of Cloyne suited Berkeley well.
Since his return from America his health had a good deal
given way, and he suffered severely from gout and colic.
He could no longer with any satisfaction to himself have
fulfilled duties which involved much bodily exertion. But

[1] One of the leading divinity schools of the Protestant Episcopal Church
in the United States has been named after Berkeley, and is still located at
Newhaven. There is a Berkeley Association at Harvard College (L. C.,
see note 2, p. 186).

he found abundant scope for an active mind and for large sympathies. He rose at four, and spent much time in reading and meditation, Plato being his favourite author, and Hooker next. Only with him reflection rarely ended in himself; 'Non sibi sed toti' was a motto which he ever kept in mind. The pages of the 'Querist,' which was published after 1735 in annual parts, witness how much his thought was occupied with the religious, social, and economic evils which were rife around him. His queries referred chiefly, though by no means exclusively, to Ireland. It grieved him to the heart to see such wretchedness, such ignorance, such laziness, among the masses; such selfishness, absenteeism, and indifference among the upper classes; such mutual distrust if not antipathy, such bitterness of religious difference, such jealousy of England, such sluggishness in trade, such waste of fertile soil. 'There was so much,' he said, 'to be done in Ireland, and so few who cared to do it.' Few leading Protestants, it is to be feared, had in that age much of Berkeley's genuine, unaffected care for the Roman Catholic poor. He was surrounded by them. For though in the whole diocese there may have been fourteen thousand Protestants, in his neighbourhood there were, to use his own words, 'comparatively none.' He would have rejoiced to see Protestantism advance among them, and suggested whether something might not be done by training preachers and catechists from an humbler class, who would speak their language and thoroughly understand their ways. He approved also of the charity schools as proselytising agencies. But such hopes could not be otherwise than faint. Quite apart from them, he longed to see the condition of the Irish poor ameliorated in any and every way. Knowing, therefore, that their priests were, far above all others, their directors, to them, in his 'Word to the Wise,' he appealed to use their best influence to raise the people to industry and self-reliance. In a similar spirit, seeing how needful it was that the guides of the poor should be themselves sufficiently taught, he asked 'whether, in imitation of the Jesuits at Paris, who admit Protestants to study in their colleges, it may not be right for us also to admit Roman Catholics into our college without obliging them to attend chapel duties, or catechisms, or divinity lectures.'[1] Meanwhile he left nothing undone which private beneficence could do to improve the material condition of the poor around him. He interested himself much in spinning and weaving looms; he had all the articles of his dress, including his wig, and all the dress of his household, made in the village of Cloyne. When famine and disease invaded the country, he set all the powers of his busy and inquisitive mind to search out the means of comfort and alleviation, studying medicine with all the care of a physician, and making his kitchen the infirmary of the neighbourhood. It was at this time he discovered, or imagined he had discovered, the inestimable virtues of tar water. Thenceforth, with an enthusiasm of humanity quite corresponding to that which he had thrown into the Bermuda scheme, he set himself to make known the properties of his great remedy, till its fame had run through England, and was much talked of even in America and on the Continent. All through the winter of the famine, besides his charities in kind, he weekly distributed twenty pounds among the poor, and throughout the summers of the hard times he employed a hundred men in works of husbandry. In strong contrast to these cares, we unexpectedly find him in 1746, when general insurrection was feared, spending some of his energies on warlike preparations. He had bought up all the muskets he could get, and had provided horses and arms for four-and-twenty of the Protestants of Cloyne.

[1] The *Querist*, No. 191.

Thus, too, in 1744, on tidings of the dispersion of the French fleet off Dungeness, he had a big bonfire before his gate, 'to keep up the drooping spirits of the Protestants.' He wrote also some not unseasonable letters to suggest improvements which should make the uniform of soldiers more favourable to alertness, endurance, and strength. Ill-health or disinclination kept him much away from Parliament, and for more than three years he did not once attend its sessions in Dublin. In the one winter of 1737–38 he was often present; but does not appear to have spoken except to move for the suppression of an impious and atheistical club. Among his correspondence during his quiet life at Cloyne should be mentioned a long letter, running almost to the length of a treatise, written to a gentleman who was proposing to join the Church of Rome. It contains several interesting passages. Such is one upon the use and abuse of the monastic life. 'It seems,' he said, 'very expedient that the world should have, among the many institutions formed for action, some also formed for contemplation, the influence whereof might be general and extend to others. But to get men and women to a contemplative life, who are neither fitted nor addicted to contemplation, is a monstrous abuse. To assist the λύσις and φυγή of the soul by meditation was a noble purpose even in the minds of Pagan philosophy. How much more so in the eyes of Christians, whose philosophy is of all others the most sublime, and the most calculated to wean our thoughts from things carnal, and raise them above things terrestrial! That the contemplative and ascetic life may be greatly promoted by living in community and by rules I freely admit. The institution of the Essenes among the Jews, or the Republic of Philosophers, that was to have been settled in a city to have been built by the direction of Gallienus, if that Emperor had not changed his mind; such institutions as these give delightful images, but very different from anything that I could ever see in a Popish convent, and I have seen and known many of them. I should like a convent without a vow or perpetual obligation. Doubtless a college or monastery, receiving only grown persons of approved piety, learning, and a contemplative turn, would be a great means of improving the divine philosophy, and brightening up the face of religion in our Church.'[1] His few words on Churchmanship must also be quoted. 'As Plato thanked the gods that he was born an Athenian, so I think it a peculiar blessing to have been educated in the Church of England. My prayer, nevertheless, and trust in God is, not that I shall live and die in this Church, but in the true Church. For, after all, in respect of religion, our attachment should only be to the truth.'[2] Several of his letters at this period were written to Samuel Johnson of Connecticut, and prove not only his great interest in the progress of religion and learning in America, but also his earnest desire that nothing should be allowed to interfere with a genial and cordial feeling between Conformists and Nonconformists. Another letter is to his intimate friend Bishop Benson, in answer to news received from him that Sir John James, the last baronet of his line, intended to leave Berkeley almost the whole of his large estate. 'Do you tell James that I will not have his fortune. Bid him leave it to his relations. I won't have it.'[3]

The relaxations of Bishop Berkeley and his family were such as became a cultured and refined home. He loved his garden, and the noble myrtles which adorned it; he inquired into the antiquities and traditions of the locality; all his family, from the greatest to the least, were great lovers of music, and their weekly concerts were reunions

[1] Fraser, iv. 276.   [2] *Id.*, p. 278.   [3] *Id.*, p. 280, note.

for all his principal neighbours; and the bishop's love of art and painting proved hereditary among his children.

It is impossible not to regret that Berkeley did not succeed to the Primacy instead of Stone. He looked forward with dread, so far as his own inclinations were concerned, to the prospect of its being offered to him. 'I am not in love,' he said, 'with feasts, and crowds, and late hours, and strange faces, and a hurry of affairs often insignificant.' Yet he would not have declined it if he had thought that by acceptance of it he could do good. That he would have done good in that important post no one can doubt. Even under the burden of rapidly declining health his energy was still great, and his thoughtful mind and generous sympathies would have had a noble field of exercise.

He remained at Cloyne till 1752, the year before his death. His son was then going up to Oxford; and Berkeley greatly desired to carry out a long-cherished ideal of spending his declining age there in quiet meditation. He tried to exchange his bishopric for an Oxford canonry. Failing in this, he tendered his resignation of it, more scrupulous in this than most bishops of his time. This, however, George II. curtly refused to accept. He might live, he said, where he pleased, but he should die a bishop in spite of himself. Jemmett Brown, the worthy Bishop of Cork, pressed him to carry out his earnest wish, and promised to undertake the care of his diocese. Accordingly, the last months of his life were spent at the university of Oxford, nor was there any one more greatly honoured there. 'On the evening of Sunday, January 14, 1753, Berkeley was resting on a couch, in his house in Holywell Street, surrounded by his family. His wife had been reading aloud to the little family party the lesson in the Burial Service, and he had been making remarks upon that sublime passage. His daughter soon after went to offer him some tea. She found him, as it seemed, asleep, but his body was already cold.'[1]

This sketch of Berkeley's life has been given at greater length than that of almost any other bishop in the century, both because it seemed impossible to shorten it further without injury to the picture of a pure and noble life, and because even readers to whom it is familiar would not wish it too much curtailed.

His philosophy has been here but slightly alluded to. It would be quite beyond the bounds of this work to enter upon it more fully; all the more so because a superficial account could only result in misrepresentation. If the main groundwork of his speculations must be summed up in one sentence, we might say of them, in Mr. Fraser's words, that 'the material world, its substance or permanence, its powers and its space, resolve themselves into a flux of significant sensations, sense ideas, or sense phenomena, which are perpetually sustained in existence by a divine reason and will.' This may be taken as a sort of general text, upon and around which Berkeley's devout, thoughtful, and ingenious mind wove his fabric of suggestive and often beautiful reflections, in which he combated the materialism of the age, and sought to inspire stronger convictions of the spirituality, omnipresence, providence, omniscience, and infinite power and goodness of God.[2] That he was often grossly, and even absurdly misunderstood, was owing partly to certain characteristics in the intellectual tendencies of the period, partly to the intrinsic nature of his speculation, partly to a certain want of clearness and of guarded statement in his writings. It is evident also that his opinions, even when carefully studied and thoroughly understood, may either be altogether questioned, or may lead to conclusions which he little contemplated. Certainly the same ideas which

[1] Fraser, p. 344. [2] 'Hylas and Philonous,' *Works*, i. 354.

deepened and intensified Berkeley's faith in the attributes of God, and in the powers and destinies of the human soul, tended to confirm Hume in a universal scepticism. In any case there can be no question that his writings had great influence on philosophic thought, both in England and Germany. It may be remarked, lastly, that his views, or modifications of them, were eagerly adopted by some writers of a mystical tendency.[1]

Of the remaining Irish bishops of the century a few only of the most distinguished can be briefly mentioned.

Peter Brown[2] (Cork 1710–35) has been already referred to in connection with Toland. Sir James Ware describes him as 'an austere, retired, and mortified man, but a prelate of the first rank for learning, and esteemed the best preacher of the age. . . . His life was one uniform course of piety and true religion.' He adds that he was very charitable, and as a bishop very strict in exacting residence. He was for some time Provost of Trinity College, Dublin. His principal writings were 'The Limits of the Human Understanding,' and 'Analogy of Things Divine and Human.' In part of the last-mentioned work he opposed Berkeley.

Robert Huntington[3] (Raphoe 1701) survived his consecration only a few months. He had been a very distinguished Orientalist. As chaplain at Aleppo he had corresponded much with several of the principal dignitaries

[1] Cf. Henry Brooke, in his *Fool of Quality*. 'Friend: "Do you think there is any such thing in nature as a spirit?" Author: "I know not that there is any such thing in nature as matter. . . . I know that thoughts and conceptions are raised in my mind; but how they are raised, or that they are adequate images of things supposed to be represented, I know not. What if this something, or this nothing, called matter, should be a shadow or vacuum in respect of spirit, wholly resistless to it and pervadable by it? or what if it be no other than a various manifestation of the several good and evil qualities of spirit?"' (Chap. iii. See also Gilchrist's *Life of Blake*, pp. 190-91.)

[2] Ware, pp. 571-72; Nichols, i. 381-82; Mant, ii. 198, 550; Fraser, iv. 18.   [3] Ware, pp. 278-80; Mant, pp. 203-4.

of the Eastern Church, and collected numerous manuscripts in Arabic, Syriac, Samaritan, Hebrew, and Coptic. He had also greatly won the affection and esteem of the Aleppo merchants. A few years before succeeding to Raphoe he had refused the Bishopric of Kilmore, apparently from reluctance to supersede the deprived Nonjuror, Sheridan.

Richard Pococke [1] (Ossory 1756–65; Meath 1765) was also an Orientalist of note, though not so distinguished as his eminent predecessor and relative, Edward Pococke. He had been a great traveller, and had written upon Eastern manners, and on various antiquarian and architectural subjects.

There were two Irish bishops of the name of Synge in the seventeenth century, and three in the eighteenth, all of the same family. Of the Edward Synge [2] who was Bishop of Raphoe in 1714, and Archbishop of Tuam in 1716 to 1741, King, when first recommending him for a see, spoke in terms of great praise. 'The Church,' he said, 'wants such men more than they want the Church.' He was a pious and learned man, and a great benefactor to his diocese. His son, of the same name,[3] Bishop successively of Clonfert, Ferns, Cloyne, and Elphin, was a college friend of Berkeley, and always intimate with him. He was author of a book, at one time much read, entitled 'The Gentleman's Religion.' Mrs. Delany speaks of him as too fond of state and magnificence.

Nathanael Foy [4] (Waterford 1691–1708) had suffered much in James II.'s time for his staunch opposition to Rome, and is spoken of by King as having, as a Dublin clergyman, won great love in very difficult times. Edward

---

[1] Nichols, v. 652; Mant, ii. 623–26.   [2] Mant, ii. 282, 312, 561.
[3] Fraser, iv. 21, 146, &c.; Delany's *Corresp.*, iii. 86.
[4] Ware, p. 543; Mant, pp. 92, 195.

Tennison [1] (Ossory 1731-85), a relation of the Archbishop of Canterbury, was a preacher of note, and a very ardent champion of the Protestant cause. John Vesey,[2] Archbishop of Tuam (1679-1716), had felt the penalties of a bill of attainder during the short period of Roman Catholic predominance. In the following reigns his counsels were valued, and he was three times Lord Justice. He wrote the life of Archbishop Bramhall. His son, Sir Thomas Vesey [3] (Killaloe 1713; Ossory 1740-50), was also held in much esteem. John Stearne [4] (Dromore 1713; Clogher 1717-45) was an excellent bishop. Swift, though not one of his friends, said of him that if he were asked who would make a good bishop, he should name him before anybody. Archbishop King thought he ought to have the busiest episcopal post in Ireland, and wished he might succeed him at Dublin. His benefactions to the Church and education were very great. He wrote a very useful little book on the Visitation of the Sick, which was reprinted in the present century. King also spoke very highly of Nathaniel Vigors (Ferns 1690-1721) as 'an eminent example of Christian piety and charity through his whole life.' Joseph Story (Killaloe 1760-62; Kilmore 1742-57) was the author of an erudite treatise on the priesthood. Nicholas Forster (Killaloe 1714-16; Raphoe 1716-44) was a great builder of churches and schools. William Burscough appears to have been much beloved at Limerick (1725-55). Henry Maule (Cloyne 1726-32; Dromore 1732; Meath 1744-58) was an early and principal promoter of the Charter Schools. Charles Cobbe (Killaloe 1720; Dromore 1727; Kildare 1732; and Archbishop of Dublin from 1743 to 1765) is spoken of with respect as a generous, disinterested man. William Nicolson of Derry (1718-21), and then Archbishop

---

[1] Ware, p. 191; Mant, ii. 507. [2] Ware, p. 618; Mant, pp. 55, 279.
[3] Mant, p. 506. [4] Mant, pp. 217, 587.

of Cashel (1721-27), has been spoken of among the English bishops, as also John Evans (Meath 1716-24).

Theophilus Bolton (Bishop of Clonfert in 1722, of Elphin in 1724, and Archbishop of Cashel from 1729 to 1744) was a very able, eloquent man, of whom much was expected. But high place did not improve his character. He threw himself with great ardour into politics in the so-called Irish interest, and became very secular and very ambitious. He did much to improve land by great works of drainage.

There was much outcry at Thomas Rundle's [1] appointment to Derry (1735-43). His nomination to the see of Gloucester in 1733 had been reversed in consequence of the vehement opposition of Bishop Gibson of London, who charged him with heretical opinions. The accusation was not very substantially grounded, and was based partly on a former intimacy with Whiston, and partly upon an expression which he was said to have used some years before in conversation. He had also been on friendly terms with Chubb, the Deist. It was true that he had constantly preached and spoken against Collins, Woolston, and Tindal, and that Dean Conybeare and other men high in the Church spoke warmly in his favour. The doubts which had been raised against him prevailed; and when, therefore, a year or two afterwards he was appointed to Derry there was very naturally a loud murmur raised in Ireland that a man who had been rejected in England was thought good enough for an Irish see. Rundle, however, quite outlived all disfavour. His humorous and vivacious wit may have betrayed him some time or other into an irreverent

---

[1] Mant, pp. 537-43; Swift's Poets, *Works*, 'On Dr. Rundle;' Pope to Swift, 1735, Swift's *Works*, iv. 367; Lyttelton's *Persian Letters*, xxix.; Whiston's *Memoirs*, p. 268; Lord Hervey's *Memoirs*, i. 448-54; Lady Sundon's *Diary*, ii. 247-48; *Gentleman's Mag.* for 1734.

jest. But all who had to do with him found he was a good man, and a bishop whom they could greatly love and esteem; nor was there anything in his life out of general harmony with the words of a letter which he wrote to a friend only three weeks before he died: 'Believe me, my friend, there is no comfort in this world but a life of piety and virtue, and no death supportable but one comforted by Christianity, and its real and rational hope.' He was a warm-hearted man, of whom all his friends spoke in terms of far more than common attachment.

Robert Clayton[1] (Killaloe 1730; Cork 1735; Clogher 1745-58) was, on the contrary, very indisputably heterodox. He had been a great friend of Dr. Samuel Clarke, and had adopted his Arianism with many strange variations of his own. His Arianism, however, was by no means an objection with Queen Caroline, to whom he was recommended by his relative, Mrs. Clayton, afterwards Lady Sundon, the special favourite of the queen.[2] It should be added that his peculiar opinions were then not very pronounced, and that he was a man of much learning and very considerable gifts, with a commanding deportment, frank and conciliating manner, and very open-handed to all in need. On entering upon a considerable fortune he had resigned his senior fellowship at Dublin University, and had spent much time in travel. Made an Irish bishop by Queen Caroline's influence, and looked upon rather as a clever gentleman of the world than an ecclesiastic or a scholar, when in 1749 he published a work of great erudition on the chronology of the Old Testament, and a dissertation on prophecy, it

[1] Lady Sundon's *Diary*, vol. ii.; Hunt's *Relig. Thought in England*, iii. 303; Delany's *Correspondence*, i. 293, 373; ii. 399; iii. 493; Warburton and Hurd's *Corresp.*, p. 93; Mant, 614-17.

[2] It is said that among Dr. Clarke's letters was found one which showed that he had refused the offer of an Irish bishopric (Seward's *Anecdotes*, ii. 320).

was scarcely believed that he could have been the author. His subsequent publications caused surprise of a different kind. In 1751 he fathered and published under his own auspices a treatise written, it is said, by a young clergyman, entitled an 'Essay on Spirit,' containing a number of wild speculations on the nature of the Trinity. In his dedication of it to Primate Stone, Clayton expressed his strong disagreement from the Articles and other formularies of the Church, and at a later date he further moved in the Irish House of Lords that the Nicene as well as the Athanasian Creeds should be expunged from the Irish Liturgy. The speech, and his action generally, gave great offence, which came to a head the next year, when his divergence from the faith of the Church was still more developed in the third part of a work on the Old and New Testament. A legal prosecution was ordered, and deprivation seemed probable. But the excitement was too great for his highly strung temperament. He was seized with a nervous fever, and died before the proceedings were opened. In his private character there seems to have been a singular mixture of worthy and unworthy elements, noble-hearted generosity by the side of mean sycophancy. He was very fond of display, pomp, and magnificence, but exceedingly abstemious in all his personal habits. His great error plainly was that he did not resign his high office in the Church when his views had become so wholly inconsistent with its doctrines.

Among the later bishops of the century, the best known to fame among ordinary readers is undoubtedly Thomas Percy [1] (Dromore 1782-1811), so well remembered by his 'Reliques of Ancient English Poetry.' He published this in 1765, while he was chaplain to his kinsman, the Duke of Northumberland. In 1769 he was appointed a chaplain

[1] Nichols, iii. 160, 753; Mant, p. 680.

to the king; in 1778 he was Dean of Carlisle. At Dromore he was much venerated as a benevolent and vigilant bishop, who resided constantly, and was as unremitting in his attention to the poor as he was kind and hospitable to all. For many years before his death he was blind. In earlier days he had taken a leading place in the best literary society of his age, with Johnson, Reynolds, and other illustrious men of letters. His 'Reliques' almost mark an era in the history of English literature, as introducing an element of mediævalism which had a most fruitful and refreshing influence on the somewhat stilted diction which had long prevailed. For a time the ruling school of critics laughed his poetry into temporary neglect in England;[1] but Bürger and other German poets at once translated and imitated, and soon Percy's ballads became appreciated in their native country. Even Dr. Johnson, who had once led the attack, quite changed his tone, and recognised, if not the simple beauty of their language, at all events the charm which poetry could borrow from antiquarianism, and render back to it in turn. 'Percy's attention to poetry,' he said, 'has given grace and splendour to his studies of antiquity.'[2] Wordsworth considered the genius of Percy in this kind of writing superior to that of any other man by whom in modern times it has been cultivated.[3]

In the national movement of 1783 there was no notable of the day more conspicuous than Frederick Augustus Hervey, Earl of Bristol and Bishop of Derry. Before coming to this title by the death of his elder brother he had been Master of Magdalen College, Cambridge, and then Bishop of Cloyne, 1767, whence he was advanced to Derry

---

[1] Wordsworth's appendix on 'Poetical Diction,' *Poet. Works*, v. 217. He adds the remark that even Percy himself, in his *Hermit of Warkworth*, was cowed into adopting the more glossy and artificial style of his day.

[2] Boswell's *Johnson*, iii. 281.   [3] Wordsworth, as above.

in 1768. His episcopal functions sat very lightly upon him, his chief merit in this respect being that he promoted his clergy to livings with scrupulous regard to merit and qualifications.[1] We find him also, very unexpectedly, more commended by John Wesley than any other Irish bishop; and if we had only his account it would naturally be inferred that he was a most exemplary prelate. 'June 4, 1775: The Bishop (of Derry) preached a judicious useful sermon. He is both a good writer and a good speaker. And he celebrated the Lord's Supper with great solemnity. . . . June 6: The Bishop invited me to dinner, and told me, "I know you do not love *our* hours, and will therefore order dinner to be on table between two and three o'clock." We had a piece of boiled beef and English pudding. This is true good breeding. The bishop is entirely easy and unaffected in his whole behaviour, exemplary in all parts of public worship, and plenteous in good works.'[2] Unhappily, whatever might be the prelate's good qualities,[3] they were rarely exercised in his diocese. A great part of his time, and all his later years, were spent in Italy,[4] where he died in 1803. It is probable that his absenteeism was desired rather than not by the chief authorities in Church and State, for no one could calculate beforehand what wild and inconvenient fancies might come into the head of the eccentric bishop.

When the Volunteer movement was set on foot in Ulster, in 1783, nominally to protect the country from invasion, but practically to reform Parliament, and to save Ireland from being governed any longer by a narrow oligarchy,

---

[1] Hardy's *Memoirs of Charlemont*, ii. 103. [2] Wesley's *Works*, iii. 46.
[3] Mrs. Thomson, in a note to her edition of Lady Sundon's *Memoirs*, mentions an amiable action of his in building a chapel for the Roman Catholic bishop, that he might not have to preach in the open air. He appended the condition that he should pray in it for the king or queen (ii. 227, note). [4] Mant, ii. 695.

delegates were chosen by every corps to meet at Dublin, and consider the national grievances. The Bishop of Derry headed the four delegates of Londonderry. The enthusiasm which he threw into his movements, his title, his wealth, his influence, his engaging manner, and the splendour he affected, dazzled the great mass of the Irish people, and made him their idol. Through every town he passed he was received with loud acclamations and martial honours, and entered Dublin in almost royal state. A troop of light cavalry, magnificently accoutred, preceded him; a similar troop followed the procession. Trumpets announced his approach. The bishop-earl[1] himself sat in a chariot drawn by six horses, richly caparisoned. He was dressed in purple; several carriages followed in his suite, horses, equipages, and outriders, all in splendid trappings and liveries. Detachments from different volunteer corps joined in the cavalcade. 'Long live the bishop!' echoed from the windows, and thus, amid the shouts and cheers of thousands, he took his seat among the delegates in the Rotunda.[2] The high-flown language of his letter to the Presbytery of Derry was quite in accord with the gorgeous bombast of this amazing entry into Dublin. 'I do own to you the very rock which founds my cathedral is less immovable than my purpose to liberate this high-mettled nation from the petulant and rapacious oligarchy which plunder and insult it. A convulsion of nature might indeed shiver the one to atoms, but no convulsion, either of nature or of the State, could slacken my purpose; it may destroy, but it cannot stagger me.'[3] It must be added that nothing very great resulted from these heroics. The bishop was not arrested, as seemed at the moment probable; but his great plan

---

[1] 'A crack-brained prelate-peer' (Goldwin Smith's *Ireland and the Irish*, p. 166).   [2] Sir Jon. Barrington's *Irish Nation*, quoted in Mant, p. 690.
[3] Quoted in Mant, p. 694.

of at once conferring the franchise on the Roman Catholics[1] was defeated, and the bishop, who could ill bear being left in a minority, gradually subsided. On the suppression of the Volunteer corps he retired to Albano.

It only remains to add, as before, a few notes of some other bishops. William Barnard, previously Dean of Rochester (Raphoe 1744; Derry 1747-68), is mentioned with praise by John Wesley as 'the good old bishop . . . with whom I spent two or three hours in useful conversation.' His son, Thomas Barnard (Killaloe 1780; Limerick 1794-1806), was more noted as a literary man, full of wit and humour, a friend of Johnson and Goldsmith. Johnson complimented his conversation in a charade in which 'My whole is a man in whose converse is shared The strength of a Bar and the sweetness of Nard.' George Morley (Dromore 1745-63) was another member of the Literary Society in which Johnson was the presiding figure. Matthew Young (Clonfert 1799-1800) and Thomas L. O'Beirne (Ossory 1795; Meath 1798-1823) are both mentioned in Lord Cornwallis's letters with particular praise. The latter especially was a most energetic and excellent bishop. He had been a Roman Catholic, but became a Protestant chiefly through the influence of Hinchcliffe of Peterborough. His brother was a Roman Catholic priest in his diocese. Joseph Stock (Killala 1798-1809, and afterwards Waterford) was a great Hebrew scholar, and the author of a short Life of Berkeley. He behaved well when in 1798 the French landed at Killala, where he was then holding a visitation. He might have escaped, but allowed himself to be arrested in hopes that he might help to preserve life and property, an object in which he materially assisted. General Humbert treated him well. Matthew Young (Clonfert 1798-1800) is described as a good bishop, and the most

[1] Charlemont, ii. 109.

accomplished man in Ireland. Denison Cumberland (Clonfert 1763; Kilmore 1772-74) has been already mentioned with honour. Isaac Mann (Cork 1772-89), Richard Chenevix, of Huguenot extraction (Killaloe 1745; Waterford 1746-79), and Robert Fowler (Killaloe 1771; Dublin 1778-1801) were all high in repute. William Bennett (Cork 1790; Cloyne 1791-1820) was an able preacher and a distinguished scholar. Archbishop Agar, afterwards Baron Somerton (Cloyne 1768-80; Cashel 1780-1801), was a great benefactor to the Irish Church. It may be added that he revived the office of rural deans. Edward Maurice (Ossory 1754-56) translated Homer into blank verse. The last who need be mentioned is Richard Woodward (Cloyne 1781-94), a pious and eloquent man, the author of a tract of 137 pages on the state of the Church of Ireland in 1787. In Parliament he spoke in favour of increased privileges to the Roman Catholic majority, and he received the thanks of both Houses for his valuable exertions in establishing houses of industry for the distressed poor.

There were throughout the eighteenth century twenty-two Irish dioceses, and it will be evident that a great number of the bishops who from time to time occupied them have not been mentioned even by name in this sketch. Of one or two of these discreditable accounts might be given, and many, it is to be feared, were careless and more or less negligent of their charge. But many others have been omitted simply because they appear to have been decent, respectable men, of whom nothing worth record has been told. It must be acknowledged that throughout the century it was very easy for an Irish bishop—even more so than for an English one—to live well up to the required standard of opinion. No one in Church or State expected him to trouble himself very much about the

Roman Catholic masses. If he took a moderate interest in the charity schools, and was charitable in times of special distress, he was doing all that could, on this point, be asked of him. Speaking generally, Protestant Churchmen, and they only, were his care. But as, in most parts of Ireland, these were comparatively few, and the dioceses were small, it could rarely be said, even of the most active bishops, that their work was laborious. It would be, to some extent, mere negative praise to say of a modern bishop that he was resident, hospitable, studious, and good ; it was very positive praise in the last century.

APPENDIX.

BISHOPS[1] from 1700 to 1800.

CANTERBURY.
1695 Thomas Tenison
1716 William Wake
1737 John Potter
1747 Thomas Herring
1757 Matthew Hutton
1758 Thomas Secker
1768 Hon. Fred. Cornwallis
1783 1805 John Moore

YORK.
1691 John Sharp
1714 Sir W. Dawes, Bart.
1724 Launcelot Blackburn
1743 Thomas Herring
1747 Matthew Hutton
1757 John Gilbert
1761 Hon. Rob. Hay Drummond
1777--1807 William Markham

For convenience of reference the remaining sees are arranged alphabetically.

ST. ASAPH.
1692 Edward Jones
1703 George Hooper
1704 William Beveridge
1708 William Fleetwood
1715 John Wynne
1727 Francis Hare
1732 Thomas Tanner
1736 Isaac Maddox
1743 John Thomas
1744 Samuel Lisle
1748 Hon. Rob. H. Drummond
1761 Richard Newcome
1769 Jonathan Shipley
1789 Samuel Halifax
1790--1802 Lewis Bagot

BANGOR.
1689 Humphrey Humphreys
1702 John Evans
1716 Benjamin Hoadly
1721 Richard Reynolds
1723 William Baker
1728 Thomas Sherlock
1734 Charles Cecil
1738 Thomas Herring
1743 Matthew Hutton
1747 Zachariah Pearce
1756 John Egerton
1769 John Ewer
1775 John Moore
1783--1800 John Warren

[1] It has not been thought necessary to append a list of Irish bishops. The list may be found in the Appendix to Bishop Mant's *History of the Irish Church.*
There will be found some discrepancies in the spelling of names and in dates here and there in the body of the work. There was frequent variation in the spelling of names; old and new style causes some confusion; and accession to a see is apparently not reckoned by all writers from the same time. In this list, as in the Index and Table of Contents, the names and dates are taken from Le Neve's *Fasti Ecclesiæ Anglicanæ,* though even his orthography of a name is not always consistent. Accessions are here reckoned from consecration, and the years from January.

APPENDIX

BATH AND WELLS.

1691	Richard Kidder
1703	George Hooper
1727	John Wynne
1743	Edward Willes
1774 1802	Charles Moss

BRISTOL.

1691	John Hall
1710	John Robinson
1714	George Smalridge
1719	Hugh Boulter
1724	William Bradshaw
1733	Charles Cecil
1735	Thomas Secker
1737	Thomas Gooch
1738	Joseph Butler
1750	John Coneybeare
1756	John Hume
1758	Philip Yonge
1761	Thomas Newton
1782	Lewis Bagot
1783	Christopher Wilson
1792	Spencer Madan
1794	Henry Reg. Courtenay
1797-1808	Folliot Cornwall

CARLISLE.

1684	Thomas Smith
1702	William Nicolson
1718	Samuel Bradford
1723	John Waugh
1735	Sir G. Fleming, Bart.
1747	Richard Osbaldeston
1762	Charles Lyttleton
1769	Edmund Law
1787	John Douglas
1791-1808	Edward Vernon

CHESTER.

1689	Nicholas Stratford
1707	Sir William Dawes, Bart.
1714	Francis Gastrell
1726	Samuel Peploe

1752	Edmund Keene
1771	William Markham
1776	Beilby Porteus
1788-1800	William Cleaver

CHICHESTER.

1696	John Williams
1709	Thomas Manningham
1722	Thomas Bowers
1724	Edward Waddington
1731	Francis Hare
1740	Matthias Mawson
1754	Sir Wm. Ashburnham, Bart.
1798-1824	Charles Buckner

ST. DAVID'S.

1687	Thomas Watson
1705	George Bull
1710	Philip Bisse
1713	Adam Otley
1724	Richard Smallbrooke
1731	Elias Sydall
1732	Nicholas Claggett
1743	Edward Willes
1744	Richard Trevor
1752	Anthony Ellis
1761	Samuel Squire
1766	Robert Lowth
1766	Charles Moss
1774	James Yorke
1779	John Warren
1783	Edward Smallwell
1788	Samuel Horsley
1794-1800	William Stuart

DURHAM.

1674	Lord Nathaniel Crew
1722	William Talbot
1730	Edward Chandler
1750	Joseph Butler
1752	Hon. Rich. Trevor
1771	John Egerton
1787	Thomas Thurlow
1791 1826	Hon. Shute Barrington

# APPENDIX

ELY.
1691 Simon Patrick
1707 John Moore
1714 William Fleetwood
1723 Thomas Green
1738 Robert Butts
1748 Sir Thomas Gooch, Bart.
1754 Matthias Mawson
1771 Edmund Keene
1781-1808 Hon. James Yorke

EXETER.
1689 Sir Jonath. Trelawney, Bart.
1708 Offspring Blackhall
1717 Launcelot Blackburn
1724 Stephen Weston
1742 Nicholas Claggett
1747 George Lavington
1762 Hon. Fred. Keppel
1778 John Ross
1792 William Buller
1797-1803 H. R. Courtenay

GLOUCESTER.
1691 Edward Fowler
1715 Richard Willis
1721 Joseph Wilcocks
1731 Elias Sydall
1735 Martin Benson
1752 James Johnson
1760 William Warburton
1779 Hon Jas. Yorke
1781 Samuel Halifax
1789-1802 Rich. Beadon

HEREFORD.
1691 Gilbert Ironside
1701 Humphrey Humphreys
1712 Philip Bisse
1721 Benjamin Hoadly
1724 Hon. Henry Egerton
1746 Lord Jas. Beauclerk
1781 Hon. John Harley
1788-1802 John Butler

LICHFIELD AND COVENTRY.
1699 John Hough
1717 Edward Chandler
1731 Richard Smallbrooke
1750 Hon. Fred. Cornwallis
1768 John Egerton
1771 Hon. Brownlow North
1774 Richard Hurd
1781-1824 Jas. Cornwallis, Earl of Cornwallis

LINCOLN.
1695 James Gardiner
1705 William Wake
1716 Edmund Gibson
1723 Richard Reynolds
1744 John Thomas (1)
1761 John Green
1779 Thomas Thurlow
1787-1820 Sir G. Pretyman Tomline

LLANDAFF.
1679 William Beaw
1707 John Tyler
1724 Robert Clavering
1729 John Harris
1734 Matthias Mawson
1740 John Gilbert
1749 Edward Cresset
1755 Richard Newcome
1761 John Ewer
1768 Jonathan Shipley
1769 Hon. Shute Barrington
1782-1816 Richard Watson

LONDON.
1675 Henry Compton
1714 John Robinson
1723 Edmund Gibson
1748 Thomas Sherlock
1761 Thomas Hayter
1762 Richard Osbaldeston
1764 Richard Terrick
1777 Robert Lowth
1787-1809 Beilby Porteus

NORWICH.

1691 John Moore
1708 Charles Trimnell
1721 Thomas Green
1723 John Leng
1727 William Baker
1733 Robert Butts
1738 Thomas Gooch
1748 Samuel Lisle
1749 Thomas Haytor
1761 Philip Yonge
1783 Lewis Bagot
1790 George Horne
1792-1805 Charles Manners Sutton

OXFORD.

1699 William Talbot
1715 John Potter
1737 Thomas Secker
1758 John Hume
1766 Robert Lowth
1777 John Butler
1788 Edward Smallwell
1799-1806 John Randolph

PETERBOROUGH.

1691 Richard Cumberland
1718 White Kennet
1729 Robert Clavering
1747 John Thomas (2)
1757 Richard Terrick
1764 Robert Lambe
1769 John Hinchcliffe
1794-1813 Spencer Madan

ROCHESTER.

1684 Thomas Spratt
1713 Francis Atterbury
1723 Samuel Bradford
1731 Joseph Wilcocks

1756 Zachariah Pearce
1774 John Thomas (3)
1793-1802 Samuel Horsley

SALISBURY.

1689 Gibert Burnet
1715 William Talbot
1721 Richard Willis
1723 Benjamin Hoadly
1734 Thomas Sherlock
1748 John Gilbert
1757 John Thomas (2)
1761 Hon. Rob. Hay Drummond
1761 John Thomas (1)
1766 John Hume
1782 Hon. Shute Barrington
1791-1807 John Douglas

SODOR AND MAN.

1697 Thomas Wilson
1755 Mark Hildesley
1773 Richard Richmond
1780 George Mason
1784-1813 Claudius Crigan

WINCHESTER.

1684 Peter Mew
1707 Sir Jonath. Trelawney
1721 Charles Trimnell
1723 Richard Willis
1734 Benjamin Hoadly
1761 John Thomas (2)
1781-1820 Hon. Brownlow North

WORCESTER.

1700 William Lloyd
1717 John Hough
1743 Isaac Maddox
1759 James Johnson
1774 Hon. Brownlow North
1781-1808 Richard Hurd

LIST OF AUTHORS AND EDITIONS

QUOTED OR REFERRED TO.

No Author referred to at second hand is included in this List.

Abbey and Overton. *English Church in the Eighteenth Century*, 2 vols. 1878.
Adventurer, The (R. Hawkesworth), 1752.
Akenside, M. *Poems*, Anderson's 'British Poets.'
Alison, Sir A. *Life of Marlborough*, 2 vols. 1852.
Allen, T. *History of Lambeth*, 1827.
Anderson's *Poets of Great Britain*, 14 vols. 1793–95.
Anderson, J. S. M. *History of the Colonial Church*, 3 vols. 1856.
Angeloni, Baptista. *Letters on the English Nation*, 1755.
Annals of England, 1848.
Apology for the Parliament, &c. 1697.
Apthorp, E. *Sermon on Consecration of Bishop Halifax*, 1781.
Arblay, Madame D'. *Diary and Letters*, 7 vols. 1842–46.
Arnold, T. *Life and Correspondence* (Stanley), 1845.
Asylum for Fugitive Pieces in Prose and Verse, 1785.
Athenian Oracle, 1706–10.
Atterbury, Bishop F. *Memoirs*, by Folkestone Williams, 2 vols. 1869.
Babington, Charles. *Macaulay's Character of the Clergy considered*, 1849.
Baird, R. *Religion in the United States of America*, 1844.
Barbauld, A. L. *Works*, with memoir by L. Aikin, 2 vols. 1825.
Barclay, R. *Apology for the Quakers*, 1849.
Barrington, Sir Jonah. *Sketches of his own Times*, 3 vols. 1869.
Barrington, Shute, Bishop. *Sermons, Charges, and Tracts*, 1811.
Bell, Dr. *Life*, by Southey, 3 vols.
Benham, W. *Diocesan History of Winchester*, 1882.
Bennett, G. *On Ecclesiastical Establishments*, 1796.
Bentham, J. *History of Ely*, 1771.
Bentley, R. *Correspondence* (Wordsworth), 2 vols. 1842.
Binckes, Dr. *Animadversions on Two Jan. 31 Sermons*, 1702.

Bingham, T. *Works* (Pitman), 9 vols. 1838-40.
Bissett, W. *Plain English Sermon for Reformation of Manners*, 1704.
Blackburne, F., Archdeacon. *On the Intermediate State*, 1772.
Blake, W. *Life*, by Gilchrist, 2 vols. 1862.
Blomfield, F. *History of Norfolk*, 11 vols. 1806.
Boulter, Archbishop. *Letters to Ministers of State*, 2 vols. 1769.
Bray, T. *Bibliotheca Parochiana*, 1696.
" *Essay on Enlarging the Means of Knowledge*, 1697.
" *On Religion in America*, 1700.
" *Account of the Design of Dr. Bray's Associates*, 1787.
Brief Defence of the Church and State of England, &c., 1706.
Brokesby, F. *Letter to R. Nelson on the S.P.G.*, 1708.
Brooke, H. *Fool of Quality, or History of Henry, Earl of Moreland,
   with Memoir* (Kingsley), 2 vols. 1859.
" *Plays and Poems*, 4 vols. 1789.
Brown, J. *Estimate of Manners, &c*, 2 vols. 1757.
Bull, G., Bishop. *Life*, by Nelson (Buxton), 1827.
Burke, E. *Reflections on the F. Rev.* (Wordsworth's Christian Institutes).
Burnet, G., Bishop. *History of his own Time* (Bohn), 1857.
Burnet, G. *Four Discourses to the Sarum Clergy*, 1694.
Burney (*see* D'Arblay).
Butler, Joseph, Bishop. *Analogy and Sermons* (Angus).
" " *Durham Charge*, 1751.
" " *Memoirs of* (Bartlett), 1839.
Byrom, J. *Poems* (Chalmers' English Poets).
" *Literary Remains*, 4 vols. 1854-58.
Cairns, J. *Unbelief in the Eighteenth Century*, 1881.
Calamy, E. *Life and Times*, by himself (Rutt), 2 vols. 1830.
Campbell, Lord. *Lives of the Chancellors*, 7 vols. 1846-48.
Campbell, T. *Life and Letters* (Beattie), 3 vols. 1849.
Cassan, S. H. *Lives of the Bishops of Sherborne and Salisbury*, 1824.
" *Lives of the Bishops of Winchester*, 1827.
Caswall, H. *America and the American Church*, 1852.
" *American Church and American Union*, 1861.
Chalmers' *Biographical Dictionary.*
Chamberlain, T. *Select Letters* (Englishman's Library).
Channing, W. E. *Correspondence with L. Aikin*, 1874.
Charlemont, J., Earl of. *Life*, by F. Hardy, 2 vols. 1812.
Chateaubriand, F. F. A. *Essai sur la Litt. Angl.*, 1836.
Chesterfield, P., Earl of. *Characters of Remarkable Personages of his
   own Time*, 1777.
" " *Letters to his Son* (Stanhope), 1774.
Chubb, T. *Works*, 1733-45.
Church of England. Vindicated from Misrepresentation, by a Presbyter, 1801.

Churchill, C. Poems (Anderson).
Churton. Letter to Hurd on his Strictures on Secker, 1796.
Claggett, N., Bishop. Sermon at the Meeting of the Charity Schools, 1739.
Clarke, S. Memoir, by Whiston, 1748.
Clergy, Hardships of the Inferior, &c., 1722.
„ Justice of Restraining, &c., 1715.
Clergyman's Advocate, 1711.
Coleridge, S. T. Life, by J. Gilman, 1840.
Collings, Dr. Animadversions on a Sermon by Dr. Tillotson, 1680.
Complaint of the Church of England against Pluralities, &c., 1737.
Connoisseur, The (Coleman and Thornton), 1754.
Considerations on the Present State of Religion, 1801.
„ „ Scheme of Methodists, &c., 1794.
Cornwallis, C., Marquis. Correspondence (Ross), 3 vols. 1859.
Cowper, W. Poems, with Life (Stebbing), 1854.
Crisis, The, 1754.
Cudworth, Rd. Works (Birch), 2 vols. 1829.
Cumberland, R. Memoirs of Himself, 3 vols. 1807.
„ Plain Reasons for Belief. To the Patrons of the New Philosophy, 1801.
Cunningham, J. Church History of Scotland, 2 vols. 1859.
Curteis, G. H. Dissent in Relation to the Church of England, 1872.
Dallaway, A. History of Sussex, 2 vols.
De Foe, D. Tour through Great Britain, 3 vols. 1724.
Deism, Growth of, and other Tracts, 1709.
Delany, Mrs. Autobiography (Llanover), 6 vols. 1861-62.
Dibdin, T. F. Reminiscences, 2 vols. 1836.
Doddridge, P. Correspondence, &c. (Humphreys), 5 vols. 1803.
„ Sermon on the Earthquake, 1750.
Dodsley, R. Poems (Anderson).
Dodwell, H. Life, by F. Brokesby, 1715.
Doran, Dr. A Lady of the Last Century (Mrs. E. Montagu), 1873.
Dorner, J. A History of Protestant Theology (Robson and Taylor) 2 vols. 1871.
Douglas, J., Bishop. The Criterion, 1807.
Drake, F. History of City and Cathedral of York, 1736.
Eachard, J. Grounds of the Contempt of the Clergy, 1672.
Edinburgh Review.
Fabricius, J. A. Salutaris Lux Evangelii, 1731.
Fellows, J. Grace Triumphant, a Poem, 1772.
Fielding, H. Works, with Life, Murphy, 10 vols. 1784.
Fleetwood, W., Bishop. Works, 1737.
Fox, C. J. Memoir, by Lord Russell, 4 vols. 1853-57.
Frampton, R., Bishop. Life, by Evans, 1876.
Franklin. Autobiography, with Narrative by H. Weld.

Free Thoughts on the Pret. Dignity of the Clergy, 1700
Freeholder, The, 1716.
Freethinker, The, 3 vols. 1718-23.
Gambold, J. *Life and Works*, 1789.
Gardner, W. *University Sermon*, 1745.
Garth, Sir S. *Poems* (Anderson).
Gay, J. *Poems* (Anderson).
Gentleman's Magazine, v. d. from 1731.
Gibbon, E. *Memoirs of his Life* (Milman), 1854.
Gibson, E., Bishop. *Pastoral Letter*, 1739.
Gilbert, J., Bishop. *Sermon before S.P.G.*, 1744.
Godkin, Jas. *Ireland and her Churches*, 1867.
Goldsmith, O. *Life* (Sir J. Prior), 2 vols. 1837.
Graves, R., Dean. *Life and Works*, 4 vols. 1840.
Gray and Mason. *Correspondence* (Milford), 1853.
Green, Mat. *Poem* (Anderson).
Green, Valentine. *History of Worcester*, 2 vols. 1796.
Grose, F. *Olio of Essays and Anecdotes*, 1796.
Grub, G. *Ecclesiastical History of Scotland*, 4 vols. 1861.
Guardian, The, 1713.
Hallam, H. *Literature of Europe*, 4 vols. 1837.
Hansard. *Parliamentary Debates*, 1700-1800.
Hart, E. *Preservative against Comprehension*, 1718.
Harte, Walter. *Poems* (Anderson).
Hartley, D. *Observations on Man*, 1801.
Hayley, W. *Memoirs of his own Life*. 2 vols. 1823.
Hearne, T. *Reliquiæ* (Bliss), 3 vols. 1860.
Herring, Archbishop. *Letters to Duncombe*, 1777.
Hervey, J., Lord. *Memoirs of Reign of George II.*, 1848.
Hervey, Jas. *Meditations, &c., with Life*, 1803.
Hildesley, Bishop. *Life*, by Rivington, 1821.
Hill, Rowland. *Life*, by Charlesworth, 1877.
Hoadly, B., Bishop. *Works*, 3 vols. 1773.
Hope, Beresford. *Worship in the Church of England*, 1874.
Horne, G., Bishop. *Life and Works* (Jones of Nayland), 6 vols. 1809.
Horne, T. H. *On the Study of the Scriptures, and Sacred Philosophy*, 1839.
Horneck, A. *Life*, by Kidder, 1698.
Horsley, S., Bishop. *Charges*, 1830.
    „   *Sermons*, 1862.
    „   *Speeches in Parliament*, 1813.
Hough, J., Bishop. *Sermon before the Societies for Reformation of Manners*, 1704.
Howard, Sir R. *History of Religion*, 1694.
Hughes, J. *Letters of Eminent Persons*, 2 vols. 1772.
Hume, D. *My own Life*, 1777.

LIST OF AUTHORS AND EDITIONS

Hunt, J. *Religious Thought in the Eighteenth Century*, 3 vols. 1873.
Hurd, Bishop. *Assize Sermon*, 1752.
  ,, *Life*, by Kilvert, 1860.
  ,, *Correspondence with Warburton* (see Warburton).
Hutton, J. *Missionary Life in the South Seas.*
Idler, The, 1758.
Jefferson, S. *History of Carlisle.*
Jenyns, S. *Poems* (Anderson).
Jessop, A. *Diocesan History of Norwich*, 1882.
Johnson, J. *Clergyman's Vade Mecum*, 1709.
Johnson, T. *Account of the Present State of the Church of England.*
Johnson, S., Dr. *Life of Boswell*, 4 vols. 1823.
  ,, *Lives of the Poets* (Anderson), 1795.
Johnson, S., of Connecticut. *Life and Correspondence* (Beardsley), 1874.
  ,, ,, *Works*, by Lynam.
Jones, W., of Nayland. *Life and Works* (Stevens), 6 vols. 1810.
  ,, *Sermon before the Sons of the Clergy*, 1782.
Jones, W. B., and Freeman, E. A. *History of St. David's*, 1856.
Jortin, J. *Memoirs of his Life and Writings* (Disney), 1792.
  ,, *Tracts, Philological and Miscellaneous*, 1790.
Ken, T., Bishop. *Life*, by a Layman, 2 vols. 1854.
  ,, ,, by Bowles, 1830.
Kennet, White, Bishop. *Life*, by himself, 1730.
Kettlewell, J. *Life and Works* (Lee), 1719.
King, W., Archbishop. *Origin of Evil* (Law).
  ,, W., Dr. *Works, with Life by Nichols*, 3 vols. 1776.
Knox, Alex. *Remains*, 4 vols. 1836.
Knox, Vices. *Elegant Extracts in Poetry.*
Lamb, C. *Memoirs*, by R. Cornwall.
Lathbury, T. *History of the Nonjurors*, 1843.
Lavington, G., Bishop. *Enthusiasm of Methodists and Papists compared* (Polwhele), 1833.
Law, E., Bishop. *Considerations on the Theory of Religion*, 1774.
Law, W. *Works*, 9 vols. 1762.
  ,, *Extracts from, and Life* by E. Tighe, 1813.
  ,, *Life and Opinions*, by J. A. Overton, 1881.
Lechler, G. V. *Geschichte des Englischen Deismus*, 1841.
Le Clerc, J. *Bibliothèque Choisie*, 1728-31.
Le Neve. *Fasti Ecclesiæ Anglicanæ* (Hardy), 1854.
Lecky, W. E. H. *History of England in the Eighteenth Century*, 1875.
Leslie, C. *Theological Works*, 6 vols. 1832.
Lloyd, R. *Poems* (Anderson).
Lowth, R., Bishop. *Letter to Warburton.*
Lyttelton, G., Lord. *Works* (Ayscough), 1775.

Lyttelton, G., Lord. *Poems* (Anderson).
Macaulay, Lord. *History of England*, 8 vols. 1858.
Mackay, Jas. *Journey through England*, 1724.
Macneven, W. J. *Pieces of Irish History*, 1807.
Mahon, Lord. *History of England*, 1713-83, 7 vols. 1854.
Maistre, Compte Jos. de. *Considérations sur la France*, 1844.
Malcolm, J. P. *Anecdotes of Manners, &c., of London*, 1810.
Mandeville, B. *Fable of the Bees*, appended to Maurice's edition of *Law's Answer*, 1846.
Mant, Bishop. *History of the Church of Ireland*, 2 vols. 1840.
Martyn, H. *Journal and Letters* (Wilberforce), 1820.
Mason, W. *Poems*, 1811.
Massey, W. *History of England*, 1745-1802, 4 vols. 1855-63.
Matter, M. J. *Histoire de Christianisme*, 1839.
Maty's Review, 5 vols. 1782-86.
Maurice, F. D. *Introduction to Law's 'Answer to Mandeville,'* 1846.
Memorial to the Clergy, 1723.
Mirror, The, 1779.
More, Hannah. *Works*, 11 vols. 1830.
  „   *Memoirs* (Roberts), 1830.
More, Henry. *Philosophical Writings*, 1712.
Mosheim, *Ecclesiastical History* (Maclaire), 5 vols. 1758.
Moss, Archdeacon. *Visitation Charge*, 1764.
Moss, R. *Sermon before the Charity Schools*, 1708.
Müller, Max. *Introduction to the Science of Religion*, 1873.
Murray, R. *Ireland and her Churches*, 1846.
Murray, T. B. *Jubilee Tract of S.P.C.K.*, 1850.
Napleton, J. *Advice to a Student*, 1795.
Nelson, R. *Life*, by Secretan, 1860.
  „   „ by Teale, 1840.
Newton, J. *Works*, 2 vols. 1828.
Newton, T., Bishop. *Works and Autobiography*, 6 vols. 1787.
Nichols, J. *Literary Anecdotes of the Eighteenth Century*, 1812-15.
Nicolson, W., Archbishop. *Letters on Various Subjects* (Nichols), 1809.
Noble, M. *Continuation of Granger's Biographical History*, 7 vols. 1804-6.
Occasional Thoughts on the Memorial of the Church of England, 1705.
Oglethorpe, Jas. *Memoirs* (Wright), 1867.
Oliphant, Mrs. *Historic Sketches of the Reign of George II.*, 2 vols. 1869.
Onslow, Ph. *Diocesan History of Worcester*, 1883.
Orford, H. Walpole, Earl of. *Memoir of Last Ten Years of George II.* (Holland), 2 vols. 1846.
  „   *Memoirs of Reign of George III.* (Le Marchant), 1845.
  „   *Journal*, 1771-83 (Doran), 2 vols. 1859.

LIST OF AUTHORS AND EDITIONS

Ormerod, G. *History of Cheshire*, 1819.
Overton, J. H. *Life in the English Church*, 1660-1714, 1885.
Oxford Essays, 1868.
Paley, W. *Works*, 1846.
  „   *Memoirs* (Meadley), 1809.
Parliamentary History, v. d.
Parr, S. *Life and Works* (Johnstone), 1828.
Paterson, Jas. *Pietas Londinensis*, 1714.
Pattison, Mark. *Tendencies of Religious Thought in England*, 1688-1755 (Essays and Reviews), 1860.
  „   *Memoirs*, 1885.
Pearce, Z., Bishop. *Life*, by himself, 1816.
Perry, G. *History of the Church of England*, 1861-64.
Pitt, Ch. *Poems* (Anderson).
Plain English made Plain, 1704.
Polwhele, R. *Introduction to Lavington.* (See Lavington.)
  „   *History of Devonshire*, 1797.
Pope, A. *Poems* (Anderson).
  „   *Works* (Croker), 8 vols. 1871-73.
Potter, J., Archbishop. *Works*, 1753.
Prideaux, H. *Life, with Tracts and Letters*, 1748.
Principles of the Reformation concerning Church Communion, 1704.
Public Characters, 1823.
Purcell, E. S. (Archbishop Manning's Essays on Religion and Literature), 1870.
Quarterly Review.
Report of Lincolnshire Clergy, 1800.
Rigg, J. H. *Churchmanship of J. Wesley*, 1878.
Roberts, G. *Social History of the Southern Counties*, 1856.
Rogers. *Letter to the Lords on the Occ. Conf. Bill*, 1704.
Romaine, W. *Essays on Psalmody*, 1775.
Romilly, Sir S. *Memoirs of his own Life*, 2 vols. 1841.
Rowe, R. *Diary of an Early Methodist* (N. Pidgeon), 1880.
Russell, M. *History of the Church in Scotland*, 2 vols. 1834.
Sacheverell, H. *Sermon on False Brethren*, 1709.
Schleiermacher, F. *Life*, by Rowan, 1860.
Schlosser, F. C. *History of the Seventeenth and Eighteenth Centuries* (Davidson), 1843-52.
Scott, J. *Short and Easy Way*, &c. (Somers Tracts), 1713.
Scourge, The, by T. L. (Lewis), 1720.
Secker, T., Archbishop. *Eight Charges*, 1769.
Seward, W. *Anecdotes of Distinguished Persons*, 4 vols. 1798.
Sewell, W. H. *Account of the S.P.C.K.*, 1874.
Shaftesbury. *Characteristics* (Hatch), 1870.
Sharp, J., Archbishop. *Life*, by T. Sharp (Newcome), 2 vols. 1825.
Shenstone, W. *Poems* (Anderson).

Sheridan. R. B. *Dramatic Works, with Life* (Bohn), 1848.
Sherlock, T., Bishop. *Works*, 4 vols. 1812.
    „   *On Religious Associations.*
Shipley, Jon., Bishop. *Works*, 2 vols. 1792.
Skeats, H. S. *History of the Free Churches*, 1688-1851, 1869.
Smith, G. *History of the Missionary Societies.*
Smith, Goldwin. *Irish History and Character*, 1861.
Smith, R. *Sermons*, 1823.
Somers, *Collection of Scarce Tracts* (Sir W. Scott), 1809-15.
Somerville, T. *My own Life and Times*, 1841.
Somerville, W. *Poems* (Anderson).
Southey, R. *Life and Correspondence* (C. Southey), 1849.
    „   *Poets, Works*, 1838.
    „   *Sermons*, 2 vols. 1823.
    „   *Specimens of Later E. Poets*, 1807.
Spectator, The, 1710-14.
S.P.G., Account of, 1706.
    „   *Collection of Papers*, 1702.
    „   *On the Danish Mission*, 1719.
    „   *Proceedings*, 1785.
Sprat, T., Bishop. *Poems* (Anderson).
Stanley, A. C. *Historical Memorials of Westminster Abbey*, 1868.
Stoughton, J. *Church of the Revolution*, 1874.
Sundon, Lady. *Memoirs and Correspondence*, 2 vols. 1847.
Surtees, R. *History, &c., of the County of Durham*, 2 vols. 1816-40.
Swift, Dean. *Life and Works* (Sir W. Scott), 19 vols. 1824.
    „   *Life*, by Craik, 1882.
Tatler, The, 1709.
Tayler, J. J. *Retrospect of Religious Life in England*, 1876.
Taylor, J. *Wesley and Methodism*, 1851.
Thirlwall, Bishop. *Literary Remains.*
Thomas, J., Bishop of Rochester. *Sermons, &c., and Life* by G. H. Thomas, 1796.
Thomson, Jas. *Poems* (Anderson).
Tillotson, J. Archbishop. *Works, with Life* by Birch, 10 vols. 1820.
Toland, J. *State Anatomy of Great Britain*, 1717.
Tomline, G. P., Bishop. *Charge of* 1794.
Toplady, Aug. *Works, with Memoir*, 6 vols. 1825.
Trimmer, Mrs. *Life and Writings*, 2 vols. 1814.
Tucker, Jos., Dean. *Tracts*, 3 vols. 1772-85.
Tyerman, L. L. *Oxford Methodists*, 1873.
Vaughan, R. A. *Hours with the Mystics*, 1856.
Verses, Collection of, 1775.
Voltaire, F. A. *Essai sur les Mœurs*, 1818.
Wagstaffe, W. *Works*, 1726.
Wakefield, Gilbert. *Memoirs*, 1792.

Walcot, M. E. C. *Customs of Cathedrals*, 1872.
Wall, W. *Dissuasive from Schism* (in Wordsworth's Christian Institutes).
Walpole (*see* Orford).
Warburton, W., Bishop. *Works*, 7 vols. 1788.
„   „   *Correspondence with Hurd*, 1809.
„   „   *Life*, by J. S. Watson, 1863.
Ware, Sir Jas. *History of the Bishops, &c., of Ireland*, 1764.
Warren, J., Bishop. *January 31 Sermon*, 1783.
Warton. *Notes to Pope's Works*.
Waterland, D. *Works, with Life* (Van Mildert), 6 vols. 1823.
Watson, R., Bishop. *Anecdotes of his own Life*, 2 vols. 1818.
Watts. *Lyric Poems* (Anderson).
Wedgwood, J. *John Wesley and the Evangelistic Reaction*, 1870.
Weekly Miscellany, 1773.
Wesley, J. *Works*, 14 vols. 1829.
Wesley, S. *Reply to S. Palmer*, 1704.
Whiston, W. *Memoirs of his own Life*, 2 vols. 1769.
Whitefield, G. *Letters*, 1772.
Whitehead, P. *Poems* (Anderson).
Wilberforce, W. *Practical View*, &c., 1797.
„   *Life*, by his Sons, 5 vols. 1839.
„   *His Friends and Times* (Colquhoun), 1866.
Wilcox, J., Bishop. *Sermon on the Irish Working Schools*, 1739.
Willis, Browne. *Survey of Cathedrals*, 3 vols. 1742.
Wilson, D. *Pilgrim Fathers*, 1849.
Wilson, H. B. *History of Merchant Taylors*, 1814.
Wilson, T., Bishop. *Life*, by Keble, 2 vols. 1862.
„   „   „   by Cruttwell, 1782.
Woodward, J. *On the Societies for Reformation of Manners*, 1711.
Wordsworth, Chr. *Social Life at the English Universities*, 1874.
Wordsworth, W. *Poems* (Moxon), 6 vols. 1849.
„   *Life*, by C. Wordsworth, 2 vols. 1851.
World, The, 1753.
Worthington, W. *Essay on Redemption*, 1745.

INDEX.

ABE

ABERNETHY, Bishop, ii. 95
Abjuration Act, i. 5
Abuses, Church, i. 371-77
Academies, i. 331
Addison, i. 43, 59; ii. 27, 29
Adulation, i. 377; ii. 23
Agar, Bishop, ii. 354
Agistment, ii. 305
Akenside, M., ii. 1
Aleppo, factory of, i. 80, 167
Allegiance, oath of, i. 5, 127
'Alliance of Church and State,' Warburton's, ii. 113-16
America, i. 56, 73-91, 349 66; ii. 125, 185-93, 336-37
American war, ii. 86, 152, 242, 213-44, 280
Analogy, argument from, ii. 57
Angeloni, Baptista, i. 214; ii. 16, 88
Anne, Queen, i. 68 n.
Anne, Queen, reign of, i. 182
Annet, P., i. 34, 227
Antinomianism, i. 291, 305-6
Apthorp, i. 366
Arian subscription, i. 38
Arianism, i. 36-39, 104; ii. 312
Armagh, see of, ii. 296-97
Arminianism, i. 39
Arnold, Dr., ii. 152
Articles, the Thirty-nine (*see* Subscription)
Ashburnham, Bishop, Sir W., ii. 72
Ashbury, ii. 133, 134
Ashe, Bishop, ii, 307
Associations, religious, i. 50-52, 116
Athanasian Creed, ii. 28
Atkins, W., ii. 286
Atonement, i. 238-39
Atterbury, Bishop F., i. 31, 39, 70, 96, 142-49, 199, 375; ii. 18, 26, 28, 29
Authority, ii. 7 8, 11

BEV

BAGOT, Bishop, ii. 187, 244-45
Baker, Bishop, ii. 31
Balguy, J., ii. 119, 127
Bamborough Castle, i. 166
Bangorian controversy, i. 36, 194; ii. 10-15, 50, 110
Baptist Missionary Society, ii. 198, 200
Barbauld, Mrs., i. 370; ii. 118, 165
Barclay, R., i. 248
Barnard, Bishops T. and W., ii. 353
Barrington, Bishop, ii. 220-23
Barrington, D., ii. 220
Barrington, Lord, ii. 221
Barrington, Sir Jon., ii. 290
Bathurst, Lord, i. 145
Beadon, Bishop, ii. 274
Beauclerk, Bishop, ii. 76
Beaufoy, Mr., ii. 88
Beaw, Bishop, i. 162
Bedell, Bishop, ii. 289
Bedford, Duke of, i. 364
Behmen, J., i. 294-95, 299
Bell, Dr., ii. 170 73
Belsham, J., i. 42
Benbow, Admiral, i. 58
Bennet, Bishop, ii. 354
Bennett, T., i. 39, 42, 203
Benson, Bishop, i. 363, 381, 385; ii. 41, 62 63, 333-41
Benson, G., i. 212
Bentley, Dr. R., i. 65; ii. 61, 64
Beresford, Lord Bishop, ii. 315
Berkeley, Bishop, i. 28, 35, 43, 63, 206, 349, 353, 379, 382; ii. 68, 312, 329-44
Berkeley, Dr., i. 310; ii. 186
Bermuda, i. 84, 349; ii. 334-36
Berridge, J., ii. 140
Berryman, W., i. 39
Beveridge, Bishop, i. 51, 135-37

B D 2

BIB

Bible Society, ii. 90
Bibles, i. 55, 346
Bingham, Jos. i. 42
Bishops, i. 92-182, 365-99; ii. 1-73, 205-74
Bishops for America, i. 57, 358, 362-64; ii. 46, 185-89
Bishops, Irish, ii. 313-56
Bisse, Bishop, i. 161
Bisse, T., i. 161
Bisset, W., ii. 174
Blackburn, Archbishop, i. 374-76; ii. 35
Blackburne, F., i. 223, 241; ii. 91, 122, 246-47
Blackhall, Bishop, i. 153-54
Blackstone, Judge, i. 216
Blair, J., i. 82
Blake, W., i. 332; ii. 154
Böhler, P., i. 304, 308
Bolingbroke, i. 19, 23, 146, 227, 229
Bolton, Archbishop, ii. 347
Bonwicke, A., i. 66
Bossuet, i. 4, 95, 134
Boulter, Archbishop, ii, 35, 282, 283, 287, 299, 301, 317-21
Bounty, Queen Anne's, i. 68 n., 114; ii. 304
Bowers, Bishop, ii. 35
Boyle, Archbishop, ii. 297, 315
Boyle, R., i. 78, 82
Boyne, Mr., ii. 89
Bradford, Bishop, ii. 34
Bradshaw, Bishop, ii. 35
Bray, Dr., i. 47, 54-57, 83-86, 340, 352
Brett, T., i. 40; ii. 104
Bristol, Earl of, Bishop, 300-2
Brokesby, F., i. 87, 113, 170
Brooke, H., i. 241, 249, 299-301; ii. 313
Brown, Bishop J., ii. 312
Brown, Dr. J., i. 230, 327, 339
Brown, M., ii. 144
Brown, N., ii. 286
Browne P. i. 28; ii. 309, 311, 312, 341
Buckner, Bishop, ii. 272
Bull, Bishop G., i. 37, 42, 47, 60, 133-35
Buller, Bishop, ii. 270
Buller, C., ii. 97
Bunyan, J., i. 119
Burke, E., ii, 110-12, 127, 157
Burnet, Bishop G., i. 43, 47, 51, 54, 70, 110-15, 132, 160, 181, 370
Burney, Miss, ii. 167, 216, 224
Burscough, Bishop, ii. 346

CLA

Busby, Dr., i. 132
Butler, Bishop John, ii. 269
Butler, Bishop Jos., i. 23 n., 62, 217, 230, 363, 381-82, 390; ii. 41, 54-61, 112
Butler, Bishop R., ii. 76
Byrom, J., i. 70, 298; ii. 60

CALAMY, E., i. 47, 72, 95, 104, 177; ii. 178
Calvinism, ii. 148
Cambridge, i. 64-72, 320-28
Cambridge Platonists, i. 119
Cameronians, ii. 176
Camisards, i. 4
Campbell, J., i. 341
Campbell, R., ii. 154, 165
Canada, ii. 193
Carey, E., ii. 200
Caroline, Queen, i. 110, 138, 192, 378-80; ii. 22, 56, 59, 65
Carter, Mrs., ii. 69
Carteret, Lord, i. 379
Catechising, i. 61
Cecil, Bishop, ii. 76
Cecil, R., ii. 144, 150
Chandler, Bishop, ii. 25-26
Chandler, Dr. S., i. 207, 212, 254; ii. 25, 41, 52
Channing, Dr., ii. 181
Chaplains, i. 139
Chardin, Sir J., i. 86
Charity schools, 1. 59-60, 333-34, 339
Charlemont, Earl of, ii. 128, 322, 325
Charter schools, ii. 283, 287
Chateaubriand, ii. 159
Chatham, Lord, ii. 95, 221
Chenevix, Bishop, ii. 354
Cherry, F., i. 170
Chesterfield, Lord, i. 329, 380; ii. 283
Christian Knowledge Society (see Society)
'Christianity as old as Creation,' i. 246-48
'Christianity not founded on argument,' i. 252-53
Chubb, T., i. 26, 34, 227, 239; ii. 17, 111
Church and State, ii. 100-22
Church-building, i. 14, 194
Church fabrics, ii. 200
Churchill, C., i. 319, 373
Claggett, Bishop, ii. 71
Clarke, Dr. S., i. 36-39, 42, 117, 147, 157, 379, 380, 381; ii. 19, 41, 54
Clavering, Bishop, ii. 35, 36

INDEX

Clayton, Bishop, i. 223, 227, 379; ii. 259, 318-49
Cleaver, Bishop, ii. 273
Clergy, i. 32, 93-94, 181, 312
Clergy, Deistical attacks on, i. 33
Clergy, poverty among, i. 68-69, 318-19
Cobbe, Bishop, ii. 346
Codrington, Gen., i. 86, 90
Coke, Dr., ii. 133-34, 136
Colchester, Col., i. 50
Colchester, Lord, i. 86
Coleridge, S., ii. 131, 154, 165, 267
Collier, Jer., i. 42, 188
Collins, A., i, 32, 35, 41, 227, 233, 235, 239, 244, 381; ii. 26
Colonial Church, i. 56, 73-91, 349-66; ii. 193-96
Commonwealth, the, i. 174
Comprehension, Church, i. 14-17, 113, 115, 205-7; ii. 89
Compton, Bishop, i. 55, 81, 85, 106-7, 301
Conant, Dr. J., i. 134
Coneybeare, Bishop, ii. 67, 85
Conversion, i. 279 81, 394
Convocation, i. 5, 12-14, 144, 193-201, 225; ii. 11, 18
Convocation, Irish, ii. 311
Cornbury, Lord, i. 91
Cornwallis, Archbishop, ii. 97, 126, 205-6, 228
Cornwallis, Bishop, ii. 76
Cornwallis, Lord, ii. 290
Cornwell, Bishop, ii. 272
Coronation sermons, ii. 23, 209
Corporation Act, ii. 87
Courayer, Dr., i. 205, 218
Courtenay, Bishop, ii. 270
Coward, Dr., i. 41
Cowper, Lady, i. 382
Cowper, Lord, i. 90
Cowper, W., i. 326, 330; ii. 80, 88, 144-45, 151, 165
Cresset, Bishop, ii. 76
Crewe, Lord, Bishop, i. 164-66
Crigan, Bishop, ii. 274
Cross, emblem of, ii. 58
Cudworth, Ralph, i. 241
Cumberland, Bishop, ii. 289, 354
Cumberland, Duke of, ii. 183
Cumberland, R., i. 122-23

DAILLE, J., i. 219
Dame schools, i. 332, 335-37
'Danger of the Church,' i. 9, 46, 202
Danish missions, i. 89

Dawes, Archbishop, i. 153-55, 230
De Maistre, ii. 98
Defoe, D., i. 338
Deism, i. 24-36, 225-29, 257, 381; ii. 51-52, 56-59, 110, 127-28, 312
Delany, Mr., ii. 309
Derby, Earl of, i. 139
Derham, W., i. 42
Dibdin, T., i. 328
Diderot, ii. 128
Discipline, Church, i. 126, 201-2
Disinterested virtue, i. 30-31
Disney, J., ii. 125
Divine right, i. 126, 201-2
Dodd, Dr., ii. 83
Doddridge, P., i. 107, 217, 230, 253, 254; ii. 47, 52, 70, 113, 235
Dodwell, H., the Elder, i. 39-41, 170; ii. 104
Dodwell, H., the Younger, i. 227, 252-53
Douglas, Bishop, i. 290, 396; ii. 187, 261-63
Downes, Bishop, ii. 282, 307, 314
Drama, ii. 29
Drummond, Bishop, ii. 76, 209
Dryden, J., i. 173
Dublin University, ii. 284
Du Moulins, i. 177

EACHARD, Dr., i. 63, 68; ii. 51
Eastern Church, i. 58, 102, 167, 192
Education (see Universities, Public Schools, Grammar Schools, Elementary Schools, Charity Schools, Charter Schools, Dame Schools, Female)
Edward VI.'s Prayer Book
Egerton, Bishop H., ii. 35
Egerton, Bishop J., ii. 219
Elementary Education, i. 332-36; ii. 168-73, 287-89
Ellis, Bishop, ii. 73
Emlyn, J., i. 36
'English interest' in Ireland, ii. 299, 318
Enthusiasm, i. 29, 394, 398; ii. 79
Episcopate, i. 366-69, and see Bishops
Erastianism, ii. 106
Essayists, i. 43-44; ii. 109
Eucharist, the, ii. 15-17
'Evangelical Magazine,' ii. 89
Evangelical movement, i. 251, 258, 312; ii. 82, 138-52, 167, 215, 243
Evans, Bishop, i. 162

Evidences, Christian, i. 252-57
Evil, Origin of, i. 31
Ewer, Bishop, ii. 274

FALCONER, Bis' op, ii. 184
Fanaticism, ii. 80, 81
Feathers Tavern petition
Febronius, ii. 94
Fellenberg, ii. 172
Fellows, J., ii. 81
Female education, i. 73, 331
Fenelon, i. 4; ii. 91
Field preaching, i. 264-65
Fielding, H., i. 216, 231, 313, 329, 338, 341; ii. 10, 35
Firmin, T., i. 104
Fleetwood, Bishop, i. 63, 120-22; ii. 37
Fleming, Sir G., Bishop, ii. 68
Fletcher, J., i. 53, 187
Fleury, Cardinal, i. 138
Forbes, Lord, ii. 178
Foreign Protestants (see Protestants)
Forster, Bishop, ii. 346
Foster, Dr. J., i. 212, 213
Fowler, Bishop E., i. 118-19
Fowler, Bishop R., ii. 354
Foy, Bishop, ii. 345
Frampton, Bishop, i. 167-68
Francke, i. 294, 347
Franklin, B., i. 352, 357, 361; ii. 152, 212
Frederic I., i. 105
Frederic the Great, i. 205
'Free and Candid Disquisitions,' i. 197, 223, 225; ii. 126
'Freethinker,' the, ii. 64, 320
Freethinking, i. 25, 233-35
French prophets, i. 394

GALE, J., i. 39
Gallican Church, i. 74, 100-2
Gambold, J., i. 307-9
Gardiner, Bishop, i. 162
Gastrell, Bishop, i. 39, 42; ii. 29
George I., i. 8, 367; ii. 23
,, reign of, i. 183; ii. 1-36
George II., ii. 22, 23, 44, 75
,, reign of, i. 183; ii. 36
George III., i. 346, 364; ii. 82, 96, 206
,, reign of, ii. 77
Georgia, i. 349-53
German Protestants (see Protestants)
Gibbon, E., i. 298, 326, 330; ii. 1, 129, 241, 257, 266
Gibson, Bishop, i. 42, 384, 385-86; ii. 19
Gilbert, Bishop, ii. 47, 48

Godolphin, Lord, i. 13
Goldsmith, O., i. 67, 313; ii. 262
Gooch, Bishop T., ii. 68
Good Friday, ii. 214
Gordon, Bishop, ii. 185
Gordon riots, ii. 84, 95-97, 261
Gower, Earl, i. 372
Grabe, E., i. 42; ii. 28
Grafton, Duke of, ii. 210
Grammar schools, i. 330; ii. 310
Granville, Lord, ii. 205, 219
Graves, Dean, i. 344; ii. 310, 313
Gray, T., ii. 80
Green, Bishop, ii. 271
Green, M., ii. 110
Grenville, G., ii. 72, 271
Grimshaw of Haworth, ii. 141
Grose, F., i. 331
Grove, H., i. 208, 212
Guildford, Lord, i. 54, 86

HALIFAX, Bishop, ii. 240
Halifax, Lord, i. 364
Hall, Bishop, i. 151-2
Hall, R., ii. 130
Hanover, i. 204
Hanway, Jonas, i. 341; ii. 83
Hardwicke, Lord Ch., ii. 49
Hare, Bishop, ii. 61-2
Harley, Bishop, ii. 274
Harris, Bishop, ii. 76
Hartley, D., i. 223, 327; ii. 116
Haweis, ii. 144
Hawes, i. 188
Hayley, J., ii. 154
Hayter, Bishop, ii. 72
Hearne, T., i. 64, 71, 111; ii. 9
Heathcote, Lord, i. 91
Herring, Archbishop, i. 46, 186, 389; ii. 10, 37-40
Herrnhut, i. 304, 307, 308
Hervey, J., i. 44 n.; ii. 142, 151, 164
Hervey, Lord, i. 371, 373
Hervey, Lord, Bishop, ii. 300-2
Hewitson, i. 91
Hickes, G., i. 8, 39, 188, 190; ii. 104
'High' and 'Low' Church, i. 9, 12; ii. 32
High Churchmanship, i. 9, 113; ii. 80
Hildesley, Bishop, i. 389; ii. 66-67
Hill, R., ii. 144, 167, 175
Hinchcliffe, Bishop, ii. 153, 243-44
Hoadly, Archbishop J., i. 327; ii. 297, 321
Hoadly, Bishop B., i. 31, 102, 145, 194-96, 222, 382; ii. 1-20, 50, 110-12

INDEX 375

HOB

Hobart, Bishop, ii. 193
Hontheim, N. von, ii. 94
Hook, Justice, i. 50
Hooper, Bishop, i. 131
Horne, Bishop, i. 292, 309, 388; ii. 126, 144, 175, 187, 257-60
Horneck, A., i. 51-53, 137
Horsley, Bishop, ii. 99, 130, 156, 159, 165, 167, 170, 187, 263-69
Hospitals, i. 340
Hough, Bishop, i. 47, 129-31, 181
Howard, J., ii. 83
Howel, L., i. 192
Hume, Bishop, ii. 73
Hume, D., ii. 39, 57, 128-29, 223
Humphreys, Bishop, i. 162
Huntingdon, Countess of, ii. 95, 147, 206
Huntington, Bishop, ii. 309, 344
Hurd, Bishop, i. 199, 389, 391; ii. 42, 72, 119, 223-27, 235
Hurdis, J., ii. 165
Hutchinsonians, i. 309-12; ii. 141, 144, 258
Hutton, Archbishop, ii. 40

IMMORALITY, i. 45, 230; ii. 77-79
Imputed righteousness, ii. 152
Inactivity in the Church, i. 368, 398
India, i. 89, 347-48; ii. 196-97
Indians, American, i. 353
Ingham, B., i. 307
Inspiration, i. 237
Intolerance, i. 22; ii. 89
Ireland, i. 365; ii. 275-355
'Irish interest,' ii. 299
Ironside, Bishop, i. 156
Irreligion, i. 229-32; ii. 77, 272
Itinerant preachers, i. 265; ii. 90

JABLOUSKI, i. 99, 106
Jacobites, i. 5-8, 70-71, 146, 174, 184-87; ii. 80, 280, 311
James II., i. 5, 50
Jebb, J., ii. 125, 130, 152
Jews, i. 214-15
Johnson, Bishop, i. 364; ii. 71
Johnson, Dr. S., i. 63, 198, 292, 327, 363, 371; ii. 28, 63, 90, 117, 164, 241, 330, 350
Johnson, Dr. S., of Connecticut, i. 155, 230, 310, 335, 360-64; ii. 341
Johnson, J., i. 318
Jones, Bishop, i. 103
Jones of Alconbury, i. 223, 216

LOC

Jones of Nayland, i. 309; ii. 144
Jones, Sir W., ii. 197
Jortin, Dr., ii. 203, 223, 241, 249
Junius, ii. 269

KAFFRARIA, ii. 199
Kaime, Lord, ii. 58
Keene, Bishop, ii. 73
Ken, Bishop, i. 6, 43, 60, 63, 108, 132, 170-72; ii. 104, 178
Kennet, Bishop, i. 86, 90; ii. 31-33
Keppel, Bishop, ii. 270
Kettlewell, J., ii. 104
Kidder, Bishop, i. 123-24
King, Archbishop, i. 31, 43; ii. 279, 292, 301, 302, 303, 305, 312, 315-19
King, P., i. 43
Knox, V., i. 327

LADIES, education of, i. 73
Lambe, Bishop, ii. 274
Lambeth degrees, ii. 30
Lancaster, Jos., ii. 173
Langhorne, ii. 79
Lardner, N., i. 37; ii. 41, 129-31
Latitudinarians, i. 102
Lauderdale, Lord, ii. 208
Laurence, i. 40
Lavington, Bishop, i. 290, 394-96
Law, Bishop, i. 224, 241, 338; ii. 89, 245-51
Law, W., i. 180, 228, 240, 242, 248-49, 276, 291-98, 301, 307, 309; ii. 14-15, 219
Lay baptism, i. 39-41, 386
Le Clerc, i. 240
Lee, F., i. 241
Leibnitz, i. 381
Leighton, Archbishop, i. 112
Leland, i. 254; ii. 44, 127
Leslie, C., i. 191; ii. 104, 309, 311
Levant, English Church in, i. 80
Libraries, parochial and diocesan, i. 56-58
Lindsay, Archbishop, ii. 317
Lindsey, T., i. 37; ii. 60, 125, 130
Lisbon earthquake, i. 341; ii. 53
Lisle, Bishop, ii. 76
Literary Club, ii. 86, 262
Liturgy, American, ii. 190-93
Liturgy, revision of (see Revision)
Lloyd, Bishop, i. 125-28; ii. 25
Lloyd, Bishop (Nonj.), i. 169-70
Lloyd, R., i. 325
Locke, J., i. 24, 213, 381; ii. 102, 251

LON

London Missionary Society, ii. 89, 198
Low Church, i. 9; ii. 7
Lowth, Bishop, i. 321, 323-24, 384, 387; ii. 61, 211-13
Lutherans, i. 74, 98, 347; ii. 28
Lyttleton, Bishop, ii. 274
Lyttleton, Lord, i. 130, 313, 330, 372

MACARTNEY, Lord, ii. 196
Mackay, J., i. 319
Mackworth, i. 86
Maclaire, Dr., ii. 91
Madan, Bishop, ii. 274
Madan, M., ii. 144
Maddox, Bishop, i. 302; ii. 69-70, 183
Madras system of education, ii. 171
Malcolm, J. P., i. 339
Malebranche, ii. 333
Man, Isle of, i. 138-42
Manchester, Dean of, i. 372
Mandeville, i. 32, 227
Mann, Bishop, ii. 354
Manners-Sutton, Bishop, ii. 209
Manningham, Bishop, i. 160-61
Mansfield, Lord, ii. 87, 153
Mansion House, i. 210
Manx, i. 58; ii. 67
Mapletoft, W., i. 154
Markham, Archbishop, ii. 210
Marlborough, Dean of, i. 1, 4
Marsh, Archbishop, ii. 297, 303, 315-17
Martyn, H., ii. 150, 197, 200
Mary, Queen, i. 83
Mason, Bishop, ii. 274
Materiality of the soul, i. 41
Maule, Bishop H., ii. 346
Maule, Bishop I., ii. 287
Maurice, Bishop, ii. 354
Mawson, Bishop, ii. 70-71
Mayhew, i. 365
Melmoth, i. 86
Meredith, Sir W., ii. 125
Methodism, i. 207, 251-92, 353-58, 382-97; ii. 81, 93, 131-39, 147, 157, 195, 262, 312
Mew, Bishop, i. 158-59
Middleton, C., i. 227
Milner, I., ii. 144
Milner, J., ii. 144
Miracles, i. 242-43
Missionary Society, ii. 175, 199
Missions, foreign, i. 88, 347-49, 351, 353; ii. 196-200, 336
'Moderation,' i. 8
Monasteries, ii. 34

OCC

Montgomery, R., ii. 165
Moore, Archbishop, ii. 167, 199, 207-8
Moore, Bishop, i. 71
Moravians, i. 142, 301-9, 351, 382; ii. 25, 70, 200
More, Hannah, i. 331 n., 339; ii. 83, 99, 119, 127, 129, 145, 157, 165, 167, 170, 215, 216, 222
More, Henry, i. 119, 241
Morgan, Dr., i. 227; ii. 17, 273
Morley, Bishop, ii. 353
Mosheim, i. 214
Moss, Archdeacon, ii. 69, 72
Moss, Bishop, ii. 271
Mysteries, i. 25-28
Mysticism, i. 240; ii. 79

NAPLETON, J., i. 121
Natural religion, i. 248-51, 311; ii. 57
Negroes, i. 80, 86, 90; ii. 194-95
Nelson, R., i. 39, 43, 47, 54, 60, 63, 66, 86, 170, 177; ii. 27
Nepotism, i. 376; ii. 24
New England, i. 84, 87 (see America, Colonial)
Newcome, Archbishop, ii. 309, 325
Newcome, Bishop, ii. 76
Newton, Bishop, i. 392; ii. 47, 91, 237-40
Newton, J., ii. 47, 91, 117-18, 126, 142, 151, 271
Newton, Sir I., i. 240, 310, 381; ii. 268
Nicolson, Bishop, i. 49, 70, 159-60, 309; ii. 346
Noailles, Cardinal De, i. 100
Nonconformity, i. 14-23, 205-13; ii. 85-90, 101, 152, 162, 270
'Non-cures,' ii. 308
Nonjurors, i. 3, 5-6, 40, 146, 154, 167-71, 187-93; ii. 177-85, 310, 332
Non-residence, i. 317-19, 376; ii. 272, 306
Non-resistance, i. 7 (see Passive Obedience)
Norris, J., i. 28
North, Bishop, ii. 218-19
Nottingham, Earl of, i. 15, 21, 23, 29, 39
Nowell, Dr., i. 202

O'BEIRNE, Bishop, ii. 308, 353
Occasional conformity, i. 17 20, 208

INDEX

Oglethorpe, Gen., i. 47, 57, 142, 204, 340-41, 349-52
Okely, i. 241, 309
Omai, ii. 198
Optimism, i. 32
Ormond, Duke of, i. 71; ii. 285
Osbaldestone, Bishop, ii. 69
Otley, Bishop, i. 241, 309
Oxford, i. 39, 64-72, 187, 322-28
Oxford, Earl of, i. 109

PAINE, J., ii. 119, 129, 157, 257
Pakington, Sir J., i. 20
Paley, Archdeacon, ii. 89, 119, 152, 164
Parnell, Archdeacon, ii. 285
Parr, Dr., ii. 85, 87, 89, 152, 153, 223, 224
Party spirit, i. 8, 11-12
Pascal, i. 4
Passive obedience, i. 7, 11, 126, 201-2; ii. 11, 332
Paterson, ii. 103
Patrick, Bishop, i. 69, 86, 115-16
Patristic divinity, i. 219; ii. 24
Patronage, Church, i. 371, 378-79; ii. 65-66, 271, 295, 302
Pearce, Bishop, ii. 63-67
Penal code, ii. 278
Penance, i. 140-41
Pepys, i. 167
Percy, Bishop, ii. 126, 241, 249-50
Perfection, i. 282-86
Pestalozzi, ii. 172
Peterborough, Earl of, ii. 333
Philanthropy, i. 337-39
Phillips, i. 86
Physical agitations (Methodism), i. 285; ii. 141
Pitt, W., ii. 94, 281
'Plain Account,' &c. (Hoadly), ii. 15, 19
Pluralities, i. 317-19; ii. 214, 306
Pocoche, Bishop, ii. 345
Pococke, Dean, i. 133; ii. 309
Poetry, sacred, ii. 201-3
Pope, Alex., i. 32, 130, 311
Porteus, Bishop, i. 318, 343; ii. 43, 87, 97, 126, 144, 155, 156, 161, 165, 167, 168, 174, 197, 213-18
Potter, Archbishop, i. 39, 42, 302, 384-85; ii. 22-25
Prayer, calmness in, ii. 17
Prayer-book (see Liturgy)
Preaching, i. 112
Preferment-hunting, i. 371; ii. 302

Presbyterianism, i. 9, 18, 93, 111, 210; ii. 85, 101
Presbyterianism, Irish, ii. 291-94
Presbyterianism, Scotch, i. 19 n., 131; ii. 175-9
Price, Dr., ii. 119
Prideaux, Dean, i. 63, 66, 82, 83, 318
Priestcraft, i. 35
Priestley, i. 37; ii. 84, 86, 119, 129-31, 162, 266
Primacy, Irish, ii. 296-97
Prisons, i. 340, 350; ii. 83
Progress, religious, i. 224; ii. 249
Prophecy, i. 241-46
Protestant interest, i. 1-5, 203-5; ii. 101
Protestants, foreign, i. 98, 203-5, 351
Provoost, Bishop, ii. 189-90
Public schools, i. 63, 328-30
Punishment, eternal, i. 239-42
Puritanism, i. 92, 152 n.; ii. 142, 258

QUEBEC Bill, ii. 95
'Querist,' the, ii. 338

RAIKES, R., ii. 83, 165-66
Randolph, Bishop, ii. 274
Reasonableness of Christianity, i. 25-28
Redemption, i. 295-97
Reformation, i. 24-25; ii. 12, 277
Reformation of Manners, Societies for, i. 46-50, 342-44; ii. 174, 313
Regium donum, i. 213
Religious associations, i. 50-52, 116
Restoration, the, i. 175
Revision of Liturgy, i. 15, 224-26; ii. 40, 52, 153, 202, 240
Revival of religion, ii. 78-79
Revolution, French, i. 238, 254; ii. 98-100, 120, 129, 153-63
Revolution of 1688, i. 1, 5, 9, 14, 173-76
Reynolds, Bishop, ii. 35, 36
Richardson, J., ii. 286
Richmond, Bishop, ii. 274
Robertson, Dr., ii. 95, 154
Robinson, Archbishop, ii. 297, 323-24
Robinson, Bishop, i. 38, 108-10
Rokeby, L., Archbishop (see Robinson)
Romaine, W., ii. 141
Romanism, i. 2-4, 216-19; ii. 19, 58, 90-100, 221
Romilly, Sir S., ii. 93, 128, 154, 155
Rooke, Sir J., i. 58
Rose, Bishop, ii. 179

INDEX

Ross, Bishop, ii. 87, 97, 269 70
Rousseau, J., ii. 128–29
Royal supremacy, ii. 103
Rundle, Bishop, i. 379; ii. 21, 71, 309, 347–48
Rutland, Duke of, ii. 289

SACHEVERELL, Dr., i. 10–12, 35, 49, 202; ii. 9, 18
Sailors, i. 58; ii. 174
St. Paul's, monuments in, ii. 69
Salters' Hall controversy, i. 211; ii. 42
Sancroft, Archbishop, i. 16, 124, 301
Sandwich, Earl of, ii. 198
Scepticism, ii. 128
Schism Act, i. 23, 62, 208
Schleiermacher, i. 307; ii. 159
Schulz, i. 348
Schwartz, C. F., i. 348; ii. 196
Scotch Episcopal Church, Scotland, union with, i. 19 n.; ii. 107
Scott, T., i. 293; ii. 143
Seabury, Bishop, ii. 133–34, 185-89
Seagrave, R., i. 253, 290, 322
Secker, Archbishop, i. 13 n., 62, 158, 186, 200, 230, 364, 382, 384, 388; ii. 6, 41–47, 55, 90, 116, 183
Seven bishops, the, i. 115, 126
Shaftesbury, Earl of, i. 28–32, 227; ii. 110
Sharp, Archbishop, i. 15, 48, 49, 63, 103; ii. 178
Shenstone, i. 335
Sheridan, Bishop, ii. 310
Sherlock, Bishop, i. 230, 249, 303, 375, 382; ii. 48–54, 183
Shipley, Bishop, ii. 88, 152, 241 43
Shirley, W., ii. 144
Sierra Leone, ii. 199
Simeon, C., ii. 144, 197
Sincerity in opinion, i. 195
Skelton, ii. 309
Slavery, i. 81, 89–90, 350, 353; ii. 162–65
Smallbrooke, Bishop (or Smalbroke), i. 39, 392; ii. 33 34
Smallwell, Bishop, ii. 274
Smalridge, Bishop, ii. 26–29
Smith, A., i. 327
Smith, Bishop, i. 159
Smith, S., i. 329
Societies, ii. 171, 174–75, 288, 313 (see also S.P.C.K., S.P.G.)
Societies, devotional, i. 50 52, 344 45
Society for Promoting Christian Knowledge, i. 46, 54–60, 334, 345–48; ii. 196
Society for the Propagation of the Gospel, i. 85 91, 348–49, 352; ii. 189, 193–94
Socinians, i. 37–38
Soldiers, i. 58; ii. 174
Somers, Lord, i. 2
Somerville, T., ii. 95, 154
Sorbonne, the, i. 100; ii. 94
Soul, nature of, i. 41
South Sea Islands, ii. 197
Southey, i. 187, 325, 330, 331 n.; ii. 131, 154, 165, 195
Spinkes, N., i. 188
Spirituous Liquors Bill, ii. 46
Spratt, Bishop, i. 149–51
Squire, Bishop, ii. 273
Staël, Madame de, ii. 159
Stanhope, Lord, i. 208-9
State and Church, ii. 100 22
Stearne, Bishop, ii. 346
Steele, R., i. 43, 59, 338
Sterne, L., ii. 82
Stock, Bishop, ii. 353
Stone, Archbishop, ii. 39
Story, Bishop, ii. 346
Stratford, Bishop, i. 161
Stuart, Bishop, ii. 274
Subscription to Articles, i. 211, 220–23; ii. 86, 122–26, 193, 246, 250
Sunday schools, i. 337; ii. 165 70
Sunday trading, i. 342; ii. 217
Swift, Dean, i. 60, 62, 162, 341; ii. 9, 104, 278, 282, 287, 293, 301
Sydall, Bishop, ii. 76
Synge, A. and E., Bishop and Archbishop, i. 28; ii. 309, 311, 345

TALBOT, Bishop, i. 157-58; ii. 42
Talbot, Lord Ch., i. 157, 178, 379; ii. 56
Tanner, Bishop, ii. 73
Tenison, Archbishop, i. 85, 86, 94 96; ii. 20
Tennison, Bishop, ii. 346
Terrick, Bishop, ii. 86, 211
Test, sacramental, i. 17–20, 209; ii. 19, 87-88
Theological books, i. 42
Theological discussion, i. 232
Thirlby, i. 39
Thomas, J., Bishop of Lincoln, ii. 75
Thomas, J., Bishop of Rochester, ii. 75
Thomas, J., Bishop of Salisbury, ii 75

INDEX

THO

Thomson, J., i. 340
Thoresby, R., i. 12, 111, 152 n.
Thornton, J., ii. 167
Thorold, Sir J., i. 334
Thurlow, Bishop, ii. 220
Thurlow, Lord, i. 370; ii. 187-88
Tillotson, Archbishop, i. 95, 136, 241, 337, 356; ii. 106
Tindal, M., i. 32, 227-28, 246-48; ii. 21, 109
Toland, J., i. 25, 32, 64, 227; ii. 110, 312
Toleration, Act of, i. 14; ii. 107
Tomline, Bishop, ii. 125, 144, 167, 240-41
Toplady, A., ii. 125, 127, 142
Tories, i. 7
Trelawney, Bishop, Sir J., i. 128-29
Trevor, Bishop, ii. 73
Trimmer, Mrs., ii. 166, 168
Trimnell, Bishop, i. 22, 155-56
Tucker, Dean, ii. 119, 152
Turner, Bishop, i. 124, 167, 170
Turretin, Professor, i. 98, 207, 222
Tyler, Bishop, i. 162

ULSTER, settlement of, ii. 291
Uniformity, ii. 85, 112
Unitarianism, i. 37-38; ii. 129
'United Irishmen,' ii. 293-94
Unity, Church, ii. 85
Universities, i. 64-72, 320-28; ii. 155
Ursinus, i. 106
'Usages,' Nonjuror, i. 191; ii. 182
Utrecht, peace of, i. 2, 109, 203

VENN, H., i. 292; ii. 140
Venn, J., ii. 144
Vernon, Bishop, ii. 272
Vesey, Archbishop, ii. 346
Vigors, Bishop, ii. 346
Village itineracies, ii. 90
Virginia (see Colonial, American)
Voltaire, i. 381; ii. 77, 128

WADDINGTON, Bishop, ii. 35, 85
Wagstaffe, T., i. 40, 41, 188
Wake, Archbishop, i. 16, 96-103, 208, 222, 302, 317; ii. 106
Wakefield, G., i. 328, 332; ii. 131
Wales, i. 139, 163, 334; ii. 64-65
Walker of Truro, ii. 139
Walpole, H., i. 130, 187, 231, 374, 380; ii. 42, 43, 47, 93, 215, 269

WOR

Walpole, Sir R., i. 202, 209, 364, 371, 374, 380; ii. 21, 65, 74, 299-300, 325-26
Warburton, Bishop, i. 28, 199, 228, 230, 232, 249, 290, 321, 376, 392-94; ii. 92-93, 116, 132-36, 140, 152, 164, 167, 174, 236, 270, 287, 351, 353
Ware, Sir J., i. 153
Warren, Bishop, ii. 273
Waterland, Dr. D., i. 39, 221; ii. 16
Watson, Bishop, i. 164, 211, 324; ii. 88, 89, 125, 127, 129, 154, 164, 196, 251-57, 299
Watts, Dr., i. 213; ii. 41, 85, 101, 113
Waugh, Bishop, ii. 35, 36
Welsh bishops, i. 163; ii. 3, 264 (see Wales)
Welton, ii. 31
Wesley, C., i. 283, 351, 353; ii. 133, 203
Wesley, J., i. 7, 207, 217, 249-50, 252-92, 299, 300, 322, 342, 351, 353-55, 383-97; ii. 92-93, 116, 132-36, 140, 152, 164, 167, 174, 236, 270, 287, 351, 353
Wesley, Mr., i. 89, 274
Wesley, S., i. 7, 15, 62, 70, 148, 352
West Indies, i. 90; ii. 194-95
Wetherell, Dr., i. 310
Weymouth, Lord, i. 171
Wheatley, C., ii. 16
Whig bishops, i. 173-75, 370; ii. 4
Whiston, W., i. 36, 54, 64, 66, 95, 147, 240; ii. 3, 16, 20, 22, 28
Whitby, D., i. 42
White, Bishop, ii. 134, 189-90
Whitefield, G., i. 2, 58, 260, 262, 276, 291, 293, 321, 342, 345, 354-57, 361, 383, 389; ii. 63, 164
Whitehead, i. 373, 375
Wilberforce, W., i. 328, 343; ii. 88, 119, 136, 145, 157, 163, 171, 196-97
Wilcocks, Bishop, ii. 35
Willes, Bishop, ii. 73
William III., i. 1, 5; ii. 176
Williams, Bishop, i. 153
Willis, Bishop, ii. 30
Wilson, Bishop, i. 60, 138-42, 303, 334, 353, 379; ii. 97
Winchester School, i. 129
Wollaston, W., i. 227, 381
Woodward, i. 52
Woodward, Bishop, ii. 354
Woolston, T., i. 34, 227, 229, 242; ii. 33, 59, 64
Wordsworth, W., i. 332; ii. 99, 154
Worthington, W., i. 224, 241; ii. 243

WOR
Wortley, Lady M., i. 73
Wotton, W., i. 67
Wyndham, ii. 152, 163
Wynne, Bishop, ii. 35, 36

YALE College, ii. 337
Yonge, Bishop, ii. 76

ZIN
Yorke, Bishop, ii. 126, 274
Young, Bishop M., ii. 353
Young, E., i. 319

ZIEGENBALG, i. 58, 89, 347
Zinzendorf, Count, i. 301, 302, 303, 308, 385, 393

THE END.

PRINTED BY
SPOTTISWOODE AND CO., NEW-STREET SQUARE
LONDON

www.ingramcontent.com/pod-product-compliance
Lightning Source LLC
Chambersburg PA
CBHW032029220426
43664CB00006B/409